6140093239

KU-186-621

The UK Economy and Europe

BRUCE R. JEWELL

PITMAN
PUBLISHING

Pitman Publishing
128 Long Acre, London WC2E 9AN

A Division of Longman Group UK Limited

First published in Great Britain 1993

© Longman Group UK Limited 1993

British Library Cataloguing in Publication Data
A CIP catalogue record for this book can be obtained from
the British Library.

ISBN 0 273 60084 2

All rights reserved; no part of this publication may be reproduced,
stored in a retrieval system, or transmitted in any form or by
any means, electronic, mechanical, photocopying, recording, or
otherwise without either the prior written permission of the
Publishers or a licence permitting restricted copying in the United Kingdom
issued by the Copyright Licensing Agency Ltd, 90 Tottenham
Court Road, London W1P 9HE. This book may not be lent, resold,
hired out or otherwise disposed of by way of trade in any form
of binding or cover other than that in which it is published,
without the prior consent of the Publishers.

Typeset by Mathematical Composition Setters Ltd, Salisbury, Wiltshire.
Printed and bound in Great Britain by Clays Ltd, St Ives plc.

The
publisher's
policy is to use
**paper manufactured
from sustainable forests**

Contents

Preface and Acknowledgements

Students of economics, business studies and related subjects require an understanding of the workings of the UK economy and its problems. Hence the intention behind the present book is to provide an introduction to the UK economy for A level (and equivalent) students. Throughout the book, reference is made to underlying theory to enable the reader to link theory with real life issues. Students may undertake more detailed study of the issues through reference to the extensive reading list at the end of the book.

It is my belief that all students of economics and of the UK economy require an historical perspective to enable them to appreciate the development of the economy to its present state. Consequently, reference is made to both economic history and economic thought. The modern UK economy is inextricably linked to the European Community and the economies of our partners in the Community. The second half of the book concentrates on EC issues, especially those policies that have an impact on key macro-economic variables. Students will need to make their own assessment of the costs and benefits of Britain's membership of the EC. This book places the main issues before the reader, without judgement.

I wish to acknowledge the hard work and efficiency of Penny and Elaine in typing the manuscript. I also wish to thank Jenny, my wife, for her support, patience, advice and practical help on the production of this work.

Bruce Jewell
March 1993

PART ONE

HISTORICAL SURVEY

CHAPTER I

The UK Economy to 1972

Entry into the European Community marked a major watershed in British political and economic history. Hence, in this chapter we will briefly survey the British economy to that date. After the spectacular development of the economy in the 19th century Britain suffered a long period of relative decline for which all kinds of solutions were sought but were found wanting.

OBJECTIVES
1 To survey the development of the British economy.
2 To develop an understanding of Keynesian theory and practices.
3 To review the experience of the Keynesian era of economic policy.
4 To account for the failure of Keynesian demand management to deliver the objectives laid down.

Historical survey

British economic history of the last two centuries is often portrayed as a century of triumph followed by a century of long, relentless decline. The triumphant first part of the period is epitomised by book titles such as *The First Industrial Nation* (by P. Mathias), *The First Industrial Revolution* (by P. Deane) and *The Workshop of the World* (by J. D. Chambers).

Britain was the first country to experience a modern industrial revolution. This involved a significant shift in the structure of the economy away from agriculture and towards the industrial sectors. At the same time, changes in the techniques and organisation of industrial production permitted an increase in output to supply both a rapidly growing population and an expanding overseas market. By the mid-19th century Britain had become a predominantly urban and industrial economy, a net importer of food and the world's leading producer and exporter of manufactured goods.

By the mid-19th century the fruits of the British Industrial Revolution were beginning to 'trickle down'. Not only did the country enjoy the highest per capita income in the world but skilled manual workers (the aristocrats of labour) were beginning to enjoy relatively high living standards. This prosperity was achieved in a private-enterprise, *laissez-faire* economy, with the role of the state confined to providing defence and a framework of law and order.

Laissez-faire in the domestic economy was accompanied by free trade in the overseas sector. Influenced by the writings of Adam Smith and David Ricardo, statesmen such as Robert Peel and William Gladstone abolished protective tariffs and other restrictions on both imports and exports. The prosperity that followed the completion of the process of freeing trade led contemporaries to associate free trade with prosperity. From 1860 to 1931 free trade remained the policy of successive governments despite:

- *the abandonment of this policy by Britain's trading partners;*

- *the desire to practise discrimination in favour of the Empire; and*

- *criticisms of the harm done to some parts of British industry by this open door policy.*

To illustrate the last point, consider the plight of the silk and cotton industries. The cotton industry was efficient in the 19th century – it had nothing to fear from overseas competition and could only benefit from universal free trade. The silk industry was less efficient than its rivals in France. Consequently, free trade with France caused a serious decline in Britain's silk industry but played an essential role in the continuing expansion of Lancashire's cotton industry. Therefore, it is not surprising that the cotton mill owners played a leading role in the campaign to achieve free trade.

Despite this apparent success there were aspects of the UK's economic performance which were both unimpressive and posed problems for the future.

1 Industrialisation was both slow and 'patchy'. Low-paid, low-productivity industry coexisted with the rapidly expanding leading sectors.

2 Growth rates were low (e.g. in the boom period of the second third of the 19th century the average annual rate of growth was 2.2 per cent according to Deane and Cole, 2.5 per cent according to Nick Crafts). Consequently, the interpretation of the Industrial Revolution as a period of sudden, rapid change has been replaced by a gradualist interpretation.

3 Productivity growth was also low despite the inventions of the Industrial Revolution, the use of steam power and the factory system of production. In fact the main feature of industrialisation in the UK was not increased productivity, but an increase in the industrial workforce.

4 Britain's exports were dominated by textiles and were increasingly sold to low-income countries.

5 'The development of the economy before 1860 was based neither on very high levels of home investment, nor on modern financial institutions. As a result, the capital market was ill-suited to ensuring an efficient use of investible funds' (N. Crafts, in *ReFresh*, Vol. 4).

6 Even during this period of economic supremacy, Britain had a deficit on its visible trade. The well-known high UK propensity to import is therefore not unique to the 20th century.

7 The trade deficit was, however, balanced by a consistent surplus on invisibles. Of growing importance in receipts from invisibles were 'interest, profit and dividends' from foreign investment. These provided the UK with a current account surplus which was then reinvested abroad. Although financially beneficial to the economy, such transactions can prove harmful in the longer run if they inhibit home investment.

The late 19th century has also provoked considerable debate among economic historians. The last quarter of the 19th century has been portrayed as a watershed (a climacteric) in British economic history. Cheap imports from the New World produced a severe crisis in arable farming. At the same time a series of intense depressions led to a sharp rise in unemployment. The rate of growth of both output and productivity (per capita output) fell sharply and Britain was overtaken by two industrial newcomers: the recently united Germany and the USA.

The relative decline of the UK is not surprising (in many respects what is more surprising is why a small, offshore island acquired such a lead in the first place) and is not in itself a matter of concern. In a growing world economy there is scope for expansion even if market share is falling. However, the extent to which Britain was falling behind did become a matter of concern to contemporaries.

Late Victorian retardation in the UK economy is explained in a variety of ways, and many of the points that are made are familiar to students considering the slow growth of the British economy in the late 20th century. The retardation is explained partly by the slow growth of demand consequent upon the industrialisation of other countries. To quote Nobel Prize-winning economist Sir Arthur Lewis: 'The principal reason for the relative stagnation of British industry was that Britain had ceased to be the workshop of the world.' The idea that others were merely 'catching-up' is sometimes accompanied by a complacent attitude (i.e. the latecomers will eventually slow down when they reach Britain's state of maturity) or by a fatalistic view (i.e. Britain was handicapped by older technology when competing against the new technology of the latecomers). Depressingly, these ideas were heard again in the 1950s and 1960s in respect of the German and Japanese economic miracles.

The other explanation concerns the supply side. It is argued that Britain suffered as a result of entrepreneurial failure. This encompasses a number of points.

1 There was a failure to adopt new technology.

2 There was a failure to develop strategically important new industries. Over-commitment to the staple industries such as cotton, coal and iron led to a neglect of the industries that were to play a key role in the 20th century (e.g. chemicals, electrical goods, motor vehicles).

3 A feature of British business enterprise was the continuation of small, family-based businesses. There was a failure to develop the large-scale, modern corporation that played a vital role in the German and American economies.

4 The financial institutions are also targets of criticism. City institutions played only a small role in raising finance for British industry, preferring to invest money overseas.

Late Victorian retardation was followed by a brief interlude of rapid (but fluctuating) growth during the Edwardian period. This was a period of renewed expansion even in the staple industries such as cotton. However, a combination of inflation and sharp downturns in the economy contributed to deteriorating industrial relations. Nevertheless, in terms of the staple industries this is seen as a high watermark in terms of output, employment and exports.

Much was to change during the First World War. Markets were lost, in many cases for ever, by a combination of:

- *inability to supply markets during the war;*

- *the development of new rivals (e.g. Japan) away from the main areas of warfare;*

- *the impoverishment of much of Europe.*

Britain also suffered as a result of capital consumption: failure to replace it during the war led to a decline in the quantity and quality of Britain's stock of real capital. At the same time, balance of payments problems during the war led to a significant decline in Britain's holdings of overseas assets. This in turn jeopardised Britain's ability to balance its overseas payments in the post-war period.

The First World War also led to the abandonment of the Gold Standard. This was a central feature of 19th-century overseas trade. National currencies exchanged for gold at a fixed rate. The system provided certainty for trading relationships and an automatic mechanism for curing balance of payments problems (*see* Fig. 1.1). However, a run on gold in August 1914 led to the suspension of the Gold Standard. It was always intended as a temporary expedient and the 1920s saw an attempt (ultimately futile) to return to gold

---

Fig. 1.1 *The 19th-century gold standard*

Deficit country	Surplus country
Balance of payments deficit	Balance of payments surplus
↓	↓
Gold outflow	Gold inflow
↓	↓
Reduction in money supply	Increase in money supply
+	+
Rise in interest rates	Fall in interest rates
↓	↓
Deflation	Reflation/inflation
↓	↓
Fall in demand for imports	Rise in demand for imports
↓	↓
Balance of payments equilibrium	Balance of payments equilibrium

as part of the hoped-for return to pre-war normality. Unfortunately for those who saw renewed prosperity in terms of a return to 1913, the war changed the world beyond all recognition.

The inter-war period (1919–39) is usually seen as a period of slump and high unemployment. For 20 years unemployment exceeded 10 per cent of the labour force and rose to even higher levels during the depressions of 1921–4 and 1931–3. The root problem was the decline of the staple industries upon which Britain's economy had relied. The textile and coal industries lost export markets in the face of low-cost competitors. The iron and steel industry not only lost overseas markets but faced a growing problem of import penetration. Engineering suffered as a result of changes which adversely affected those parts of the industry in which Britain was strong.

The decline of the staple industries was accompanied by expansion in the new industries (chemicals, electrical goods, motor vehicles). In what we can call the 'revisionist view' of the inter-war period, stress is laid on growth in the economy and on rising living standards. The low and even negative inflation of the period meant that people in employment enjoyed growing prosperity. Unfortunately, this growth coexisted with depression and unemployment in the traditional industrial areas. The coexistence of expansion and unemployment is explained partly by immobility of labour (occupational and geographical) and by the inability of the new industries to absorb the unemployed from the declining industries.

The economic problems of the inter-war period were aggravated by government policy.

1 The attempt to restore the Gold Standard led to the overvaluation of sterling in the period from 1925 to 1931. This harmed Britain's exports and necessitated high interest rates.

2 Financial orthodoxy meant balanced budgets and, in a time of declining tax yields, cuts in government expenditure. Such policies further reduced demand in the economy and led to further job losses. A policy of public works to create jobs (as suggested by Keynes and trade union leaders) was rejected by the Treasury. It was argued that public works would merely 'crowd out' private enterprise. Interestingly, many of the economic debates of the 1980s and 1990s parallel those of the 1920s (e.g. the 'Treasury view' in the 1920s is similar to the 1980s concern over the PSBR and crowding out).

The other feature of UK economic policy in the 1920s was the continued commitment to free trade (despite the Conservative desire for Imperial Preference – the policy of mutual tariff concessions for Empire and Commonwealth nations). Opponents of free trade argue that it was an inappropriate policy at a time when others were raising tariffs. In this argument Britain is seen as playing 'by the rules' while others take advantage of the open door presented by the British government. The contrary view is that in the 1920s the real problem was the loss of export markets rather than import penetration by Britain's rivals. As we move into the 1930s, import penetration becomes a greater problem. This, together with a desire to use UK import controls as a bargaining weapon, led in 1931–2 to the abandonment of Britain's free trade policy. Britain had succumbed to the worldwide trend towards tariffs and other import controls. 'Beggar my neighbour' policies were pursued by all the major industrial nations in the hope that it would solve their own economic problem. However, as import controls are also export controls, the result was a further decline in world trade. The world-wide slump of 1931–4, heralded by the 1929 Wall Street Crash, was aggra-vated and prolonged by this worldwide resort to import duties. Each nation was plunged further into crisis by desperate and futile measures to solve its own problems.

In the late 1930s the UK economy saw renewed growth (associated with rearmament), but unemployment remained high until 1940. It then ceased to be a problem but six years of war led to further lost markets and capital con-sumption on a scale even greater than during the First World War. However, the experience of high unemployment and world war led to a strong desire to build a new and better world. Part of the new world was the Keynesian revolution in economic policy.

The Keynesian era: John Maynard Keynes

The most significant English economist of the century, John Maynard Keynes (1883–1946) studied under Alfred Marshall at Cambridge University. On leaving Cambridge he joined the civil service and served on the Royal Commission on Indian Currency and Finance (1913–14). During the First World War Keynes was a Treasury civil servant and rose to be the Treasury's principal delegate at the Paris Peace Conference in 1919. However, he was very critical of the reparations clauses in the Treaty of Versailles, which, he argued, would cripple the German economy, alienate the German people and have economic and political repercussions on the victorious allies. His attack on the reparations terms is contained in his book *Economic Consequences of the Peace* (1919).

On resigning from the Treasury, Keynes returned to Kings College, Cambridge while at the same time pursuing a career in the City. He gained, lost and regained a fortune both for himself and for his college. He was also a member of the Bloomsbury group of writers, painters and other intel-lectuals. This interest in the arts is reflected in his work towards the establish-ment of the Arts Council.

During the 1920s Keynes was a critic of government policy. His pamphlet 'Economic Consequences of Mr Churchill' (1925) was an attack on the govern-ment's decision to return to the Gold Standard at a level which overvalued sterling. He also wrote pamphlets on economic policy for Lloyd George's Liberal Party and was a member of the Macmillan Committee on Finance and Industry.

Keynes's major theoretical works were published in the 1930s: *Treatise on Money* (1930) and *General Theory of Employment, Interest and Money* (1936). This latter book contained the essence of Keynesian macro-economics. However, the Keynesian revolution in policy had to await the Second World War.

In 1940 Keynes wrote a pamphlet entitled 'How to pay for the War' in which he analysed the problem of inflation in a wartime situation of excess demand. By now Keynesian ideas were accepted by Treasury officials and politicians. Keynes became a director of the Bank of England and in 1942 was given a peerage as Lord Keynes of Tilton. Two years later he was a major participant in the Bretton Woods Conference which established the post-war international monetary system.

The IMF, the IBRD (World Bank) and the system of managed exchange rates emerged from Bretton Woods but Keynes's plan for paper gold (the 'Bancor') proved unacceptable to the Americans – only to reappear in the guise of Special Drawing Rights (SDRs) in a later age. Shortly after the end of the war Keynes died of a heart attack – although by then Keynesian economics was accepted as orthodox macro-economics.

The Keynesian revolution in economic theory

John Maynard Keynes brought about a revolution not just in economic policies pursued by governments in the UK but also those in other industrial democracies. The impact of Keynes's ideas so dominated the 30 years after the Second World War that economic historians can look back upon it as the 'age of Keynesian economics'.

The details of Keynesian macro-economic theory are well covered in text-books such as those by Beardshaw, Maunder *et al* and Anderton. Although it is not necessary to go through the details of Keynesian theory it is useful to extract the essence of Keynesianism. Keynes, it should be remembered, produced his most important writings at a time of high unemployment during the 1930s. The depression of the 1930s, coupled with the rise of a new ideology and a new model for society in the Soviet Union, provides an essential backdrop to Keynes's writings. Unemployment represents a waste of resources and therefore involves an opportunity cost in terms of lost production. This is in addition to the hardship it imposes upon the unemployed and their families. Keynes feared that continuing high unemployment would threaten the social order; that government's inability and unwillingness to reduce it might lead to a British revolution. (It should be appreciated that, before the horrors of Stalin's purges were revealed, substantial parts of the British left showed considerable sympathy for the Soviet experiment.) Keynes's writings were an attempt to improve the operation of the market by replacing a free market with a guided market. For Keynes (a 'new' liberal, as opposed to a Gladstonian or *laissez-faire* liberal), a reformed market was needed if the market or capitalist economic system was to be saved.

Pre-Keynesian economists believed that the economy was always moving to a full employment equilibrium. The basis for this belief was quite simple: in micro-economics we learn that the equilibrium price is the one at which the amount demanded exactly equals the amount supplied. The equilibrium price therefore 'clears' the market, ensuring neither surplus nor shortage. Price cuts lead to an extension in demand not just in the product market but also in that for labour. Hence in the long run, when wage cuts made it worthwhile to employ more people, unemployment would disappear.

Pre-Keynesian economists did not naively believe that unemployment was impossible. (The experience of the 1920s would have quickly disabused them of that idea.) They did, however, consider it to be a temporary phenomenon as the market adjusted to the new conditions of supply and demand. When unemployment appeared to persist, the explanation lay in market imperfections (especially monopolistic activities of unions) which prevented wages falling, to bring about the extension of demand for labour. For the Conservative government of Stanley Baldwin the solution to the problem of unemployment was for trade unions to accept wage cuts and so increase the attractiveness of employing labour. Keynes (an academic without influence on government policy in the 1920s) argued that wage cuts would not only not solve the problem but would aggravate it. This is because a reduction in wages would lead to a further reduction in demand not just for goods and services but also for labour. Wage cuts would produce a spiralling down to a new and lower equilibrium.

Belief in equilibrium in the macro-economy was shared by both pre-Keynesians and Keynes. However, the nature of the equilibrium was different. The pre-Keynesian equilibrium involved full employment at a market-clearing wage. The Keynesian macro-economic equilibrium was the level of national income at which aggregate demand equalled aggregate supply. In other words, it was the point at which the planned supply was exactly equal to planned expenditure. A basic feature of Keynesian economics is that supply responds to demand. Hence a rise in demand will result in increased output (assuming that idle resources exist to be put to work). Hence the level of national income (Y) will rise to satisfy the aggregate demand for goods and services.

Aggregate demand and therefore Y is equal to $C + I + G + X - M$, where C is consumer demand, I investment demand, G government demand, X export demand and M is home demand for imported goods and services.

Equilibrium occurs not when Y equals $C + I + G + X - M$ in an actual or *ex post* sense but when it does in a planned or *ex ante* sense. The economy will either be at, or moving towards, this point. However, this does not necessarily mean full employment: if the macro-economy is in equilibrium below full employment, unemployment will persist. The *laissez-faire* approach to the problem of unemployment was based on the belief that unemployment was temporary and would be solved by market forces. Keynes had demonstrated (Fig. 1.2) that equilibrium (the point to which the economy was moving) did not guarantee an end to the misery of unemployment.

Keynesian demand management is based on the belief that as the market fails to solve the problem of unemployment, it is necessary for the state to intervene to ensure full employment. The intervention took the form of managing the level of aggregate demand to ensure that it was sufficient to create full employment (usually defined as a situation in which the number of vacancies equalled the number of people searching for work so that there was no demand deficiency unemployment). As the level of aggregate demand was crucial, it is necessary to consider its components.

1 Consumer demand (C): this is determined partly by the level of disposable income (over which governments have some control via taxation). Hence tax changes can be a method of influencing the level of C and therefore Y.

2 Investment demand (I): this refers to investment by firms in plant and stock and is the most volatile component of aggregate demand. As interest rates

Fig. 1.2 *Keynes's deflationary gap*

The deflationary gap provides an explanation of persistent unemployment. At the full employment level of national income (Y^f) there is shortfall in aggregate demand. This deficiency of demand is known as the deflationary gap. Y falls back to the equilibrium level (Y^e) at which aggregate demand is equal to planned output. However, to produce this level of output it is not necessary to employ all who seek a job – consequently there will be some demand deficiency unemployment.

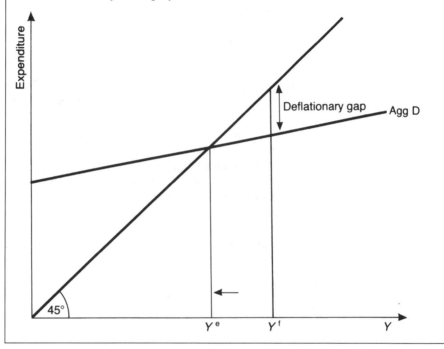

affect investment decisions it should be possible to control or at least influence I via changes in interest rates.

3 Government demand (G): as this is undertaken by the state it is surely possible to adjust G in the interests of controlling aggregate demand. As we will see later, however, numerous technical problems are involved in controlling G.

4 Export and import demand (X – M): logically, aggregate demand can be increased and unemployment reduced by either an increase in exports (e.g. prompted by government subsidy) or a reduction in imports (e.g. through import control). However, 'beggar my neighbour' policies of creating jobs by interference in overseas trade were tried in the 1930s and prolonged the slump. In the 1940s when Keynesian theories were accepted by governments such interference was against the 'spirit of the age'. In addition it should be remembered that, as a liberal, Keynes believed in free trade. Hence he was an interventionist in the domestic economy, but a non-interventionist in its overseas sector. For these reasons, Keynesian demand management concentrated on the C, I and G components of aggregate demand and left X and M alone.

As mentioned earlier, investment demand is especially volatile and as a result occupied a large part of Keynes's theory. In fact, we should see the theory as being made up of:

- liquidity preference theory: *this explains how the market rate of interest is determined by the interaction of the supply of money and the demand to hold money;*

- marginal efficiency of capital: *this explains the level of investment by reference to the rate of interest;*

- the multiplier: *this shows the extent to which the change in investment produces a multiple change in Y. The nature of the change in Y depends upon the level of employment. As Keynesians assumed that supply is elastic at below full employment, the resulting change in Y is 'real'. That is, there is a rise in the physical quantity of output. At full employment, supply is inelastic and therefore the change in Y is brought about by higher prices for the same quantity produced. For Keynesians any rise in aggregate demand will lead to increased output and unemployment when there are spare resources, but to inflation when spare resources are not available.*

These building blocks of Keynesian theory can now be expressed as

$$\Delta MS \to \Delta i \to \Delta I \to \Delta Y$$

Where MS is money supply
i is the rate of interest
I is the level of investment
Y is the level of national income and Δ is a 'change in'.

I and therefore Y can be increased by a reduction in interest rates, which in turn is achieved by an increase in the money supply. However, the linkages that make up Keynesian theory are not only indirect but also uncertain. Take, for instance, the impact of a rise in the money supply. Keynes did not argue that it has no impact. The logic of the notation above is that a change in the money supply affects the real economy and can cause inflation. However, the impact is via interest rates and investment and Keynes analysed a situation (known as the liquidity trap) in which a change in the money supply has no impact at all. This is seen as the ultimate impotence of monetary policy and explains the Keynesian preference for fiscal policy.

The link between interest rates and investment assumes that investment is elastic with respect to interest rates. Keynes himself argued that the link was not clear cut and that other factors (business psychology and changes in the growth of demand via the accelerator) affected investment.

Although the multiplier linkage is beyond doubt, the nature of the rise in Y (real or money) depends upon the level of unemployment.

The Keynesian revolution in policy

As the years pass and government documents become available to historians, the nature and timing of the Keynesian revolution in government economic policy are disputed among economic historians. The traditional view is that Keynes was a 'heretic' and ignored by officialdom during the inter-war period. Consequently, it is assumed that had Keynesian ideas been adopted during that period, unemployment would have been solved. Keynesian heresy became orthodox macro-economics in the post-war period as government practised Keynesian demand management. If one event symbolises this transformation it is the 1944 White Paper on Employment Policy which committed the government to 'the maintenance of a high and stable level of employment'.

The revisionist view of the Keynesian revolution in policy suggests that the transformation was less clear cut and less complete. There was some acceptance of Keynesian ideas before 1939, some continuing scepticism even after 1944. However, there is 'general agreement that during the war years the essential theoretical message of the Keynesian revolution – that capitalist economies were not self-financing by virtue of some automatic market mechanism – had been firmly established. At this date few economists would have denied that if the economy fell into a depression . . . government intervention would be needed to stimulate demand and help get the economy back to full employment' ('The Rise and Fall of the Management Economy', R. Middleton in *ReFresh*, Vol. 5).

Demand management

By demand management we mean managing the level of aggregate demand in the economy to achieve some desirable outcome. Those that governments sought during the Keynesian era were:

- full employment, *defined as unemployment no greater than 2.5–3 per cent of the labour force; alternative definitions of full employment were a situation of zero demand deficiency unemployment or a situation in which the number of unemployed equals the number of vacant jobs;*

- price stability, *or at least only mild inflation;*

- balance of payments equilibrium: *this was necessary to maintain the value of the currency within a narrow band either side of parity as defined in the Bretton Woods agreement of 1945;*

- economic growth, *or a rise in the productive capacity of the economy. This was important in facilitating the rise in living standards that the population required and expected.*

These policy objectives were to be achieved by various policy weapons. In the early Keynesian era (to the late 1960s) fiscal policy was used to maintain full employment, stimulate growth, control inflation and manage the balance of payments to support the target exchange rate. Budget deficits (increases in government spending with no corresponding rise in tax revenue) were used to reflate the economy in the interests of full employment and growth. Budget surpluses (increases in tax revenue with no corresponding rise in government spending) were used to reduce inflationary pressure and to combat balance of payments deficits. Monetary policy was assigned a role in relation to management of the national debt. As the nation's largest borrower the government was anxious to keep down the cost of borrowing.

In the late Keynesian era (late 1960s to mid-1970s) fiscal policy remained an essential weapon in the management of the economy. However, it was now supplemented by incomes policy to control inflation. A growing problem for Keynesians was how to explain the coexistence of high unemployment and rising prices when Keynesian theory stressed these problems as opposites. By the 1960s it was argued that much of the inflation of the period could be attributed to cost-push pressure. Unlike demand-pull inflation, cost-push inflation did not require full employment. It could occur at any level of employment provided imperfections in the market permitted producers to pass on cost rises. The existence of trade unions, national wage bargaining and the government commitment to full employment were sufficient to create the conditions of imperfection needed to produce cost-push inflation.

Another change in the late Keynesian period was a more active exchange rate policy. The 1967 devaluation was soon followed, in 1971, by the general collapse of the Bretton Woods system of managed exchange rates. Therefore, rather than managing the economy to achieve an exchange rate target, the government could use the exchange rate to achieve other objectives.

Despite these changes in the late Keynesian period, the emphasis remained on demand management via fiscal policy. In many respects it was, or appeared to be, a successful policy. Unemployment remained low throughout the period. Britain did experience inflation but it was relatively mild (2–3 per cent) compared with later years. Full employment and low inflation were the primary aims of government economic policy and governments did at least achieve these objectives. Admittedly, the balance of payments and growth performance were less satisfactory but at least Britain enjoyed full employment. (*See* Fig. 1.3.)

Euphoria at the success of Keynesian fiscal policy should be tempered by the fact that, although low by standards of later years, the trend in both unemployment and inflation was upwards. Each downturn in the business cycle brought a rise in unemployment, to levels exceeding those of previous downturns. Even the high levels of employment that were achieved can be attributed to factors other than the success of government economic policy. In other words, a combination of post-war reconstruction, a consumer boom and the high levels of military expenditure during the Cold War might provide a better explanation of full employment. Simply because it coincided with the Keynesian era is not proof that full employment was the result of Keynesian demand management.

By the early to mid-1970s Britain experienced a combination of high unemployment and high inflation: something Keynesians found difficult to explain and to solve. Deflationary policies designed to reduce inflation aggravate the unemployment problem; similarly, reflationary policies to reduce unemployment aggravate inflation. Stagflation (a situation in which prices

Fig. 1.3 *Unemployment: Keynesian analysis*

Type	Description and Cause	Remedy
Demand deficiency unemployment	A shortfall in aggregate demand	Raise the level of demand by reflation
Frictional	Job changing unemployment	Improve the flow of information about job vacancies
Seasonal	Seasonal fluctuations in activity	Diversification in the local economy
Structural/ regional	Long-term decline of major industries	Retraining Regional policy
Technological	Labour-saving technology causes job losses	Retraining

and unemployment are both rising but output is not) in Britain and elsewhere played a major role in undermining Keynesian macro-economics in the face of the 'monetarist counter-revolution'.

Before looking at monetarism (in chapter 3), it would be useful to survey criticisms of Keynesians' fine-tuning: the use of discretionary policy measures to manage the level of aggregate demand in order to achieve the economic objectives. These criticisms can be divided into two types. First, there are a number of technical points relating to the operation of the policy. These do not disprove Keynesian theory but suggest that implementing policy is considerably more difficult than textbooks suggest. The second group of criticisms are more fundamental and attack the foundations of Keynesian theory.

Technical problems

1 If one accepts Keynesian analysis there is a problem relating to conflicting aims. Over-stimulation of an underemployed economy will cause over-heating and thus inflation. Excessive deflation will cure the inflation problem, but plunge the economy into unemployment. Textbooks suggest that it is possible to manage the level of demand to achieve full employment without inflation, but in practice it is difficult to achieve the correct balance.

2 Keynes's deflationary and inflationary gaps suggest that the transition from unemployment to inflation is a sudden one. In practice, long before the economy approaches full employment there is upward pressure on prices as skill shortages occur.

3 The impact of demand management measures depends on the uncertain response of the private sector. For instance, can governments be certain that tax increases will reduce, or tax reductions increase, consumer spending? In textbook theory we are given the marginal rate of withdrawal (MRW) and, therefore, we can calculate the multiplier impact on the national economy. In the real world the MRW cannot be estimated with any great certainty. Consequently, over- or under-stimulation of the economy can easily occur. Consider an example: the deflationary gap is £1 billion and MRW is 0.8. The multiplier is assumed to be 1.25 and, to close the gap, the government should increase spending by £0.8 billion. (Rise in $G \times 1/0.8 = £1$ billion; $= £1$ b $\times 0.8$; $= £0.8$ billion.) However, if the MRW is actually 0.66, the multiplier is 1.5. The total rise in national income will then be £1.2 billion, thus replacing a deflationary gap by an inflationary one.

4 The success of the policy depends upon the accuracy of data and the speed with which it is made available to decision-makers. Unfortunately, there are inevitable delays in:

(a) data collection and interpretation (statistics are historical);
(b) perceiving a problem;
(c) deciding on action;
(d) implementing a policy change;
(e) producing the desired result.

Time lags mean that the 'medicine' will work only after a lapse of time. Sometimes it produces results only after the problem has solved itself. Consequently, rather than acting in a counter-cyclical manner, Keynesian policies can sometimes aggravate the problem (i.e. deflationary measures start to work as unemployment rises).

5 Similarly, it is argued that public expenditure cannot be turned on and off like a tap in the way textbooks seem to imply. Public investment has to be planned and labour must be complemented by other factors – hence building motorways (the often quoted solution to unemployment) involves considerable practical problems. Cuts in public expenditure are also more difficult than textbooks imply. Most government expenditure is committed (politically, legally, morally) well in advance. For instance, short-term cuts in education expenditure have to concentrate on consumable items like paper or purchases of textbooks for the simple reason that most of the money is earmarked for wages and salaries to which the local authority or school is contractually committed.

Fundamental criticisms To the technical problems associated with demand management we can add a number of fundamental criticisms.

1 Government commitment to full employment had a long-term impact on behaviour in the labour market. It affected attitudes to work and wage claims. For instance, critics of trade unions argue that by protecting workers from unemployment government policy contributed to irresponsible wage claims. The removal of the commitment to full employment would have led to greater responsibility in wage bargaining.

2 The textbooks portray economic management as alternating between deficit (to cure unemployment) and surplus (to cure inflation). In practice there was an inbuilt bias towards deficit because governments were reluctant to cut

Fig. 1.4 *The stop–go cycle*

A persistent problem of the UK economy has been the alternation of expansion and contraction. The expansionary phase results in inflationary pressure and a worsening of the balance of payments. To correct these problems governments have to deflate the economy. Long-term growth has therefore been constrained by the balance of payments. A political interpretation of the cycle links it with the parliamentary cycle. A newly elected government anxious for economic success overheats the economy and is forced to pursue deflationary measures in the middle years of a Parliament. However, as the next election approaches it is necessary to reflate the economy to avoid electoral unpopularity.

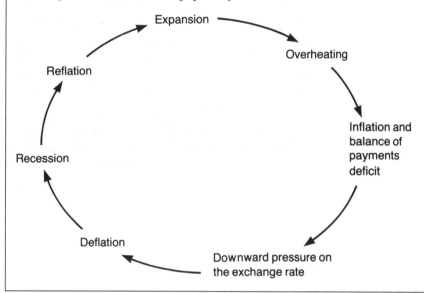

public spending and/or raise tax rates. Therefore, critics of Keynesian demand management argue that there was an inflationary bias in the policy.

3 Keynesian demand management involves short-term adjustment to solve the immediate problem, whether it be unemployment, inflation or a balance of payments deficit. Keynesian policy can be destabilising and, therefore, discourage investment which is vital for growth. During the Keynesian period the long-term objective of growth to raise living standards was frequently sacrificed (*see* Fig. 1.4).

4 The monetarist case against Keynesian policy is that it both ignores the monetary effects of fiscal policy and produces purely short-term benefits. The first point relates to the rise in the money supply that follows a budget deficit financed by borrowing from banks. Monetarists argue that a rise in the money supply is a necessary and sufficient condition for inflation. Hence the Keynesian budget deficit, designed to reduce unemployment, actually causes inflation. The second point is best understood by reference to the Phillips curve. In the original curve, shown in Fig. 1.5, government can trade off

Fig. 1.5 *The Phillips curve*

The economist A. W. Phillips gathered data on unemployment rates and wage increases for the UK for the years 1861–1913 and 1923–58. The data was plotted as a scatter diagram from which a 'line of best fit' was constructed. This became known as the Phillips curve, and suggested that there was an inverse relationship between the two variables.

It should be appreciated that on the vertical axis Phillips plotted the percentage rise in wages, although this was seen as a proxy for inflation, and that he identified a relationship between two variables rather than constructing a theory of inflation. Other writers then used the curve in support of their theories of demand-pull and cost-push inflation.

The Phillips curve suggests that there is a 'trade-off' between unemployment and inflation – that is, the cost of reducing unemployment is higher inflation and the cost of reducing the inflation rate is higher unemployment. Although this suggests a painful choice, at least it implies the government can opt for its preferred combination of unemployment and inflation.

The Phillips curve trade-off has since been the source of great controversy. Milton Friedman rejected the idea of trade-off except in the short run; others dispute even a short-run trade-off. Nevertheless Phillips's research had a profound and lasting influence on policy-makers during the Keynesian era and the Phillips curve provided a foundation on which others (including Friedman) could build.

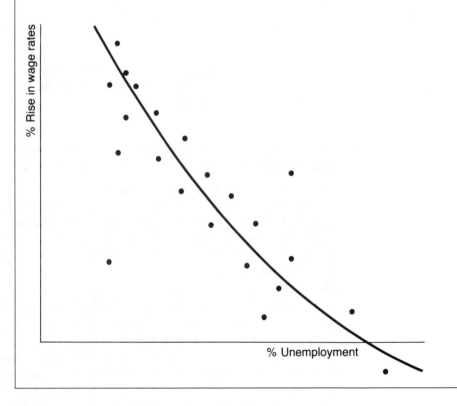

inflation against unemployment (and vice versa). The monetarist version is that the trade-off is a purely short-term phenomenon. In the long run unemployment returns to its natural level but the consequence of the trade-off is an acceleration in the inflation rate.

Keynesian macro-economics was undermined by stagflation in the 1970s. The symbolic end of the Keynesian era was not the election of Mrs Thatcher's Conservative government in 1979 but the IMF's imposition of a monetarist policy on the UK in the aftermath of the 1976 sterling crisis. Tight control of the public sector borrowing requirement (in the interests of controlling the money supply) dates from this period.

Statistical appendix

Average UK inflation rate (%)

1900–14	0.7
1915–20	16.5
1921–38	−1.5
1939–45	6.3
1945–50	4.3
1950–67	3.8
1968–73	7.5
1974–80	15.9
1980–87	6.9

GDP growth per year (%) 1950–73

Germany	6.0
Italy	5.5
France	5.1
Netherlands	4.8
UK	3.0
USA	3.7

Unemployment – OECD standardised percentage rates

	1960	1968	1974
Germany	1.0	1.2	2.1
Italy	5.5	5.6	5.3
France	1.1	2.6	2.8
Netherlands	0.7	1.4	2.7
UK	1.3	2.1	2.1
USA	5.4	3.5	5.5

Source: adapted from Crafts, N. and Woodward, N. *The British Economy Since 1945*, OUP

CHAPTER 2

The Development of the European Community to Britain's entry

After the disasters of two world wars the nations of Europe were anxious to live in peace and harmony through greater co-operation and economic integration. In the first decade after 1945 there were a number of initiatives, most of them achieving only partial success. Undaunted by the task, however, statesmen of Europe eventually concluded a series of agreements from which emerged the present European Community. In the early years Britain remained aloof from emerging institutions but a changed position in the world coupled with continuing economic problems convinced many in Britain that its future lay with membership of the EC.

OBJECTIVES   1 To outline the initiatives leading to the establishment of the EC.
2 To outline the objectives behind the Communities.
3 To explain Britain's initial aloofness from the EC.
4 To explain Britain's eventual acceptance of Community membership.
5 To survey the long process of membership negotiations.

Chronology of events

1947   Benelux customs union.

1947   Marshall aid offered by the USA.

1948   Organisation for European Economic Co-operation.

1949   North Atlantic Treaty signed.

1949   Council of Europe established.

1950   Schuman Plan for European coal and steel industries.

1950/4 Negotiations on the aborted European Defence Community.

1951   European Coal and Steel Community (ECSC) Treaty signed.

1954   Western European Union Treaty signed by the ECSC states plus the UK.

1955   Messina Conference on Further European Integration.

1957   EEC and Euratom Treaties signed in Rome.

Fig. 2.1 *The European Community*

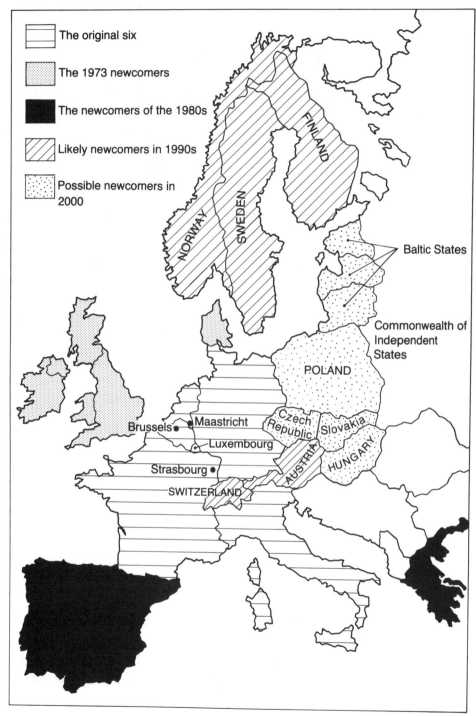

Fig. 2.1 shows the EC, starting with the six original members and giving developments since then – and potential future members.

The desire for unity

Although this book is concerned mainly with economic matters, it is important to appreciate that the movement toward greater European co-operation and even integration extends beyond the economic field. Indeed the three organisations that constituted the European Economic Communities (later known as the European Community) were not the only ones that attempted to unite European nation states after the Second World War: numerous other organisations and initiatives were launched in the aftermath of 1945. Some concentrated more on political or diplomatic aims while others were rooted more in economic affairs. Some proposals had strictly limited aims; others had a supra-national or federal structure as the ultimate goal. Moreover, there were different objectives behind each initiative (and indeed participating states often had different reasons for favouring particular proposals). However, the main reasons for this interest in European integration can be distilled into the following.

1 A desire for peace, harmony and prosperity after two devastating world wars which had been ignited by European national rivalries.

2 A desire to promote trade and economic interdependence by creating a European market to replace national markets.

3 Mutual co-operation to promote reconstruction and growth.

4 A desire (especially on the part of the French) to contain German power and thereby prevent a repetition of the events of 1914 and 1939.

5 A desire to rid Europe of the two 'outsiders', namely the superpowers that controlled much of Europe in the aftermath of the collapse of the Third Reich. European unity was seen by some as a way of removing both American and Soviet influence and control.

6 Increased links with European neighbours came to be seen as a substitute for the loss of colonies. Most of the EC member states were or had been colonial powers. The loss of empire led to renewed interest in Europe. (We should not, however, exaggerate the importance of this factor since at the time the EEC was founded both France and Belgium had extensive empires and no immediate intention of relinquishing them.)

Early moves towards European integration took the form of the Organisation for European Economic Co-operation (1948) and the Council of Europe (1949). Neither body is an EC organisation even though individual EC countries are members of these organisations.

The OEEC was established to administer American aid for post-war European reconstruction (known as Marshall aid, after the American Secretary of State, George Marshall). In addition, it aimed to liberalise and to multilateralise European trade and payments. These objectives are shared with both the EC and, on a worldwide level, with the General Agreement on Tariffs and Trade (GATT), signed in Havana in 1948.

By 1961 the reconstruction role of the OEEC was complete and the trade liberalisation role was taken over by the EC and the European Free Trade

Fig. 2.2 *Europe's other organisations*

Organisation	Main Function	Membership
Bank for International Settlement (1930) Basle	Promotion of co-operation between national central banks	Most European countries plus Australia, Canada, Japan, South Africa, USA
Conference on Security and Co-operation in Europe (1973) Prague	To develop friendly relations and co-operation between participants	Most European states plus USA
Council of Europe (1949)	To achieve greater unity between members, to encourage economic and social progress, to uphold the principles of parliamentary democracy and promote human rights	26 Western European states, including all 12 EC members
Economic Commission for Europe (1947) Geneva	Discuss economic, environmental and technological issues, and recommend action	Most European states plus Canada and USA
European Bank for Reconstruction and Development (1990) London	Reconstruction of private enterprise in Eastern Europe	Most European countries, the USA, Japan, the EC and European Investment Bank
European Free Trade Association (1960) Geneva	Promotion of free trade in industrial goods between members	Seven Nordic and Alpine states
Group of Seven (G7)	Forum for discussing economic problems	Canada, France, Germany, Italy, Japan, UK, USA
Group of Ten (1962)	Forum for discussing international monetary arrangements	G7 plus Belgium, Netherlands and Sweden
Nordic Council (1952) Stockholm	Promotion of co-operation	Denmark, Finland, Iceland, Norway, Sweden
North Atlantic Treaty Organisation (1949) Brussels	Defence pact	Canada, Iceland, Norway, Turkey, USA plus EC states except Ireland (neutral); France is a member of the alliance but not of the military structure
Organisation for Economic Co-operation and Development (OECD) (1961) Paris	Forum for discussion and co-ordination of economic and social policies	EC and EFTA states plus Australia, Japan, New Zealand, Turkey and USA
Western European Union (1955) London	Collective defence organisation of nine states; defence link between NATO and EC	EC members except Denmark, Ireland and Greece

Association (EFTA). Hence in that year the OEEC was transformed into the Organisation for Economic Co-operation and Development (OECD). The deletion of Europe from the title reflected the inclusion of non-European states such as Australia, Canada, Japan, New Zealand and the USA. Its basic role now is to provide a forum for representatives of the governments of the industrialised democracies to discuss and co-ordinate policies in relation to economic and social matters.

The Council of Europe should not be confused with the EC Council of Ministers. (Neither should we be confused by the fact that it shares the Strasbourg Assembly Building with the European (EC) Parliament – this is equivalent to football clubs sharing a ground.) The Council of Europe aims to:

- *achieve greater unity between the 26 nations represented;*

- *encourage economic and social progress;*

- *uphold the principles of parliamentary democracy.*

European federalists had hoped that the establishment of the Council of Europe in 1949 would lead to a federal Europe. However, national governments (including the UK Labour government under Attlee) were opposed to the Council evolving into a European government. Consequently, the 177 members of the Council of Europe Parliamentary Assembly were and are nominated by national parliaments and are not directly elected by voters of the member states. The Assembly is a forum for the exchange of views and has few powers. The other Council of Europe institution is the Committee of Ministers of Member States, which meets twice yearly.

The Council of Europe is primarily a political institution dealing with social, cultural and, increasingly important today, environmental issues. Perhaps its greatest achievement was the 1950 European Convention for the Protection of Human Rights and Fundamental Freedoms and the establishment of the European Commission on Human Rights and the European Council of Human Rights.

To reiterate, the institutions so far mentioned sprang from the same desire for co-operation that led to the creation of the EC but overlapping membership is coincidental and these organisations are not connected to the EC. Fig. 2.2 lists these 'other organisations'.

The establishment of the European Coal and Steel Community (ECSC): 1951

The first EC organisation to be established was the ECSC, founded in 1951 – six years before the Treaty of Rome. The inspiration behind the ECSC was Jean Monnet, who is often seen as the 'father of European unity'. Monnet was the civil servant in charge of French economic planning. It should be pointed out that French indicative planning was both more extensive and more successful than equivalent British attempts at planning (e.g. Britain's National Plan of 1965). Moreover, the French system of government enables civil servants both to be more influential and to have a higher profile than their British counterparts. Monnet was a federalist but favoured a strategy of European integration in a piecemeal fashion, sector by sector.

The choice of heavy industry as the first sector to be subjected to Monnet's federalism reflected the geographical position of the industry in the border-lands of Europe, and the economic and political interests of France. In the late 1940s coal was in short supply and Monnet regarded access to Germany's Ruhr coalfields as vital for his modernisation plan. At the same time there was a steel surplus and Monnet was anxious to prevent trade barriers blocking French access to European markets. As well as these industrial and economic considerations there were political motives. By placing heavy industry under the High Authority of the ECSC France sought to tie Germany into an arrangement which would make it difficult (if not impossible) for it again to threaten European peace. (Interestingly, a century earlier British free traders Richard Cobden and John Bright argued for the abolition of tariffs on the grounds that it would reduce both the danger and possibility of war. Increased trade leads to both prosperity and interdependence, making it both less likely and more difficult for nations to engage in war.)

Monnet's ideas were incorporated in the Schuman Plan (1950), advanced by the French Foreign Minister Robert Schuman. On 18 April 1951 representatives of the governments of Belgium, France, Italy, Luxembourg, the Netherlands and the Federal Republic of Germany (West Germany) signed a treaty establishing the ECSC (*see* Illustration 2.1). Article 2 of the treaty states:

> The European Coal and Steel Community shall have as its task to contribute, in harmony with the general economy of Member States and through the establishment of a common market . . ., to economic expansion, growth of employment on a rising standard of living in Member States. The Community shall progressively bring about conditions which will of themselves ensure the most rational distribution of production at the highest possible level of productivity, whilst safeguarding continuity of employment and taking care not to provoke fundamental and persistent disturbances in the economies of Member States.

To this general aim the treaty added more specific objectives in terms of:

- *an orderly supply of coal and steel products to the common market;*

- *ensuring that comparable consumers have equal access to sources of production;*

- *creating and maintaining conditions that will encourage expansion of the industry concerned while at the same time preventing 'unconsidered exhaustion of natural resources';*

- *improving and harmonising working conditions and living standards for employees of the industries concerned;*

- *promoting the growth of international trade.*

Although the ECSC had a remit limited to two (albeit important) sectors of industrial production, its objectives, principles and institution provide the

---

Illustration 2.1 *Preamble to the Treaty of Paris 1951, which established the European Coal and Steel Community*

[The sovereign rulers of the six countries]

CONSIDERING that world peace can be safeguarded only by creative efforts commensurate with the dangers that threaten it,

CONVINCED that the contribution which an organized and vital Europe can make to civilization is indispensable to the maintenance of peaceful relations,

RECOGNIZING that Europe can be built only through practical achievements which will first of all create real solidarity, and through the establishment of common bases for economic development,

ANXIOUS to help, by expanding their basic production, to raise the standard of living and further the works of peace,

RESOLVED to substitute for age-old rivalries the merging of their essential interests; to create, by establishing an economic community, the basis for a broader and deeper community among peoples long divided by bloody conflicts; and to lay the foundations for institutions which will give direction to a destiny henceforward shared,

HAVE DECIDED to create a European Coal and Steel Community

---

embryo of the far more comprehensive body that emerged in later years. The 1951 treaty referred to a common market without barriers and specified the following matters that are incompatible with it:

- *import and export duties;*

- *discriminatory practices relating to price, delivery terms, transport rates;*

- *measures which interfere with a purchaser's free choice of supplier;*

- *subsidies or aids granted by states;*

- *restrictive practices which tend towards the sharing or exploiting of markets.*

The 1951 treaty included a social dimension in relation to conditions of work and life for the workers employed in the sectors it covered. It also created a series of institutions that were replicated in the wider organisation that followed the 1957 Treaty of Rome. The ECSC institutions comprised:

- *a High Authority (eventually the EC Commission);*

- *a Common Assembly (European Parliament);*

- *a Special Council of Ministers;*

- *a Court of Justice;*

- *a Court of Auditors.*

The role of these institutions is investigated in chapter 10, but for the moment it should be stressed that the 1951 treaty was an important step towards the creation of a common market, albeit only in the heavy industrial sector.

The creation of the European Communities

European integration received a setback with the abandonment in 1954 of a scheme to pool military resources in a European Defence Community. European nations were clearly not ready for such a far-reaching measure in the field of defence and so attention returned to the Monnet policy of 'integration, sector by sector'. Monnet proposed that the next sector for integration should be the newly emerging atomic energy industry. Remember that, at the time, atomic energy was seen as a source of cheap, clean energy, and would therefore provide the key to future prosperity.

Belgium, the Netherlands and Luxembourg (the so-called Benelux countries) proposed that the principle of a customs union that they had adopted after the war should be extended to all Western European countries. The Benelux customs union involved free trade between members and a common tariff against goods from other countries.

The two proposals (Monnet's Atomic Energy Community and the Benelux customs union) were the subject of negotiations at the 1955 Messina conference. Although Britain sent an official observer to Messina, the Conservative government preferred the existing OEEC to any new supranational body. Consequently, Britain withdrew from Messina and it was clear that any resulting agreements and institutions would be limited to the six existing ECSC states.

The Messina conference was followed by work on the details of two proposed treaties. Political instability in France, and the fear of the replacement of a pro-integrationist government by the anti-integration General de Gaulle, led to renewed urgency in the negotiations (the 'Rush to Rome' as it has been called). On 25 March 1957 the six states that made up the ECSC signed a treaty which established the European Atomic Energy Community (Euratom).

Three weeks later, on 17 April 1957, the same states signed a treaty establishing the European Economic Community (EEC), concerned with a common commercial policy and the progressive abolition of restrictions on international trade. The three communities (ECSC, Euratom and EEC) had a common membership and eventually common institutions. Consequently, they came to be regarded as a single entity with the term 'European Community ' encompassing them all.

The 1957 Euratom treaty states:

> It shall be the task of the Community to contribute to the raising of the living standards in the Member States and to the development of relations with the other countries by creating the conditions necessary for the speedy establishment and growth of nuclear industries.

In particular Euratom is required to:

- *promote research and ensure the dissemination of technical information;*

- *establish uniform safety standards to protect the health of workers and of the general public;*

- *facilitate investment and ensure the establishment of the basic installations necessary for the development of nuclear energy in the Community;*

- *ensure that all users in the Community receive a regular and equitable supply of ores and nuclear fuels;*

- *make certain, by supervision, that nuclear materials are not diverted to purposes other than those for which they are intended;*

- *exercise the right of ownership conferred upon it with respect to special fissile material;*

- *ensure wide commercial outlets and access to the best technical facilities by the creation of a common market in specialised materials and equipment, by the free movement of capital for investment and by freedom of employment for specialists within the community;*

- *establish with other countries and international organisations such relations as will foster progress in the peaceful uses of nuclear energy.*

The April 1957 treaty which established the EEC is more wide-ranging. The preamble to the treaty (*see* Illustration 2.2) clearly states that the EEC extends beyond the field of trade and economics. It refers to 'ever closer union' and the pooling of resources to preserve and strengthen peace and liberty. Like the ECSC treaty, it has both political and economic objectives.

Illustration 2.2 *Preamble to the Treaty of Rome 1957, which established the European Economic Community*

[The sovereign rulers of the six countries]
DETERMINED to lay the foundations of an ever closer union among the peoples of Europe,
RESOLVED to ensure the economic and social progress of their countries by common action to eliminate the barriers which divide Europe,
AFFIRMING as the essential objective of their efforts the constant improvement of the living and working conditions of their peoples,
RECOGNIZING that the removal of existing obstacles calls for concerted action in order to guarantee steady expansion, balanced trade and fair competition,
ANXIOUS to strengthen the unity of their economies and to ensure their harmonious development by reducing the differences existing between the various regions and the backwardness of the less favoured regions,
DESIRING to contribute, by means of a common commercial policy, to the progressive abolition of restrictions on international trade,
INTENDING to confirm the solidarity which binds Europe and the overseas countries and desiring to ensure the development of their prosperity, in accordance with the principles of the Charter of the United Nations,
RESOLVED by thus pooling their resources to preserve and strengthen peace and liberty, and calling upon the other peoples of Europe who share their ideal to join in their efforts,
HAVE DECIDED to create a European Economic Community

Article 2 states:

> The Community shall have as its task, by establishing a common market and progressively approximating the economic policies of Member States, to promote throughout the Community a harmonious development of economic activities, a continuous and balanced expansion, an increase in stability, an accelerated raising of the standard of living and closer relations between the States belonging to it.

Article 3 then goes on to detail the activities of the Community:

- *the elimination of customs duties and quantitative restrictions on imports and exports between member states;*

- *the establishment of a common customs tariff and of a common commercial policy towards third countries;*

- *the abolition of obstacles to freedom of movement between member states for persons, services and capital;*

- *the adoption of a common agricultural policy;*

- *the adoption of a common transport policy;*

- *ensuring that competition in the common market is not distorted;*

- *the application of procedures by which the economic policies of member states can be co-ordinated and disequilibria in their balances of payments remedied;*

- *the approximation of the laws of member states to the extent required for the proper function of the common market;*

- *the creation of a European Social Fund to improve employment opportunities for workers and to contribute to raising their standards of living;*

- *the establishment of a European Investment Bank to facilitate the economic expansion of the Community by opening up fresh resources;*

- *the association of the overseas countries and territories in order to increase trade and to promote jointly economic and social development.*

The activities outlined in article 3 illustrate the wide-ranging nature of the commitment member states were entering into by accepting the treaty (the UK acceded in 1972). Their exact nature is dealt with in subsequent chapters, but article 3 provides the essence of the activities that constituted the common market. Although the road to European unity proved long and difficult, it was clear from the start that the EC rather than the OEEC would be the vehicle for European integration. As early as 1958 the UK applied for associate status, fearing that a major opportunity had been lost. Associate status would provide the benefits of access to the free trade area without accepting the supra-national nature of the EC (British governments have always preferred links between European governments rather than European institutions that begin to have supremacy over national governments), or the common external tariff (which posed a particular problem for Britain, whose trade policy had for 30 years favoured Commonwealth countries). Britain's application was rejected and it had to wait 15 years to 'catch the European bus that she missed in 1957'.

The Luxembourg Agreement 1966

The first great crisis in the history of the EC occurred in 1965 after the Commission President, Walter Hallstein, made a series of proposals on financing the common agricultural policy and the provision of independent revenue for the EC. Although acceptable to five member states and approved by the Parliament, these measures proved unacceptable to the French government. Not only did the French block progress in the June 1965 Council of Ministers meeting, but for the remainder of that year withdrew representatives from all EC meetings. This French boycott, the 'empty chair policy' as it was known, led to a suspension of decision-making within the EC and threatened to break up the young institution.

The French were eventually tempted back to the Council of Ministers for a meeting held in Luxembourg in January 1966. This meeting was dominated by the constitutional issue of decision-making within the Council and the role of the Commission. The French argued that in questions of vital national interest, only unanimous agreement was politically acceptable.

In the Luxembourg compromise the French did not achieve their full aim, but it was agreed that:

> when issues very important to one or more member countries are at stake, the members of the Council will try, within a reasonable time, to reach solutions which can be adopted by the Council while respecting their mutual interests, and those of the Community, in accordance with Article 2 of the Treaty.

The Merger Treaty 1965

The 1951 and 1957 treaties created separate communities: the ECSC, Euratom and the EEC. Technically, the three were entirely separate although (coincidentally) sharing a common membership. In 1965 the Communities were merged together with common institutions: there was to be one Assembly (Parliament) and the Commission was to be the executive arm for the merged Community. The merger reflected the growing perception of the Community as a single entity. Instead of the European Communities we can now refer to the European Community.

Founding fathers of the EC

Winston Churchill, *British Prime Minister 1940–45 and 1951–55*. He spoke in favour of a United States of Europe – but without Britain.

Jean Monnet, *French civil servant*. He drafted the Schuman Plan and was first President of the High Authority of the ECSC; often called the father of European unity.

Konrad Adenauer, *German Chancellor from 1949 to 1963*. He brought West Germany into the movement for integration.

Robert Schuman, *French Foreign Minister 1948–1953*. He promoted the Schuman plan, and worked for Franco–German *rapprochement* through ECSC.

Paul Henri Spaak, *Belgian Foreign Minister and Prime Minister*. He was the 'creative force' behind the Treaty of Rome.

Walter Hallstein: *a German, and first President of the Commission*. He forged the common market.

Charles de Gaulle, *French President 1959–1969*. He sought a ' *Europe des patries'*, to resist US influence.

Chronology of UK accession to the EC

1957 Treaties of Rome led to the establishment of the Communities.

1960 Stockholm Convention established the European Free Trade Association (EFTA), comprising Austria, Denmark, Norway, Portugal, Sweden, Switzerland and the UK.

1961 Ireland, Denmark and the UK requested negotiations on membership of the EC.

1962 France's President de Gaulle vetoed UK membership.

1967 Second application for membership. Again brought to an end by a French veto.

1969 The new French President (Pompidou) stated that he was not opposed to the principle of UK membership.

1970 Negotiations started between the EC and four applicants: Denmark, Ireland, Norway and the UK.

1972 Treaty of Accession, signed by the applicants.

1972 In referenda Danish and Irish electors voted for accession. The Norwegian electorate voted against.

1973 (1 January) Accession of Denmark, Ireland and UK to the EC.

1975 The UK's continued membership of the EC was supported by voters in the first ever nationwide referendum.

The long road to British membership

As the six original members completed the process of establishing the two Communities to operate alongside the ECSC, the British Conservative government put forward its own, more limited plans. These concentrated on free trade between member states rather than a common commercial policy involving a common external tariff, and would have enabled Britain to maintain its policy of giving preference in trading to the Empire and Commonwealth. Britain also feared the loss of both its national sovereignty and the assumed special relationship with the USA.

The free trade area proposal was pursued during 1956 and 1957, but was resented by the six as an attempt to break up the process that culminated in the Treaty of Rome. Britain then sought association with the institutions that made up the EC: association would enable it to obtain trade advantages without adding to its international obligations. Britain could export industrial goods to the six yet continue to import Commonwealth food and raw materials. Britain's attempt was blocked by the new French President, de Gaulle. Historians attribute de Gaulle's anti-British stance from 1958 to 1968 to resentment at his treatment as Free French leader during the Second World War and to his dislike of the pro-American stance of successive British governments.

With association blocked, Britain now worked to establish a free trade area with those OEEC states which felt unable to accept the requirements of EC membership. The result was the Stockholm Convention of 1959, by which Britain, Austria, Denmark, Norway, Portugal, Sweden and Switzerland established the European Free Trade Association (EFTA). EFTA was (and still is) a more limited arrangement of states than the European Community. Its objectives were:

- *to promote economic expansion in member states;*

- *to ensure that trade between members took place in conditions of fair competition;*

- *to contribute to the harmonious development and expansion of world trade and the progressive removal of tariffs;*

- *to avoid significant disparities between members in conditions of supply of raw materials produced in the area.*

The aim was free trade in industrial goods but no common external tariff, no common agricultural policy and no attempt at full economic and monetary union. EFTA was a grouping of national governments but did not involve the establishment of supra-national institutions. Its limitations were soon clear, however: EFTA countries had low tariffs prior to 1959 and thus there was little benefit from the modest reductions that did occur; apart from Britain the EFTA countries were the smaller countries of Western Europe, and were not 'industrial giants'.

Disappointment with EFTA was accompanied by an acceleration in the process of decolonisation. Between 1957 and 1965 independence was granted to almost all major territories in the British Empire (the exceptions being Hong Kong, the rebel colony of Rhodesia and a number of small dependencies). The independence of the African, West Indian and Asian colonies was followed by a decline in the importance of trade with the Empire/Commonwealth. Events such as Suez (1956) demonstrated that Britain was not a superpower or in the same league as the USA or Soviet Union. The assumed special relationship with the USA was very much a one-way affair, especially as the Americans were prepared to shift investment from Britain to the EC countries. Britain's economic performance was also disappointing: relatively slow growth, balance of payments deficits and the emergence of a pattern of 'stop–go' in economic management.

By 1960 the British Conservative government was coming round to the idea of applying for full membership of the EC. In part this was because the six existing members, and Community leaders such as Monnet, made it clear that association was not on the agenda: it was full membership or nothing. At the same time the attitude of President de Gaulle seemed in line with British thinking. He was a French nationalist who favoured a co-operative confederation of nation states rather than a supra-national United States of Europe. This, after all, had been a major reservation of British government in the long series of negotiation that culminated in the Treaty of Rome.

It was against this background that, on 31 July 1961, Prime Minister Harold Macmillan and pro-Europe ministers such as Edward Heath gained the support of the bulk of the governing conservative party. There were of course some opponents: those concerned about the impact of a change in trade policy on industry and agriculture and those on the right wing of the party who feared the loss of sovereignty and of links with the Empire and Commonwealth. There was also a division of opinion within the Labour opposition. The centre–right Labour leadership was in favour of British entry but the bulk of the party, especially the left wing, opposed it. It was argued that the EC 'was a conservative, Catholic, capitalist club which would hinder the objectives of Socialism in Britain' (Greenwood, *Britain and European Co-operation since 1945*, p. 84). It is interesting that – then as now – the opponents of European integration within British politics tended to be on the right wing of the Conservative Party and the left wing of the Labour Party, although their reasons for opposing membership were/are different.

The British negotiation team was led by Foreign Office Minister Edward Heath. Problem issues included future trade with the Commonwealth, especially those countries that were heavily dependent upon Britain for export earnings. Since the 1930s Imperial Preference had been a major principle of British trade policy and this gave Britain access to cheap foodstuffs. Moreover, the system of support for Britain's efficient agricultural sector would be jeopardised by the EC's common agricultural policy. Then there was the issue of the commitment Britain had recently entered into with its partners in EFTA.

Despite these problems, real progress was made until 1962 but all came to naught in January when President de Gaulle declared that Britain was unfit for membership. Historians put forward numerous theories for de Gaulle's '*Non*'. Undoubtedly a major factor was his preference for a community led by a reinvigorated France rather than one in which Britain was seen as the 'Trojan Horse' for the Americans: 'In the end there would appear a colossal Atlantic community under American dependence and leadership which would swallow up the European Community' (de Gaulle).

The second British application for membership was in 1967. The Conservatives had now been replaced by Harold Wilson's Labour government. When it took office in 1964 the new government hoped to reverse the decline of Britain by economic planning to secure, in Wilson's words, the benefits of the 'white heat of the technological revolution'. However, economic success proved as illusory under Labour as it had been under the Conservative governments of the 1950s and early 1960s. Balance of payments problems and a futile attempt to maintain an unrealistic exchange rate ($2.80) meant a continuation of the stop–go policies of the Conservative era. As a result British economic growth was below that of EC countries. Britain was forced to withdraw defence commitments east of Suez, adding to American scepticism of British pretentions to be anything more than a European power.

Wilson accepted that EFTA and the Commonwealth were not the answer to British economic problems. To compete in world markets Britain needed access to the large common market of the EC. Like Macmillan before him, Wilson believed that de Gaulle's preference for a confederation of nation states would make it easier for Britain to fit into the EC. However – also like Macmillan – Wilson underestimated de Gaulle's opposition to British membership. The French President stated that Britain was still not ready for membership. To his previous comments about British preference for the Atlantic link he now added British economic weakness as a reason for his second '*Non*'. The devaluation of sterling in 1967 suggested that Britain could be an economic liability. Consequently, France's partners accepted de Gaulle's rejection of the second British application for membership.

The third British application was made in more promising circumstances. De Gaulle had retired from politics and his successor Georges Pompidou was markedly less hostile to Britain; in 1969 he stated that he had no objection in principle to British membership of the EC. Second, the new Conservative Prime Minister, Edward Heath, was the most pro-European of all British post-war prime ministers and he had good working relationships with both Pompidou and West German Chancellor, Willy Brandt. Third, although within both major political parties there continued to be strong opposition to Britain joining the EC, there was growing popular support for membership. This was not due to any support for a federal Europe but simply because membership seemed to promise greater economic prosperity.

The 1971 White Paper on the EC entry states: 'HM Government is convinced that our country will be more secure and our people and our industries more prosperous if we join than if we remain outside'. The White Paper emphasised:

- *the growing importance of trade with the EC six;*

- *the importance of securing access to a large domestic market;*

- *the dynamic repercussions of membership in terms of greater specialisation and the sweeping away of archaic attitudes and practices;*

- *the prospects of improving the growth rate of the British economy.*

The controversial issue of the future of Commonwealth preference was reduced in importance. Decline in Commonwealth trade even before entry led to a decline in British attachment to this 40-year-old policy. It was only the question of safeguards for West Indian sugar producers and New Zealand dairy farmers that remained on the agenda. It was agreed that Britain's preferential trade in these commodities would be phased out over four years.

A more important problem was the EC's common agricultural policy (CAP), which would raise food prices in Britain. Added to this was the budgetary issue. As the EC budget is based on revenues from imports of non-EC goods, Britain, as an open economy with continuing links with the wider world, would be a major source of EC revenues. At the same time Britain would not be a major recipient of EC expenditure. This was because the CAP absorbs the bulk of the EC budget and Britain's small but efficient agricultural sector would attract only small amounts of CAP funds. Heath hoped that membership would switch British trade increasingly towards the EC, thus reducing British liabilities to the EC budget and, hence, the cost of membership, and that the EC would create a regional development fund from which Britain would derive benefit.

In October 1971 Parliament approved the principle of British membership. As with most major parliamentary votes on the EC, the two main parties were divided. On this occasion pro-Europeans in the governing Conservative Party were supported by the Liberal Party (consistently pro-European) and pro-European elements within the Labour opposition. The parliamentary majority was opposed by an anti-EC combination of right-wing Conservatives and the bulk of the Labour Party.

In January 1972 the British government signed a treaty of accession with the six existing members, by which it acceded to the Treaties of Paris (ECSC) and Rome (EEC and Euratom). The terms of entry included the following points.

1 Tariffs between the UK and the other members would be eliminated in a phased way over five years.

2 Britain would enjoy equal voting rights and equal representation with France, West Germany and Italy ('the big four').

3 There would be no EC interference with the size and status of the British Steel Corporation and the National Coal Board.

4 There would be a gradual transition from government subsidies on food to import levies.

5 Special arrangements were made for New Zealand butter and West Indian sugar.

6 Associate member status was offered to independent Commonwealth countries.

Britain, Ireland and Denmark became members of the EC on 1 January 1973. The simultaneous admission of the three countries reflected their close links. Both Denmark and Ireland accepted that if Britain joined it was essential for them to join at the same time. In a popular referendum the fourth candidate for admission, Norway, rejected membership, fearing that an EC common fishing policy would jeopardise the Norwegian fishing industry.

British membership was not the end of the saga, however, since 1974 saw the re-election of a Labour government. Labour was deeply divided over the issue of Europe. Prime Minister Wilson's strategy to deal with the problem of party disunity was to renegotiate the terms of entry. This enabled the government to appease the anti-Europeans while at the same time leading pro-Europeans to believe that Britain would remain within the Community. Britain's partners agreed that Britain would be the chief claimant on the new Regional Fund. The newly signed Lomé Convention with the so-called ACP states offered trade opportunities to Commonwealth countries. There was agreement on future budget rebates to ease the problems of Britain's contribution to EC finance. At the same time a rise in world food prices diverted resentment over the CAP. Lastly, there seemed little prospect of economic and monetary union – which throughout the years had troubled Britain.

Wilson presented renegotiation as a triumph for his government. Greenwood argues that 'Deep down ... [it was] a sham'. The renegotiators merely tinkered with the Treaty of Accession, and neither France nor Germany resisted British requests. After the 'triumph' of renegotiation Wilson proposed to put the question of British membership to the people in an unprecedented national referendum. This was a unique event in British history: pro-Europeans of all parties stood on the same platform speaking against anti-Europeans, also drawn from all parties. It must be remembered that the referendum was a vote on whether Britain should *remain* a member (not whether or not to *join*). This affected the result, which was two to one in favour of staying. 'While the referendum gave legitimacy to Heath's move into Europe and Wilson's renegotiation, it was essentially the approval of a confused and bored population voting for the status quo' (Greenwood, *Britain and European Co-operation since 1945*, p. 102).

The EC and sovereignty

Both left- and right-wing critics of Britain's membership of the EC point out that it involves a loss of sovereignty. Moreover, as the process of European integration deepens the loss is intensified. 'Parliament is no longer sovereign and can thus be pushed into the background as far as the laws are concerned. If by chance British legislation were to conflict with EEC legislation, the latter would be upheld by the European Court and enforced by British courts whatever Parliament said' (Tony Benn, *Policy and Practice, the Experience of Government*).

Before examining the issue further, it is necessary to define a number of terms: whereas 'power' is the ability to make things happen, 'authority' is the rightful or lawful exercise of that power. A hijacker can have *power* in that, by threatening hostages, he or she can give orders which others will obey. However, the hijacker does not have *authority*: the power is exercised in an unlawful manner. In the UK authority is ultimately derived from the sovereign body – the Crown in Parliament. Unlike the USA (where the Supreme Court can overturn legislation from Congress) laws passed by the two Houses of Parliament and given Royal Assent cannot be challenged or overturned. That at least *was* the situation.

Since accession, there has been a loss of three types of sovereignty.

1 *Parliamentary*: EC regulations are law as they stand. In the case of directives, the principles are enacted in EC institutions and all that is left to the UK Parliament is to decide on the actual form of what really is delegated legislation.

2 *Legal*: British courts may no longer take British law as the sole source of their judgements. Moreover, Community law and decisions of the European Court of Justice take precedence over UK law and over the highest court in Britain: the House of Lords.

3 *Political*: British governments, elected by British voters, are required to comply with EC policy. In a growing number of areas the EC is a constraint on decision-making. Membership of the Exchange Rate Mechanism, for example, means a loss of independence over monetary policy, and economic and monetary union even more so.

This concern about loss of sovereignty has been expressed by Euro-sceptics of both the left and the right. The former feared that the EC would impose capitalist, free market principles to constrain a radical Labour government. The right fear that the EC involves 'backdoor socialism' against the wishes of Parliament and the electorate.

The counter to this concern about loss of sovereignty runs as follows.

1 Entry in 1972 and confirmation in 1975 were voluntary.

2 Although there is no mechanism for secession, in reality it is difficult to see how or why the EC member states would oppose any member determined to secede. (Although no state has seceded, Greenland, an autonomous area under the Danish crown, did leave the EC.)

3 Absolute sovereignty is illusory in the modern world. The needs of international trade, defence and diplomacy mean that countries have to accept limitations on their sovereignty, e.g. the GATT treaty involves a voluntary surrender of autonomy over trade regulation.

4 The power of the Commission is exaggerated since it only proposes legislation. All major decisions require agreement (either unanimous or by qualified majority depending on the type of decision) in the Council of Ministers.

5 The concern over the lack of democratic control over the Commission (the so-called democratic deficit) can also be criticised. It is because of the desire to retain as much national sovereignty as possible that national governments (most notably the British) have opposed an extension of powers for the European Parliament.

6 The benefits of economic integration outweigh the loss of sovereignty.

The evolution of the EC: an outline

Regional groupings of economies are not uncommon in the world. As we have seen, Britain was a member of EFTA before it joined the EC. What makes the EC unusual (if not unique) is that co-operation extends further than a mutual agreement to abolish tariffs and other import controls. The creation of a free trade area was but the first stage in European co-operation or, as some would say, European unity. We can identify the stages in this process (and *see* Fig. 2.3).

Stage 1: a free trade area This is a group of states which have abolished tariffs and quotas on trade but retain independent tariffs on goods from outside the area.

Fig. 2.3 *Forms of integration across national boundaries*

	Abolition of Tariffs Between Members	Common External Tariff	Harmonisation	Single Currency	Common Fiscal Policy
Free trade area	√				
Customs union	√	√			
Common market	√	√	√		
Monetary union	√	√	√	√	
Economic and monetary union*	√	√	√	√	√

* EMU goes further than monetary union as it involves a common fiscal policy.

Stage 2: a customs union This goes further, with the imposition of a common external tariff from imports from outside the area.

Stage 3: a common market This combines a free trade area and a common external tariff with an attempt to harmonise economic policies in certain key areas. In addition, a common market allows the free movement of labour and capital across national boundaries.

In its first quarter-century the EEC (as it was then called) strove to create a 'common market'. The objective was to create a situation in which trade between members was no different from trade within a member state. However, frustration at the slow progress led to renewed effort by governments to complete the process. In 1985 European heads of government committed themselves to the creation of a single market by the end of 1992.

The Single European Act (SEA) defines the single market as 'an area without internal frontiers in which the free movement of goods, persons, services and capital is ensured'. Progress towards the single market was enhanced by changes in decision-making within the EC. Under the SEA, majority voting (rather than unanimous agreement) was 'extended to most major areas of the single market programme'.

Readers should note the subtle change in terminology. The European Economic Community became the European Community, emphasising that the EC has a wider brief than trade and economic affairs. The common market now became the single market, emphasising that we should see EC members as participants in a single domestic market.

By the end of 1992 all barriers (tariff and non-tariff) to trade were due to be eliminated. These can be classified as:

- physical barriers – *customs controls, documentation, border stoppages (although action to prevent movement of illicit drugs, terrorists and immigrants from third countries will still be permitted);*

- technical barriers – *national product standards, technical regulations, conflicting business laws, public procurement policies;*

- fiscal barriers – *especially differing rates of VAT and excise duties.*

The EC has reached the end of this stage. The two remaining stages are matters of controversy and conjecture.

Stage 4: economic and monetary union

The EC will not be a single market for as long as exchange rates fluctuate. The essential difference between domestic and international trade is the presence in the former and absence in the latter of a single, common currency.

Most members of the EC are part of the Exchange Rate Mechanism, whereby currency fluctuations are kept within a certain band. With the exception of the UK, EC members have committed themselves to a single currency. If, or when, this is achieved the EC will have reached a new stage on the road to unity. Already the national governments of the EC have surrendered considerable discretion over economic policy. Those who favour the EC argue that the benefits of close involvement with the world's largest market coupled with the anti-inflation discipline that will be imposed will more than outweigh the loss of sovereignty. Euro-sceptics continue to reject this loss of sovereignty.

Stage 5: political union

Supporters of political union (so-called Euro-federalists) see the EC evolving in the same way as the USA. A federal Europe will result in a Europe-wide federal government responsible for certain issues, with national governments dealing with other issues.

As stated before, stages 4 and 5 remain controversial and very much in the future. The Conservative government of John Major has clearly stated both its support for the free trade aspects of the EC and its scepticism of (if not opposition to) the wider ideals of economic and political union.

PART TWO

UK ECONOMY

CHAPTER 3

Macro-economic Policy

We saw in chapter 1 that disillusionment with Keynesian policies led to a revival of pre-Keynesian ideas that came to be known as monetarism. As a result of a shift in economic theory there was a change in the nature of macro-economic policy. This chapter looks at these changes and then sets the scene for subsequent chapters which cover aspects of the performance of the economy.

OBJECTIVES
1 To explain monetarism and monetarist policies.
2 To describe and analyse monetary policy in the period of Conservative rule.
3 To describe and analyse the changing nature of fiscal policy in the era of monetarism.

Economic policy-making

As a broad definition we can say that economic policy consists of those choices made or rejected by government, designed to affect the production of goods and services in the economy. To understand policy-making it is necessary to distinguish between objectives, instruments and targets or indicators.

1 *Objectives* are what the government is seeking to achieve by its economic policy. During most of the post-war era this comprised full employment, price stability, balance of payments equilibrium and income redistribution. The order of priorities has changed over the years: for instance, full employment was the main objective of economic policy for the first three decades after 1945, but not today. Conservative governments since 1979 have stressed long-term expansion as the ultimate aim of policy, and that price stability is an essential precondition for achieving this aim. Since 1979 a single-minded pursuit of the goal of low or even zero inflation has been at the heart of government economic policy-making.

2 *Instruments* are the means by which the government seeks to control the economy. They can take a variety of forms:

(a) taxation;
(b) government spending;

(c) interest rates;

(d) exchange rate;

(e) control of the money supply.

The choice of instrument will depend upon circumstances, the prevailing theory and the choice of target. For instance, for much of the post-war era one of the targets of government economic policy was to keep sterling within a narrow band either side of a central exchange rate. With this as a target of economic policy the exchange rate cannot be used as an instrument of that policy; if the target is abandoned, the exchange rate can be used as an instrument.

3 *Targets* can be seen as intermediate rather than ultimate goals. For instance, monetarists stress the importance of targets for the growth of the money supply. The money supply will be monitored to see if the government is 'on target'. However, control of the money supply is not the ultimate aim of policy. Control of the money supply is an intermediate aim *en route* to the objective of controlling inflation, which in turn is seen as a precondition for long-term growth and improved living standards.

Both policy-makers and students of policy must therefore distinguish between:

- *objectives – what is to be achieved;*

- *instruments – how it is to be achieved;*

- *targets or indicators – evidence that progress has been made toward the achievement of the objective.*

The monetarism counter-revolution

In chapter 1 we saw that Keynesianism was dominant in the first three decades after the Second World War. Keynesian economics was orthodox macro-economics and the economic policy of both Labour and Conservative governments was based on Keynesian principles. Faith in Keynesian economics and Keynesian policies declined in the 1970s – especially during the period of stagflation in which rising unemployment was accompanied by rising inflation. The failure of Keynesian theory to explain and provide a solution to this problem gave a major impetus to the revival of pre-Keynesian ideas that came to be known as monetarism.

Even during its heyday Keynesianism had its critics, the Austrian economist Friedrich Hayek being an early one. He was especially critical of the increase in state activity resulting from policies of demand management: the creeping extension of the state would pose a threat to freedom. Another early critic was Henry Simons of the University of Chicago, who favoured control of the money stock to achieve a stable price level. However, it was Milton Friedman, one of Simons's successors at the University of Chicago, who was to be the driving force behind monetarism (a term first used in 1968 by the American economist Karl Brunner).

It should be appreciated that monetarism is more than the view that inflation is caused by excessive growth in the money supply. We can define monetarism as 'the view that the quantity of money has a major influence on economic activity and the price level and that the objectives of monetary policy are best achieved by targeting the rate of growth of the money supply' (Cagan, in Eatwell, Milgate and Newman (eds), *Money* (a section of *Palgrave's Dictionary of Economics*), p. 195).

Friedman's most important work was *A Monetary History of the United States, 1867–1960*, written in 1963 with Anna J. Schwartz. In this lengthy book Friedman and Schwartz demonstrated that fluctuations in monetary growth preceded peaks and troughs of all US business cycles since the Civil War. For instance, the US slump of the early 1930s was preceded and caused by a large contraction in the US money supply in the aftermath of the Wall Street Crash

---

Illustration 3.1 *Key propositions of monetarism*

1. The rate of growth of the quantity of money is related to the rate of growth of nominal income. Hence if the quantity of money grows rapidly, so will nominal income, and conversely.

2. The velocity of circulation, though not constant, is fairly predictable.

3. There is a six- to nine-month time lag between changes in money growth and changes in nominal income.

4. The impact of change in monetary growth affects output first and then prices. The total delay between a change in monetary growth and in the rate of inflation is 12–18 months.

5. Monetary changes affect output only in the short run.

6. In the long run, the rate of monetary growth affects only prices.

7. What happens to output in the long run depends on 'real' factors.

8. Inflation is always and everywhere a monetary phenomenon, in the sense that it cannot occur without an increase in the quantity of money exceeding the rise in output.

9. Government spending will lead to inflation, if it is financed by printing currency or creating bank deposits at a faster rate than output is growing, or crowding out, if it is financed by taxes or by borrowing from the (non-bank) private sector.

10. An increase in cash balances will lead to increased spending on a wide range of assets.

11. Monetary policy is important and what is important about monetary policy is its effect on the quantity of money, not on bank credit or interest rates.

12. Wide swings in the rate of change of the quantity of money are destabilising and should be avoided.

13. Monetarists disagree about the policy implications but Friedman consistently argues that not enough is known about the relations between changes in the quantity of money on the one hand, and in prices and output on the other, to ensure that discretionary policy will do good rather than harm. Hence his preference for the 'fixed-throttle' automatic approach to policy.

of 1929. By the 1970s the monetarist proposition that monetary changes affected economic activity was widely accepted by both economists and rising politicians such as Ronald Reagan in the USA and Sir Keith Joseph and Margaret Thatcher in the UK.

Friedman has stated his 'key propositions' of monetarism in a number of publications (e.g. his contribution to *Palgrave* on 'Money'), and a simplified version is given in Illustration 3.1. However, the essence of monetarism is that:

1 Fiscal policy (the preferred weapon of Keynesians) has no independent effect on prices or on the level of output. The impact of fiscal measures exists only to the extent that the central bank turns a budget deficit into money.

2 Monetary growth has a transitory influence on output and employment. Consequently Friedman accepts that monetary expansion can increase real output and employment but only in the short run. This means that the Phillips curve trade-off is only a short-run phenomenon.

3 In the long run, output is determined by the real forces of supply and demand.

4 As a result of 3 above and of the stability of the demand for money and therefore the velocity of circulation in the Fisher equation (*see* chapter 6), the long-term impact of monetary expansion is on prices. Hence monetary growth results in inflation.

5 In all cases there are time lags in the relationships. Consequently a rise in the money supply results in inflation after 12–18 months. Moreover, it is not possible to predict exactly the result of changes in monetary aggregates.

Policy implications

The most important policy implication of monetarism relates to the abandonment of discretionary policy in favour of an automatic approach. Keynesian demand management involved short-term adjustments to deal with the immediate problem whether it be unemployment, inflation or balance of payments deficit. This can be compared to a pilot steering a ship up an estuary and adjusting speed and direction to avoid sandbanks and rocks. Monetarists reject this approach as destabilising. The frequent policy changes tend to aggravate problems rather than solve them, due to the uncertain and lagged response to changes in the supply of money. Monetarists prefer governments to adopt an automatic rule and to stick to it without deviation. Hence, instead of being a pilot controlling speed *and* direction, the monetarist chancellor is like a train driver who can control only speed. The automatic rule preferred by Friedman is controlled, or 'fixed-throttle', growth of the money supply. Monetary growth of 5 per cent per year, allowing for productivity gains, will permit the purchase of additional output without causing unacceptable price rises.

Monetarists see control of inflation as vital not just for its own sake but as a necessary condition for market forces to operate properly. Correctly operating market forces will produce, in the long run, both high levels of employment and economic growth. These are the ultimate objectives of economic policy although the control of inflation is an essential intermediate objective. There is also a difference between Keynesians and monetarists in the way inflation is perceived: Keynesians are willing to tolerate mild inflation as the price of full employment; monetarists are intolerant of inflation because of the harm caused to market forces.

To control inflation it is essential to control the growth of the money supply. This means controlling both private sector borrowing (via interest rates or other weapons) and public sector borrowing. The public sector borrowing requirement (PSBR) is a particular target of monetarist criticism. PSBR will be financed in one of four ways (and each method causes a particular problem for the economy):

- *printing money, thus adding to inflation;*

- *borrowing from banks, thus adding to the money supply and therefore inflation;*

- *borrowing from the non-bank sector, thus pushing up interest rates and causing 'crowding out';*

- *borrowing from abroad, thus adding to balance of payments problems in subsequent years.*

A tight fiscal stance means either cutting public expenditure to reduce or avoid a PSBR or raising taxes. As monetarists share supply-siders' dislike of high taxation because of the impact on incentives, the preferred method of reducing the PSBR involves reductions in public expenditure or, more likely, reductions in the planned growth of public expenditure. Supply-side policies, which tend to accompany monetarist macro-economic policies, are designed to make the market more competitive (*see* chapter 4).

Rational expectations: the new classical economics

The rational expectations school builds on both classical theory from Smith onwards and the monetarism of Friedman and others. We have seen that Friedman rejected the discretionary approach to economic policy associated with Keynesian demand management. Instead he favours an automatic approach based on a controlled growth of the money supply. This is because of the failure of Keynesian reflation to reduce unemployment except in the short run. The rational expectations school takes it a stage further by disputing the existence of even a short-run trade-off.

The rational expectations hypothesis starts with the proposition that participants in the market do not ignore or 'throw away' information and predictions about the future course of events in the economy. Rather, they rationally anticipate the consequences of government policy and react accordingly. Consumer and producer reaction will thus partly or totally counteract the intended effects of the government's discretionary fiscal and monetary policy.

This can be illustrated by the Phillips curve. Remember that in Keynesian economics there is a trade-off, but in monetarist theory a purely short-term one. The rational expectationists argue that monetary expansion intended to reduce unemployment will produce an expectation of inflation with no change in real wages. Friedman suggests that in the interval between monetary expansion and inflation there is a rise in employment as people believe that there has been a rise in real wages, but that these same people withdraw from employment when they realise that they have been victims of the money illusion.

The rational expectations school argues that ultimately – after learning has taken place and expectations are adjusted accordingly – the policy-makers have no impact on the economy. In other words, the trade-off does not exist even in the short run.

Thatcherism

Margaret Thatcher was Prime Minister from 1979 to 1990 – the longest continuous period of premiership for one and a half centuries. Although not an original thinker in the way that Keynes was, the combination of political, economic and social policies pursued during the Thatcher years was so distinctive compared to previous Conservative and Labour governments that the term 'Thatcherism' is justified.

Thatcher had been Education Secretary under Edward Heath (1970–4). The Heath government ended with an acceleration of the rate of inflation (the 'Barber dash for growth') and a high degree of social discontent (e.g. the miners' strike and overtime ban which led to electricity cuts and a three-day working week). Within the Conservative Party there was considerable discontent with the failure of Heath's policies and his unenviable record of losing three out of four general elections in which he was party leader. Keynesian policies did not provide an answer to stagflation of the period and the scene was set for the revival of pre-Keynesian ideas known as monetarism. Milton Friedman, the Professor of Economics at Chicago University, was highly influential in right-wing or free-market 'think tanks' such as the Institute for Economic Affairs. Friedman together with Professor Alan Walters of the LSE convinced a large number of Conservative-minded intellectuals of the validity of monetarist theories. Included in this group were Sam Brittan (of the *Financial Times* and elder brother of Leon Brittan, the present European Commissioner) and Sir Keith Joseph, a cabinet minister under Heath who had become critical of the inflationary consequences of Heath's economic policy. In a later interview Joseph stated that at this time Professor Walters refused to shake his hand since he (Joseph) had been party to the debasement of the currency. Joseph was without doubt the first and the leading monetarist in the Conservative Party, by now in opposition. Supporters wanted him to challenge Heath for the leadership of the party but, realising that his talents were those of a 'thinker' rather than a leader, he declined.

This opened the way for Thatcher, also on the right of the party, to challenge for leadership in 1975. To the surprise of many she became

Conservative leader and therefore leader of the opposition at a time when the Wilson and Callaghan government faced the problem of inflation, a sterling crisis and growing trade union problems. In the 1979 general election the defeat of the Callaghan government led to the appointment not only of Britain's first woman Prime Minister but one who was to impose on Britain a distinctive style of government and of policy. The main features of what became known as Thatcherism were a belief in monetarism, economic liberalism and individualism.

A belief in monetarism

As we have seen, monetarism is the view that inflation is caused by excessive growth in the money supply, which is in turn caused by public sector borrowing. The solution is therefore to control the growth of the money supply by controlling public sector borrowing and therefore also public sector spending.

'Sound money' is important to eliminate inflation while at the same time reducing unemployment in the long run, and creating a stable non-inflationary framework in which private enterprise can flourish.

It should be appreciated that the ultimate objective of economic policy remained a high growth in living standards but the strategy to achieve the objective was to be different from that in the Keynesian era. Elimination of inflation was seen as the key to the ultimate achievement of other economic goals. This also meant a switch away from the discretionary style of policy associated with Keynesian demand management. Keynesian policy is essentially short-term adjustment to tackle immediate policy; monetarism stresses an automatic approach to policy over the medium term.

Economic liberalism

Thatcherism involved less state intervention in the economy. This 'rolling back of the state' under Thatcher took the form of:

- *the privatisation of public enterprise;*
- *deregulation (e.g. of the buses);*
- *minimal intervention rather than planning;*
- *free trade;*
- *flexibility in labour markets;*
- *tax reductions to provide incentives.*

These measures are designed to stimulate the supply side of the economy, thus contributing to a rise in output, employment and living standards. Like all supporters of a free-market approach, Thatcherites believed the benefits of any growth will (eventually) 'trickle down to all groups in society'. Consequently, although the initial beneficiaries of Thatcherism might be a narrow section of the community (the yuppies of the early 1980s), eventually growth would benefit all.

Another aspect of Thatcherite economic liberalism was its 'anti-corporatism'. To promote free and competitive enterprise it was felt necessary to reduce powerful vested interests such as trade unions and professional associations.

The legal position of unions was steadily weakened over the 1980s, a decade in which high unemployment and a change in the structure of industry would of itself weaken the union movement. The monopoly privileges of some professional associations (solicitors over conveyancing, and opticians) were removed as part of the same policy of opposition to vested interests.

Individualism The major feature of Thatcherite social policy was self-reliance. In an enigmatic statement Thatcher argued that 'there was no such thing as society – only individuals'. By this she meant that people had a responsibility to support themselves and their families and should not rely upon the state to provide them with a living. It was argued that the welfare state had created a 'culture of dependency' which sapped the drive of many sections of the community (as well as contributing to high taxation that was also disliked by Thatcherites). This dependency culture had to be replaced by an enterprise culture, thus bringing about not just a reversal of Britain's economic misfortunes but a fundamental change of attitude in society.

When Thatcher formed her first government in 1979 there was a determination to alter fundamentally the nature of society and the economy in Britain not only to eliminate inflation through a monetarist policy but create a competitive, free enterprise economy through supply-side measures.

Monetary policy

Keynesian era Until the late 1960s the monetary policy of the UK government focused on the management of the national debt. The priority was to stabilise interest rates to hold down the cost of government. It is true that at times during the 1950s and 1960s credit squeezes were imposed to reduce the rate of growth of money supply. However, such measures were temporary crisis measures and were removed because of government unwillingness to countenance high interest rates and the consequent damage that would be done to the economy and government popularity. This was the age of 'permissive' monetary policy in which the quantity of money was allowed to adjust to sustain target rates of interest. The government, reflecting the prevailing Keynesian orthodoxy, had no particular interest in the quantity of money and did not publish money supply figures. After all, why should the government be concerned about the money supply? The Keynesian liquidity preference curve (*see* Fig. 3.1) shows that the impact of the money supply is indirect via interest rates and investment – and even then the liquidity trap points to a situation in which changes in the money supply have no impact at all.

Although the monetarist counter-revolution is usually associated with the late 1970s, in fact there were signs of a shift in policy even in the 1960s. The government letter of intent to the IMF in 1968 noted the intention of the Treasury to control the growth of the money supply.

'Competition and Credit Control' (1971) marked a shift in policy away from support of the gilt-edged market and towards the control of money and credit. The details of these changes are too rooted in history to warrant retelling but the results were unfortunate. Instead of controlling the growth

Fig. 3.1 *Keynes's liquidity preference curve*

Keynes analysed interest rates in terms of the demand for money and the supply of money. At M supply of money the market rate of interest is r. An increase in the supply of money to M_1 will (other things being equal) lead to a fall in the market rate of interest to r^1.

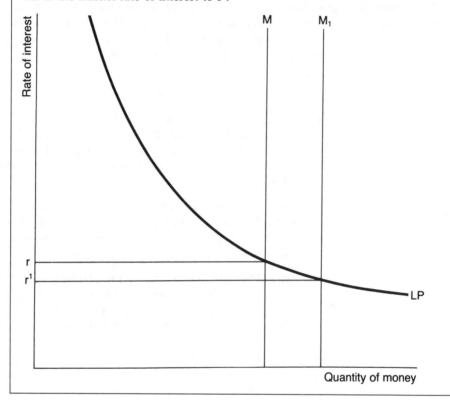

of money supply, the changes produced an unprecedented rise in the money supply. The 'dash for growth' during the Barber boom (named after the then Chancellor of the Exchequer) led to a 30 per cent rise in £M3 and was followed (in the manner predicted by Friedman) by massive inflation in the mid-1970s. This experience played a major part in the rise of monetarism in Britain and the replacement of Edward Heath by Margaret Thatcher as Conservative leader.

The 1974–9 Labour government faced a sterling crisis and in 1976 sought IMF assistance. The conditions imposed by the IMF included a commitment by the UK to stick to annual monetary targets – that is, the government was required to keep to a target annual growth rate of £M3 (the then preferred measure of the money supply). In turn this meant that the PSBR became a target of policy. The PSBR had to be controlled to control the growth of £M3 – no longer would it be an outcome of policy; rather, it would be the centre of policy.

The change to a monetarist approach preceded Thatcher's time in office but whereas Labour pursued the policy as a necessary evil, Thatcher was firmly committed to the elevation of monetary policy and the downgrading of fiscal policy. This change is seen in the drafting of the Medium Term Financial Strategy.

The Medium Term Financial Strategy (MTFS)

The MTFS was a crucial element in the economic strategy of the first Thatcher government, a government determined to eliminate inflation without recourse to income policy. In the MTFS target rates for the growth of broad money (defined then as sterling M3) were set for four-year periods, together with a planned reduction in the PSBR.

The basis behind the MTFS was:

- *the monetarist view of inflation;*

- *the belief that a PSBR not financed by an inflationary increase in the money supply would be financed by debt issue, which would in turn crowd out private sector investment; as both were regarded as undesirable it was essential to reduce public sector borrowing, hopefully without increasing the level of taxation;*

- *recognition of the importance of expectations in the behaviour of economic agents. As expectations play a part in the inflationary process, so acceptance by firms, unions and others of government commitment to reduce inflation (at all costs) will reduce inflationary pressure.*

In the early 1980s the MTFS involved inflexible targets which aggravated the unemployment problem. Moreover, the rise in unemployment increased the PSBR through a fall in tax yield and a rise in welfare spending. Consequently, the MTFS had only limited success in controlling the growth of the money supply.

From 1983 the MTFS lost much of its prominence in government economic policy. The strict monetarism of the early years gave way to a more pragmatic approach. Problems of controlling the money supply meant that emphasis was now placed on M0 (notes, coins and balances at the Bank of England) rather than the broader £M3.

Middle 1980s to 1990: the Lawson years

The MTFS was successful in reducing the inflation rate over the medium term. However, this was at the expense of output and employment. Keynesian economists, such as the American James Tobin and the Briton James Meade, argued that deflation had mainly reduced output and employment, and that this would always be the case unless the government adopted an incomes policy. There were also technical problems relating to monetary targets. £M3 grew rapidly in 1980/1 despite the acknowledged tight monetary conditions. The behaviour of £M3 was attributed to the re-intermediation following the removal of direct controls on bank lending (i.e. the removal of supplementary special deposits).

The result was a change in policy within the introduction of new monetary targets. Instead of one intermediate target, the government planned to assess monetary conditions 'in the light of movements, in narrow and broad money, and the behaviour of other financial indicators, in particular the exchange rate' (Financial Statement and Budget Report 1987). The indicators now took in M0 (narrow money), M4 (broad money), the exchange rate and asset prices. £M3/M3 was dropped because it was behaving in an unpredictable fashion. M0 was targeted because of its clear correlation with inflation. However, broad money could not be ignored and so M4 (which includes building society deposits) was included. Asset prices were included because of their impact on liquidity. Finally, the exchange rate was included in the indicators because of international desire for currency stability and national concern about the impact of exchange rate fluctuations on importing and exporting. These were the indicators: the objective remained the defeat of inflation and the policy weapon was to be interest rate changes. As shown in Illustration 3.2, the effect of interest rate rises is to discourage borrowing and therefore investment and other forms of spending. In Keynesian terms this represents a fall in the level of aggregate demand. For monetarists the important impact is on bank lending and therefore the supply of money.

Illustration 3.2 *The impact of a rise in interest rates*

A *On the macro-economy*

1 A rise in the cost of borrowing.

2 A fall in the level of investment.

3 A rise in mortgage rates resulting in:

   (a) a fall in discretionary income
   (b) a fall in consumer spending
   (c) slow-down in the housing market.

4 A rise in exchange rates resulting in:

   (a) a fall in export competitiveness
   (b) a rise in competitiveness of imports.

5 The downturn in the economy is likely to be accompanied by job losses but a reduction in inflationary pressure.

B *On a particular business*

1 A fall in the volume of sales due to (a) the fall in discretionary income and/or (b) interest rate on credit sales perhaps discouraging people from buying on credit.

2 A rise in the cost of (past and present) borrowing.

3 A cutback in the firm's investment plans (a higher internal rate of return is needed if investment is to be made).

4 It raises the cost of working capital (investment in stocks).

5 It increases the opportunity cost of converting liquid reserves into stock.

6 Destocking might occur.

7 Cash flow problems.

8 Possible short-time working or staff lay-offs.

9 Company shares are less attractive to shareholders.

Exchange rate targeting

By 1988 it was clear that one indicator above all others dominated the conduct of monetary policy: the exchange rate, which was shadowing the Deutschmark at the rate of £1 = 3DM. The explanation for this policy of shadowing was:

- *the exchange rate has a significant impact on the real economy;*

- *for Chancellor Lawson (but not Thatcher) shadowing was the prelude to membership of the Exchange Rate Mechanism;*

- *this, in turn, was seen as a way of joining the 'low inflation club';*

- *it provided a degree of external discipline on the domestic economy. To keep within the target range it is essential that monetary policy is used to keep the inflation rate in line with the country whose currency is being shadowed.*

The immediate impact of shadowing the Deutschmark was not greater monetary discipline in a deflationary sense but, instead, cuts in interest rates. The Deutschmark was weak and to prevent a currency inflow (which would have pushed up the exchange rate, thus endangering export industries) it was necessary to reduce UK interest rates. Coinciding with this cut in interest rates were:

- *a reduction in income tax (to 25 per cent standard rate, 40 per cent higher rate);*

- *deregulation of the financial sector, which increased the competition for customers to borrow money;*

- *a desire to ease monetary conditions to prevent the Black Monday (October 1987) fall in share prices producing a worldwide slump like the one that followed in the wake of the 1929 Wall Street Crash.*

The Lawson boom of 1987–8 quickly led to overheating of the economy since, although GDP rose by 4.7 per cent in both 1987 and 1988, domestic demand rose even faster. Consequently, although unemployment fell to below 10 per cent the retail prices index showed that inflation was moving upwards and, as usually happens, the current account of the balance of payments was moving into deficit.

The resurgence of inflation brought a shift in policy by 1987. The emphasis shifted towards domestic monetary conditions. This meant, first, high interest rates to keep within M0 targets and, second, the running of a public sector debt repayment (PSDR). The PSDR is the opposite of a PSBR and is thus deflationary rather than inflationary. When attention turned again to the exchange rate, the objective was to keep it high. A high rate keeps down the cost of imported goods and this was considered more important than the adverse effect a high rate has on exporters.

The combination of a high pound, high interest rates and the planned PSDR was to produce a recession in the UK.

Central bank independence

As part of its policy of nationalisation, the Labour government of 1945–51 nationalised the Bank of England in 1946. Prior to this date the Bank had been a joint stock company – in other words, a bank in the private sector. Even before 1946, however, the Bank of England had a unique role in the banking system as:

- *the sole note-issue bank in England and Wales;*
- *the holder of the government's accounts;*
- *the bank for other banks.*

Over the 19th century the Bank slowly took on the responsibility of lender of last resort. This is shown by the Bank's indifference to banking collapses in the early part of the century but intervention in the later part.

Until 1914 Britain, that is sterling, was on the Gold Standard. The currency was both convertible into gold at a fixed rate and backed by an equivalent account of gold in Bank of England vaults. (Apart from a fiduciary issue of notes which developed as a result of relinquishing of note-issue powers by other English and Welsh banks.) The Gold Standard provided a check on the growth of the money supply and an automatic mechanism to correct the balance of payments (*see* Fig. 1.1). This automatic-rule approach to policy was consistent with the non-interventionist stance of 19th-century governments. The fact that the Bank of England was in the private sector (though accepting the responsibilities that went with its privileged position in the banking system) was not questioned.

At the end of the First World War there was a desire to return to normality. This meant restoration of the Gold Standard, which was partly achieved in 1925. The Standard was seen as essential to stable trading relations and was favoured by the banking community, especially the Bank of England and its then Governor, Montagu Norman. However, the decision to return to gold at its pre-war parity was criticised by the opposition parties, by trade union leaders and by John Maynard Keynes. The pound was overvalued by 10 per cent, thus harming the export performance of already hard-pressed industries. The return to gold can be compared to applying the brakes while cycling uphill. The left regards the bankers, especially Norman, as the villains of the piece. Hence it was not surprising that the Bank of England become a Labour target for nationalisation.

The Labour government nationalised the Bank of England in 1946. It should be remembered that Keynesian macro-economics was accepted as orthodox economics from 1940 onwards. Governments (both Labour and Conservative) accepted demand management as a way of achieving the economic objectives of full employment, price stability and balance of payments equilibrium. Monetary policy, especially in terms of determining short-term interest rates, was seen as an important weapon of government economic policy. Consequently, control of the Bank of England was seen as a prerequisite of successful economic policy formulation. This would avoid the situation that applied in the 1920s, of bankers pursuing policies that conflicted with the objectives of the elected government.

From 1946 it was accepted that the central bank should be publicly owned and subject to Treasury control. Like other nationalised industries of the period, the Bank of England was separate from the government but major policy initiatives and key appointments were subject to Treasury control. In carrying out monetary and exchange rate policy, the Bank of England acted as the agent of the Treasury.

The monetarist counter-revolution led by Friedman brought a questioning of the desirability of political control of the Bank of England. Friedman rejected the use of fine tuning to manage the economy. Keynesian reflation would lead to inflation with no reduction in unemployment except in the short run. Monetarists argued that vote-seeking governments will be tempted to pursue expansionist (i.e. inflationary) monetary policy in what is a futile attempt to reduce unemployment by Keynesian methods.

The British situation may be contrasted with that in Germany. The German Bundesbank is constitutionally independent of the government and is charged with the duty of pursuing the policy objective of price stability. Hence the elected federal government determines fiscal policy and the Bundesbank adjusts monetary policy to ensure that, when combined, the result is non-inflationary.

The case for an independent central bank is based on the following points:

- *such a bank has no incentive to deviate from the objective of price stability;*

- *because monetary policy is flexible an independent central bank can neutralise the inflationary tendencies of the elected government;*

- *there appears to be a correlation between the degree of central bank independence and low national inflation rates;*

- *an independent central bank will command greater credibility, thus reducing inflationary expectations.*

Critics of central bank independence base their case on the concept of democratic deficit. If the central bank is not subject to political control it is not accountable. It is possible that the central bank, as in the Montagu Norman era, will pursue unacceptably restrictive policies at the expense of employment levels. However, such criticisms are based on Keynesian notions of the ability of governments to exert a long-term impact on unemployment.

The issue of central bank independence is also relevant to economic and monetary union (EMU) within the EC. The Maastricht Treaty provides for the establishment of a European Central Bank which, it is envisaged, will enjoy the same degree of independence as is currently enjoyed by the Bundesbank. Acceptance of EMU will mean a transfer of monetary sovereignty, and Euro-sceptics argue that this is an unacceptable transfer of sovereignty. Supporters of EMU argue that the independent Central Bank would remove the temptation for politicians to reflate (which for monetarists means inflate) for party political advantage.

Fiscal policy

The role of taxation and fiscal policy has changed over the years. In the mid-19th century the great Chancellor of the Exchequer William Gladstone saw his duty as raising sufficient revenue to cover the government's expenditure commitments. The level of both government spending and taxation should be kept to a minimum and the government should run neither a deficit on the budget (seen as setting a bad example) nor a surplus (seen as an unwarranted confiscation of taxpayers' money).

In the 20th century the budget took on additional functions, primarily at the behest of two other Liberals. David Lloyd George, Chancellor of the Exchequer in the years before the First World War, gave the budget an expressly redistributive role. His famous and controversial 1911 budget sought to redistribute wealth and income – in particular away from the landowning class. A generation later Keynes convinced people that the budget should take on the role of economic management. Hence during the Keynesian years students would make the following points in answer to the familiar questions about the functions of taxation:

- *to raise revenue to finance the provision of goods and services that are inadequately provided by the market (i.e. public and merit goods);*

- *to redistribute wealth and income;*

- *to discourage the consumption of demerit goods;*

- *to tax away monopoly profits;*

- *to protect home producers;*

- *to regulate the economy, in particular the use of taxes to curb demand.*

Perceptions of the role of taxation changed with the monetarist counter-revolution of the 1970s. When faced with the question 'What are the legitimate functions of taxation?' a supporter of free-market and monetarist principles would argue that there is only one legitimate function: to raise revenue to finance government activity – and such activity should be kept to a minimum. The redistributive function is criticised as being harmful to incentives on which future prosperity is based. In other words, we should not attempt to 'redistribute the cake' if such activity jeopardises 'baking a larger cake'. Free-market supporters also reject the right of the state to interfere with consumption by taxing demerit goods. They would not support the use of tariff barriers to restrict imports and, most important of all, they reject the idea of managing the economy by discretionary fiscal policy.

Monetarists favour an automatic fiscal rule of balancing the budget. Hence the prime duty of the Chancellor of the Exchequer is to ensure that government raises sufficient revenue to cover its spending commitments. In the early Thatcher years, when monetarism was particularly dominant in policy decisions, the government's aim was to reduce the public sector borrowing requirement. Logically this involved either cuts in government spending or increases in taxation but increases in taxation clashed with the government aim of reducing the burden of taxation to stimulate the supply side. For

Fig. 3.2 *The Laffer curve*

Laffer pointed out that a tax rate of zero per cent would raise zero revenue but so too would a rate of 100 per cent: it would not be worthwhile working if the state confiscated the whole of one's income. Consequently there is certain tax rate (x per cent) which maximises tax yield and any rise above x will reduce tax yield. Two further conclusions can be drawn. First, it is possible to raise the tax yield by reducing the tax rate – the tax reduction produces incentives which raise output and income thus increasing tax yield. Second, at rates below x per cent it is possible to detect the disincentive effect. Where tax yield rises by a lower proportion than tax rate the tax is having a disincentive effect. This is shown in a line tangential to the curve. If the line is at an angle of more than 45 degrees then the disincentive effect is present. The Laffer curve is based on a simple idea and it has been very influential – its greatest weakness is the difficulty of predicting the tax rates which produce a disincentive effect or which maximise tax yield.

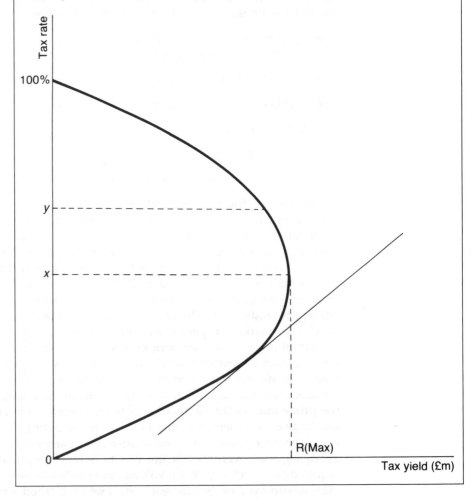

monetarists, controlling the PSBR was more important than achieving low taxation, and so there was a constant threat that if the PSBR could not be reduced by other means, tax increases would be imposed. Nevertheless, the preferred method of curbing the PSBR was to reduce the level of government spending – or to be more exact, to reduce the planned increase in government spending.

The aim of reducing the PSBR, both in money terms and as a percentage of GDP, was at the heart of the Medium Term Financial Strategy. However, the recession of the early 1980s kept the PSBR stubbornly high. This was because unemployment causes both a fall in tax receipts and a rise in welfare expenditure.

By the late 1980s the government recorded a surplus on its finances. Public sector debt repayment (PSDR) is a surplus on current income over expenditure and, as the name suggests, involves a repayment of the national debt.

The recession of the early 1990s has brought a revival of the PSBR. A fall in tax receipts coupled with a rise in welfare spending led to a shortfall in government finances. In the 1992 budget the Chancellor forecast a £28-billion PSBR. By the autumn statement of 1992 this was reassessed as £37 billion, possibly rising to £48 billion. The more relaxed attitude to the PSBR compared with the early 1980s illustrates the way in which strict monetarism has been succeeded by a more pragmatic view. A drastic reduction in the PSBR would involve tax rises (which would further delay recovery) or cuts in government expenditure (which are difficult and unpopular). There is now a tendency to distinguish between that part of the PSBR caused by temporary downturn in activity and the remainder caused by an unwillingness or inability to raise taxes sufficiently to cover expenditure. In this way the government takes comfort from the fact that, but for the recession, the PSBR would be considerably lower.

The Thatcher and Major governments favour a low tax economy, although Fig. 3.2 demonstrates that the effect of government policy can have a perverse effect. These governments also favour a shift in the balance of taxation from direct to indirect. Direct taxes, imposed on income and wealth, are usually seen as progressive (although the community charge, or poll tax, was an exception) and therefore contribute to income and wealth redistribution. However, they are seen as harming effort and enterprise. Conversely, indirect taxes (usually seen as regressive) are applauded as being 'voluntary' and not harmful to enterprise (*see* Fig. 3.3).

The first budget of the Thatcher era involved a significant shift from income tax to expenditure taxes. Although the main, but not the only, beneficiaries were the more prosperous citizens, Chancellor Sir Geoffrey Howe did announce the government's intention to reduce the burden of income tax. Over a decade later, in 1992, Chancellor Norman Lamont introduced a lower rate of 20 per cent as the prelude to an eventual standard rate of 20 per cent. This commitment to lower income tax acts as a political constraint on increasing taxation and so, at the time of writing, tax increases to reduce the PSBR seem most likely to take the form of increases in indirect taxes. These could involve either increasing the rate of VAT (productive of revenue but unpopular) or extending its coverage. As we will see in chapter 11, reducing

Fig. 3.3 *Direct v. indirect taxation*

Advantages of Direct Taxation	*Advantages of Indirect Taxation*
1. Usually progressive	1. Convenient; payment is spread
2. Redistribution in favour of low-income groups (whether this is beneficial is a matter of opinion)	2. 'Voluntary'
3. Yield rises as income rises	3. Does not harm effort and initiative
4. Anti-inflationary	4. Less chance of evasion
5. Incidence (burden) is easy to determine	5. Flexible
	6. Can be used for specific purposes

Disadvantages of Direct Taxation	*Disadvantages of Indirect Taxation*
1. Disincentive effect	1. Regressive
2. Stifles initiative and enterprise	2. Penalises certain forms of consumption
3. Evasion and avoidance encouraged	3. Harms the industry concerned
4. Discourages investment, including investment from abroad	4. Raises prices
5. Expensive to collect	5. Incidence (burden) is difficult to determine
6. Reduces savings	

the extent of zero rating would be popular among the other EC member states although guaranteed to be unpopular at home.

Appendix 3.1 Conservative budgets 1979–1993

This appendix highlights some of the major budget changes in taxation. In most budgets allowances and exemptions against direct taxation are raised in line with inflation – in fact, a failure to raise them is more headline grabbing. Similarly, in most budgets specific excise taxes (which are related to quantity rather than value) are raised to maintain yield in real terms.

Date	*Chancellor*	*Major changes*
1979	Howe	Cut in basic rate of income tax: 33 to 30%
		Cut in highest rate: 83 to 60%
		Rise in VAT to 15%
		Cuts in planned public expenditure
1980	Howe	MTFS: aim to reduce PSBR to 2% of GDP
		Targeting of benefits
		No significant changes in taxation
1981	Howe	Public expenditure cuts
		Tax allowances not raised in line with inflation

Date	Chancellor	Major changes
		Rise in taxes on North Sea oil, alcohol, tobacco, motoring
		One-off tax on bank profits
1982	Howe	Tax thresholds raised by more than inflation (to make up for 1981)
		Cut in national insurance surcharge
		Rise in specific excise duties
1983	Howe	Reflationary budget
		Rise in allowances by more than inflation
		Cut in national insurance surcharge
		Rise in specific excise duties
		Rise in mortgage interest relief
		Incentives for the unemployed to become self-employed
1984	Lawson	Rise in specific excise duties
1985	Lawson	Cuts in capital transfer tax
		Rise in specific duties
		Expansion of youth training
1986	Lawson	Cut in basic rate income tax to 29%
		CTT replaced by inheritance tax
		Rise in some specific duties
1987	Lawson	Cut in basic rate income tax to 27%
		Portable pensions with tax relief
		Higher than planned increase in public spending
		No change in specific duties except 5p cut in tax on unleaded petrol: the higher rate on leaded petrol is a 'pollution tax'
1988	Lawson	Basic rate income tax cut to 25%; aim to reduce to 20%
		Top rate cut from 60 to 40%
		Allowances increased by twice the rate of inflation
		Separate taxation for husbands and wives
		Mortage interest tax relief limited to one mortage payer per home
		Rise in excise duties
1989	Lawson	Budget to curb demand in the face of renewed inflation
		Reform of national insurance to diminish the poverty trap
		Rise in allowances
		Of the excise duties only the tax on unleaded petrol was increased
1990	Major	Abolition of joint taxation for married couples
		TESSAs launched to encourage saving
		No major changes in income tax
		Rise in exemptions on capital taxes
		Rise in excise duties
1991	Lamont	£140 per head reduction in community charge (poll tax)
		VAT rose from 15 to 17.5%
		End of mortgage tax relief at higher tax rates
		Rise in excise duties
		Rise in exemptions in capital tax
1992	Lamont	Reduction in income tax on first £2,000 of taxable income (from 25 to 20%)
		Rise in excise duties
1992	Lamont	In the autumn statement, car tax was abolished

Date	Chancellor	Major changes
1993	Lamont	The last spring budget. Future budget announcement will occur in the autumn when spending plans are announced
		No increase in allowances
		VAT introduced on domestic fuel

Appendix 3.2 Schools of economic thought

1. *Classical economics*
The economic thought of the 18th and early 19th centuries associated with Adam Smith, David Ricardo, Thomas Malthus, and J. S. Mill. Classical theory concerned growth and development and set out to investigate the nature and causes of the 'wealth of nations' and the distribution of the national product. Capital accumulation, the expansion of markets and division of labour played a crucial role in classical theory.

2. *Neo-classical economics*
Theory developed in the 19th century which used marginal analysis to analyse the pricing of goods, services and factors of production in competitive markets. In competitive situations, equilibrium price will 'clear' the market. Hence neo-classical economists accepted that market forces will produce a full employment equilibrium.

3. *Keynesian economics*
Macro-economic theory developed in the 1930s by Keynes and extended by Keynesian economists after his death in 1946. Keynes stressed the importance of aggregate demand in determining the level of economic activity and demonstrated that the market system did not guarantee a full employment equilibrium. Hence Keynes advocated intervention in the form of demand management to achieve the government's macro-economic objectives.

4. *Monetarism*
A school of economic thought which argues that instability in the economy is caused primarily by disturbances within the monetary sector – in particular it is argued that 'inflation is always and everywhere a monetary phenomenon'. Monetarists such as Milton Friedman argue that the duty of government is to prevent rapid increases or decreases in the money supply. This 'fixed-throttle' approach contrasts with the discretionary approach associated with Keynesianism. Although modern monetarism is associated with the last quarter of the 20th century, many of the basic principles originated in classical theory.

5. *New classical macro-economics*
This is a restatement of classical economics but with stress laid on rational expectations and a natural rate of unemployment. Although often treated as synonymous with modern monetarism, there is a vital difference. Friedman

and other monetarists accept the Phillips curve trade-off in the short run – new classical economists reject even a short-run trade-off. Keynesian demand management policies are seen as futile and so governments should concentrate on supply-side measures to make markets work better.

Appendix 3.3 Important economic indicators

Indicator	What it measures	Its significance
Capacity utilisation	Extent to which plant and machinery is being used	Indicates (a) room for growth and (b) inflationary pressure
Capital account flows	Flow of capital into and out of a country	Affects exchange rate. Outflows represent the acquisition of assets overseas
Consumer confidence	Consumers' perception of well-being	Determines spending in the immediate future
Consumer spending	Spending by households	Key element in the determination of GDP
Current account balance	Receipts from trade in goods and services less expenditure on goods and services	Must be balanced by capital flows and changes in official reserves
Disposable income	Personal income after taxation and other adjustments	Personal disposable income is the basis for consumption and saving
Employment	Number employed plus the number self-employed	Indicates current potential output
Gross domestic product (GDP)	Measures the extent of economic activity in terms of current prices	Measures the total level of production
Gross national product (GNP)	GDP plus net property from abroad	Measure of national income
Gross domestic fixed capital formation	Capital investment	A determining factor in future output
Housing starts	Number of new houses started	Indicates construction activity
Labour or workforce	Total of those employed plus self-employed plus unemployed	Indicates maximum potential output
Money supply	Notes, coins and bank deposits	Indicator of the level of transactions and future inflation
Orders	New orders received by producers	Indicates output in the immediate future
Productivity	Output per unit of input	Indicates efficiency and potential total economic output
PSBR/PSDR	Net total of government revenue over expenditure: PSBR is a deficit; PSDR is a surplus	Indicates the government's fiscal stance

Indicator	What it measures	Its significance
Real GDP	Measures economic activity at constant prices	Provides a measure of growth of output over time
Retail prices index	Changes in the price of a basket of goods: weighted average change in prices	Measure of inflation experienced by an average household
Retail sales	Total value of sales by retailers	Indicates consumer demand
Stocks/inventories	Stocks of goods held by firms	Indicates demand pressure
Savings ratio	Savings as a proportion of income	Major influence on investment and interest rates
Terms of trade	The ratio of changes in export prices to changes in import prices	Indicates changes in the volume of imports that can be bought with a given volume of exports
Unemployment	The number of people out of work but ready and able to work	Indicates spare capacity in the economy
Wholesale and Producer prices	Changes in average prices at the factory gate	Leading indicator of future retail price inflation

Appendix 3.4 Regular publications from the Central Statistical Office

Annual Abstract of Statistics Covers every aspect of economic, social and industrial life

Business Monitors Statistics on industry and the distributive trades

Economic Trends Published once a month, it includes all main economic indicators

Family Expenditure Survey Annual survey of household spending based on a sample of 11,500 households

Financial Statistics Published once a month, it includes key financial and monetary statistics

Monthly Digest of Statistics Covers population, employment, prices, wages, production, output

Regional Trends Annual source of official statistics about UK regions

Social Trends Annual survey of population, education, employment, income, wealth, health and social services

UK Balance of Payments The annual 'pink book' contains information on visible trade, invisible trade and capital movement

UK National Accounts The annual 'blue book' contains data on national income

UK Social and Business Statistics Annual publication covering key social and economic statistics

Economic Trends Annual Supplement Statistics on the UK economy from 1950

CHAPTER 4

Micro-economic Policy

We saw in chapter 3 that since the interventionist period of the Keynesian era governments in the UK have adopted a more *laissez-faire* stance on the economy. In micro-economic or industrial policy the UK has continued this free-market, or supply, approach in which government is confined to improving the operations of the market by making it more competitive. This chapter commences with the issue of interventionism and non-interventionism before moving on to a more detailed look at particular micro-economic policy issues.

OBJECTIVES
1 To analyse the case for and against intervention in the private sector.
2 To explore the supply-side approach.
3 To analyse the government's small-firms policy.
4 To analyse competition policy.
5 To analyse the policy of privatisation.

The rationale for government intervention

The zenith of *laissez-faire* in the UK came in the mid-19th century. The state played a minimal role in economic and social affairs, confined mainly to the provision of public goods such as law and order and defence. In fact, the bulk of government expenditure went towards financing past, present and future wars. The state merely 'held the ring' to allow private enterprise to prosper by responding to consumer needs.

This minimalist role of government was in line with classical economic theory that developed from Adam Smith onwards. It was believed that the 'invisible hand' of market forces would produce an optimum result.

1 Resources are allocated to produce the goods and services demanded by consumers.

2 The market system is a flexible and continuous referendum by which consumers signal their desires.

3 The profit motive ensures that supply will respond to demand and that resources will be used in the most productive way.

4 Competition provides a spur to efficiency.

5 Income from the provision of factors of production will ensure that all will benefit from the wealth produced. Competitive forces in the factor markets will ensure an equitable return on factor inputs.

Despite this belief in market solutions, problems emerged that produced a sub-optimum outcome when the economy was left to market forces. For instance, the competitive railway system of the 1830s was replaced by regional monopoly. As early as 1844 there were plans to nationalise the railway track. Victorian private enterprise produced environmental health problems that necessitated government intervention. The provision of education was inadequate and therefore large sections of the community were denied access to it. These and other instances of market failure provided the justification for state intervention in the second half of the 19th century.

Economists based their case for intervention on the proposition that markets do not always work in the smooth frictionless way suggested in classical economic theory. The market either fails to solve a problem or it actually creates a problem. This failure is the result of distortion caused by the absence of competition or by the divergence between the private and the social (i.e. private plus external) costs and benefits of an economic activity.

Consider monopoly and other imperfections in the market. All statements in support of an unregulated market are based on the assumption that the market is competitive. Productive and allocative efficiency will only be achieved when all markets are perfectly competitive and when trading takes place at equilibrium price in all markets. Only then will the social optimum situation of price equalling marginal cost occur in all forms of production. In imperfect markets price (average revenue) exceeds marginal costs. Consequently, at the profit maximising output the price paid by consumers exceeds the additional cost of producing the last unit of output. As price reflects marginal utility, we can conclude that welfare will be enhanced if output of that product is increased since the additional utility to the consumer will exceed the additional cost to the producer. However, the monopolist will decide not to increase output since to do so would reduce profits. As monopoly produces an unsatisfactory situation some form of state intervention is considered necessary. This can take the form of breaking up the monopoly, nationalising it or regulating it (see later).

Market failure in the form of divergence between private and social costs and benefit takes a number of forms.

1 The social cost of an activity exceeds private costs by the extent of external costs such as pollution.

2 The social benefits of certain forms of consumption (e.g. education and health) exceed private benefits, which in any case are not fully appreciated. This provides the *raison d'être* for state provision of merit goods.

3 The social return from innovation exceeds the private return. This provides the justification for state support for research and development, especially in the case of those projects which take a long time to payback.

4 The social benefit from production in the less well-off parts of the country exceeds private benefit. This provides the justification for regional aid.

Intervention to correct market failure led to state provision of goods and services neglected by private enterprise (i.e. public and merit goods) and to taking over production of goods and services where it can be more efficiently undertaken by the state. The result is known as a 'mixed economy' although two points must be appreciated.

1 All economies are in practice mixed, although the balance will vary, with some leaning towards free enterprise and others towards the planned economy (*see* Fig. 4.1).

2 The mixture takes two forms:

(a)   private versus public enterprise;
(b)   market versus non-market provision.
      In (a) the distinction between sectors is based on ownership of the means of production; in (b) on the mechanism for allocating resources (*see* Fig. 4.2).

The trend in the UK during most of the 20th century was towards a larger public and non-market sector and a smaller (in proportionate terms at least) private and market sector. Hence earlier decades of the century saw an increase in central and local government provision of services (e.g. education, the National Health Service). In the main these services are free at the point of consumption and are financed out of general taxation. This is the non-market sector. The other component of the public sector is (increasingly this should be 'was') the nationalised industry sector. Nationalised industries in the UK are/were publicly owned but operated in the market sector. In other words, they sold their goods and services in the market place, albeit one in which they were not exposed to full competition.

In addition to state provision of goods and services, the 20th century has seen increased state intervention designed to guide the economy towards some desirable outcomes and away from some undesirable ones. This intervention has taken the form of:

■ *discouraging or even banning demerit goods;*

■ *control and regulation of monopoly;*

■ *encouraging greater regional balance in the economy;*

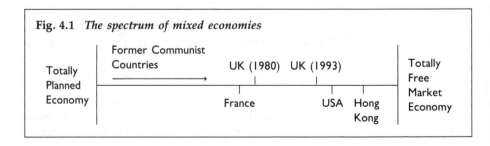

Fig. 4.1 *The spectrum of mixed economies*

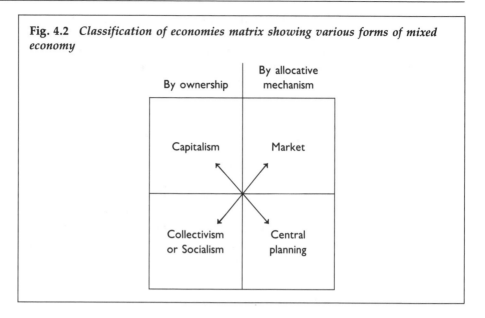

Fig. 4.2 *Classification of economies matrix showing various forms of mixed economy*

- *control of external costs;*

- *subsidies to encourage activities that produce substantial external benefits (to non-consumers);*

- *action to reduce inequality;*

- *modifying the price system where shortages would produce hardship (e.g. in housing);*

- *protecting groups (e.g. employees and consumers) who might otherwise be placed in a weak position;*

- *correcting macro-economic problems.*

Until the mid-1970s, there was a broad consensus about the desirability of government intervention in the market place. Even many Conservatives accepted the need for some state involvement in the form of providing goods and services or in terms of regulating private enterprise. In fact a ratchet effect was in operation: more radical governments increased state intervention in the economy and these governments were followed by more conservative governments that tended to accept the status quo. This trend towards greater state intervention began to be questioned in the mid-1970s, coinciding with the monetarist counter-revolution associated with Friedman and Hayek. We can attribute the reaction against state intervention to:

- *concern about the excessive power of the modern state;*

- *a growing belief in the superiority of competitive markets;*

- *disenchantment with the performance of government management and regulation of the economy.*

The 1979 election of a Conservative government under Margaret Thatcher was a prelude to a concerted attempt to roll back the state. In addition to privatisation, the Thatcher and Major governments have pursued a variety of policies to deregulate markets, opening them up to greater competition and to the free play of market forces.

Supply-side economics

Keynesian economics emphasises the importance of aggregate demand and it is assumed that supply will respond to demand. The emphasis in supply-side economics is on the productivity capability of the economy. Advocates of supply-side economics have a distrust of government intervention, the results of which are unpredictable, perverse and destabilising. Hence they believe in the old classical view that governments should merely provide a framework for the operation of market forces. This framework should include:

- *the provision of public goods;*

- *a balanced budget;*

- *low taxation;*

- *controlled growth of the money supply;*

and *either* a fixed *or* a cleanly floating exchange rate (in neither case should there be scope for discretionary action by the government).

Supply-siders believe in market forces: the market is calm and orderly, and the price mechanism provides the necessary signals and incentives and it produces an optimum allocation of resources. However, rigidities and imperfections impair the smooth functioning of the market – especially the market in the factors of production that are crucial in the productive capacity of the economy. Therefore supply-side measures are micro- rather than macro-economic. They can be characterised as measures designed to make markets work better so as to increase the creation of wealth. At the same time they can be seen as counter-inflationary (anything which increases supply relative to demand helps to reduce inflationary pressure) and as aiding the reduction in unemployment (reducing the natural rate of unemployment).

We can categorise the major elements in supply-side policies pursued by Conservative governments in terms of:

- *incentives to encourage enterprise, effort, savings and investment;*

- *measures to improve the efficiency of the market by allowing greater freedom;*

- *labour market measures.*

Incentives The most effective incentive is to reduce the burden of taxation – especially taxes on income and profits. Economists have always argued that the disincentive aspect of taxation is not its overall burden (the average rate of taxation) but its marginal rate. By reducing the tax levied on the final pound of income, it is expected that incentives will be greater. The Laffer curve illustrated in chapter 3 has highly influenced Conservative tax cutting in the 1980s and 1990s although difficulties in reducing public spending (coupled with concern over public borrowing) act as a constraint on tax reductions.

As well as reducing the overall burden of taxation, it is important to minimise its distorting effect. Logically this should mean a broader-based VAT and a reduction in the specific duties. Nevertheless, for reasons of externalities and social equity, the UK has preferred the present system of a relatively narrowly based (by EC standards) VAT and heavy specific duties on certain items (tobacco, petrol, alcohol, betting).

In addition, there are other, more immediate incentives such as assistance for new start-up businesses and, for employees, profit-related pay and share option schemes, and wider share ownership generally.

Market freedom Measures have included:

- *privatisation;*
- *deregulation;*
- *removal of other government controls (e.g. incomes policy);*
- *limitations on trade unions;*
- *the end of exchange controls (1979);*
- *removal of institutional barriers in the capital market;*
- *abolition of dividend controls;*
- *abolition of controls on bank lending;*
- *increased freedom of action for building societies;*
- *removing monopoly powers of professional associations (e.g. conveyancing, opticians' services);*
- *compulsory competitive tendering (market testing).*

Measures in the labour market These have been designed to improve the quality and quantity of labour, remove rigidities in the labour market and reduce the natural rate of unemployment. They include:

- *removing the poverty/unemployment trap by cuts in income tax for those in work;*
- *sale of council houses to increase the geographical mobility of labour;*
- *reforms in the pension system to encourage 'portability', thus reducing labour immobility;*
- *training and re-training schemes;*
- *reduction in trade union power by a series of Employment Acts;*

■ *removal of wage-fixing Wages Councils;*

■ *relaxation of some of the earlier employment protection measures;*

■ *opposition to the EC Social Charter.*

Small and medium-sized enterprises

In the past, small firms were frequently ignored by both governments and economists. There was a strong belief in the benefits of large-scale production, resulting in a 'big is best' mentality. Economies of scale result in average costs falling as the scale of production rises. Some economies are available only when there is an increase in the size of the factory or other production unit (these are 'plant level economies'). Other economies are 'firm-level economies' and are available to firms which grow by increasing the number, rather than the size, of plants.

Focusing on plant size alone we can identify the minimum size necessary for efficient lowest-cost production. This is known as the minimum efficient plant size (MEPS), which is shown in Fig. 4.3 as output level 0X. If the scale of production is below 0X the producer will be at a significant cost disadvantage compared with rival firms at home and abroad. Competitive forces will lead to the elimination of a small independent firm producing below the MEPS. This is achieved either by means of closure (voluntary or involuntary) or take-over.

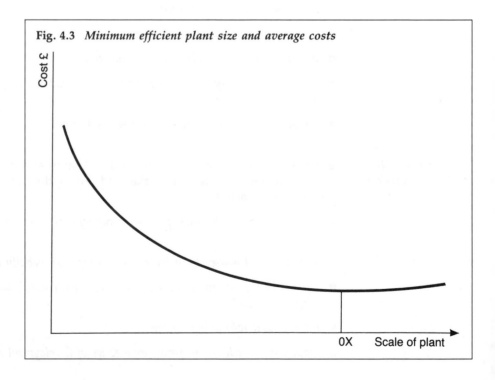

Fig. 4.3 *Minimum efficient plant size and average costs*

Cost £

0X   Scale of plant

Britain's failure to compete in world markets was often attributed to the small size of British firms, especially in manufacturing industry, relative to competitors abroad. Consequently, in the 1960s and 1970s governments promoted industrial mergers to create large-scale firms. The Industrial Reorganisation Corporation was established for this purpose even though its activities during the 1960s and 1970s might appear to have run counter to UK competition policy. The need for economies of large-scale production when competing in world markets was greater than any fears of sponsoring monopolistic tendencies in the market.

During this period small firms were seen in a rather negative light: as firms that through lack of finance, drive, ambition and market opportunity failed to grow. These negative factors can be divided into supply factors which limited size:

- *limitations of the owner–manager;*
- *entrepreneurial preference for small scale;*
- *institutional factors which stunted the growth of enterprise;*
- *the absence of substantial economies of scale in the sector concerned;*

and demand factors which limited size:

- *low level of demand;*
- *market imperfections resulting in a fragmentation of the market in terms of geography or other forms of segmentation.*

These are negative points which explain the persistence of small firms in terms of failure to grow despite the economies of scale that should have been available.

There were some additional, more positive explanations for the continued existence of small firms:

- *they had advantages in terms of better staff and customer relations;*
- *the process of vertical disintegration (e.g. in the motor industry) provided opportunities for small firms to supply components;*
- *co-operation in joint projects enabled smaller firms to compete.*

Despite these last points there was still a tendency to see small firms as an aberration rather than being valuable in their own right.

A growing interest in the small-firms sector

The belief that 'big is always best' was questioned in the early 1970s. An influential book, *Small Is Beautiful* by Ernst Schumacher, provided a slogan for those who came to appreciate the attractions of small-scale, 'human-sized' units of production. A number of factors provided the stimulus for this growing interest in the positive benefits of small firms.

First, the performance of the large units created in the 1960s and 1970s was very disappointing. They proved to be less flexible, less innovative and less efficient than was hoped. It was shown that large firms had increased in size not through internal or organic growth but by acquisitions. The post-merger financial performance of many of these companies proved disappointing. This was attributed either to the problems of integration and reorganisation after the acquisition or to the folly of the decision to expand by acquisition in the first place. Second, as expansion of large companies was due primarily to an increase in the number of plants owned (rather than in the size of the individual plant) the large firms were not acquiring the plant level technical economies of scale. This being the case, it suggested that small firms were not so disadvantaged in the competition for markets. Third, there was evidence that small firms made a major and often overlooked contribution to the economy in terms of jobs, innovation and exports.

The contribution of the small-firms sector

The contribution of small and medium-sized enterprises (SMEs) should be seen in terms of:

- *employment;*

- *output;*

- *exports;*

- *innovation;*

- *competition in what would be an increasingly monopolistic and oligopolistic market.*

Evidence does seem to suggest that in the first two decades after the Second World War the contribution of SMEs to both employment and output was declining. This decline in relative importance was reversed in the late 1960s and the decades since have seen a steady rise in their relative importance. As a source of employment, the new small firm epitomised the 'enterprise culture' which Conservative governments of the 1980s and 1990s sought to nurture. The independent-minded entrepreneur was motivated by profit to develop his or her business and in so doing would provide employment. Entrepreneurs who sought self-employment as an alternative to unemployment would reduce the unemployment totals. Moreover, it was hoped that in their expansion they would provide job opportunities for others. In many respects this was a naive hope since most very small businesses fail to expand beyond the point of providing employment for the entrepreneur. Many, indeed, fail completely after a short existence (although the entrepreneurial drive often leads the same entrepreneur to try again). As a policy to reduce unemployment, assistance to small firms should be seen as part of the supply-side measures.

As a source of innovation the evidence is mixed. The science-based small company founded by an inventor anxious to develop his or her ideas is not typical of small firms as a whole. Not only do the majority of small firms not develop new technology and products, but they are slow to adopt new ideas developed by others. Any failure to be innovative can be attributed to the following disadvantages:

- *lack of expertise;*

- *inability to afford investment in research and development;*

- *lack of economies of scale, resulting in barriers to entry;*

- *problems in acquiring and protecting patent rights;*

- *problems in coping with complex government regulations.*

Conversely, small firms do enjoy substantial advantages in terms of flexibility, the absence of bureaucratic impediments to progress, and superior communications within the organisation.

Although we might be tempted to think that new technology always contributes to what seemed in the past to be a relentless march to larger and larger units, some technological developments have been beneficial to SMEs. First, innovation in terms of new products provides market opportunities for new businesses. Second, some new technological processes have reduced the advantages of scale. New printing techniques have reduced the break-even level of output for newspapers. As a result new openings have been available to businesses interested in newspaper publication. Some of the same printing technology coupled with the rise of a new business relationship (the franchise) has created opportunities for small firms in the fast-printing business.

As a source of competition to inhibit monopolistic practices the role of small firms is somewhat doubtful. Theories of monopoly and oligopoly suggest that large firms will create barriers to entry or will pursue policies (e.g. price wars) designed to eliminate new competition. Small firms usually develop a niche within the market selling to a particular segment. They do this rather than face large firms in direct competition.

In its 1991 publication *Competing with the World's Best*, the Confederation of British Industry gave its view of SMEs:

... the UK needs a stronger infrastructure of SMEs. This is particularly important to the strength of the UK manufacturing base.

1 The natural pattern of growth suggests that at least some of the large companies of tomorrow will be the smaller companies of today.

2 Smaller companies tend to be more flexible and dynamic than larger companies ...

3 Smaller companies also have a key role to play in innovation. The Government's Advisory Committee on Science and Technology point out: 'Smaller firms are entrepreneurially driven and form an important seedbed out of which innovation experiments flow to be tested in the wider context.'

4 SMEs form a vital link in the supply chain of components and sub-assemblies which support and feed larger companies. The absence of an adequate supporting infrastructure has contributed to the relatively high penetration of imports into the UK market ...

Problems confronting small firms

There are a number of problems peculiar to SMEs:

- *absence of full economies of scale;*

- *lack of specialist expertise;*

- *greater exposure to risk especially in view of limited product range;*

- *shortage of suitable premises;*

- *problems in raising finance.*

The financial problems suggest an element of discrimination against small firms. They have limited access to City institutions (the smallest firms have none at all). Share issues are not available as a source of finance in the way that they are to the large public company. A high gearing ratio, resulting from a need to borrow funds for a high proportion of the firm's finance, increases the vulnerability of the business to failure. Inability to pay interest on loans leads to legal action, unlike any failure to pay a dividend to risk-taking shareholders. It is also argued that banks treat small firms less favourably when loans are sought. This is because of the absence of a long track record, the dependence upon a single entrepreneur, the high gearing ratio and the lack of a diversified product range.

The relative importance of these factors is open to debate, but research by WINtech for the Welsh Development Agency produces the following conclusion: 'Managerial factors tend to dominate the factors cited [as barriers to growth]. Process and product technology is also an important constraint. Somewhat surprisingly, financial factors appear to play a relatively minor role' (*Competing with the World's Best*, CBI, 1991).

Assistance for small firms   The problems facing small firms provide the rationale for special assistance for them. The *laissez-faire*, non-interventionist approach to economic policy assumes a 'level playing field'. Hence if the market system does discriminate against SMEs there is a sound case for intervention to redress the imbalance.

In recent decades governments have provided substantial assistance to small firms and encouraged other institutions to assist in the development of such firms. UK government assistance to SMEs has taken three forms.

1 Increasing access to finance by changes in taxation and sponsorship of changes in the capital market.

2 Provision of information and advice by means of the Small Firms Service.

3 Exemptions from constraints imposed by regulation and legislation.

Taxation and finance   The rate of corporation tax has declined over the last decade. More important for small companies, preferential tax treatment means that they are subject to a 25 per cent rate (rather than the 33 per cent imposed on other companies). This provides an incentive for enterprise as well as enabling companies to retain more of their profits for the purposes of reinvestment.

Under the Loan Guarantee Scheme (introduced in 1981) the government guarantees 70 per cent of a loan granted by financial institutions to small firms (up to a maximum loan of £75,000). The borrower is required to pay interest above market rates and to pay an insurance premium in respect of the guarantee. The benefit of the scheme, and its *raison d'être*, are that it covers situations where banks would be reluctant to lend money because of the risks involved and the inadequacy of collateral offered by the borrower. It is known that more than 20,000 SMEs have received loans under the Scheme – although this should be set against the total number of SMEs. Moreover, any evaluation of the Scheme is complicated by the impossibility of knowing what would have happened in its absence. It is reasonable to assume that some at least of the loans would have gone ahead without the Scheme. It is also the case that a high proportion of the loans (some 33 per cent in the mid-1980s) went to companies that subsequently failed.

Under share buy-back small firms are permitted to sell shares and have the option of purchasing them back in the future. This is beneficial to firms that do not want to surrender equity permanently.

The Enterprise Allowance Scheme is designed to encourage the unemployed to establish new businesses. An allowance of £40 a week is granted to those who set themselves up in business. One limiting factor is that the unemployed person must have £1,000 (or access to £1,000) to invest in the business. Further assistance with skills and management advice is available through local Training and Enterprise Councils (TECs).

Under the Business Expansion Scheme (BES) there were tax concessions for individuals who invested in unquoted companies and who retained their shareholding for a minimum of five years. Despite the major contribution that the BES made to the financing of SMEs it was phased out in 1993. A further initiative that appears to be destined for elimination is the Unlisted Securities Market (USM). This is a market in the shares of medium-sized companies that do not seek a full Stock Exchange quotation. The limited success of the USM has encouraged talk of its closure, thus cutting off a useful supply of funds for SMEs.

Information and advice

The Small Firms Service was established to provide advice to small businesses, and was expanded in the Enterprise Initiative launched by the DTI in 1988. The purpose was to assist companies use their initiative to identify and exploit business opportunities. Government grants were made available for firms seeking consultation on design, marketing, exporting, planning, research, financial information systems and quality assurance. The success of the scheme in terms of the assistance given is diluted by the fact that it reaches only a small minority of companies eligible for assistance (45,000 out of 1,250,000 by 1991).

Exemption from regulation

State help for small firms has also taken the form of reducing government interference in their affairs. Included in this is the exemption given to small firms in issues relating to maternity reinstatement and industrial tribunals. The White Paper *Lifting the Burden* (1985) led to simplified administrative requirements being imposed on small firms. This is consistent with the supply-side economic measures of the Thatcher government. Supply-side economists take as a starting point the idea that the greatest service that can be performed for small business is to reduce the level of interference, thus freeing enterprise.

Competition policy

A large part of economic theory is designed to demonstrate the advantages of a competitive market and the undesirability of monopoly. Unfortunately, economies of scale have produced a trend toward dominant firm and/or oligopoly situations in which price competition has been replaced by tacit or even formal collusion. Faced with this trend towards dominant forms and oligopoly, government can take one of three policy stances:

- *accept the situation as the natural outcome of the market;*

- *adopt an automatic-rule approach to prevent such situations;*

- *adopt a discretionary or pragmatic approach which looks at the merits of individual cases.*

In general the UK tradition has been to adopt a discretionary approach policy that has contained elements of automatic rule.

In view of the different treatment of merger, monopoly and restrictive practice it is necessary to look at the three separately.

Restrictive practices

Restrictive trade practices have taken a number of forms:

- *full-line forcing (forcing retailers to take the manufacturer's full range of goods);*

- *resale price maintenance (dictating prices at which retailers sell goods);*

- *aggregated rebates;*

- *price-fixing cartels, which aim to ensure that members are able to charge higher prices than if they competed with one another;*

- *market-sharing cartels, where members agree who should win a particular contract, or otherwise divide up the market to eliminate competition.*

The impact of each of these measures is to reduce the intensity of competition and replace it by some degree of collusion, at the expense of customers.

Under various statutes (most notably the Fair Trading Act 1973) all restrictive practices have to be registered with the Office of Fair Trading. The Restrictive Practices Court has power to decide whether a restrictive practice should be allowed to continue. The parties to the agreement have to prove both that the restrictive practice (RP) confers some benefit on the public in the form of one of the 'gateways' and that the benefits outweigh the disadvantage to the public. The gateways can be seen as the permitted defences of an RP, which arise if it:

- *protects the public from injury;*

- *prevents local unemployment;*

- *maintains exports;*

- *gives assistance to exports;*

- *operates against existing restrictions on competition;*

- *supports another acceptable RP;*

- *promotes fair trading terms for buyers and suppliers;*

- *does not, in fact, restrict competition.*

The onus of proof in RP cases is on the parties to the agreement. Unless they can demonstrate that it confers some net positive benefit on the public, the RP will be declared illegal.

The Restrictive Practices Court has dealt with relatively few cases although it is claimed to have had a deterrent effect. Supporters of the current system argue that the clear guidelines about what is and what is not acceptable have resulted in firms not attempting to pursue restrictive practices which are harmful to the public interest. 'It is generally recognised that the restrictive practices legislation has been highly effective in controlling the more formal price fixing and market sharing agreement once prevalent in UK industry' (Ferguson in *Developments in Economics*, Vol. 9, p. 112). However, loopholes continue to exist and the unearthing of secret cartels suggests that problems remain. This is demonstrated by recent literature from the Office of Fair Trading seeking aid in detecting cartels. The OFT asks customers to consider the following questions to aid detection.

1 Does the industry or the product have characteristics which make it easier to organise, police and sustain a cartel? For example, are there few sellers; homogeneous products with little scope for competition in quality, service, or delivery; and similar costs of production and distribution for all suppliers?

2 Are there factors which encourage suppliers to make a cartel agreement at a particular time, for example the development of widespread excess capacity or a recession?

3 Do prices change or behave in ways that would not be expected in the prevailing circumstances without some form of contract? For example, are prices increased by the same amount or at the same time in a period of excess capacity; has the spread of quoted prices suddenly narrowed; or are discount levels or structures suddenly changed?

4 Do price changes over time reveal so regular and systematic a leader/ follower situation as to be inexplicable without some kind of contact between suppliers?

5 Are similar phrases or explanations used in announcing price changes?

6 Are 'give-away' phrases sometimes used in correspondence or conversation, for example 'the industry has decided that margins must be increased to a more reasonable level'?

7 Do suppliers exchange information, for example on sales, market shares, forecasts or investment plans? Generally, agreements to exchange information are registrable under the Restrictive Trade Practices Act only if they concern information on prices.

8 Do suppliers get together frequently, socially or for business purposes, for example at trade association meetings on statistics or standards? Of course there is no suggestion that such meetings are in themselves reprehensible.

Parties to a secret and therefore illegal RP are referred to the Court, which has powers not just to order the abandonment of the agreement but also to fine and imprison those involved in what is actually contempt of court. Moreover, anyone harmed by such an unlawful agreement can sue for damages.

Monopolies Under the 1973 Fair Trading Act two distinct types of monopoly situation are defined.

1 *Scale* – where at least 25 per cent of goods or services of any description in the UK (or in a defined part of it) are supplied by or to (in the case of services, by or for) a person, company or members of an interconnected group of companies.

2 *Complex* – where at least 25 per cent of goods or services of any description in the UK (or in a defined part of it) supplied by or to (in the case of services, by or for) persons or companies who are members of a group (not being an interconnected group of companies) who conduct their respective affairs, by agreement or otherwise, in such a way as to prevent, restrict or distort competition in connection with the production of such goods or the supply of such goods or services, the goods or services concerned need not necessarily be supplied by or to (or for) every member of such a group.

References to the Monopolies and Mergers Commission (MMC) are made either by the Secretary of State for Trade and Industry or by the Director General of Fair Trading, one of whose duties is to monitor behaviour in markets and to evaluate allegations of monopoly abuse. The reference specifies the goods or services to which it relates and generally asks the MMC to establish:

- *whether a monopoly situation exists and in favour of what person or persons;*

- *whether any steps (by way of uncompetitive practices or otherwise) are being taken by any such person to exploit or maintain that situation;*

- *whether any action or omission on the part of any such person is attributable to that situation; and*

- *whether any facts found by the MMC in its enquiry operate, or may be expected to operate, against the public interest.*

After investigations, the MMC reports to the Secretary of State. The report will describe the market, the company or companies concerned and the views of the parties. It will also:

- *give definite conclusions on each of the questions raised by the reference;*

- *specify, if a monopoly situation has been found to exist, any facts which operate against the public interest and the particular effects adverse to the public interest which these facts have; and*

■ *consider and, if it thinks fit, recommend what action should be taken for the purpose of remedying or preventing those adverse effects.*

Illustration 4.1 shows the summary findings of an MMC enquiry.

It is for the Secretary of State to decide the action to be taken (if any). This might take the form of asking the Director General to obtain undertakings or to make an order to prevent or remedy the particular adverse effect.

The major criticisms of monopoly policy are that:

■ *the MMC lacks real teeth;*

■ *there are comparatively few references;*

■ *recommendations are frequently ignored; and*

■ *concentration has increased within the UK.*

Illustration 4.1 *An MMC monopoly investigation: summary findings*

Structural Warranty Services in Relation to New Homes

Referred   23 May 1990
Completed: 14 December 1990
Published: 6 March 1991

The Commission found that a scale monopoly situation existed in favour of the National House Building Council (NHBC).

The Commission found that the NHBC provides structural warranty cover for over 90 per cent of new private sector homes under its Buildmark scheme. The effect of NHBC's Rule 12 is broadly to require its members to pre-notify to it all the homes they propose to build and thus trigger the process of inspection, insurance and payment of the current fees. The result is roughly to double the unit warranty costs of an NHBC member who wishes to submit new homes to another scheme either on a sampling basis or a long-term basis as a second source of warranty services.

The Commission found that Rule 12 *operates and might be expected to operate* against the public interest because by preventing, without financial penalty, dual sourcing and the sampling of alternative schemes, it restricts competition. The Commission found that other rules of the NHBC contribute to the restriction of competition and *operate or might be expected to operate* against the public interest. They made recommendations to remedy these matters by making amendments and certain additions to NHBC's rules. One member dissented from the Commission's conclusions and related recommendations on Rule 12.

Source: MMC, *Annual Report 1992*

Mergers Since 1965 mergers and proposed mergers can be referred to the MMC by the Director General of Fair Trading or the Secretary of State for Trade and Industry. For a merger situation to qualify for investigation by the MMC, the criteria are that two or more 'enterprises' (at least one of which is carried on in the UK) 'cease to be distinct' and that either one or both of the market share test or the assets test (*see* below) are satisfied. An 'enterprise' means the activities, or part of the activities, of a business.

A merger is most dramatically illustrated by a take-over bid by one company for another. With or without this feature, a merger giving rise to a reference often involves the acquisition, or prospective acquisition, of 'control' of one company (and the enterprise or enterprises which it carries on) by another. This may mean the acquisition (or prospective acquisition) of a controlling interest, which can usually, in practice, be equated with over 50 per cent of the relevant voting power. However, it may also include, in the absence of a controlling interest, the ability materially to influence the policy or the ability to control the policy of a company or of any person carrying on an enterprise.

Some merger references are made following the completion of a merger but, more frequently, they are made in anticipation of one, in particular where there has been an offer by one company to the shareholders of another with a view to acquiring control of the latter. A reference after the completion of a merger can normally not be made more than six months after the merger has occurred.

The market share and assets tests mentioned above are, respectively, that as a result of the merger, at least 25 per cent of goods or services of any description which are supplied in the UK, or in a substantial part of it, are supplied by or to (in the case of services, by or for) one person or, if this was already the case, such supply is enhanced (market share), and that the gross value of worldwide assets taken over exceeds £30 million (assets test).

Illustration 4.2 *An MMC merger investigation: summary findings*

Southern Newspapers plc

Referred:	*24 July 1991*
Completed:	*23 October 1991*
Published:	*27 November 1991*

This enquiry concerned the proposed acquisitions of a controlling interest in Southern Newspapers plc by four companies: EMAP plc, Pearson plc, Reed International plc, and Trinity International Holdings plc. Separate references had been made in respect of each of these.

Southern's principal business is the publishing of local newspapers in Hampshire, Dorset, Wiltshire and Somerset, including evening newspapers in Southampton, Bournemouth and Weymouth. It is the 13th largest publisher of regional and local newspapers in the United Kingdom with 2.5 per cent of the market.

The Commission unanimously concluded that the transfer of a controlling interest to any of EMAP, Reed or Trinity *might be expected not* to operate against the public interest. The majority came to the same conclusion in respect of Pearson. One member dissented because of the effect on competition and choice in two particular geographical areas but in other respects agreed with the conclusions of the majority.

Source: MMC, *Annual Report 1992*

If a merger is referred for investigation the MMC considers all relevant aspects but with special reference to:

■ *maintaining and promoting effective competition;*

■ *promoting the interests of consumers, purchasers and other users of goods and services with regard to the prices, quality and variety of the goods and services supplied;*

■ *promoting through competition the reduction of costs and the development and use of new techniques and new products, and facilitating the entry of new competitors into existing markets;*

■ *maintaining and promoting the balanced distribution of industry and employment;*

■ *maintaining and promoting competitive activity in overseas markets.*

If the Commission decides that the merger does not operate, and may be expected not to operate, against the public interest, then no further action is taken. In fact the Secretary of State has no power to overrule such a recommendation, an example of which appears in Illustration 4.2.

Alternatively, the MMC might decide that:

---

the merger does or may be expected to operate against the public interest. The Secretary of State may overturn or disregard such a finding, although in practice this has rarely occurred. The Commission must specify what the adverse effects are, and also consider what action (if any) should be taken to remedy or prevent these, which may include a recommendation that the merger should not be allowed or that it should be unscrambled if it has already taken place. The Commission may recommend that the merger should not be allowed unless the acquirer gives some statutory undertakings. The Secretary of State must take any recommendations into account and also any advice the Director General of Fair Trading offers.

The Secretary of State's decision is usually announced at the same time as the Commission's report is published. The Director General of Fair Trading may be asked to seek any undertakings that may be required, and to keep under review any undertakings given or orders made in respect of mergers, and to advise the Secretary of State if any further action seems necessary. [MMC Fact Sheet 4]

The 'output' of the MMC appears rather low. From 1965 (when mergers were brought within its scope) to 1992, it has reported on only 149 mergers. In 1991, for instance, only a third or less of all mergers and proposed mergers were found by the Office of Fair Trading to qualify for a reference. Of the 183 mergers that qualified, only seven were actually referred to the MMC. Although the MMC is used rather sparingly, it might be said to have a deterrent effect in discouraging the most blatantly anti-competitive mergers. It is often the case that parties to a merger will abandon the proposal rather than suffer the six-month delay (and therefore uncertainty) while an investigation takes place.

Other aspects of the work of the MMC

In addition to investigating mergers and monopoly situations, the MMC has acquired additional powers under the Competition Act 1980, the Broadcasting Act 1990 and the Fair Trading Act 1973.

General reference

Under the Fair Trading Act, the Secretary of State may require the MMC to report on the general effect on the public interest of any practice adopted as a result of or to preserve monopoly situations or which appears uncompetitive. Examples have included refusal to supply, parallel pricing, tie-in sales (where the sale of one item requires the sale or purchase of another) and full-line forcing (where a manufacturer's complete product range is required to be sold).

Restrictive labour practices

The MMC will find out whether the practices described in the reference exist, whether they are restrictive and whether they operate, or may be expected to operate, against the public interest and with what adverse effects. A restrictive labour practice in this context refers to any restrictions not exclusively relating to remuneration, connected with employment or work done in specified commercial activities in the UK, which is not necessary or is more stringent than necessary and which could be discontinued without contravening any legal requirement.

Competition references

The Competition Act 1980 introduced a means whereby specific anti-competitive practices by particular persons (usually an individual firm), as opposed to whole markets, could be investigated to see if they were against the public interest.

Public sector references

The 1980 Act enables the Secretary of State to refer to the MMC questions concerning the efficiency and costs of, the service provided by, and the possible abuse of, a monopoly situation by nationalised industries and certain other public sector bodies such as the Post Office and British Rail. The MMC may also be required to report on whether the body concerned is pursuing a course of conduct which operates against the public interest. These enquiries are sometimes described as efficiency audits.

Privatised industry references

Under various privatisation acts, the regulator (OFTEL, OFGAS, OFWAT, etc.) is able to refer matters relating to the conduct of privatised industries to the MMC. For instance, the MMC investigated chatlines and message services for OFTEL.

Broadcasting

The MMC has a new role relating to the competition aspects of networking arrangements between holders of regional Channel 3 licences. Following an investigation by the Director General of Fair Trading, the Independent Television Commission or a licence-holder may refer to the MMC, for investigation and report (although its decision is determinative), certain questions relating particularly to the competition test described in the Broadcasting Act 1990.

Privatisation

Privatisation has been one of the distinctive features of the Conservative governments that have been in power since 1979. It is clearly in line with the free-market, supply-side policies associated with the modern Conservative Party. However, before considering it further we should be clear about its meaning and how it relates to other policies. Privatisation has taken two distinct forms.

1 The sale of public sector industry to the private sector – this is what in a previous age we would have called denationalisation.

2 The provision of public sector services by private sector firms, e.g. the contracting out of refuse services by local authorities.

Two related policity initiatives have been involved.

1 Deregulation, which means the removal of government regulation that promotes monopoly and barriers to entry, e.g. deregulation of bus services.

2 Marketisation, which means shifting non-market sector services into the market sector, e.g. encouragement for private health care.

In this section we shall focus on the denationalisation of the former public corporations. This has been undertaken by the Thatcher and Major governments with such vigour that in 1993 there remain only three nationalised industries of any significance: Nuclear Electric, whose power station decommissioning costs have made privatisation unattractive; British Coal, which is being slimmed down to make it a candidate for privatisation; and British Rail, which is set for a unique form of privatisation (of which more later).

The basic objectives of the privatisation exercises were to:

- *improve efficiencies by making these large industries more responsive to market forces;*

- *reduce the power of public sector unions;*

- *increase competition within the industries concerned;*

- *promote share ownership by employees, in the belief that by giving them a stake in the new companies labour relations, morale and productivity will be improved;*

- *promote wider share ownership and 'popular capitalism';*

- *raise revenue and thereby reduce the PSBR.*

Supporters of privatisation point out that as well as the initial benefit to public sector finances there are longer-term benefits in relieving government of future financing responsibilities. Fig. 4.4 summarises the pros and cons of privatisation.

The larger nationalised industries were sold off by an issue of shares to which the general public were invited to subscribe. In most cases the allocation of shares was deliberately weighted towards the small shareholder as part of the policy of extending share ownership. By this method the

---

Fig. 4.4 *The pros and cons of privatisation*

Arguments for Privatisation of Nationalised Industries	*Arguments against Privatisation of Nationalised Industries*
1. Managements freed to make their own decisions	1. State monopolies have been converted into private monopolies
2. Government constraints removed	2. Will lead to a neglect of the social function (e.g. uneconomic but socially vital services)
3. More responsive to customer demand	
5. Discipline of the market	3. Privatisation involves the sale to taxpayers of national assets which in effect they already own
6. Greater efficiency	
7. Reduces power of the public sector unions	4. Threat to jobs in new profit-seeking privatised concerns
8. Wider share ownership encouraged	

---

government hoped to reverse the long-term decline in private shareholding, create a share-owning (as well as a house-owning) democracy and counter the domination of the stock market by the large (and usually cautious) institutional investors. Some of the smaller state-owned enterprises were sold to other companies (e.g. Rover was sold to British Aerospace), and in a few instances there were management and employee buy-outs. Table 4.1 lists the various UK privatisations.

Rail privatisation will take a unique form. With its diverse nature and unprofitable sectors, BR cannot be sold off as a single unit. Consequently, it is planned to separate track from operations, and to allow private operators access to the track on a franchise basis. Illustration 4.3 describes the benefits of privatisation of BR, and Illustration 4.4 outlines the government's plans.

A major dilemma in most privatisation initiatives is that each one converts a public sector monopoly into a private sector monopoly. Indeed, a traditional argument for nationalisation was that public sector ownership was always preferable to private ownership of a natural monopoly. Disappointment with the performance of the nationalised industries led to a reassessment of this view. It is now argued that the benefits of private enterprise are so substantial that the dangers of monopoly should not impede privatisation. In any case, the argument runs, ownership of the industry is not a prerequisite for preventing the abuse of monopoly power. Regulatory authorities can and have been established to ensure that a monopoly position is not abused. This has often taken the form of the regulator (OFTEL, OFGAS, OFWAT) restricting price rises to a formula such as RPI plus/minus k (where the RPI is the current inflation rate and k is a number chosen by the regulator).

Table 4.1 *UK privatisation*

Organisation	Industry	Date	Method	Receipts (£m)
Amersham International	Radio chemicals	1982	Shares	64
Associated British Ports	Port owner	1983	Shares	97
British Aerospace	Aircraft	1981	Shares	390
BAA	Airports	1987	Shares	1,223
British Airways	Airline	1987	Shares	854
British Gas	Gas supply	1986	Shares	7,000
British Petroleum	Oil company	Various	Shares	6,000
British Rail Hotels	Hotels	1983	Sold to trade	
British Shipbuilders	Shipyards	Various	Employee buy-out and trade sales	
British Steel	Steel production	1988	Shares	2,430
British Telecom	Telecommunications	1984	Shares	4,700
Britoil	North Sea oil	1982/85	Shares	1,053
Cable & Wireless	Telecommunications	Various	Shares	1,021
Electricity companies	Electricity supply	1990–1	Shares	
Jaguar	Car maker	1984	Shares	
National Freight Company	Road haulage	1982	Employee buy-out	354
Rolls-Royce	Aero engines	1987	Shares	1,032
Rover Group	Car maker	1988	Sold to BA	150
Royal Ordnance	Arms maker	1987	Sold to BA	186
Sealink	Ferries, harbours	1984	Sold to British Ferries	
Short Brothers	Aircraft	1989	Sold to Canadian company	30
Holdings of British Technology Group		Various	Shares sold to institutions and firms	
– ICL	Computers			
– Fairey	Engineering			
– Ferranti	Electronics			
– Inmos	Silicon chips			
Water companies	Water supply	1989	Shares	1,903

Illustration 4.3 *The benefits of private sector involvement and liberalisation*

Improved services for passengers and freight customers will come from:

(a) More concern for the customers' needs. Management and employees in the private sector have greater incentives to provide the services which the consumer wants. The profitability of their company – and at the end of the day their jobs – depend on providing a service which attracts custom. Nationalised industries do not face such acute pressures.

(b) Competition and ending the monopoly. New operators will be allowed to provide services, giving customers a choice and stimulating improved services and value. Already a number of companies have indicated an interest in introducing new freight or passenger services.

(c) Management freedom. Railway management should be free to get on with its main task of running services to the satisfaction of passengers and customers. The Government's proposals will provide for greater participation by the private sector in railway operation, with less scope and justification for Government involvement in managerial issues.

(d) Clear and enforceable quality standards. The Franchising Authority will specify and monitor the level of services which passenger operators will be required to meet. For the first time standards such as punctuality, reliability and overcrowding will be written into contracts. A franchisee failing to perform to the required standards will be in breach of contract and subject to penalties including, in extremis, the loss of the franchise.

(e) Motivation. Franchising passenger services to reflect regional or local identities will help to boost the pride that all employees take in providing a high quality service to the travelling public.

(f) Efficiency. Smaller operating companies will bring more localised manage-ment closer to the public and greater opportunities to cut out waste and otherwise reduce costs, without sacrificing quality.

Source: *New Opportunities for the Railways*, HMSO

In some instances the government has opened up the market to new com-petitors (e.g. Mercury Communications in the telecommunications industry) but a dominant firm position remains and often the business has derived rather more benefits than domestic consumers.

Privatisation is now established and accepted by most (but not all) people. The Labour Party, which in the early 1980s threatened to return the privatised industries to the public sector, has accepted the principle of privatisation in most cases. Hence the real question for students of economics is not the case for and against privatisation but, rather, whether privatisation has produced the benefits expected by its supporters. Profitability is one criterion on which to judge the success of a private enterprise, but two problems remain: high profits might be the result of monopoly power and inadequate regulation; and we should also judge these industries (especially dominant firm situations) by other criteria.

A York University study used various criteria including accounting ratios, labour productivity and employment efficiency. The conclusion reached was:

Illustration 4.4 *The government's plan for BR*

The Government's objective is to extend the involvement of the private sector in the operation of the railways, ensure continuity of services, assure safety, and provide value for money. This is the best way to improve the service to customers. The Government intends ...:

(a) to sell BR's Freight and Parcels businesses to the private sector;
(b) to establish a Franchising Authority and to franchise a substantial number of passenger services;
(c) to restructure BR to own and operate track and infrastructure separately from the operation of services;
(d) to establish rights of access for new operators to the rail network;
(e) to establish an independent Regulator to protect the interests of consumers and to supervise access to all track and charges for its use; and
(f) to provide opportunities for the sale or leasing of stations.

Source: *New Opportunities for the Railways*, HMSO

'The hypothesis that a movement away from political control improves performance was generally supported' (D. Parker in Healey, *Britain's Economic Miracle: Myth or Reality*, p. 186).

Given the public service nature of many of these industries we should also evaluate privatisation in terms of quality of service. In a competitive market a dissatisfied consumer will go elsewhere – in a monopoly situation the consumer is in a weak position. In the public sector, service is increasingly evaluated in terms of performance in satisfying customer needs. For instance, under the Rail Passengers Charter there are refunds if trains run late. In a privatised monopoly similar monitoring of performance is necessary, and is undertaken by the regulator.

Micro-economic policy: key concepts

Anti-competitive practice A practice which restricts, distorts or eliminates competition in the market.

Competition policy A policy which aims to promote effective competition between suppliers by regulating mergers, restrictive practices and dominant firm situations.

Concentration ratio A measure of seller concentration. Hence the five-firm concentration ratio is a measure of the proportion of market held by the five largest firms.

Deregulation Removal of legal and other regulations impeding free enterprise.

Dominant firm One that accounts for a significant proportion of the market.

Efficiency The relationship between factor inputs and output. Technological efficiency measures the relationship in physical terms, economic efficiency in cost terms. Allocative and distributive efficiency relates to the performance of the market in allocating resources to satisfy consumers' needs.

Industrial policy Government measures to promote industrial efficiency and technological progress.

Merger The combining together of two or more firms.

Nationalisation Public ownership of industry.

Popular capitalism Extension of share ownership to give more people a stake in the wealth-creating sector.

Privatisation Denationalisation, or transferring an industry from the public to the private sector.

Productivity Output per unit of input.

Supply-side economics That part of economic analysis concerned with the productive capability of the economy.

Supply-side measures Policies to improve the flexibility of factors markets so as to maximise output for a given level of aggregate demand.

Take-over The acquisition of one company by another.

CHAPTER 5

Unemployment

Unemployment represents a waste of scarce resources and yet, for the second time in a decade, UK unemployment has reached three million (*see* **Fig. 5.1**). **In the past the government's reaction would have been to reflate the economy, thereby increasing the level of demand for goods and for labour. Governments both in the UK and elsewhere argue that such action is merely inflationary and that the only solution to this problem is to make markets more competitive so that the market will solve the problem.**

OBJECTIVES
1 To analyse the problems involved in measuring unemployment.
2 To explain and analyse causes of unemployment.
3 To explain supply-side solutions to the problem.
4 To explain and analyse regional policies.
5 To survey recent trends in unemployment.

The measurement of unemployment

Any analysis of unemployment, its causes and solutions must be preceded by a measure of the extent of unemployment. This is the first source of controversy: there are differences of opinion about the number of people unemployed at any one time. UK government statistics on unemployment are based on the 'claimant count' undertaken by Unemployment Benefit Offices on a given day each month. This reflects the fact that for statistical purposes a person is unemployed if he or she is capable of and willing to work but is unable to find a job and is in receipt of benefit. Anyone who is not registered and is not receiving benefit is therefore not included in the count.

During the Thatcher period there were a number of changes to the system of unemployment benefit. Critics accuse the government of manipulating the figures to reduce the number unemployed. This charge is countered by the claim that the new definition gives a truer picture of those who are 'genuinely unemployed'. Whatever the truth of the matter, there is little doubt that the

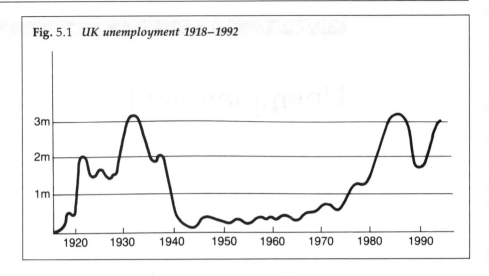

Fig. 5.1 *UK unemployment 1918–1992*

net effect of the following changes was to reduce substantially the number of people included in the unemployment total:

1980 School leavers unable to claim until September of the year in which they leave.

1981 Men over 60 in receipt of benefit for one year did not have to sign on and were switched to a new benefit.

1982 Clerical count replaced by computer count.

1983 All men over 60 were not required to sign on.

1986 Publication of monthly figures delayed to eliminate those no longer unemployed.

1986 Abolition of right to claim partial benefit for those with insufficient contributions.

1987 Period of disqualification from benefit (i.e. for those who voluntarily leave a job) extended from six to 13 weeks.

1988 Abolition of benefit for those under 18. It was assumed that all 16–18-year-olds were in education, training or work, thus removing the 'option of unemployment' from this age group. It means that for statistical purposes the minimum age for unemployment in the UK is 18.

Even before the changes introduced by the Thatcher government there was a difference between the UK official definition (based on those claiming benefit) and the definition used by the International Labour Organisation (ILO) and OECD for the purposes of international comparison. The ILO/OECD definition is based on the excess of labour supply (willing, able and ready to work) over demand. The *Labour Force Survey* uses the ILO/OECD definition for a sample survey of 60,000 adults in Great Britain. A comparison of the figures from the survey shows that the UK claimant count does understate the true extent of unemployment. 'Under-registration' can take the form of:

- *those not entitled to benefit;*
- *those under 18;*
- *men over 60;*
- *those on Special Employment Measures or on training schemes (such as Employment Training);*
- *those seeking work without registering.*

In addition, there are people on short-time working or who are deterred from seeking work by the presence of high unemployment. It is not surprising that the government critics argue that true unemployment is one million in excess of government statistics.

At the same time there is likely to be some 'over-registration' in the sense of inclusion in the claimant count of people who are not 'genuinely' unemployed:

- *those making fraudulent claims while being employed in the 'black' or 'hidden' economy;*
- *those voluntarily unemployed;*
- *job changers who are unemployed for very short periods of time;*
- *the unemployable.*

Government supporters on the right of the Conservative Party argue that, because of over-registration, the claimant count exaggerates the problem of unemployment. Objective analysis suggests that the claimant count does understate the problem, but not by the amount suggested by opposition politicians.

The unemployment statistics can be expressed either as a stock (in thousands) or as a percentage of the workforce. Like most economic statistics there will be a long-term trend with fluctuations around that trend. The fluctuations that are particularly relevant here are seasonal ones. We should expect unemployment to rise in winter and fall in summer. To obtain a better picture of unemployment than is gained from crude figures it is necessary to filter out the changes in unemployment caused by purely seasonal factors. This results in what is known as the seasonally adjusted figure, which is likely to be above the crude figure in summer but below it in winter.

Causes of unemployment

An analysis of the cause of unemployment is essential before determining policy prescriptions to reduce or eliminate the problem. However, different schools analyse the problem in different ways and so – before looking at policy – it is necessary to survey the major schools of thought.

Classical (pre-Keynesian) theory

Classical economists saw the market as self-correcting: the price mechanism adjusts until all shortages and surpluses are removed. The market-clearing mechanism applied both to the market in goods and to that in labour. Hence unemployment (a surplus of labour) would drive down wage rates, thus extending the demand for labour until once more it came into balance. This view of the labour market does not rule out unemployment. Structural change in a dynamic economy will lead to job losses. However, the problem of unemployment was seen as essentially temporary until such time as wage rates adjusted to bring long-term equilibrium at full employment.

A cardinal principle of classical theory was Say's law, which basically states that supply creates its own demand. By employing factors of production, goods and services are supplied. The same factors of production receive incomes which enable them to purchase the goods and services that they produced. It was argued that income would not be 'lost' from the system because the leakages and injections (that appear in the Keynesian circular flow model) tend to equality in the long term. The public sector budget balances because of government commitment to financial orthodoxy: savings and investment balance at the equilibrium rate of interest in the loanable funds theory, and the Gold Standard provided a mechanism to correct imbalances in the balance of payments.

In terms of both Say's law and the market clearing mechanism, classical economists believed that the economy tended towards full employment. Consequently, government intervention in the labour market was unnecessary.

Keynesian theory

Classical economists explained the continuing unemployment of the 1920s and 1930s in terms of market imperfections. Because of immobility and monopolistic forces in the market, the price mechanism failed to 'clear the market'. However, Keynes argued that wage cuts (the classical solution to unemployment) would aggravate the problem by reducing aggregate demand. Keynes based his argument on the fallacy of composition, which basically states that what is true in the singular is not necessarily true in the aggregate. An individual prepared to accept a wage cut will increase his or her chances of gaining or retaining employment. However, wage cuts across the whole labour force would result in a reduction in aggregate demand, leading to further job losses. Keynes accepted that the economy moved towards an equilibrium – but this was an equilibrium in terms of the level of national income. The equilibrium level of national income did not guarantee full employment.

Keynesian unemployment is unemployment caused by a deficiency in the level of aggregate demand. In addition to cyclical unemployment resulting from lack of demand during a downturn in the cycle, we can also identify persistent unemployment associated with a deficiency of demand at the equilibrium level of national income.

As well as Keynesian unemployment caused by a general deficiency of demand, we can also identify unemployment caused by a mismatch of demand and supply. Hence the overall level of demand might be adequate but, for a variety of factors, the unemployed might not be able to fill the vacancies that exist. The other forms of unemployment are:

1 *Structural* – associated with changes in the structure of the economy.

2 *Regional* – associated with the decline of regional industry.

3 *Technological* – caused by labour-saving technology.

4 *Seasonal* – associated with seasonal variations in the level of business activity.

5 *Frictional* or *transitional* – while job changing.

These types of unemployment resulting from the mismatch of supply and demand can be attributed to immobility (either occupational or geographical) of labour. The unemployed are unable to transfer into the expanding areas of employment due to:

- *the housing market;*

- *family and social ties;*

- *lack of skills;*

- *lack of qualifications;*

- *impediments in the market (e.g. trade unions, barriers to entry).*

The solution to all these was to increase the mobility of factors of production.

Whether we are referring to deficiency of overall demand or the mismatch of supply and demand, Keynesian theory suggests that unemployment can be solved, albeit at the cost of rising prices, through the Phillips curve trade-off. The monetarist counter-revolution led to a new perspective on the problem of unemployment, suggesting that it was not easily solved.

Monetarist and new classical perspectives on unemployment

Milton Friedman rejected the Phillips curve trade-off and instead put forward the notion of the natural rate of unemployment, to which the economy will always return. The natural rate (*see* Fig. 5.2) is the equilibrium rate of unemployment and is determined by frictions in the labour market: discrimination, training facilities, level of benefits relative to wages, trade unions and employment legislation.

At the natural rate of unemployment a constant rate of inflation is possible: it might be 0 per cent, 5 per cent or any level, depending upon the growth of the money supply. The natural rate of unemployment is therefore the non-accelerating inflation rate of unemployment (NAIRU). Any attempt to reduce unemployment below the natural rate is futile: it results in accelerating inflation and works only in the short term.

For Friedman there is no long-run trade-off. (For another group of economists, known as the rational expectations school, the trade-off does not apply even in the short run.) However, this does not mean that unemployment cannot be reduced. By reforms in the labour market to remove obstacles and encourage labour mobility, it is possible to reduce the natural rate of unemployment. This means that government effort to reduce unemployment

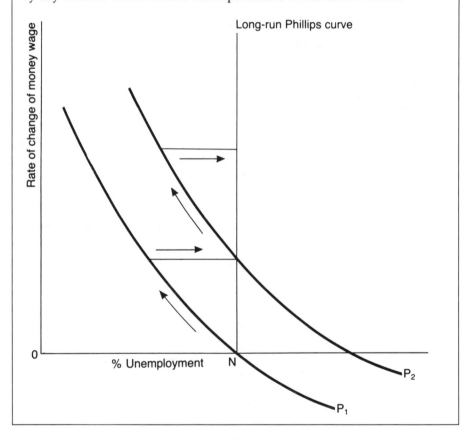

Fig. 5.2 *Friedman's long-run Phillips curve*

Faced with unemployment at N per cent, a government adopting Keynesian principles would reflate the economy and in so doing trade off some inflation against the reduction in unemployment. However, the trade-off is purely short term – as the newly employed realise that the rise in wage rates does not lead to a rise in real wages they will return to their previous state of being voluntarily unemployed. Successive trade-offs have no long-term impact on unemployment but they do produce successively higher rates of inflation.

Friedman saw 0N per cent unemployment as the natural rate of unemployment. At the natural rate the labour market is in equilibrium and a constant rate of inflation is sustainable. Any attempt to reduce unemployment below the natural rate is futile except in the short run and leads to accelerating inflation. Although it is not possible to keep unemployment below the natural rate, it is possible to reduce the natural rate by any measure which reduces the imperfections in the labour market.

has switched from macro-economic policy measures to micro-economic, or supply-side, measures such as training, reforms in the housing market and removal of restrictions in the labour market.

The other key feature of the modern analysis of unemployment is the distinction between involuntary and voluntary unemployment. Involuntary unemployment suggests that the unemployed person seeks a job but is unable to obtain one. In the Keynesian era it was assumed that most if not all unemployment was involuntary and that only a tiny minority of workshy people could be classed as voluntarily unemployed. The distinction needs to be more precisely defined, however. By involuntary unemployment we mean an inability to obtain a job at the current wage rate. Voluntary unemployment, on the other hand, is caused by unwillingness to accept a job at current wage rates (*see* Fig. 5.3).

Search unemployment is voluntary. The term refers to a situation where an unemployed person continues to search for a particular job rather than accept any job. Search unemployment is caused by people being 'choosy' about which jobs to accept.

Fig. 5.3 *Voluntary unemployment*

At the market clearing wage 0X, 0W workers obtain employment. This is less than the current labour force but the logic of the supply curve suggests that the remaining workers (shown as distance *a*) were unwilling to work at current wage rates. In classical theory these people are regarded as being voluntarily unemployed.

The workers' trade union obtains a minimum wage of 0U and as a result employment falls to W_1. Distance *b* represents involuntary unemployment resulting from unions pricing members out of work.

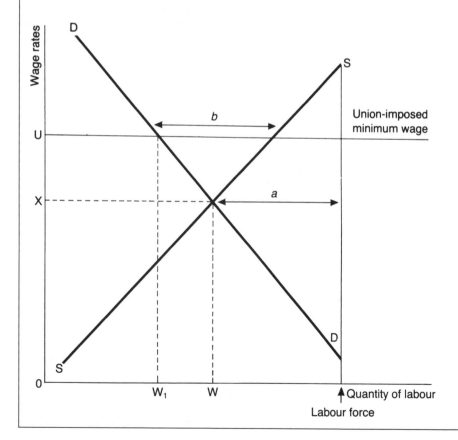

The low paid can be caught in the unemployment trap, which is a particular form of the poverty trap. The unemployment trap applies to a situation in which take-home pay is less than, or little better than, benefits received when not working. As we assume rational behaviour, we should not be surprised when individuals opt for benefits in these circumstances.

Trade union activity is also criticised by monetarists and new classical economists. Whereas, in the past, trade unions were blamed for inflation, today they are seen by the Conservative government and right-wing economists as causing unemployment. This is not a case of the individual volunteering for unemployment but, rather, of organised labour pricing itself out of jobs (*see* Fig. 5.3).

Having surveyed different perspectives on the causes of unemployment let us now turn to government policy to cure the problem.

Policies to reduce unemployment

Policies to tackle the problem of unemployment must be linked to its perceived causes. In the Keynesian era unemployment was regarded as wholly involuntary and could be tackled by a combination of reflation, to raise the level of aggregate demand (*see* Fig. 5.4), and measures to increase the mobility of factors of production.

Reflation typically took the form of increases in government spending, cuts in taxation and lower interest rates. The rise in government spending would trigger off a multiplier increase in national income, output and employment. Although tax reductions would achieve similar results Keynesian economists have always seen public sector spending as a more potent weapon than tax reductions simply because the latter might lead to an increase in savings rather than in consumer spending. Illustration 5.1 demonstrates the greater potency of the multiplier when government spending rather than taxation is changed.

These fiscal measures might be accompanied by interest rate reductions which, it was hoped, would stimulate capital investment. However, the interest rate reduction will achieve its desired result only if investment is interest-elastic. In both the classical loanable funds theory and the Keynesian marginal efficiency of capital theory the reduction in interest rates will increase the level of investment. However, Keynes himself pointed out that there are other factors, most notably the famous 'animal spirits', which influence the level of investment. In a slump such as the 1930s – or indeed the early 1990s – a reduction in interest rates might prove insufficient encouragement for business people to undertake investment.

The increase in aggregate demand will, it is hoped, have a beneficial effect on the level of employment although evidence shows that in recovery from a slump a rise in employment/fall in unemployment usually follows the upturn in other economic variables (such as output, income, orders). Moreover, in addition to this time-lag problem there are a number of more fundamental problems.

First, even in the Keynesian era it was accepted that reflation had to be accompanied by measures to increase factor mobility to ensure that the

Fig. 5.4 *Reflationary measures and the multiplier*

To combat demand deficiency unemployment a government will reflate the economy, by increasing the level of government spending while leaving tax rates unchanged. In the situation below the government seeks to raise the level of national income to the full employment level (Y^f). However, it is not necessary to raise government spending by the full extent of the deflationary gap. The multiplier leads to an increase in national income larger than the increase in government spending – we can see the extent of the multiplier effect by comparing the rise in G and the rise in Y.

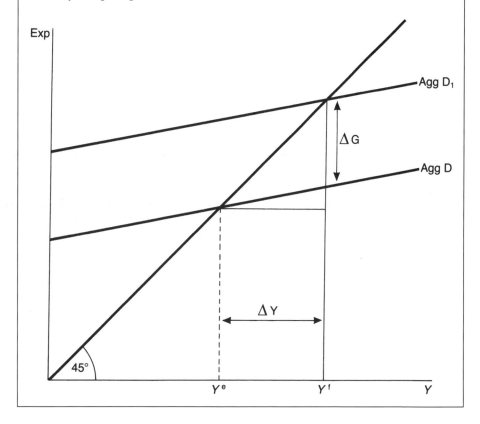

unemployed were able to take advantage of the job opportunities that became available. Training and re-training schemes are methods of increasing the occupational mobility of labour. Regional policy which (as we will see later in this chapter) concentrated on increasing the mobility of capital was necessary to ensure that jobs were available in the areas of high unemployment.

A second problem concerns the purchase of imports. Reflation in the UK will lead to increased spending on imported goods and services. The UK has particularly high marginal propensity to import, with the result that UK reflation is likely to produce a multiplier stimulus to the German or Japanese economy. In theory, depending upon the relative sizes of the marginal rates of withdrawal, it is possible for the impact of UK reflation to be greater abroad than it is in the UK. Keynes himself was a Liberal and therefore believed in

---

Illustration 5.1 *Reflation by increase in government expenditure or tax cuts*

From a Keynesian perspective an increase in government spending (G) is always more potent than an equivalent cut in taxation (T). The proof lies in the multiplier.

Assume a closed economy with government expenditure but only a flat-rate tax. The marginal propensity to save (mps) is 0.25.

The multiplier is $1/1 - mpc$ (marginal propensity to consume) or, in this case, $1/mps$, i.e. $1/0.25$.

A £1 million rise in G leads to a rise in Y of £1 million multiplied by $1/mps$. Hence £1 million $\times 1/0.25 = £4$ million.

A £1 million cut in taxation leads to a £0.75 million first round increase in consumer spending – the remainder being saved.

Hence the increase in Y is £0.75 million $\times 1/0.25 = £3$ million.

Conclusion: Keynesians recommend increased government spending rather than tax reductions to reflate the economy.

---

free trade. As stated earlier, he was an interventionist at home but a non-interventionist in the international economy. Consequently, demand management measures concentrated on C, I and G and left X and M alone. The spirit of the post-war age, reflected in the GATT, was opposed to trade barriers and so this problem of the benefits of reflation leaking abroad remained. Some economists (e.g. the New Cambridge School in the 1980s) favoured reflation accompanied by protection to prevent leakage abroad of the benefits. Protectionists are, however, in a minority; the majority of economists, politicians and business people see import controls as:

- *barriers to trade;*

- *impediments to change;*

- *promoting monopoly;*

- *contrary to free choice.*

The election of the Thatcher government in 1979 and the UK's increasing involvement in the EC after 1973 meant that import controls were no longer on the agenda of practical politics.

A third problem of Keynesian reflation concerns its likely inflationary consequences. The original Phillips curve suggests a trade-off between unemployment and inflation. Keynesian reflation will reduce unemployment but at the cost of a rise in the rate of inflation. It was always accepted that mild inflation was a small price to pay for full employment and so governments were prepared to trade off some inflation for reduced unemployment. This acceptance of the trade-off was undermined by the stagflation of the 1970s, in which Keynesian economists found it difficult to explain high unemployment at a time of unprecedentedly high inflation. A more fundamental attack on accepted wisdom came from Milton Friedman, who rejected the traditional Phillips curve in favour of a long-run vertical curve. This suggested that:

- *there was a natural, or equilibrium, rate of unemployment to which the economy would always return;*

- *the trade-off worked only in the short run and therefore Keynesian reflation was futile;*

- *any attempt to reduce unemployment below the natural rate would lead to accelerating inflation.*

Acceptance of Friedman's ideas led to a fundamental shift in policy objectives and weapons. First, the main objective of government economic policy ceased to be the maintenance of full employment (which became a discarded concept) and instead became combating inflation. Low, even zero, inflation was seen as essential for long-term growth and prosperity. Nothing, not even the maintenance of high levels of employment, was to interfere with the zero inflation objective of the Thatcher and Major governments.

Second, Keynesian macro-economic policy was rejected. No longer would fiscal and/or monetary policy be used to control the level of employment. This does not mean that UK government ceased to be concerned about the plight of the jobless although there was a major shift from macro-economic policy (the concern of the Chancellor of the Exchequer) to micro-economic policy (the concern of other economic ministries such as the DTI and the Department of Employment). This shift to micro-policy was a result of the

Fig. 5.5 *Supply-side measures to tackle unemployment*

Policy measure	Rationale
1. Reduce direct taxation	To eliminate the unemployment and poverty traps and provide an incentive to work
2. More selectivity in benefits	To increase the incentive to work
3. Portable pensions	To increase labour market flexibility
4. Reforms in the housing market, e.g. sale of council houses, relaxation of rent controls	To increase geographical mobility of labour
5. Improved training and re-training	To increase occupational mobility of labour
6. Reduce overhead cost of labour, e.g. reduce minimum standards of working conditions	To reduce labour costs and make it more attractive to employ
7. Reduce direct costs of labour, e.g. abolition of Wages Councils, reducing power of unions	To reduce labour costs and make it more attractive to employ
8. Encouragement of self-employment, e.g. tax changes, Enterprise Allowance	To encourage the unemployed to seek an alternative to employment

monetarist/new classical 'counter-revolution' in economics. Friedman had argued that, although it was not possible to reduce unemployment below the natural rate, it was possible to reduce the natural rate itself. The natural rate is determined by structural rigidities in the labour market (e.g. trade unions forcing up wages, the pension system which 'ties' people to certain jobs, occupational immobility of labour). Only measures which reduce labour market imperfections will reduce the natural rate of unemployment (*see* Fig. 5.5).

At the same time as the monetarist counter-revolution there was renewed interest in the supply side of the economy. Keynesian policy concentrated on the demand side and it was always assumed that supply would respond. Supply-side economists argue that enterprise has to be encouraged not by cash hand-outs from the state (which were usually used inefficiently) but by tax reductions. Keynesians favour reducing taxes to increase demand; supply-siders to provide an incentive for enterprise, initiative and effort. Tax cuts enable people to keep more of their income, thus encouraging both the self-employed and wage earners. It also increases the differential between take-home pay for low-paid workers and benefits from unemployment, thus helping to reduce the problems of the poverty and unemployment trap.

Regional problems and regional policy

The term 'regional problem' has a variety of meanings, depending upon our focus of interest. It is often equated with regional differences in unemployment although there are other dimensions to this issue. For instance, although the South East is traditionally seen as prosperous and (until the recession of the early 1990s at least) experiencing low unemployment, in many ways it is a problem area, facing congestion and overcrowding. While this is a different kind of problem from that of various parts of the North, it is still a regional problem.

If we take a multi-faceted view we can say that regional problems involve:

- *the uneven distribution of industry in the UK;*

- *the uneven distribution of population, with some areas experiencing depopulation and others congestion;*

- *regional differences in income and wealth;*

- *regional differences in the quantity and quality of the social infrastructure and social services (e.g. in access to health care);*

- *unequal opportunities for people in the various regions;*

- *regional differences in the rate of unemployment.*

Regional policy has usually focused upon the regional differences in unemployment, with assistance given to two kinds of areas:

- *those of declining industry (e.g. the North East, South Wales, Central Scotland);*

■ *those which have not developed industry and which have relied upon low-productivity, low-wage and highly seasonal activities such as farming, fishing and tourism (e.g. the South West, Central Wales, Scottish Highlands).*

Before looking at interventionist measures, we should consider the free market solution to the problem. Regional differences in unemployment will lead to regional differences in the price of factors of production such as land and labour. Consequently, capital will be repelled from prosperous areas such as the South East by high costs and attracted to the less prosperous ones by low rents and low wages. At the same time, there will be some movement of labour away from the areas of unemployment. The process continues until equilibrium between regions is restored. The free market solution has logical appeal and its critics should remember that capital (in the form of multi-national corporations investing abroad) and labour (in the form of economic migration) both move in search of, respectively, inexpensive resources and improved living standards. If it happens across national borders, there is no reason to doubt that it can occur within national boundaries.

The interventionist approach to regional problems is based on one of three propositions.

1 The free market approach does not work.

2 The free market approach involves an unacceptable delay before equilibrium is restored.

3 The free market solution involves unacceptable disparities in income and living standards.

For the free market solution to work it is necessary to have substantial wage (and rent) differences between regions. This is due to the 'Golden Triangle' effect that attracts new investment to the South East. Given the distance between, say, Newcastle and both the prosperous South East and the Channel routes to the EC, there must be substantial differences in factor rewards to compensate for the higher transport costs. In the past most have seen these large wage differences as socially divisive and politically unacceptable. However, the modern advocates of free-market economics see wage differences as an essential part of the solution to the problem. As is well known, trade unions bargain on a national basis (with additional local or plant bargaining on bonuses). National wage rates prevent wage differentials opening up to solve the problem. This is an example of institutional impediments to the free market solution. In other words, it suggests that the market would work if it were allowed to operate freely.

Those who argue that the free market solution does not work base their case on the following.

1 Labour immobilities prevent the unemployed from either migrating or taking up the newly created jobs.

2 Firms do not act rationally to seek the optimum (lowest cost) location but instead seek a satisfactory one. Consequently, they ignore the advantages of locating in a (slightly) lower cost location in the regions in favour of the South East.

Fig. 5.6 *UK Assisted Areas, designated 1984*

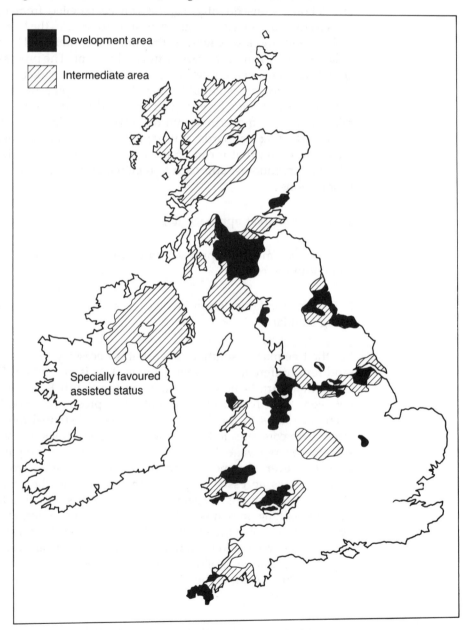

3 Labour migration distorts the population structure of the regions. The areas of outward migration acquire an ageing population, with lower skills and less enterprise. This is because younger, more skilled and more enterprising people leave. As a result the area of high unemployment becomes even less attractive to new firms.

4 Labour migration will also lead to a decline in regional demand and therefore further job losses.

5 Any migration of population will lead to (a) a waste of social capital in the area of outward migration and (b) overcrowding, congestion and a shortage of social capital in areas of inward migration.

6 The areas of high unemployment in the UK tend to be on the periphery of the EC 'Golden Triangle' and hence unattractive to new development.

The assumed inability of the free market to solve the problem has led to an interventionist approach which dates back to the 1930s although it was pursued more forcefully after 1945. During the half century in which regional policy has been pursued, a variety of measures have been used. In general there has been a preference for encouraging expanding firms into less prosperous areas rather than helping the unemployed to move to the more prosperous areas (in other words, 'taking work to the workers' has been preferred to 'taking the workers to the work'). At times, governments have used industrial development certificates to block expansion in the more prosperous regions. However, the 'stick' is an impotent weapon in a time of high unemployment. Instead governments have preferred the 'carrot' of incentives to encourage expansion in the less prosperous areas (known as Development Areas) – *see* Fig. 5.6.

The incentives (available to firms expanding in Development Areas) take the form of (and *see* Illustration 5.2):

- *investment grants equal to 15 per cent of the cost of buildings and machinery (50 per cent in Northern Ireland);*

- *additional selective grants on a discretionary basis for buildings, machinery and business start-ups;*

- *training grants of up to 40 per cent of basic wages and training costs;*

- *low-rent (or initially rent-free) premises;*

- *government loans;*

- *assistance for the movement of key workers;*

- *50 per cent remission of rates in Scottish Development Areas (75 per cent in Northern Ireland);*

- *the establishment of Regional Development Agencies to attract new firms by means of loans, advice and assistance with identifying sites;*

- *infrastructure development in industrial estates;*

- *Enterprise Zones to revive specific, derelict areas by reducing the burden of government on firms in such areas.*

Illustration 5.2 *1988 reforms to regional policy*

1. Regional Development Grant abolished. Savings in expenditure to be transferred (at least initially) to other regional assistance schemes such as Regional Selective Assistance.

2. Small firms under 25 employees:
   (i) eligible for 25 per cent investment grant up to a maximum of £15,000;
   (ii) eligible for an innovation grant of 50 per cent up to a maximum of £25,000 to support new products and new methods of production.

3. Firms with under 500 employees will qualify for grants to meet the cost of employing management consultants under the Business Development Initiative Scheme: two-thirds of the cost to be met by the government (compared to one-half in non-assisted areas).

4. Regional Selective Assistance: more money to be made available to offset the reduced expenditure on Regional Development Grants. Only projects that would not otherwise go ahead to be supported.

In addition to government help there is also assistance from the EC. This takes the form of additional sources of funding for infrastructure development in areas of high unemployment. As we will see in chapter 16, assistance is available from the EC Structural Funds, the ECSC and the European Investment Bank. However, we should also appreciate that the EC acts as a constraint on regional assistance. For instance, the Regional Employment Premium was a subsidy to firms for all workers employed in manufacturing industry in the assisted areas between 1967 and 1972. It was abolished at the time of Britain's entry to the EC because it was incompatible with EC rules on assistance to industry. The EC allows member states to aid investment in depressed regions but prohibits government subsidies to enable firms to reduce their operating costs. The latter are considered to distort the market.

The Conservative governments of Thatcher and Major have pursued a minimalist regional policy, in contrast to previous Labour governments. In part this reflects the different economic philosophies of the two main parties in the UK. It can also be explained by the apparent failure of regional policy over the decades. Despite regional policy, differences between the various regions of the UK have persisted. The failure of regional policy can be attributed to the following.

1 It does not 'create' jobs, but merely shifts them.

2 Capital grants encourage capital-intensive industry.

3 Most regional aid went to helping the declining manufacturing sector.

4 The performance of new firms in Development Areas was often disappointing and these factories were often the first to close in a period of downturn in trade.

5 Logically, regional policy is designed to encourage firms to move to a less than satisfactory location, and one that they would not ordinarily have chosen. Consequently, it means that firms choose a sub-optimum, high-cost site which makes it difficult to compete in world markets.

6 Taxpayers' money is wasted when:

(a) firms are given grants for actions that they would have taken in the absence of a grant; or
(b) firms accept grants but close down their branch factory at the next downturn in the economy.

7 It subsidises inefficiency.

8 It encourages resistance to change.

Defenders of regional policy would counter by arguing that if regional aid has not actually cured the problem it has prevented it getting worse. It could also be said that the concept itself is sound but that its lack of success is due to the small amount of assistance, spread very thinly, and the fact that individual measures were inappropriate and were subject to frequent change.

Unemployment: the record

The unemployment statistics have a higher profile than many economic statistics, because of the hardship caused to those who are unemployed and the fear of unemployment engendered in those who are in work. Nevertheless, the number out of work is not the only, or even the most accurate, data on the state of the economy. In fact, unemployment is a 'lagging indicator': the peak occurs not in the depths of a recession but after a time lag. This can be seen in the data in Table 5.1.

Looking at the figures in the table one might assume that the depths of the recession occurred in 1984/5 when unemployment peaked. In terms of

Table 5.1 *UK unemployment rate (%) 1979–1992*

Year	Rate
1979	6.0
1980	7.7
1981	11.0
1982	12.8
1983	13.0
1984	13.4
1985	13.2
1986	11.4
1987	9.4
1988	7.6
1989	5.9
1990	6.5
1991	9.1
1992	10.2

downturn in output, however, the recession was concentrated in the early years of the 1980s, and by 1984/5 the UK experienced a short-lived boom attributed to the so-called supply-side miracle of the middle Thatcher years. What was happening was that as the UK recovered from recession, the lagging indicator of unemployment continued to rise.

If we look at the late 1980s we notice the opposite lagged effect. Unemployment fell in 1989 after the Lawson boom had collapsed. It continued to rise as the UK entered a period of prolonged recession in the early 1990s. Even if the UK experiences recovery in 1993 or 1994 it is likely that unemployment will continue to rise for some time.

The number and percentage of people unemployed do not tell the full story. Government ministers often make the point that high unemployment (relative to the 1950s and 1960s) has been accompanied by a rise in the number of people in work as shown in Table 5.2. The figures seem to support government claims about rising employment (as well as unemployment). However, closer inspection of this (admittedly incomplete) time series shows that the number in employment fell during the first half of the 1980s, only to rise in the late Thatcher years. This rise can be explained either by a rise in the working age of the population or an increase in the economic activity rate. However, even the rise in the late 1980s should be qualified. The 'workforce in employment' includes not only those in employment but also the self-employed and participants in work-related government training programmes. When we look at the number of 'employees in employment' the improvement is less impressive. The number of employees in employment in the 1980s was below 23 million (and for most of the decade below 22 million). Equivalent figures for the 1960s and 1970s show a higher number of people in employment, although the government would argue that high employment/low unemployment in the past was the result of overmanning which had the effect of hiding the extent of the problem. What the discrepancy between the rise in employment and the rise in the number of employees in employment does suggest is that the 1980s saw a rise in self-employment. Although in part this can be attributed to desperation about prospects of finding a job, it can also be seen as the result of government supply-side policies. The annual percentage rise in self-employment between 1985 and 1990, according to the Department of Employment, was:

- *1985   4.2*
- *1986   2.4*
- *1987   7.5*
- *1988   5.7*
- *1989   7.0*
- *1990   1.5*

The Department of Employment publishes statistics on the number of vacancies notified to Job Centres. This is a useful indication of the state of the labour market and tends to reflect immobilities and imperfections in the market (*see* Table 5.3). The low figure of 1981 was a reflection of the intense

Table 5.2 *Numbers in work in the UK 1980–1990*

	Workforce in employment (millions)	Employees in employment (millions)
1980	25.3	22.9
1982	23.9	21.4
1984	24.2	21.2
1986	24.6	21.4
1988	25.9	22.3
1990	26.9	22.9

Source: *Economic Trends*

Table 5.3 *Notified vacancies (000) 1980–1990*

1980	135
1981	91
1982	114
1983	137
1984	149
1985	162
1986	188
1987	235
1988	248
1989	218
1990	173

recession of the early Thatcher years. The number of vacancies increased to nearly a quarter of a million by the late 1980s, suggesting that, in an expanding economy, skill shortages led to problems in obtaining labour. However, the recession of the early 1990s has led to an inevitable fall in the number of vacancies.

In 1981 there were 2.5 million unemployed for 91,000 vacancies, an average of 27.5 unemployed for each vacant job. By 1988 the average had fallen to less than 10 but the recession of the 1990s pushed it back up to 30, again presenting a depressing prospect for the unemployed.

The incidence of unemployment does not fall evenly over the population. To gain a complete insight into the problem, we look at disaggregated figures, showing unemployment by:

- *region;*
- *gender;*
- *age group;*
- *skill;*

■ *duration;*

■ *ethnic origin (although this is an issue which tends to be neglected by the economist and by government statistics).*

Regional differences in unemployment are well known to students of economics. Since the First World War unemployment has consistently been higher in the regions of the declining staple industries. However, although the regional hierarchy of unemployment levels remains virtually intact, the experience of the 1980s and early 1990s should lead us to reassess this simplistic view of high unemployment in the north and low unemployment in the south. As Table 5.4 shows, the 1980s and 1990s saw unemployment rise in all areas of the country, although the shake-out from manufacturing caused particularly high unemployment in northern regions. However, the West Midlands (for most of the century an area of low unemployment and high living standards) was hard hit by the decline of the motor and related engineering industries. Consequently, we find that this region experienced unemployment worse than the national average for the first time since the war.

The South East, still experiencing low unemployment relative to many other regions, has faced major problems in the recession of the early 1990s as the 'shake-out' during this recession has been particularly severe in the service sector. It should also be remembered that unemployment in the South East, although relatively low in percentage terms, is high numerically, given the large population of this region.

Disaggregation by gender shows a disproportionate increase in male unemployment in the early 1990s. Between August 1990 and August 1992, male unemployment rose from 7.4 to 13.3 per cent; female from 3.7 to 5.8 per cent. This can be attributed to two factors. First, there has been a long-term trend against heavy manufacturing industry, in which males predominate. At the same time many of the growth areas of employment have been

Table 5.4 *UK regional unemployment 1970–1991*

Region	Percentage unemployment				
	1970	*1975*	*1980*	*1985*	*1991*
North	4.5	4.2	7.7	15.6	10.2
Yorks and Humberside	2.8	2.8	5.1	12.0	8.5
East Midlands	2.2	2.5	4.2	9.9	7.0
East Anglia	2.1	2.5	3.6	8.1	5.6
South East	1.6	2.0	2.9	8.1	6.7
South West	2.8	3.3	4.3	9.3	6.8
West Midlands	1.9	2.9	5.2	12.8	8.4
North West	2.7	3.9	6.2	13.8	9.2
Wales	3.8	4.0	6.5	13.7	8.5
Scotland	4.1	3.6	6.8	12.9	8.6
Northern Ireland	6.6	5.4	9.1	16.0	13.7
UK	2.6	3.0	4.8	10.9	7.9

female-intensive. A second factor is that this data might reflect the gender bias in statistics. Unemployment figures based on the claimant count underestimate the extent of female unemployment.

It is more difficult to analyse unemployment by skill or by industry. It has been a severe problem for the less skilled, especially those previously employed in the declining manufacturing industries. However, to talk about an 'unemployed coalminer' or an 'unemployed car worker' is a contradiction in terms. If a person is unemployed he is not a coal miner, and vice versa. Consequently, it is not meaningful to produce figures for unemployment by skill or industry.

Mobility of labour is related to age. In general, mobility (in both senses of the word) declines with age. Consequently, unemployment is a particular problem for the older worker whose prospects of being re-engaged are low. Occupational mobility is much higher among younger workers who find it easier to re-train. However, geographical mobility is affected by the state of the housing market. Hence workers of all ages have found it difficult to move region during the prolonged slump in the housing market that commenced in 1988.

The duration of unemployment tends to rise with the level of unemployment. In 1989, 38 per cent of the unemployed had been out of work for one year or more. (This compared favourably with the EC average of 52 per cent being long-term unemployed.) By 1992, however, the long-term unemployed had risen as a percentage of the total: over 50 per cent have been unemployed for six months or longer. The explanation is that the flow of people into joblessness increases during a recession and the flow of people into new jobs tends to slow down. Long-term unemployment is a particular problem since it tends to create hardship, low morale and unemployability. The long-term unemployed have declining prospects of re-employment as any vacancy tends to be taken by the more recently unemployed.

As mentioned above, economists tend to ignore the ethnic bias in unemployment and government statistics tend not to collect data on this issue. It is well known that unemployment tends to be higher among the Afro-Caribbean community, although in part this is a function of the problems of inner cities. Among the Asian community self-employment is especially well developed, resulting in a lower rate of unemployment.

UK unemployment and the EC

A question that needs to be addressed is the extent to which UK unemployment has been affected by membership of the EC. It is difficult, if not impossible, to give a definite answer to this, because we cannot know what unemployment would have been had the UK not joined the EC. All we can do is to speculate on this issue, based on our understanding of economic principles.

In the absence of the EC, Britain would have had greater autonomy in its trade policy. Hence it could have imposed various forms of trade barriers which might have reduced import penetration. On the other hand, import controls would have limited UK exports to European countries, with resulting job losses. It is also true that without the competitive spur of the EC single market, British industry would have been even less competitive when selling to the rest of the world. This might have led to further job losses.

Most informed commentators accept that, on balance, EC membership produces commercial and trade advantages for Britain and that with these advantages go job prospects and higher living standards. There is less agreement on the other trade aspect of the EC: the exchange rate. For most of Britain's time in the EC, sterling has floated freely and therefore the EC did not pose an exchange rate problem. In the late 1980s, when sterling shadowed the Deutschmark, and in the early 1990s, when sterling was in the Exchange Rate Mechanism (ERM), a high sterling exchange rate did cause problems for industry. The high pound limited Britain's exports and high interest rates harmed investment. This aspect of Britain's involvement with the EC might have cost jobs. Against this, however, managed exchange rates add a degree of stability to trading and an artificially high pound does keep inflation down. Supporters of the ERM would argue that these advantages outweigh the problems of the ERM.

In conclusion, it is not possible to state categorically what has been the impact of EC membership on jobs but it is certainly not the case that membership has led to the high unemployment Britain has experienced since joining the EC in 1973.

Unemployment: key concepts

Cyclical fluctuations   Short-term movements in unemployment caused by changes in the business cycle

Cyclical unemployment   Unemployment resulting from a downturn in the business cycle

Deflationary gap   The shortfall in aggregate demand at the full employment level of national income. This was Keynes's explanation of persistent unemployment

Demand-deficiency unemployment   Keynesian unemployment caused by a deficiency in the level of aggregate demand

Demand management   Managing the level of aggregate demand to achieve macro-economic objectives

Depression (or slump)   The phase in the business cycle characterised by a severe decline in the level of economic activity

Disguised unemployment   Where people wishing to work do not register as unemployed (as they do not believe it will increase their chances of obtaining work)

Frictional unemployment   Short-term unemployment while changing jobs

Full employment   Full utilisation of all available labour resources so that the economy produces at the limits of potential GNP. It is usually defined as unemployment of no more than 3 per cent, or a situation in which the number unemployed equals the number of vacancies

Hidden unemployment   A situation where people are in a job but their productivity is zero. It takes the form of overmanning

Natural rate of unemployment   Underlying level of unemployment consistent with a stable rate of inflation. The non-accelerating inflation rate of unemployment

Phillips curve A curve depicting an observed relationship between the levels of unemployment and the rate of change of money wages. The inverse relationship suggested that there was a trade-off between the two

Recession A phase in the business cycle characterised by a modest downturn in the level of economic activity

Regional policy Policy designed to reduce regional differences, especially in the level of unemployment

Voluntary unemployment Unemployment resulting from an unwillingness to accept a job at current market wages. Involuntary unemployment is unemployment caused by an inability to obtain a job at current market rates

CHAPTER 6

Inflation

The monetarist counter-revolution led to a major shift in the government's attitude to inflation. No longer regarded as the price of full employment, it was now seen as the only economic variable over which the government had control. Combating inflation was seen as the prerequisite of long-term growth and prosperity.

OBJECTIVES

1 To explain and analyse the causes of inflation.
2 To survey Britain's inflation record.
3 To investigate approaches to the cures for inflation.

Meaning and measurement of inflation

Inflation can be defined as the process in which there is a rise in the general level of prices resulting in a fall in the value of money. As the rise must be in the *general level* of prices, a single price rise is not in itself inflation. A rise in the general level of prices does not mean that all prices are rising or are rising at the same rate. During inflation prices rise by an average amount, but some may actually fall.

Another source of confusion about the meaning of inflation concerns changes in the inflation rate. A 'rise in inflation' means a rise in the rate of price increase. A 'fall in inflation' does not normally mean a fall in prices (that would be negative inflation), but that prices rise at a slower rate. Therefore, when we refer to a change in the inflation rate we mean an acceleration or deceleration of (positive) price rise rather than any change in the direction of price movements.

The inflation rate most widely quoted in the UK is the Index of Retail Prices (RPI). This is a weighted average of price rises which is then expressed as an index number. The weighting given to each category of goods reflects their relative importance in the 'shopping basket' of the average family. The data on expenditure patterns is derived from the *Family Expenditure Survey*, a sample survey of the expenditure of the average family in the UK. Data on price rises is then collected by government statisticians, who produce an average figure, taking weighting into account.

There are a number of problems associated with the RPI.

1 Although it provides a measure of inflation's impact upon the 'average household', it is not valid for other households. Pensioner, single-parent and low- and-high income households, for example, all have expenditure patterns significantly different from the 'average'. Moreover, even in apparently average households (i.e. average income, 2.4 children, etc.) there is no certainty that they spend their income in an 'average' way. All these non-average households will experience inflation differently from the 'average'.

2 International comparison of inflation rates is made difficult because of inconsistency in the way in which the data is collected and processed. For instance, the UK's RPI includes the cost of accommodation and is therefore affected by changes in the mortgage rate. Equivalent indices in other countries do not record such changes.

3 The RPI encompasses changes in indirect taxes and local taxation but not changes in direct taxes. Consider two shifts in taxation during the period of Conservative rule. First, in 1979 Chancellor Geoffrey Howe reduced income tax (especially at the high bands) but raised VAT. This shift from direct to indirect taxation pushed up the RPI since the VAT rise fed through to the RPI but the reduction in income tax did not. Not surprisingly, the government brought in a new index (known as the Tax and Price Index) in which changes in both taxes were included. However, the Tax and Price Index did not gain widespread acceptance. Second, in 1991 Norman Lamont raised VAT from 15 to 17.5 per cent to pay for a £140-a-head reduction in the community charge (the unpopular and now abandoned system of local taxation). The community charge reduction lowered the RPI but the VAT increase raised it. The net effect was to leave the RPI unchanged but the point is that anomalies are created by the inconsistent treatment of different forms of taxation. It can also be argued that, within certain constraints, governments can manipulate the RPI by changes in the mortgage rate or taxation.

Given these reservations about the RPI it is practice now to distinguish between the 'headline' rate shown in the RPI and the 'underlying rate', from which mortgage, tax and seasonal factors have been excluded.

4 Changes in the quality of goods and services and the development of new products also pose problems for statisticians attempting to compare the cost of a basket of goods over a period of time. The changing composition of the basket makes historical comparisons difficult except in the very short run. Therefore, even though long time series are often produced, their value is limited by these technical problems.

5 Finally, the RPI is one of the most widely quoted of economic statistics. The prominence given to it affects the behaviour of economic agents (householders, unions, firms) and can contribute to inflation – by, e.g., encouraging people to seek larger pay rises, raise prices, etc.

Inflation can be classified in terms of different rates of price rises.

Suppressed inflation   Inflation is suppressed when pressure exists for prices to rise but price controls and/or subsidies are used to prevent them. This situation is interesting in that it means that the cause of inflation can exist in the absence of the most obvious symptom. Suppressed inflation leads to shortages, queues and black markets.

Creeping inflation   This is the situation that Britain has experienced for most of the post-Second World War period. Prices rise steadily by up to 5 per cent a year.

Strato-inflation   Once inflation rises beyond 10 per cent it starts to accelerate, and remedial action is essential to avoid any movement toward Latin American-style inflation.

Hyper-inflation   This is runaway inflation caused by excessive printing of money coupled with a loss of confidence in the currency. As the population attempts to rid itself of a rapidly depreciating currency, money ceases to fulfil its normal functions of medium of exchange, store of value, and standard for deferred payment. Not surprisingly normal economic activities break down. Hyper-inflation is normally associated with political crises and it is useful to reflect on the fears expressed at the time of the 25 per cent inflation in the mid-1970s. Pessimists argued that any further rise in the inflation rate would have grave consequences for the future of democracy in the UK.

The causes of inflation

Pre-Keynesian   Classical (pre-Keynesian) economists attributed inflation to a rise in the money supply. In the era of money of intrinsic value and, later, the era of the Gold Standard, when the currency was backed by gold, inflation was the result of either debasement of the coinage or chance discoveries of gold and silver bullion. Examples of the former include the frequent exercises in recoinage undertaken by medieval kings. To create more money to pay for castles and wars they invariably added base metal into the melted-down coinage that was called in. Famous examples of bullion discoveries included South American silver brought to Europe by the Spanish in the 16th century and the gold discoveries in California in 1849. Both events were followed by inflation in Europe, thus reinforcing the ancient view that a rise in the quantity of money leads to a fall in its value. This is another way of saying that prices rise as a result of the increase in the money supply.

    The 'crude quantity theory' referred to above was modified in 1911 by an American mathematician and economist, Irving Fisher. Fisher's Equation of Exchange has been called the '1066' of economics: that is, it is the one formula that students can always remember long after the examination. It tells us that the stock of money multiplied by the velocity of its circulation (MV) is equal to the general (or average) level of prices multiplied by the number of trans-actions (PT). As MV is really the total amount of spending it must be equal to PT, which is merely the total value of goods and services purchased. There is no disagreement about the validity of the equation since the total amount spent must equal the total value of purchases: MV must equal PT. However, there is disagreement about the usefulness of the equation in analysing the relationship between M and P.

The pre-Keynesian view was that V was constant since it was determined by institutional factors such as the frequency of payment. T was determined by the level of output. Classical economists believed that the economy was either at or moving towards a full employment equilibrium. At full employment output is fixed (in the short run at least). If output cannot rise, neither can the volume of transactions (T). Consequently, pre-Keynesian economists argued that both V and T were stable and that there was a direct and causal relationship between M and P. A rise in M would lead to a rise in P.

The Keynesian view

Keynes criticised the Fisher equation and in so doing rejected the idea of a direct, causal link between the money supply and the general level of prices. He argued that T was stable only in a situation of full employment and, as was pointed out in chapter 1, the essence of the Keynesian revolution in theory was to reject the idea that the economy tended towards a full employment equilibrium. Keynes also rejected the notion that V was constant. Analysing the demand for money (the demand to hold wealth in a liquid form) Keynes argued that the demand for money (and therefore V) was not constant. If neither V nor T is constant, the impact of a rise in M is uncertain. It could:

- *be countered by a fall in V, leaving PT unchanged; or*

- *lead to a rise in T, with P unchanged; or*

- *lead to a rise in the general level of prices.*

This last point is important since Keynes did not state that a rise in the money supply could not lead to inflation – merely that the link was not certain and predictable.

Combining the various elements of Keynesian theory (liquidity preference, marginal efficiency of capital, the multiplier) we can see that a rise in M can cause inflation:

$$\Delta M \rightarrow \Delta r \text{ of } i \rightarrow \Delta I \rightarrow \Delta Y \begin{cases} \nearrow \text{Higher prices} \\ \searrow \text{Higher output} \end{cases}$$

However, the link is indirect via liquidity preference, MEC and the multiplier, and it can be broken.

For instance, in the liquidity trap a change in the money supply has no effect on interest rates and therefore no effect on the economy. Similarly, the link between interest rates and investment assumes that investment is elastic with respect to interest rates. Finally, and most importantly, the multiplier will increase the level of national income (Y) by an amount in excess of the original injection. However, whether it produces a rise in real Y or merely a rise in money Y through inflation depends upon the level of employment. At full employment real output cannot rise and therefore the effect of any expansion in the economy is inflation. At less than full employment it is possible to increase output with the result that the rise in Y is real rather than merely monetary.

Keynesians do not deny that a rise in the money supply is an essential condition for inflation (we need more money to finance our expenditure). However, as correlation is no proof of causation we should not assume that the rise in the money supply is the cause of inflation – it is possible that it is the result of inflation rather than its cause. Some Keynesians accept that a rise in the money supply *can* cause inflation but this is far short of the monetarist insistence (best summed up in Friedman's statement that 'a rise in the money supply is a necessary and sufficient condition for inflation') that it is the sole cause of inflation.

Fig. 6.1 *Keynes's inflationary gap*

Y represents the equilibrium level of national income at which aggregate demand equals aggregate supply. However, this is not necessarily the point of full employment in the economy. In the diagram Y^f is the full employment level of national income. With no spare resources it is not possible to raise output in the short run. Consequently, the rise in national income to the equilibrium level is brought about by a rise in prices: that is, national income rises as a result of an increase in the monetary value of existing real output.

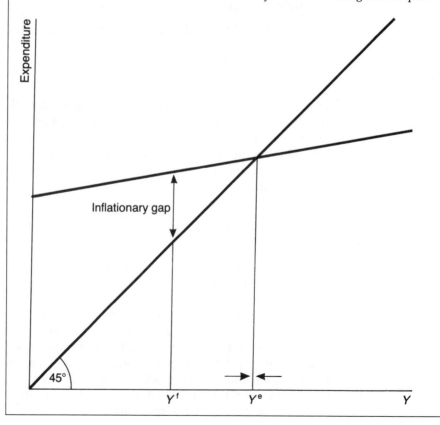

If a rise in the money supply is not the cause of inflation, Keynesians need a theory (or theories) to explain inflation. During the 1930s Keynes developed his explanation of unemployment caused by deficiency of demand. In the 1940s the problem facing British governments was excess demand in conditions of full employment. If the deflationary gap explains persistent unemployment, the inflationary gap (*see* Fig. 6.1) explains inflation. Pressures within the economy raise national income (Y) to the equilibrium level. As this cannot be achieved by a rise in real output it is achieved by price rises.

The excess demand, producing demand–pull inflation, can be caused by a rise in:

- C – *consumer spending;*

- I – *investment spending;*

- G – *government spending;*

- X – *foreign spending on UK goods and services;*

- M – *domestic spending on imported goods and services.*

Hence a boom in consumer, investment, government and export demand and/or a shortage of imports (caused by external factors or import controls) can result in demand–pull inflation. It is interesting that exports (usually seen as desirable) can be inflationary while imports (often seen as undesirable) are, in fact, disinflationary.

The Phillips curve, referred to in chapter 3, provided some evidence to support the demand–pull view of inflation in that full employment was associated with price rises whereas high unemployment was associated with low inflation or even price stability. However, it should be appreciated that the Phillips curve (even if valid) does not provide an explanation for inflation; indeed, it was not Phillips's intention to produce a theory to explain it. What the curve can be used to demonstrate is the fallacy of the simplistic view that up to full employment only output rises, whereas beyond full employment prices rise. The real situation is that as the economy approaches full employment shortages (especially of skilled labour) begin to occur. It becomes more difficult to squeeze additional output out of the economy and so prices start to rise (*see* Fig. 6.2).

The major deficiency of Keynesian demand–pull theory of inflation is that it assumes full or near full employment. It was difficult to sustain the theory during the period of stagflation in the 1970s and even more so during the high unemployment of the 1980s and 1990s. In fact an alternative 'Keynesian' view of inflation had been developed long before the 1970s: the cost-push or structuralist theory of inflation. Quite simply, this attributes inflation to cost rises that are then passed on in price rises. The only condition necessary for cost-push inflation is imperfections in the market. From your knowledge of micro-economics you will remember that perfectly competitive firms are price takers and monopolists are price makers. Some degree of monopoly power (not necessarily pure monopoly) is essential for cost-push inflation to occur. Given the imperfections that exist in the market this is a reasonable assumption.

Fig. 6.2 *Aggregate supply curves in Keynesian theory*

In diagram (a) the aggregate supply curve (AS) is shown as a backward L. This suggests that real output is perfectly elastic up to the full employment level of national income (Y^f) and perfectly inelastic beyond this point.

In diagram (b) increased output becomes more difficult as a result of skill shortages even before Y^f is reached. Consequently, supply is no longer perfectly elastic up to full employment. Prices start to push upwards even before full employment is reached.

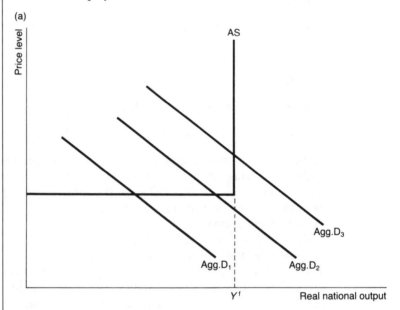

(a)

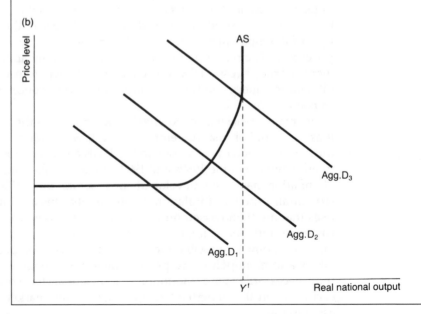

(b)

Cost-push inflation can take the form of a rise in:

- *the cost of imported materials (imported inflation occurs when the exchange rate is fixed, whereas floating insulates the country from inflation abroad);*

- *administered prices (this is known as profit-push inflation);*

- *interest rates;*

- *wage costs in excess of productivity gains; or*

- *a fall in exchange rate which raises the cost of imported goods.*

Of the variety of forms of cost-push inflation most attention is given to wage-push inflation. The labour market is characterised by imperfections:

- *monopoly supply of labour by unions;*

- *monopsony demand by large employers or employers' associations;*

- *government commitment to full employment in the pre-Thatcher period;*

- *legal constraints (admittedly lessened since 1979);*

- *bargaining to maintain pay differentials irrespective of the true situation in the market;*

- *employee–employer collusion.*

All these factors conspire (or did conspire) to produce upward pressure on wages which was passed on in price rises, producing a wage–price spiral. In fact we can develop the theory further by arguing that inflation is caused by a battle over shares in national income. Some would argue that peculiar sociological features of Britain produce pressure on wages and prices to rise. Once the process has commenced it is reinforced by expectations of further inflation. This causes economic agents to alter their behaviour (e.g. 'real wage bargaining'), thus aggravating the problem. Expectations of inflation are a self-fulfilling prophecy.

The monterarist view These Keynesian theories were rejected by Friedman and other modern monetarists. Keynesian demand–pull cannot explain inflation during periods of high unemployment. The cost-push or structuralist theory appears plausible but, according to monetarists, deals with symptoms rather than causes. Monetarists return to the pre-Keynesian quantity theory and are dogmatic in their insistence that 'inflation is everywhere a monetary phenomenon' and 'a rise in the money supply is a necessary and sufficient condition for inflation' (both quotations from Milton Friedman). To say that a rise in the money supply is a necessary condition for inflation is to argue that, because of price rises, we require more money to buy the weekly shopping basket. Keynesians would not argue against a rise in the money supply as a necessary condition for inflation. However, they and monetarists part company about whether it is a sufficient condition for inflation to occur. This means that a rise in the money supply by itself causes (rather than merely permits) inflation.

Friedman explained the relationship between the money supply and inflation with reference to the Fisher equation (MV = PT). First, he revived the classical dichotomy (also known as the classical veil). This pre-Keynesian idea separated the money economy from the real economy. Changes in the money supply influence prices but not (except in the short run) output or employment. This means that aggregate supply is inelastic in the short run, restoring Fisher's stable T in the equation (*see* Fig. 6.3).

Friedman also argued that V was stable although not constant. He developed the monetarist transmission mechanism to explain how a rise in M would eventually lead to a rise in spending. With V and T relatively stable any increase in the money supply will eventually lead to price rises. The word 'eventually' is important in the analysis since time lags form a fundamental feature of Friedman's analysis. A rise in the money supply will produce inflation, not immediately, but after a time lag of 18 months. Hence, when looking at time series data on money supply and inflation (e.g. in a data response question) remember the time lag. When the independent variable (M) peaks we should expect to see a lagged peak in the dependent variable. This uncertainty in the length of the time lag is a major factor in Friedman's preference for an automatic-rule approach to policy as distinct from Keynesian-style discretionary policy (*see* chapter 3).

Fig. 6.3 *Fisher equation of exchange (Total amount of spending MV = PT total value of purchases)*

Classical View:	Keynesian Criticism:	Modern Monetarists:
1. T is fixed by the level of output	1. The equation is a truism	1. Demand for money is stable – therefore V is stable
2. The economy tends towards full employment	2. In conditions of unemployment T can rise	2. A rise in M will lead to a rise in spending (monetarist transmission mechanism)
3. V is determined by institutional factors such as frequency of payments	3. V is not stable: demand for money changes	3. Classical veil – rise in M has little impact on real output
4. Therefore T and V are stable	4. Therefore we cannot predict the outcome of a rise in M: – fall in V – rise in T – rise in P	4. There is a causal link between M and P, although a time lag is involved
5. A rise in M leads to a rise in P		

Inflation: the record

The defeat of inflation has been at the core of government economic policy since 1979. Inflation was seen as the only indicator over which the government had control and low/zero inflation was seen as the prerequisite of long-term growth and prosperity. The year-end inflation rates are shown in Table 6.1.

In the early Thatcher years, the inflation rate was alarmingly high and was initially made worse by a substantial rise in VAT. However, the policies outlined in the Medium Term Financial Strategy (control of the money supply) brought down the rate, albeit at great cost in terms of public expenditure cuts and rising unemployment. By 1986 inflation was down to the levels last experienced in the 1960s and so this prerequisite of growth was now in place.

The tight control over the money supply was relaxed in 1987/8 especially to avert a slump in the wake of the 1987 stock market crash. Hence the Lawson boom of the 1980s was accompanied by a renewal of inflation so that by 1990 inflation was back in double figures. It was left to the new Chancellor, John Major, to reduce high inflation by a high interest rate and high exchange rate policy. Slowly Major and his successor as Chancellor, Norman Lamont, forced the inflation rate back down again during the prolonged recession of the early 1990s.

By the end of 1992 the UK's inflation rate (3.7 per cent) was below the EC average of 4.1 per cent although it was still higher than that of Germany (3.3 per cent), France (2.9 per cent), USA (3.2 per cent) and Japan (1.7 per cent). The relative inflation rate is especially important in assessing a country's competitiveness in trading. For many years the UK has suffered high relative inflation, with consequent damage to its trade, industry and employment.

Table 6.1 *Inflation rate 1980–1992*

Year	Inflation rate (%)
1980	19.0
1981	11.0
1982	8.0
1983	5.0
1984	5.0
1985	6.0
1986	3.0
1987	4.0
1988	6.5
1989	7.5
1990	10.2
1991	4.2
1992	3.7

For instance, taking a base year of 1985 (= 100) the consumer price index in 1990 for various countries was as follows:

- EC average 123

- *Netherlands 104*

- *Germany (Western) 107*

- *Japan 107*

- *France 116*

- *USA 121*

- *Italy 132*

- *UK 133*

Over the five-year period, UK prices rose by one-third and those of its main trading partners (and rivals) by rather less. Although consumer prices are not a measure of international competitiveness, it is inevitable that a sustained higher rate of inflation in the UK will reduce export competitiveness and contribute to import penetration, with resulting consequences for the balance of payments and jobs. By reducing the UK inflation rate relative to other countries, the government hopes to preserve industry's competitiveness in world markets.

We can attribute the fall in UK inflation to:

- *monetary policy involving high interest rates and ERM membership to September 1992;*

- *moderation in wage settlements keeping down producer costs;*

- *low levels of consumer demand during a prolonged depression.*

Hence, in the 'Red Book' for the 1992 budget, the Chancellor forecast not only 3.25 per cent consumer inflation by the second quarter of 1993 but also 1.5 per cent producer output inflation by the same time. This is an important indicator of future trends in consumer prices.

Since the 1992 'Red Book' was published, sterling has left the ERM and has effectively been devalued by 10 to 15 per cent. This will increase the cost of imports, including imported materials. When coupled with lower interest rates following the exit from the ERM, a record high PSBR, and recovery from the recession, it is likely that inflation will start to push upwards. The problem for any chancellor is to achieve recovery without a return to the inflation of the late Lawson period.

Inflation: key concepts

Cost-push inflation   A general increase in prices caused by an increase in the cost of factor inputs. The increased costs are passed on as higher prices

Deflation A reduction in the level of national income accompanied by a fall in inflationary pressure. A deflationary policy is designed to reduce inflation and improve the balance of payments

Demand–pull inflation Inflation caused by an excess of aggregate demand over supply in conditions of full employment

Expectations augmented Phillips curve A reformulation of the Phillips curve that allows for the effect of expectations in money wage increases. In Friedman's analysis the national rate of unemployment is the non-accelerating inflation rate of unemployment

GNP deflator A price index used as a means of adjusting money GNP values to obtain real GNP values

Hyper-inflation Chronic or runaway inflation

Indexation Automatic adjustment of payments in line with changes in the price index

Inflation An increase in the general price level sustained over a period of time

Inflationary gap Excess aggregate demand at the full employment level of national income (Y). To reach the equilibrium level of Y, prices rather than real output rises

Inflationary or wage–price spiral A self-sustained increase in the inflation rate caused by the interaction of price and wage rises

Medium Term Financial Strategy (MTFS) A financial policy introduced in 1980 which sets out targets for growth of the money supply and of the PSBR

Monetarism Theory of inflation based on excessive increase in the money supply. Monetarists also believe that discretionary macro-economic policy can reduce unemployment only in the short term and governments can do little to affect economic capacity and output by policies that operate on the demand side

Money supply Amount of money in circulation

Phillips curve A curve depicting an observed relationship between the level of unemployment and the rate of change of money wages (which was treated as a proxy for inflation)

Prices and incomes policy A policy concerned with combating inflation by directly controlling wage and price rises

Public sector borrowing requirement (PSBR) Excess of public sector spending over taxation receipts. The PSBR causes a rise in the money supply or interest rates (depending on how it is financed)

Quantity theory of money A theory which posits a direct relationship between the money supply and the general level of prices: $MV = PT$

Real wages or real income Money wages divided by the general price level

Retail Prices Index A weighted average of price rises over time

CHAPTER 7

Economic Growth

Economic growth to achieve higher living standards should be seen as the ultimate objective of economic policy. Britain's growth has frequently been disappointing and as a result Britain has slipped behind in terms of output and living standards. It was to achieve higher growth through increased trade that Britain joined the EC in 1973, and a decade later the supply-side policies of the Thatcher government promised a fundamental change in Britain's fortunes. Both these panaceas had some success but Britain's overall performance remains disappointing.

OBJECTIVES   1 To explain the nature and causes of growth.
2 To survey growth trends.
3 To account for Britain's slow growth.

Economic growth: meaning and measurement

Economic growth is clearly more than a rise in national income over time. The problem is, however, that we define growth in various ways depending upon our purpose.

1 It can be seen as a growth in the real output of an economy over time. To produce a figure for growth in real national income, it is necessary to eliminate the inflation element. This is done by multiplying national income by the national income deflator, thus making it possible to compare national income over time at constant price (*see* Illustration 7.1). The major defect of this measure of growth is that it does not, in itself, tell us anything about living standards.

2 Growth can be seen as a rise in real national income per capita. To produce such data it is necessary to divide the data for real national income for each year by the population size. Clearly, if population growth is zero the percentage change in real national income will be the same as the change in real per capita income. If the population is increasing, however, rising total real income can be accompanied by a fall in per capita real income. The value of 'real per capita' figures is that they provide a basis for measuring the change in average living standards over time. It is also possible to compare living

---

Illustration 7.1 *National income deflator*

To calculate the growth in real output from one year to another it is necessary to eliminate that part of the rise in national income resulting from inflation. Consider the following data:

Year   National income (Y)
1   £220 billion
2   £250 billion

National income rose by 13 per cent, but this is explained partly by a rise in prices giving the existing output a higher value. To disentangle the increase resulting from a rise in physical output from that resulting from inflation it is necessary to deflate the national income figure for year 2 by the following formula:

$$Y \text{ for year } 2 \times \frac{\text{index of prices for year 1}}{\text{index of prices for year 2}}$$

Assume that inflation during the year was 5 per cent:

$$Y \text{ (year 2 at constant year 1 prices)} = £250 \text{ bn} \times \frac{100}{105} = £238.1 \text{ bn}$$

From this we would conclude that real output rose by £18.1 billion or 8.2 per cent.

---

standards (and changes in living standards) on an international basis, provided real per capita national incomes are compared against a common measuring rod. For all international comparisons, the data is expressed in dollar terms (although the validity of this exercise depends upon the extent to which the exchange rate against the dollar reflects differences in the purchasing power of different currencies).

3 Growth is a rise in the productive potential of the economy. A rise in real per capita national income can be achieved by setting more of existing factors of production to work. For instance, the existence of high unemployment means that unused resources are available. If put to work, output could rise. Keynes was concerned about greater use of existing resources, shown by a movement from A to B in the production possibility curve (*see* Fig. 7.1). In the 1940s and beyond, the emphasis shifted from greater use of existing resources of the economy to the acquisition of more resources (shown by an outward shift in the production possibility curve). Hence Sir Roy Harrod (the first biographer of Keynes) took Keynesian theory a stage further than Keynes himself. He developed a theory of unemployment and inflation in a dynamic, growing economy. Although the Harrod–Domar theory is beyond the requirement of A level (and equivalent) syllabuses, an essential conclusion of the model is that if population grows more rapidly than the economy the result will eventually be unemployment. Conversely, any attempt at economic growth beyond the growth of resources will lead to inflationary pressure.

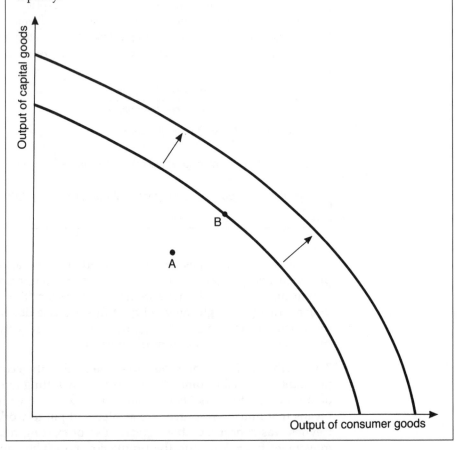

Fig. 7.1 *Production possibility curve*

At point A resources are under-utilised since the economy is not producing at the limit of possibility. Hence, a movement from A to B can be achieved by making better use of existing resources (e.g. by increasing the level of employment). Growth in the sense of increasing the productive capacity of the economy is shown by an outward shift of the production possibility curve. In the 1930s Keynes was concerned primarily with the movement from A to B. After the Second World War attention turned to raising productive capacity.

This third definition of growth concerns the production capacity of the economy rather than its current output. This is the best definition of growth, although problems in collecting data on productive potential mean that for statistical purposes economic growth is usually expressed in terms of real per capita national income.

Determinants of growth

An increase in national output can be achieved by increasing either the inputs into the production process or the output from a given quantity of inputs (e.g. productivity gains by new technology or improved organisation).

An increase in quantity and an improvement of the quality of the workforce

Population growth is a major source of growth. Not only does it increase the demand for goods and services but it provides (potentially anyway) a greater supply of labour. However, population growth through a rise in the number of births increases the labour supply only after a considerable time lag (16 years or more in the case of the UK). Population growth through a fall in the death rate is likely to increase the number of dependants rather than the working population. Only immigration provides an instant increase in the working population.

An increase in the labour supply can be achieved by ways other than a rise in the number of people within the economy.

1 An increase in the working week means an increase in the number of hours of labour supplied.

2 A change in the age structure of population could alter the balance between workers and dependants.

3 An increase in the participation rate will result in a higher proportion of the population being economically active. Logically the participation rate can be increased by:

(a) lowering the education-leaving age;
(b) raising the retirement age;
    (these are both measures that run counter to trends in modern industrial society)
(c) enabling and encouraging women to return to work sooner after the birth of children.

Improvement in human capital will increase the productivity of labour. Such improvements require considerable investment in training, health and welfare measures. Although this type of investment can be very productive, the return is uncertain and involves a considerable time delay.

An increase in the quantity and an improvement in the quality of natural resources

Although land is the factor of production given by nature, it can be 'increased' or improved by the application of man-made resources. For instance, irrigation and fertilisers increase the yield from farm land. Technological progress can make accessible previously inaccessible resources: for instance, North Sea oil has existed for thousands of years, but became a commercial resource only as a result of technological changes in the 1960s and 1970s.

An increase in the quantity and an improvement in the quality of capital

In classical growth theory, special emphasis was placed upon capital accumulation. Investment was seen as the route to growth since a mere increase in the labour force will eventually lead to diminishing marginal returns as extra labour is applied to fixed quantities of land and capital. Capital-widening is investment to maintain the existing ratio of labour to capital. Hence, as the workforce grows it is necessary to equip those additional workers, if diminishing marginal returns are to be avoided. Capital-deepening is investment to increase the amount of capital per worker. This will increase the productivity of the workforce to achieve higher levels of growth.

Investment is necessary merely to maintain the existing stock of capital. This is because capital depreciates with use. Therefore what we are really seeking is net investment (gross minus depreciation) at a rate that exceeds the growth in the labour force. However, investment always involves a sacrifice of current consumption: if $Y = C + I$ then $I = Y - C$. Consequently, a short-term sacrifice is needed for longer-term benefit.

Technical progress

Technical innovation (new products and new processes) increases the productivity of the factors of production. In this way growth rates can be increased by a series of new inventions.

Improvements in efficiency in the use of resources

There are two aspects to this point. First, improvements in organisation (e.g. the 19th-century factory system) enable entrepreneurs to obtain increased output from existing resources. Second, changes in the way resources are allocated also raise productivity. Manufacturing has always been seen as the sector with the greatest prospect for productivity gains. In the 1960s the economist Nicholas Kaldor argued that because of the small agricultural sector in the UK (the shift out of agriculture having occurred in the 19th century) the country had less scope for growth by switching from agriculture to manufacturing than was the case elsewhere in the developed world. This view led to a series of policy measures (regional policy, selective employment tax) which discriminated against the service sector to try to shift resources back into manufacturing. In later decades this preference for manufacturing as the source of growth was seen in the debate on de-industrialisation.

Whether or not an economy realises its growth potential depends upon the level of aggregate demand

Aggregate demand must be high enough to ensure that the increased productive capabilities of the economy can be fully utilised. This brings us back to macro-economic policy – about which more is said later.

Growth and living standards

The debate about the cost and benefits of growth (*see* Fig. 7.2) is sufficiently well known not to require further coverage. The question of growth and living standards, however, is central to the understanding of the economy.

For economists, the best measure of living standards is real output per head. This informs us of the average standard of living for people in the economy. Ignoring the issue of capital and defence goods (which do not raise living standards) we can say that a rise in real national income per head is a rise in average living standards. The reason for this is that in the last analysis,

Fig. 7.2 *The costs and benefits of growth*

Costs	Benefits
1. Investment involves a sacrifice of present consumption	1. Rise in real per capita income
2. Short-run fall in living standards	2. Long-run rise in living standards
3. External costs – congestion – pollution – resource depletion – threat to wildlife – landscape destroyed	3. Increase in tax yield to pay for public services
4. Often results in increased pressure at work and a decline in the quality of life	4. Reduces poverty without the need for redistribution
5. In the case of the UK it often results in a balance of payments deficit as imports are sucked in	5. Increased provision of public goods without reduction in private goods
	6. We live in a world of rising expectations – we expect to be better off and are disappointed when we are not
	7. Growth is necessary to support the growing proportion of dependants
	8. More of everything and more for all

living standards are determined by the quantity of goods and services available to the population.

Data on living standards is valid only if comparisons can be made. Economists make two types of comparison: international, between different countries; and historical, over time. The international comparisons are fraught with difficulties, due to differences in:

- *accounting methods;*

- *validity of data;*

- *life-styles;*

- *proportion of national output used to produce capital and defence goods;*

- *the distribution of income.*

As an illustration of the last point, Kuwait's per capita national income is higher than the UK's. However, this does not mean that the 'typical' Kuwaiti enjoys higher living standards than does the 'typical' resident of the UK.

Historical comparisons are more valid. An increase in real per capita income is likely to raise the living standards of most people in the UK unless growth is accompanied by increased inequality. There is evidence to suggest that inequality increases in the early years of industrialisation. Hence, it is possible for growth to be accompanied by growing poverty for a substantial minority, if not majority, of the population. This is, however, associated with newly industrialising countries; for a mature economy, like that of the UK, it is unlikely that growth will be accompanied by an increase in absolute poverty.

It is possible, however, for the benefits of growth to be unevenly distributed, suggesting that some people become more affluent while others experience no rise in living standards. This will increase relative but not absolute poverty. The distinction between these concepts of poverty is that a person is absolutely poor if his or her income is below a certain level, determined by physiological needs. A household whose income is below that necessary to buy food, heat and other basic essentials is in absolute poverty. Relative poverty obviously involves a comparison. We might say that a household whose income is below that necessary to enjoy the normal goods and services of the society in which it resides is in relative poverty even though it can afford all the basic essentials of life. For statistical purposes we can say that households with incomes that are, say, 66 (or perhaps 50) per cent of average are in relative poverty.

Growth is likely to reduce absolute poverty (although it is not guaranteed to reduce relative poverty) unless some sectors of the community gain at the expense of others. The fruits of growth will be unevenly distributed between regions and between different income groups. Some will derive great benefits, others lesser ones, and some will be no better or even worse off. The question is what, if anything, should be done about this state of affairs.

Defenders of the free market would argue that, provided the market is sufficiently competitive, the benefits of growth will eventually be spread over the whole country and among all groups in society. This process is known as 'trickle-down' – the benefits will eventually trickle down to include everyone. For example, when the initial beneficiaries of growth spend their enhanced incomes, there is additional employment and income for other sections of the community. If trickle-down does occur then there is no need for state intervention in the process – it can be safely left to the market.

Critics of the free market argue that either trickle-down occurs too slowly or it fails to encompass all sections of the community. As mentioned above, trickle-down assumes sufficient competition in the market. Imperfections in the form of monopoly power could prevent the fruits of growth trickling down. If this is the case, growth will not cure poverty and the alternative strategy of income redistribution will be necessary if the government wishes to reduce poverty. Income redistribution takes the form of taxing some sections of the community to provide welfare benefits for the less well-off. Within the UK there is considerable support for some income redistribution with the state fulfilling a 'Robin Hood' function of taking from the rich to give to the poor. However, there is considerable dispute abut the desirable degree of equality or inequality. Some degree of inequality is necessary to provide incentives for people to work harder, and to encourage movement of labour and people to take on additional responsibilities. Complete equality is seen as being harmful to the economy by undermining incentives and retarding economic growth.

The Thatcher governments of the 1980s placed less emphasis on redistribution because of their beliefs that, in a market system, trickle-down will occur and, at the same time, the alternative policy of redistribution is harmful to growth. Going a stage further, it could be argued that the redistribution associated with the welfare state played a major role in the disappointing growth of the UK economy in the post-Second World War era. It is to Britain's growth rate that we now turn.

Britain's slow growth rate

For much of the post-war period, Britain's growth rate has been considered unsatisfactory, especially in comparison with other industrial economies (*see* Table 7.1). The argument that Germany and Japan were merely catching up after the devastation of war seemed plausible in the 1950s but was wearing thin by the 1960s. In the search for the reasons for slow growth, numerous alleged culprits were identified.

Size of the domestic market It was argued that Britain had a small (by international standards) domestic market and a slow rate of population growth. This meant that the market was both small and growing only very slowly, thus depriving domestic industry of the economies of scale enjoyed by American and Japanese firms. The belief that Britain was 'too small' to remain in the top league was a major factor in its desire to enter the EC.

Management v. labour The two sides of industry blame each other for the poor performance of the economy. Labour was accused of being backward looking and inflexible. Restrictive labour practices in the 1950s, 1960s and 1970s led to overmanning and high-cost production. This reduced unemployment by hiding it in overmanned factories, but it undermined the competitiveness of industry.

The alleged poverty of British management is attributed to the social class and education systems perpetuating the 'amateurism' that has long been a feature of British society. This was symbolised in the Gentlemen v. Players cricket matches that were a feature of the British summer until comparatively recently. (Before 1939 the professional 'players' were admitted to cricket grounds through different entrances from the amateur 'gentlemen'.) The gentlemen v. player distinction remains a feature of British society.

Table 7.1 *GDP growth rates*

	Annual average rate %		
	1960–73	*1973–79*	*1979–89*
UK	3.2	1.5	2.2
UK (non-oil)	3.2	0.8	2.2
EC	4.8	2.5	2.1
OECD countries	4.9	2.7	2.1
G7 countries	4.8	2.7	2.8

Occupational distribution

Reference was made above to the impact of occupational distribution on growth. It is argued that the manufacturing sector has the greater potential for productivity gains. Hence, high growth rates can be achieved by shifting resources out of low-productivity agriculture and into high-productivity manufacturing. With a small agricultural sector, Britain has little scope for growth by this means.

A persistent concern of politicians and economists has been the growth of the service sector (*see* de-industrialisation, in chapter 9). To discriminate against the service sector and in favour of manufacturing is to undermine what has been the growth sector of the UK economy in favour of the sector that has suffered long-term decline.

Lack of investment

Lack of investment is seen as a major cause of slow growth. This is not surprising when we remember the emphasis placed by economists (especially in classical theory) on investment as *the* source of growth. It is argued that investment in the UK economy has persistently been below that of its main trading rivals. A variation on this theme is that the problem lies not with the overall level of investment but with the nature of it. A high percentage of UK investment has been in social capital (houses, hospitals, etc.), which has a lower growth-inducing potential than private sector investment in manufacturing. It is further argued that under nationalisation investment was misplaced (e.g in declining industries). Hence, the productivity gains from UK investment were below those of elsewhere. Supporters of the market argue that this state-directed investment was commercially unsound and wasteful.

Assuming that the problem was a deficiency in overall investment, we require an explanation of why this occurred. Numerous points have been made over the years and, clearly, they reflect the subjective views of their different exponents. Some of the criticisms have been addressed by the Thatcher and Major governments, although these governments have created new problems. The usual explanations for low UK investment are as follows.

1 High taxation destroyed the incentive to invest in the pre-Thatcher period.

2 The UK has a preference for present consumption and for social capital as distinct from private sector capital investment.

3 Union restrictive practices led to overmanning in the pre-Thatcher period. This reduced the profitability of investment.

4 Managerial deficiencies meant that opportunities were missed.

5 City institutions failed the nation by diverting funds into property and into overseas hands. This criticism of the UK capital market has a long history but the Wilson Commission of the late 1970s found no evidence to substantiate the claim that UK industry was starved of funds.

6 Wage levels can be used to support opposing arguments on the issue of low UK investment. Unions claim that low wages in the UK remove the incentive to invest in capital equipment, management claim that the explanation is the reverse. High wage costs (especially in view of the lower productivity of UK

workers) have reduced the profitability of investment in the UK. In what management sees as the 'bad old days' when unions were strong and militant, squabbling over shares of 'the national cake' seemed to take precedence over 'baking a larger cake'.

Balance of payments difficulties

The balance of payments acts as a constraint on growth. Growth in the UK economy usually results in inflation (as the economy approaches the short-run ceiling) and a rise in imports. The UK has a high marginal propensity to import (income elasticity of demand), with the result that imports of consumer goods, capital equipment, raw materials and services (such as foreign holidays) are 'sucked in' as incomes rise. Between 1945 and 1971, and then again between 1990 and 1992, sterling moved within a comparatively narrow band. As sterling approached the 'floor', governments were required to act to maintain the exchange rate. Although the nature of the action varied, the effect was always the same: deflation of the economy. This reduced inflationary pressure and the balance of payments deficit but at the expense of jobs, investment and long-term growth.

Between 1971 and 1990, and now since September 1992, sterling floated. The major advantage of a floating exchange rate is that, provided certain conditions are in place (*see* chapter 8), there is an automatic mechanism to solve balance of payments problems. If the balance of payments takes care of itself, it no longer acts as a constraint on growth. This is an important factor in the controversy over the ERM and monetary union in the EC (*see* chapter 15).

Inadequate or misguided state intervention

Growth has been one of the four objectives of macro-economic policy in the post-war era. Apart from in certain sectors of the environmental movement, growth is seen as a desirable objective. Politicians and the public might differ over how it should be achieved and how the benefits of growth should be distributed, but there is a clear majority in favour of economic growth and rising living standards.

Frustrated by disappointing growth rates, governments have intervened in the market. This intervention took the form of public sector investment in the nationalised industries; the channelling of funds via state bodies such as the Industrial Reorganisation Corporation and National Enterprise Board; investment grants to aid desirable projects such as job creation in the areas of high unemployment; tax incentives, the Business Expansion Scheme and the most ambitious scheme of all – the National Plan of 1965. These measures were associated with interventionist governments, both Labour and pre-Thatcher Conservative. Free market supporters argue that such intervention is misplaced and leads to a misallocation of resources. They also argue that state intervention is harmful in other respects.

1 Keynesian demand management concentrated on achieving short-term objectives (such as full employment) and neglected longer-term growth. In fact, Keynesian fine-tuning is characterised by frequent changes in policy to solve the immediate problem. This led to unsettling policy changes (which in turn discouraged investment) and a cycle of expansion and contraction.

2 There are also frequent micro-economic policy changes (e.g. in regional policy) which discourage private sector investment.

3 Critics of the welfare state argue that the quest for egalitarianism undermined incentives. Despite the well-meaning motives of the founders of the welfare state, it produced a culture of dependency harmful both to the individual recipient and to the economy as a whole. Recent Conservative governments have attempted to reverse the process by creating a culture of enterprise but this has often been at the expense of disadvantaged groups within society.

4 'Crowding-out' became a fashionable phrase in the 1980s. Monetarists argued that a public sector borrowing requirement financed by borrowing from the 'non-bank' sector (households and firms) pushes up interest rates, thus reducing private sector investment. As a result manufacturing industry is 'crowded-out' by excessive government spending.

The term 'crowding-out' is also associated with Bacon and Eltis's famous account: *Britain's Economic Problem: Too Few Producers*. Readers should note that 'problem' is in the singular, and is what the authors saw as the relentless growth of the non-market sector. This is not synonymous with the public sector although there is considerable overlap.

The size of industries in the market sector is determined by demand. The size of the non-market sector is not subject to such a constraint. The public's 'desire' (not demand in the economic sense since these services are free at the point of consumption) for non-market services grows and grows. To finance state activities additional taxes and/or borrowing is required. Both methods of financing crowd out private, market sector activities.

Finance via taxation crowds out by reducing disposable income. Finance via borrowing from the non-bank sector crowds out by raising interest rates. The solution to this problem is to control or even reverse the growth of the non-market sector of the economy. Obviously this is in keeping with the free market ideas associated with the incoming Conservative government of 1979.

Economic growth: key concepts

Balanced growth A dynamic condition of an economy where all real variables are growing at the same proportional rate

Capital accumulation Net investment to build up the capital stock

Capital-deepening The accumulation of capital at a faster rate than the growth of the labour force. Capital-deepening increases the ratio of capital to labour

Capital intensity Ratio of capital to labour employed in production

Capital-intensive methods Techniques in which a high proportion of total costs are capital costs

Capital stock The sum of capital goods in the economy

Capital-widening Capital accumulation at the same rate as the growth of the labour force

Classical growth theory A market-orientated approach which emphasises capital accumulation

Consumption The act of using goods and services in order to satisfy wants

Crowding-out A fall in private investment resulting from a rise in public sector spending

De-industrialisation A fall in the share of GDP taken up by the secondary or manufacturing sector

Economic growth An increase in real national income

Export-led growth Expansion stimulated by an increase in exports

Human capital Investment in human resources to improve the productivity of labour

Indicative planning The use of centrally determined targets to co-ordinate output and investment decisions, e.g. Labour's National Plan of 1965

National income A measure of the value of goods and services becoming available to the economy as a result of economic activity. National income equals national output equals national expenditure

Neo-classical growth theory Growth models in which emphasis is placed on substitution between factors to achieve growth

Net investment The addition to the stock of capital

Poverty, absolute A definition of poverty based on minimum levels of income necessary to sustain life

Poverty, relative A definition based on income relative to other groups in society

Productivity Output per unit of input (e.g. output per man hour)

Secular trend Trend computed for a long run of data – that is, with seasonal and cyclical factors eliminated

Stop–go Alternation of reflation and deflationary policy. The stop part of the cycle is intended to correct a balance of payments deficit

Trade cycle Fluctuations in the level of economic activity forming a regular pattern of expansion (boom) and contraction (slump)

Wealth Anything which has a market value and can be exchanged for goods or money

CHAPTER 8

Balance of Payments

Britain's balance of payments has been and still is a matter of concern. Whereas in the short run a deficit enables the people to enjoy higher living standards than they would otherwise, in the longer run a deficit cannot be sustained. Consequently, all economies require mechanisms to deal with a deficit. It is to the mechanisms for adjustment and to the balance of payments performance of the UK economy that we now turn.

OBJECTIVES
1 To explain the balance of payments as a set of accounts.
2 To explain and analyse mechanisms for curing a deficit.
3 To analyse the problem of a balance of payments surplus.
4 To survey Britain's recent balance of payments performance.

The balance of payments

Before looking at Britain's balance of payments it is useful to remind the reader of the nature and purpose of a balance of payments account. The basic purpose is to summarise the transactions between residents of a country (firms, government agencies and households) and those of other countries. Note that the word 'resident' rather than 'citizen' or 'national' is used. The passport held by participants in the transaction is irrelevant: the essential point is where those people are normally resident. Analyses of transactions enable economists and others to analyse the flow of money into and out of the country.

The format used to present the accounts has changed over the years and students should ensure that they are familiar with the format currently used in government statistics. The current format for Britain's balance of payments was adopted in 1987 and is shown in Fig. 8.1.

The current account deals with trade in (a) goods and (b) services (such as insurance, tourism, transport and banking). The selling of goods and services abroad produces an inflow of money into the country. Consequently, these are positive items in the balance of payments. On the other hand, the purchase of goods and services from abroad leads to an outflow of money and is therefore a negative item. Fig. 8.1 shows that the balance on visibles (also known as the balance of trade) is equal to the value of exports less the value

Fig. 8.1 *The balance of payments*

	£m
Current account	
Visible trade (value of exports minus value of imports)	(a)
Invisible trade (receipts from invisibles minus payments for invisibles)	(b)
A Current balance	(a) + (b)
External assets and liabilities	
Transactions in assets	(c)
Transactions in liabilities	(d)
B Net transactions	(d) − (c)
C Balancing item	(e)
A + B + C	= 0

of imports. In the case of the UK this is typically in deficit, meaning that the value of imports exceeds the value of exports.

In normal years the deficit on visibles is cancelled out by a surplus on invisibles, i.e. the value of services sold exceeds the value of services bought from abroad. If the invisible surplus cancels out the deficit on visibles the country is said to have a surplus on the current account. Conversely, the surplus on invisibles might be insufficient to cancel out the deficit on visibles and the result is then a deficit on the current account. The current balance is therefore simply the sum of the visible and invisible balance, bearing in mind that one or both of them might be minus numbers.

The next section of the account deals with transactions in assets and liabilities. In earlier years it was known as the capital account. Transactions in assets include:

- *purchase of shares in foreign-based companies;*

- *purchase of subsidiary companies abroad;*

- *loans to foreign banks;*

- *repayments to the IMF and/or foreign banks;*

- *purchase of property abroad.*

The common point about each of these is that they lead to an outflow of funds and it is for this reason that they are shown as a negative item in the balance of payment. It is true that in subsequent years they might generate an inflow (i.e. interest, profit or dividend which is recorded in the 'invisible' section of the current account) but initially the result is an outflow of funds. Transactions in liabilities refer to the inflow of funds from abroad to:

- *purchase shares in a British company;*

- *purchase property in Britain;*

- *purchase British companies and operate them as subsidiaries of a multinational corporation;*

- *lend to the UK government.*

As the transaction involves an inflow it is recorded as a positive item on the balance of payments. It is shown as a liability because the new foreign-based owner has a claim on the British economy. In subsequent years it will generate an outflow of interest, profit and dividend which will become a negative item on the balance on invisibles. Nevertheless the initial impact of the transaction is an inflow.

Net transactions will be equal to the inflow of funds (liabilities) less the outflow (assets). The pre-1987 accounts separated capital movements resulting from normal transactions from any 'accommodating movements', such as IMF loans, to finance a deficit. These accommodating movements were recorded as official financing but in 1987 it was decided to discontinue this practice because the distinction was not clear cut.

The final item on the balance of payments is known as the balancing item. This is designed to take care of errors and omissions. Given the vast number of transactions it is little surprising that some are not recorded or the information is not yet to hand. The reader might be puzzled as to how accountants and statisticians are able to calculate the errors and omissions. The answer lies in the fact that transactions are double-sided: the export of goods is balanced by inflow of funds. Data from the banking system provides government accountants with a method of checking data from other sources. Hence if there is a large, unexplained inflow of funds across the foreign exchanges, one (or a combination) of three things must have happened:

- *unaccounted for exports of goods;*

- *unaccounted for sales of services abroad;*

- *unaccounted for capital inflows.*

Normally the accounts are published in a provisional form and then revised as new information comes to hand. Logically each successive revision of the year's figures should see a reduction in the balancing item as transactions are explained.

As is well known to students, the balance of payments always 'balances' – at least in the bookkeeping sense. This is not an example, as some students think, of accountants' sleight of hand or cooking the books. Instead it is the inevitable consequence of the double-entry method of bookkeeping. All purchases are balanced by an outflow, all sales by an inflow. Consequently, if the country has a deficit on the combination of its current account and normal commercial capital transactions, there must have been a corresponding movement across the foreign exchanges to finance the deficit. These movements might have taken the form of running down the country's reserves of gold and foreign currency *or* of loans from the IMF or foreign central banks. If, on the other hand, the country enjoyed a surplus on 'normal' transactions then somehow the surplus must have been disposed of by a combination of:

- *additions to foreign currency reserves;*

- *repayment of loans to foreign banks;*

- *loans to foreign banks;*

To illustrate this principle consider a household budget. If weekly expenditure of £220 exceeds weekly income of £200, the family must have developed a means of financing the extra £20. Most probably it would have involved raiding past savings and/or borrowing in some way (loans, overdraft, credit cards, etc.) The family that receives £200 per week but spends only £180 has to find a way of disposing of the surplus. This is likely to be by adding to family savings and/or repaying past debt. The basic point is that deficits always have to be financed and surpluses always have to be disposed of. Hence in a purely accounting sense, the nation's payments always balance.

A balance of payments deficit

A balance of payments deficit means that the nation is buying more goods, services and assets from abroad than it is selling and, as a consequence, is either accumulating international debt or running down its reserves of foreign currency. Although we tend to think of a deficit as 'undesirable' we must appreciate that a nation or economy in deficit is obtaining imports without equivalent exports: the rest of the world is supplying more goods and services to the deficit economy than it obtains back. A deficit enables the residents of an economy to enjoy a higher standard of living than would otherwise be the case whilst at the same time, by reducing the pressure of demand, a deficit helps to counter demand–pull inflation.

Unfortunately, a deficit cannot be sustained indefinitely since reserves of foreign exchange and goodwill on the part of overseas bankers will eventually run out. Consequently, a deficit is usually seen as a 'problem' to be solved. However, the nature of the solution will depend upon the exchange rate regime adopted by the country:

- *fixed exchange rates, e.g. 19th-century Gold Standard or EMU;*

- *managed exchange rates, e.g. the Bretton Woods system 1945–71 and ERM 1990–2 (see Fig. 8.2);*

- *floating exchange rates, e.g. UK from 1971 until the policy of Deutschmark shadowing in 1988, and since September 1992.*

The fixed and floating regimes each provide an automatic adjustment to correct an imbalance on the economy's overseas payments. Under the 19th-century Gold Standard, a deficit on the balance of payments was accompanied by an outflow of gold. Because of the need to back the currency with gold, the outflow triggered a rise in interest rates, which would have two effects: it would reverse some of the gold outflow, and would have a deflationary impact on the economy. This would stem the tide of imports and thus improve the balance of payments. It should be noted that this automatic adjustment was at the expense of the domestic economy – slumps were induced to solve the problem of the deficit.

Fig. 8.2 *Managing the exchange rate*

Under both Bretton Woods and the ERM sterling was allowed to fluctuate within a band either side of a central rate.

(a) As the exchange rate approached the ceiling the monetary authorities were required to act by selling sterling (an emergency measure), reducing interest rates, and/or taking other steps to reflate/inflate the economy.

(b) To keep the exchange rate above the floor the monetary authorities were required to act by using reserves to buy sterling (again, an emergency measure), raising interest rates, and/or taking other steps to deflate the economy.

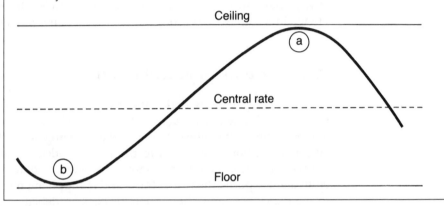

Floating exchange rates can also correct the balance of payments. A deficit will lead to high demand for foreign currencies and low demand for sterling (*see* Fig. 8.3). Consequently, a deficit produces a fall in the exchange rate, which makes exports cheaper to foreigners and imports more expensive to British residents. Paradoxically this worsening of the terms of trade can result in a rise in export earnings and/or fall in the import bill, provided the quantities change sufficiently to counteract the adverse movement in prices. The exact mechanism will be dealt with later, but for the moment we can see the automatic mechanism as (M = imports, X = exports): deficit → depreciation → rise in price of M and fall in price of X → fall in quantity of M and rise in quantity of X → fall in import bill and rise in export earnings → improvement in the balance of payment. The great advantage of this automatic mechanism is that it impacts upon the foreign exchange market rather than upon the domestic economy (*see* Fig. 8.4).

Under a managed exchange rate, there is no automatic mechanism to correct the deficit. After all, 'managed' suggests discretionary action by the government. The measures used to correct a deficit are:

- *import controls;*

- *export subsidies;*

- *deflation;*

- *devaluation.*

Fig. 8.3 *Intervention in the foreign exchange market*

1. Starting with curves SS and DD the equilibrium exchange rate is DM 3.
2. Excess demand for imports shifts the supply curve to S_1S_1 and as a result the exchange rate falls to DM 2.8.
3. Bank of England intervention in the form of buying sterling shifts the demand curve to D_1D_1 and as a result the target exchange rate of DM 3 is maintained but at a cost in terms of foreign exchange reserves.

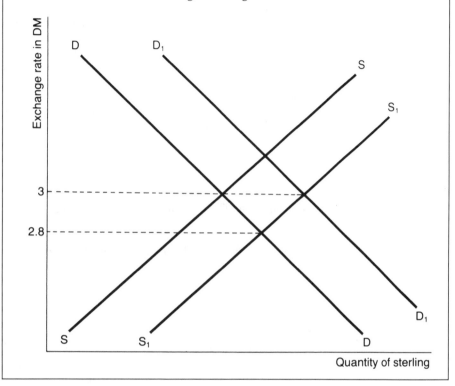

The first measure is no longer available to the UK government as a result of international obligations to GATT and to the EC. In any case, import controls also limit exports by reducing overseas ability and willingness to buy British goods.

Export subsidies are also illegal under both GATT and the EC treaties. The reason is that subsidies lead to dumping, which is seen as the unneighbourly act of exporting unemployment. With import controls and export subsidies unavailable, the choice is between deflation and devaluation.

Deflation reduces aggregate demand, including the demand for imports. If $Y = C + I + G + (X - M)$ then $(X - M) = Y - (C + I + G)$. The left-hand part of the second equation is the current balance. The right-hand part is the level of national output minus the total amount of goods and services absorbed by the economy. If national output exceeds domestic absorption the right-hand part of the equation will be positive, as will the current balance; if less than domestic absorption the right-hand side will be negative, as will the

---

> **Fig. 8.4** *Advantages and disadvantages of floating exchange rates*
>
> *Advantages*
> 1. Automatic adjustment of the balance of payments.
> 2. Adjustment occurs via the exchange rate rather than by inflicting deflation on the domestic market.
> 3. Reduces the need to hold large reserves.
> 4. Exports remain competitive since the exchange rate falls to compensate for inflation.
> 5. Provides protection from imported inflation in that inflation abroad leads to a rise in the exchange rate.
> 6. Monetary policy can be conducted independently of the exchange rate.
> 7. The balance of payments does not act as a constraint on policy-making.
>
> *Disadvantages*
> 1. Adds to the risks and uncertainty of international trade.
> 2. Contributes to a decline in trade.
> 3. The removal of external discipline might lead to irresponsible government.
> 4. Depreciation adds to inflationary pressure.

current balance. The way to ensure that $Y - (C + I + G)$ is positive is to hold down:

- *consumer spending, by fixed and monetary measures;*

- *investment spending, by high interest rates;*

- *government spending.*

Obviously, the balance of payments will improve only if there is no adverse effect on Y. This approach to the balance of payments, known as the absorption approach, is an extension of Keynesian macro-economic theory and provides us with an invaluable insight into economic policy-making.

Unfortunately, correcting the deficit by deflation means inflicting misery on the economy to solve the balance of payments. Import controls (in the usual sense of the word) might be banned but deflation and unemployment are a very effective, though painful, import control. An alternative way of achieving the result of improving the balance of payments without the pain of deflation is devaluation of the currency. Devaluation and depreciation both involve a fall in the exchange rate but we use 'devaluation' for a reduction brought about by deliberate policy decisions, 'depreciation' for a fall brought about by market forces.

At the lower exchange rate, exports are more competitive in world markets and imports are more expensive. On the face of it, this is undesirable: more exports are needed to purchase a given quantity of imports. In other words, a fall in the exchange rate represents a worsening of the terms of trade. Paradoxically, this adverse movement in the terms of trade can improve the balance of trade and the balance of payments. But for this improvement to occur, the price rise must produce a substantial fall off in the volume of imports, and/or the price reduction must produce a substantial rise in the volume of exports. This gives rise to the so-called elasticities approach to the balance of payments. As expressed in the Marshall–Lerner Condition, the balance of payments will improve if (and only if) the sum of the price elasticity of demand (PED) for exports and the PED for imports exceeds one (ignoring minus signs). Hence, if the PED for exports is −0.7 and that for imports −0.4, the combined effect is to improve the balance of payments by means of a change in quantity resulting from the change in relative prices. A follow-up to the basic rule is that the greater the sum of the elasticities, the greater the improvement in the balance of payments.

The downside of the Marshall–Lerner Condition is that if the sum of the elasticities is less than one, the fall in the exchange rate will lead to a further

Fig. 8.5 *The J curve*

The initial effect of devaluation is to worsen the balance of payments. This can be explained in terms of elasticities of supply and demand. As supply tends to be inelastic in the short run domestic producers will find it difficult to take advantage of export opportunities in the immediate aftermath of devaluation. Similarly, demand for imports and the demand for exports tend to be inelastic in the the short run. Consequently, change in the quantity of exports and imports is insufficient to counteract the change in prices. In the long run both supply and demand are more elastic, thus producing the quantity changes necessary for an improvement in the balance of payments.

In the reverse J curve the effect of upward revaluation is to increase the balance of payments surplus before it starts to decline.

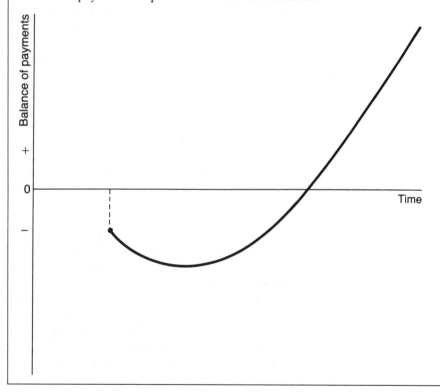

rise in the size of the deficit. Thus the floating exchange rate will not provide an automatic mechanism to correct the balance of payments. However, assuming the sum of elasticities exceeds one, the balance of payments will *eventually* benefit from a fall in the exchange rate. 'Eventually' because, as we learn in micro-economics, demand (as well as supply) tends to be inelastic in the short run. As a result it is probable that the immediate impact of devaluation/depreciation is a worsening of the deficit before it begins to improve. This is illustrated by the J curve, shown in Fig. 8.5.

The Marshall–Lerner Condition (and the whole elasticities approach) is a matter of great controversy. The best that can be said for it is that it is a necessary but not sufficient condition for successful devaluation. What it ignores is supply: are producers in a position to take advantage of the export opportunities? In 1967, when the pound was devalued from $2.8 to $2.4, the determining factor in the ability of exporters to take advantage of devaluation was the existence of spare capacity. As this was a time of relatively full employment, devaluation worked only because it was followed by deflationary measures introduced by Chancellor Roy Jenkins. In fact it is debatable whether eventual improvement in the balance of payments (after the predictable J curve effect) can be attributed to devaluation or to deflation.

In the aftermath of the 'Black Wednesday' (1992) devaluation, the constraining factor was the state of the manufacturing sector. Government critics argue that the damage done to industry over the preceding decade has impaired the ability of British manufacturers to respond to the new opportunities.

Before leaving the topic of devaluation/depreciation, one grave disadvantage must be mentioned. The rise in the cost of imports following devaluation raises industry's costs. These will be passed on in the form of higher prices in the domestic and world markets and will eventually undermine the benefit of the fall in the exchange rate. Consequently, the long-term success of devaluation does depend upon successful counter-inflation policies.

Balance of payments surplus

For students in a country where a deficit is a common problem (e.g. the UK), it might seem strange to refer to the problems of a balance of payments surplus. Nevertheless a surplus can be a problem which has to be tackled.

A balance of payments surplus is inflationary. In terms of Keynesian economics, a surplus is a net injection into the circular flow triggering off a multiplier increase in national income. If aggregate demand exceeds aggregate supply prices start to rise. Monetarists analyse the inflationary consequences of a surplus in terms of a rise in the money supply as the monetary authorities issue notes to intervene in the foreign exchange market.

A surplus is harmful in other respects. First, because the nation is absorbing less from abroad than it is supplying, logically it is experiencing living standards lower than it would otherwise experience. Second, a surplus tends to bring about currency appreciation endangering exports, output and employment in the future. Third, as one country's surplus is another's deficit (i.e. over the whole world the balance of payments sums to zero), other countries might resort to import controls to improve their own balance of payments. Again this endangers the exports of the surplus country.

The cures for a surplus will obviously be the opposite of those for a deficit:

- *the removal of exchange controls and all import controls to open up the economy;*

- *reflation of the economy in the expectation that, with a positive marginal propensity to import, the volume of imports must rise;*

- *currency appreciation (in a floating regime) or upward revaluation (in a managed regime). In this connection readers should reverse the analysis of depreciation/devaluation and envisage a reverse J curve, in which the balance of payments improves before it worsens.*

Balance of payments: the record

During the quarter-century after 1945 sterling was managed in the Bretton Woods system of exchange rates. As import controls were frowned upon as unneighbourly under GATT and as devaluation was available only in a situation of chronic deficit (e.g. 1967), the only way to correct a deficit was by deflation. This was the period of 'stop–go', when the balance of payments acted as a severe constraint upon growth so that, as other countries' economies grew, Britain was forced to lag behind. Whenever it tried to speed

---

Fig. 8.6 *Major sterling crises 1931–92*

Date	Government	Situation	Action
1931	Labour	Deficit during slump	Deflation, Gold Standard abandoned
1947	Labour	Dollar shortage	Import controls
1949	Labour	Deficit during recession	Devaluation
1951	Labour/ Conservative	Overheating during Korean War	Import controls
1955	Conservative	Overheating during boom	Credit squeeze
1956	Conservative	Suez crisis	IMF loan
1961	Conservative	Deficit during slowdown of the economy	Pay pause
1964	Labour	Deficit during boom	Surcharge on imports
1966	Labour	Deficit	Deflation
1967	Labour	Deficit during recession	Devaluation
1972	Conservative	Surplus	Sterling floated
1992	Conservative	Deficit during recession	ERM membership suspended; sterling floated down

up the growth rate the balance of payments deteriorated and often led to a sterling crisis (*see* Fig. 8.6, which lists those between 1931 and 1992).

From 1971/2 sterling floated against all other currencies. As floating provides an automatic mechanism to correct the balance of payments the constraint on growth was removed. The balance of payments problem eased in the 1980s for another reason: North Sea oil came on stream, both to reduce UK oil imports and to provide export earnings. However, as North Sea oil production was expected to be of short duration there was growing concern about what would happen when the oil ran out. North Sea oil disguised the continuing deterioration in the country's trade position. It was for that reason that it became accepted that the non-oil trade and economic position should be highlighted in statistics by separating them out from the rest of the economy. Not only did North Sea oil disguise the deterioration in the economy but it contributed to it – by raising the exchange rate North Sea oil reduced the competitiveness of British manufacturers in both home and overseas markets. The surplus on the oil account was paralleled by a growing deficit on the non-oil account.

Over the 1980s the visible balance deteriorated and, as Table 8.1 shows, the usual surplus on invisibles was progressively less able to cancel out the deficit.

As well as a failure of exports there was also a growing problem of import penetration. Imports of raw materials and machinery are usually taken as a sign of growth and prosperity in domestic industry. Unfortunately, a growing proportion of UK imports took the form not only of manufactures but also of consumer goods, suggesting deep malaise within British industry. In 1955, 23 per cent of UK imports took the form of semi- or finished manufactures. By 1975 this was up to 54 per cent and by the end of the 1980s nearly 80 per cent of UK imports took the form of manufactured goods. By the early 1980s the UK had become a net importer of manufactured goods for the first time since the Industrial Revolution (*see* Table 8.2).

Import penetration can be accounted for by a decline in the UK's relative price competitiveness. Despite the alleged supply-side miracle of the mid-1980s, UK prices remained higher as a result of differential rates of inflation and of productivity growth. A second possible explanation was a decline

Table 8.1 *UK balance of payments 1984–92*

Year	Visible balance (£bn)	Balance on invisibles (£bn)	Current balance (£bn)
1984	−1.0	3.5	2.5
1985	−4.0	5.0	1.0
1986	−2.0	5.0	3.0
1987	−8.5	7.5	−1.0
1988	−20.8	6.2	−14.6
1989	−24.0	4.0	−20.0
1990	−19.0	4.5	−14.5
1991	−10.5	4.0	−6.5
1992	−14.0	2.0	−12.0

Table 8.2 *Ratio of exports to imports of manufactured goods*

	1965	1975	1985	1991
United States	1.55	1.38	0.60	0.83
Britain	1.78	1.29	0.90	0.94
France	1.40	1.31	1.12	0.97
Italy	1.92	1.72	1.47	1.18
Western Germany	1.71	1.89	1.69	1.22
Japan	4.22	4.58	4.25	2.58
OECD average	1.29	1.36	1.12	1.06

Source: OECD

in UK non-price competitiveness. Sales of British goods suffered as a result of poorer quality, poorer reliability in terms of delivery dates and poorer after-sales service. In addition, the British marketing effort is also criticised as being inadequate.

Government economic policy can also be blamed for the problems of the visible balance. The alternation of expansion and contraction during the Keynesian era discouraged investment. As a result British industry was less able to supply markets during expansionary periods. When the discretionary approach was abandoned, especially by strict monetarism in the early 1980s, the structure of British industry was so undermined that it could not respond during the boom of the mid-1980s and imports continued to be sucked in. Even though exports grew by up to 9.5 per cent per year in the late 1980s they were still outpaced by a 13.7 per cent a year rise in imports. One issue of concern during the early 1990s recession is the continuing high volume of imports and therefore trade deficit. Normally the balance of payments improves during a recession since unemployment acts as an import control. As the economy recovers from recession it is likely that the balance of payments will deteriorate further.

As Table 8.3 reveals, the post-Second World War era has seen an increase in the EC's relative share of trade with Britain. In part this is because of Britain's membership, which has inevitably had a trade-diverting effect. However, this growth in the significance of Western Europe in Britain's trade predates EC membership and is in part a reflection of changes in the world and Britain's position within it.

In most years there is a net capital outflow from the UK. This shows up as a negative figure for net transactions in assets and liabilities. The outward migration of investment funds was facilitated by the removal of all exchange controls in 1979. Investment overseas is often criticised as being harmful to UK manufacturing but by generating receipts of interest, profit and dividend in future years can be seen as beneficial in the long run. By 1988 UK residents had external net assets of $162 billion and although this was less than German or Japanese holdings it was larger as a percentage of both GNP and exports, as Table 8.4 shows. By contrast, the USA had a large overseas deficit.

Table 8.3 *UK trade in goods (proportion of total)*

Imports from:	1955	1965	1975	1985	1990
EC	12.6	23.6	36.5	48.9	52.6
Rest of Western Europe	13.1	12.2	14.9	14.2	12.5
North America	19.5	19.6	13.3	13.8	13.4
Other developed countries	16.9	16.3	10.8	9.7	8.1
Oil exporters	9.2	9.8	13.5	3.3	2.4
Other developing countries	28.7	18.4	11.0	10.0	11.0
Total developed countries	59.4	67.4	72.4	84.4	86.6
Exports to:	*1955*	*1965*	*1975*	*1985*	*1990*
EC	15.0	26.3	32.3	48.8	53.4
Rest of Western Europe	13.9	15.5	17.0	9.5	8.8
North America	12.0	14.8	11.8	17.0	14.5
Other developed countries	22.2	17.7	12.7	7.0	6.1
Oil exporters	5.1	5.6	11.4	7.6	5.4
Other developing countries	31.8	20.1	14.8	10.1	11.8
Total developed countries	61.4	71.4	70.5	80.1	82.8

Source: *Annual Abstract of Statistics*, CSO

Table 8.4 *External net assets 1988*

	Total ($bn)	As % of GNP	As % of exports
UK	162	19	83
Japan	291	10	76
Germany	199	17	52
USA	−544	−11	−126

Balance of payments: key concepts

Appreciation A rise in the exchange rate through market forces

Balance of payments A statement of a country's trade and financial transactions with the rest of the world over a period of time

Balance of trade (**visible balance**) This concerns trade in goods only. Numerically it is the value of exports minus the value of imports

Capital account The section of the balance of payments account which records movements of funds linked with (i) purchase or sale of assets and (ii) borrowing or lending

Current account A statement of a country's trade in goods and services with the rest of the world over a period of time

Deflationary policy Reduction in the level of aggregate demand to reduce inflation and/or balance of payments deficit

Depreciation Fall in the exchange rate through market forces

Devaluation   A deliberate reduction in the exchange rate in order to effect a beneficial change in the balance of payments

Exchange control   A means of limiting access to foreign currency in order to control trade

Exchange rate   The rate at which one currency exchanges for another

Fixed exchange rate   An exchange rate regime in which the value of one currency is fixed in relation to another, e.g. 19th-century Gold Standard

Floating exchange rate   A system of determining exchange rates by the interplay of market forces. It is usual to distinguish between clean floating (no intervention) and dirty floating (some intervention to effect a beneficial change in the exchange rate)

J curve effect   The tendency for a country's balance of payment deficit to deteriorate after devaluation before moving into surplus

Managed exchange rate   An exchange rate regime in which the central bank intervenes in the foreign exchange markets to maintain a currency within a specified band, e.g. the Bretton Woods system, ERM

Marginal propensity to import   The proportion of additional income spent on imports

Marshall–Lerner Condition   The condition necessary if devaluation is to be successful in reducing a balance of payments deficit. Successful devaluation requires that the sum of the price elasticities of demand for imports and exports exceeds one

Protectionism   A policy of protecting domestic producers by means of tariffs, quotas and other import controls

Revaluation   A deliberate increase in the exchange rate

CHAPTER 9

Sectors of the Economy

In this final chapter on the UK economy we look at the significance and performance of selected sectors of the economy. In particular we will look at these sectors' contribution to national output and employment and how they fare over the last decade.

OBJECTIVES
1 To analyse the significance of selected sectors of the economy.
2 To develop an understanding of issues relevant to particular sectors.
3 To identify and account for trends in individual sectors.
4 To consider the extent and causes of de-industrialisation in the UK economy.

Economic development and sectors

Developing (or underdeveloped) countries are characterised by a high proportion of the population engaged in primary activities, especially hunting, agriculture, forestry and fishing. The industrial and manufacturing (secondary) sector tends to be small in comparison and what industrial activities there are tend be be small scale, workshop-based and often carried out in a domestic setting. One major distinction between underdeveloped and developed economies is that, in the former, work in the form of production to gain a living is usually in a domestic and family setting. As the economy matures beyond a certain size work starts to separate from domestic and family life.

As the economy develops the relative importance of the primary and secondary sectors changes, and shifts towards the latter. This process occurred in Britain during the Industrial Revolution of the early 19th century, and the 1851 census is significant in that, for the first time, Britain's urban and industrial population is seen to exceed the rural and agricultural population. It should be appreciated that these changes are relative – the relative decline of agriculture does not mean that the sector declined in absolute terms. In fact it remained prosperous and buoyant until the last quarter of the 19th century, when cheap imports from the New World led to a major contraction and massive migration off the land. In the 20th century the absolute decline in agriculture was reversed by government (and later EC) support for the sector, but the relative decline in terms both of share of GDP and of employment has

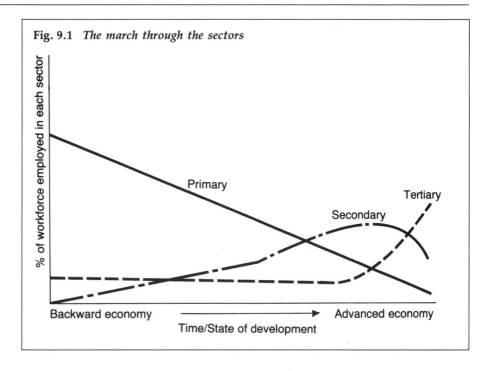

Fig. 9.1 *The march through the sectors*

continued. Consequently, although output might have risen in quantity and value it has been at a slower rate than that in the rest of the economy. The explanation for the shift from agriculture to industry lies in differences in income elasticities of demand. That for foodstuffs is low, with the result that any rise in real incomes beyond a certain level leads to only a small increase in demand for food but (its income elasticity being high) a large increase in demand for the products of manufacturing industry.

This shift in the importance of the sectors of the economy is depicted in Fig. 9.1. It should be noted that a feature of a mature, or advanced, economy is the growing importance of the tertiary (or service) sector. However, we should not assume that the tertiary sector is absent from a pre-industrial society. In 19th-century Britain, for instance, domestic servants formed the second largest occupational group. The large country houses employed hosts of them but the 20th-century change to a more egalitarian society, and a severe decline in the real income and wealth of the landed aristocracy, have led to the contraction of domestic service. But this decline has been accompanied by a rise in other tertiary pursuits. Again, this can be explained in terms of income elasticity of demand: as we enjoy higher living standards an increasing proportion of our income goes on entertainment, travel, tourism, health care, education and financial services such as savings schemes and insurance. This growth in demand explains why in a mature and affluent (by world standards) economy a growing proportion of UK output and employment is service in nature (*see* Table 9.1). The process appears universal although, as we will see later, there is considerable debate about whether (and if so, why) it has gone too far in the UK.

Table 9.1 *GDP shares at constant 1985 prices 1971–91*

	1971	1980	1985	1991
Agriculture, forestry and fishing	1.4	1.5	1.4	1.8
Energy and water supply	5.6	9.2	7.6	5.7
Manufacturing	28.5	24.1	22.8	21.0
Construction	7.2	5.5	6.0	6.8
Services				
distribution	13.4	12.2	13.3	14.7
transport and communication	6.3	6.6	7.3	7.0
banking and finance	9.5	12.2	18.6	17.7
other services	28.1	28.6	22.9	25.3

Source: CSO, National Accounts

Agriculture

Agriculture contributes a small, and still declining, share of the UK's GDP, as the following figures show:

- *1979–81   2.1 per cent*
- *1986   1.8 per cent*
- *1987   1.7 per cent*
- *1988   1.4 per cent*
- *1989   1.5 per cent*
- *1990   1.4 per cent.*

However, the declining share of GDP should not obscure the fact that, in real terms, the output of agriculture as a whole rose during the late 1980s. At constant 1985 prices its contribution to GDP rose from £4.1 billion to £5.5 billion.

This rise in output was achieved with a declining number of people engaged in the sector: from 649,000 in 1980 to 561,000 in 1990, the latter figure representing 2.1 per cent of the workforce in employment. Over the same period, the area under agriculture also declined – but only from 18.9 to 18.5 million hectares. The differential decline can be explained in terms of:

- *a change in the nature of farming, towards less labour-intensive methods;*
- *greater use of machinery and factory farming methods;*

■ *the impact of EC common agricultural policy (CAP) reforms* (see *chapter 16);*

■ *the need to reduce costs in a difficult environment.*

The price of farm inputs rose substantially in the 1980s – none more so than labour: the index of labour costs for agriculture rose from 66 in 1980 to 140 in 1990 (1985 = 100). The cost of animal foodstuffs, fertilisers, energy and capital equipment also rose. At the same time, the price of agriculture was undermined. The index of the ratio of product to input prices fell from 110 in 1980 to 97.3 in 1990. Consequently, British farmers depend upon farm support from both the government and the EC. However, the CAP has notoriously led to overproduction and, as we will see in chapter 16, the UK government has consistently sought reform of the CAP in the form of:

■ *setting a limit on CAP market support;*

■ *lower support prices. This is in line with the free-market philosophy of the UK government but has an adverse effect on the farming community.*

The trend towards larger farm units has been a feature of British agriculture. By the late 1980s the largest holdings constituted 12 per cent of the total but accounted for 56 per cent of agricultural activity. Conversely, the small farm group comprised 44 per cent of farmers but provided only 2.6 per cent of activity. The larger units tend to be arable farms, especially in eastern England. The greater use of tractors, combine harvesters and other equipment on arable farms has been at the expense of farm employment. The acreage under arable crops fell during the 1980s from 3.9 to 3.7 million hectares but wheat, the main cereal, increased at the expense of other crops. The acreage given over to vegetables and horticulture also fell, but the increased use of fertilisers has enabled the yield per acre to rise. There is a similar differential impact on livestock numbers, with dairy cows subject to the greatest decline. The CAP milk quota system has imposed a limit on dairy production and it has proved a particularly difficult problem for British farmers.

Britain has been a net importer of food since the mid-19th century. The UK imports £22 billion of 'food, feed and beverages' annually, but also exports around £12 billion. The ratio of imports to exports is consistently around two to one, although it should be appreciated that the 'food, feed and beverages' categories are broader than the primary products of the agricultural sector. The UK government and the food industry have sought to increase exports via the promotional 'food from Britain' campaign. One result of farm support over many decades has been a steady rise in the UK's self-sufficiency in food. The UK produces 56 per cent of its 'food and feed' and 74 per cent of the 'indigenous type food and feed'. The latter category refers to foods that the UK is capable of producing. If greater self-sufficiency is the result of increased efficiency and competitiveness it is to be welcomed; if it was the result of distortions in the market it would be at the expense of the food consumer.

The industrial sector

Energy Historically, Britain has been rich in energy resources in the form of both land-based coal and oil and gas from the UK continental shelf. Around 70 per cent of UK energy is derived from oil and coal although the relative importance of the two changed over the 1980s. A further quarter of the UK's energy needs comes from gas.

The significance of the continental shelf is demonstrated by the following 1991 statistics. Oil and gas production from it accounted for 1.5 per cent of GNP. Revenues from the sale of gas totalled £2.8 billion, and from oil £8 billion. The offshore industries employed 33,000 and the Exchequer received taxes and royalties of £1 billion from North Sea production. The industries were responsible for 21 per cent of UK industrial investment and 5 per cent of gross domestic fixed capital formation. These figures are very impressive but many would argue that North Sea developments have been at the expense of the manufacturing sector.

Oil was first brought ashore in 1975 and in the next decade output rose steadily, although the *Piper Alpha* fire in 1988 had a serious impact on both output and the balance of trade in oil. From 89 million tonnes in 1981 it rose to 126 million tonnes in 1986 but in the 1990s fell back again to its early 1980s level of around 88 million tonnes per year. Daily output is around a quarter of a million tonnes, making the UK the world's ninth largest oil producer. Known reserves are 1.2 billion tonnes, which means that at current levels of output they will last for 13 years. Reserves could be as high as 7 billion tonnes, however, and the oil could last until well into the 21st century. Certainly the government expects Britain to remain self-sufficient in oil until the mid-1990s and then to be a significant producer until well into the next century. Oil exploration and production are in the hands of 250 or so private enterprise firms licensed by the UK government, to which royalties as well as taxes are paid. There is also a small amount of onshore production but it remains very small compared with that from the continental shelf.

In the 1980s the UK was a net exporter of both crude petroleum and natural gas liquids and of refined petroleum products. Certain grades of product had to be imported because of the nature of the reserves, but on balance the UK exported more than it imported. In the middle years of the decade exports of crude products were double the imports. However, the depletion of reserves (especially in the larger reservoirs) coupled with the loss of *Piper Alpha* led to the gap between exports and imports closing.

One aspect of North Sea oil of particular interest to economics students concerns its impact on the economy. For this we need to consider:

- *the multiplier effect of investment in the industry;*

- *the employment effects in the oil and in related industries;*

- *the direct balance of payments effects in terms of trade in oil products;*

- *the indirect balance of payments effects in terms of exchange rate and the impact of exports of other products;*

- *the impact on government finances.*

In most cases the impact is beneficial but the exchange rate effect, especially in the early 1980s, is usually seen as harmful to the manufacturing sector.

Historically, Britain obtained gas by burning coal to produce what was known as town gas. Since 1967 gas has come from the continental shelf, thus reducing the demand for coal but also contributing to a cleaner Britain. Natural gas accounts for over 25 per cent of total primary fuel consumption and this proportion is set to rise as a result of the electricity generators' 'dash for gas' policy. At expected depletion rates, reserves will last well into the mid-21st century.

One issue of significance to economists concerns the structure of the industry. Unlike electricity, gas was privatised as a single and, therefore, near-monopolistic concern. It is debatable whether British Gas plc's 1991 profit of £1.7 billion on a sales turnover of £10.5 billion was due to efficiency or its monopoly position. The privatisation measure did allow for rival companies to supply a share of the industrial and commercial market through the British Gas pipe network. Concern over the lack of competition led to a review by the Office of Fair Trading and British Gas undertaking to reduce its share of the industrial and commercial market from 95 to 40 per cent. This measure is designed to help the large industrial user, however, not the domestic consumer.

The 20th century has seen a significant if intermittent decline in the coal industry since its 1913 peak when output was 292 million tonnes (of which 74 million tonnes were exported) and employment exceeded one million. By 1991 output was down to 91 million tonnes, of which 71 million came from deep mines, 17 million from open-cast mines, and 3.4 million from licensed mines. The nationalised British Coal had shed nearly 700,000 miners and had closed 800 pits between 1955 and 1992, at which point there were 50 operational pits and 44,000 miners. The industry relied heavily on contracts from the electricity generators – over 75 per cent of coal output went to them. This left the industry vulnerable to any change in the policy of the generators, which as private sector firms have no obligation to burn coal. Their 'dash for gas' policy led to a loss of contracts for the coal industry with an inevitable loss of jobs and further pit closures. A plan to close a further 31 pits led to a major controversy in 1992. The government argued that there was insufficient demand to justify existing capacity and that EC rules on state aid for industry (*see* chapter 13) did not allow state subsidies, which in any case conflicted with its free-market philosophy. Critics argue that the slimming down of the industry coupled with the strategy of increasing productivity by concentrating on the largest and most efficient pits is all part of preparations for the privatisation of the coal industry. The exact extent of coal closure is uncertain but it is clear that the 1990s will see the further diminution of this once great industry.

When the electricity industry was privatised generation was placed in the hands of two companies (National Power and PowerGen), distribution under the National Grid Company and supply to customers under 12 regional electricity companies for England and Wales. Separate arrangements were made for Scotland. Nuclear Electric, which remained under state ownership, is responsible for 15 per cent of output.

Manufacturing   In 1991 manufacturing accounted for 21 per cent of both GDP and employment, which, as we will see in chapter 11, is low by the standards of most of Britain's partners. Despite its relatively small size, the sector has always been seen as crucial to the success of the British economy because of its contribution to visible trade (80 per cent of exports), to productivity growth and overall economic growth. Because of the qualitative importance attached to manufacturing there has been concern about the alleged de-industrialisation of the UK economy. Table 9.2 shows the relative importance of different parts of the sector.

The manufacturing sector was especially hard hit by the recession of the early Thatcher years. This led to a considerable shake-out, which left the sector 'leaner and fitter' to take on new competition. The aim was to reverse the long-term decline in relative productivity.

The productivity gains of the 1980s were impressive and for the first time in decades UK productivity rose faster than many of its rivals (*see* Table 9.3). This is not to say that productivity was high in absolute terms, however. The figures in Table 9.3 show an impressive growth in output per unit of labour input but it should be appreciated that the rise in productivity took the form of a fall in output lower than the fall in employment in the manufacturing sector: from 5.8 million people in 1982 to 4.7 million in 1991. A rise in productivity can be achieved either by producing the same output from a smaller number of workers or by producing more with existing workers (or some combination of the two). Although the former kind of rise is beneficial in terms of aiding the competitiveness of British industry, the latter is more desirable.

The rise in productivity was achieved by a high level of investment during the so-called 'miracle years' of the 1980s (*see* Table 9.4). Investment is important for two reasons: as the most volatile element in aggregate demand

Table 9.2 *The relative importance of different parts of the manufacturing sector*

	Net output (£ billion)	Employment (000)
Metals and minerals	8.9	326
Chemicals	10.8	303
Other metal goods	6.1	283
Mechanical engineering	12.6	660
Electrical and electronic	13.7	587
Motor vehicles	6.0	216
Aerospace and other transport	6.7	211
Food, drink and tobacco	13.6	496
Textiles	2.9	175
Clothing and footwear	3.3	261
Paper and printing	11.6	465
Other manufacturing	9.5	539
TOTAL MANUFACTURING	105.8	4,522

Table 9.3 *Labour productivity growth in manufacturing*

	Average annual percentage growth		
	1950–73	1973–9	1979–89
UK	3.4	1.1	4.8
USA	2.8	1.3	3.4
Japan	9.5	5.1	5.4
France	5.7	4.6	3.2
Italy	5.4	5.8	4.0

Source: *Treasury Bulletin,* Summer 1992

Table 9.4 *Investment in manufacturing 1981–91*

	Gross investment in plant and machinery		Gross investment in buildings	
	£ billion	% change on previous year	£ billion	% change on previous year
1981	6.1	−20.4	0.8	−27
1982	6.0	−2.4	0.7	−8
1983	6.0	0.4	0.6	−14.5
1984	7.1	17.9	1.0	45.9
1985	8.3	15.5	1.2	22.2
1986	8.3	1.5	1.1	−6.8
1987	8.3	0.7	1.2	6.5
1988	9.2	12.1	1.3	16.9
1989	10.1	9.6	1.6	16.1
1990	9.8	−3.1	1.4	−12.4
1991	8.8	−10.5	1.5	−10.5

Source: *Economic Trends,* 1992

it both reflects and induces changes in the overall level of activity; and it is a major factor in the long-term growth and prosperity of any industry. However, the statistics also show a decline in investment levels during the recession of the early 1990s. This decline was both a cause and effect of recession.

The rise in industrial and manufacturing output during the 1980s took place only after they declined in the recession of 1980–4. Table 9.5 shows the index of production using 1985 as the base year. In any time series data the choice of period and (especially) base year can have a significant impact upon perception of the data. For instance, if 1981 rather than 1985 were chosen as the base, the rise in production in the later 1980s would appear more dramatic. As the data shows, by 1985 output had returned to its long-term trend after a temporary but nonetheless severe reduction in output.

The data in Table 9.5 informs us that industrial output (which includes non-manufacturing activities such as energy production and mining) rose

Table 9.5 *Production indices 1980–92*

	Industrial output	*Manufacturing output*
1980	92.6	96.7
1981	89.6	90.9
1982	91.4	91.1
1983	94.7	93.7
1984	94.8	97.6
1985	100.0	100.0
1986	102.4	100.9
1987	105.7	106.6
1988	109.6	114.2
1989	109.9	119.0
1990	109.1	118.3
1991	106.1	112.2
1992 (provisional)	105.0	111.0

Source: OECD; *Economic Trends*; *Britain: A Handbook*, HMSO

9.9 per cent between 1985 and 1989; if we confine the data to manufacturing alone, the rise was a more impressive 19 per cent. However, there was a considerable fall-back in output in the recession that occurred from 1989/90 onwards. Manufacturing output fell by 0.5 per cent in 1990, 5.2 per cent in 1991 and 0.8 per cent in 1992 as the government searched for the long-promised 'green shoots' of recovery.

As Tables 9.6 and 9.7 show, the performance of different parts of the sector varied.

Table 9.6 *Performance of selected industries*

	Index of output (1985 = 100)		*Export/Import Ratio (%)*
	1989	*1990*	
Extraction of metal ores	70	67	2.5
Metal manufacture	125	122	91
Extraction of minerals	108	100	92
Non-metallic minerals	121	115	94
Chemicals	119	118	122
Man-made fibres	114	118	132
Metal goods	113	107	79
Mechanical engineering	110	111	115
Electrical and electronic	118	118	88
Motor vehicles	125	121	62
Other transport	129	129	123
Food, drink, tobacco	105	106	61
Textiles	97	92	54

Source:OECD; *Economic Trends*; *Britain: A Handbook*, HMSO

Table 9.7 *Industrial sector: percentage change in output 1992 compared with 1991*

All manufacturing	−0.8
Mechanical products	−5.3
Metals	−4.7
Minerals	−4.4
Transport equipment	−3.5
Metal goods	−2.6
Electrical goods	−1.1
Textiles	−0.5
Drink and tobacco	+0.1
Clothing and footwear	+0.4
Vehicles and parts	+0.5
Chemicals	+1.5
Paper and printing	+1.6
Food	+1.7
Artificial fibres	+1.9

Source: *Financial Times*, February 1993

We saw in chapter 8 that as a result of the loss of competitiveness in world and domestic markets Britain became a net importer of manufactured goods during the early 1980s. In 1991 Britain had a £6 billion deficit on manufactures although some industries performed better than others, as Table 9.8 shows.

The overall ratio of exports of manufactures to imports was 93 per cent in 1991. If we look at the EC ratio (*see* Table 9.9), we find that in the early 1980s it fell to 68 per cent although it has since risen to a more respectable 98 per cent. This suggests that manufacturing's performance in trade with the EC

Table 9.8 *Industrial imports and exports 1991*

	Exports (£ billion)	Imports (£ billion)
Chemicals	13.7	10.9
Textiles	2.3	3.7
Iron and steel	3.0	2.6
Non-ferrous metals	1.9	2.5
Metals	2.1	2.5
Other semi-manufactures	6.0	9.0
Machinery	29.5	29.4
Vehicles	8.5	10.2
Clothing and footwear	2.2	5.2
Scientific instruments	4.2	4.0
Other manufactures	12.0	11.5

Table 9.9 *UK trade in manufactures with the EC*
(£ billion) 1970–91

	Exports	Imports	Balance	Export/Import Ratio %
1970	2.2	1.5	+0.6	142
1971	2.3	1.9	+0.4	123
1972	2.5	2.5	+0.1	102
1973	3.3	3.7	−0.4	90
1974	4.7	5.2	−0.5	91
1975	5.1	5.7	−0.6	90
1976	7.3	7.8	−0.5	94
1977	9.3	9.8	−0.5	95
1978	10.3	12.0	−1.8	85
1979	12.7	15.3	−2.6	83
1980	14.2	15.3	−1.1	93
1981	13.3	16.0	−2.7	83
1982	14.6	19.2	−4.5	76
1983	16.0	23.5	−7.6	68
1984	18.9	27.4	−8.5	69
1985	21.8	31.0	−9.2	70
1986	24.0	34.5	−10.6	69
1987	28.0	38.9	−10.9	72
1988	31.8	44.6	−12.8	71
1989	37.5	51.6	−14.1	73
1990	43.2	52.6	−9.4	82
1991	47.0	47.3	−0.7	98

Source: *Developments in the EC*, 1992, HMSO

was better than with the world as a whole. However, the importance of manufacturing is such that anything less than 100 per cent should be seen as a cause for concern.

De-industrialisation

De-industrialisation involves a structural change in the economy, away from manufacturing and towards the tertiary or service sector. In many respects it is a natural process associated with the continuing development of a mature economy. In what we can call the 'march through the sectors' model of development we see a progressive shift of resources out of agriculture into manufacturing (the industrial revolution) and later out of manufacturing and into the service or tertiary sector (*see* Fig. 9.1). This process is explained in terms of income elasticity of demand. As living standards rise, so the demand for services grows more rapidly than that for primary or manufactured goods.

However, the decline in the UK manufacturing sector is not just relative but is also absolute. The UK has experienced an absolute decline in manufacturing employment, symbolised not just by the decline in the 19th-century staple industries (coal, steel, cotton, shipbuilding), but also some major 20th-century ones (cars, electrical goods, aircraft manufacture). Job losses and factory closures in both the early 1980s and early 1990s suggest that the industrial base of the UK is being undermined – that one by one Britain's industries are being destroyed.

The first point to consider is whether or not de-industrialisation really matters. A number of economies (for example Switzerland, Kuwait, New Zealand, some offshore islands) enjoy high per capita incomes despite having a small manufacturing sector. Living standards do not depend solely upon the industrial sector and, in theory, an economy could prosper by exporting services in return for importing primary and secondary goods. However, the UK is too large to rely on services and it lacks the characteristics necessary for prosperity based on tourism.

De-industrialisation does matter because job losses from manufacturing lead to unemployment. In the past those made redundant from manufacturing were absorbed by the tertiary sector. This is no longer the case because the sector has not grown fast enough and labour-saving developments in the sector have reduced its need for an ever-growing labour force. The manufacturing sector, traditionally at the heart of the UK economy, is crucial for its growth-inducing and export-creating qualities. Without a strong manufacturing sector it is difficult for Britain to experience growth and to pay for its much needed imports.

History also provides an interesting insight into the dangers of de-industrialisation. Nationalist historians in India attribute much of the poverty of the sub-continent to the de-industrialisation that started in the mid-18th century. They argue that in pre-British India there was a strong industrial base (admittedly dependent upon handicraft rather than factory production). Contact with Britain destroyed much of Indian industry, however. British rule opened up India to the low-cost textile producers of Lancashire, and Indian cotton was unable to compete. This historical analogy is not intended to imply that Britain will suffer the same fate as India but it does illustrate the problems of exposing high-cost producers to the 'blast of competition'.

De-industrialisation clearly does matter; we must now consider why it has occurred and what can be done to reverse it. The problem can be attributed to:

- *import penetration;*

- *low investment;*

- *low productivity;*

- *uncompetitiveness;*

- *labour relations problems;*

- *inadequate development of sunrise industries;*

- *misallocation of resources in 'propping up' declining and doomed industries;*

- *endemic inflation leading to balance of payments problems and deflation (i.e. the stop–go cycle);*

- *misplaced government intervention;*

- *restrictive practices by both firms and labour;*

- *the social structure of the UK;*

- *the education system.*

Although these points are commonly made, they do not reach the heart of the problem. Throughout the years three different explanations have been espoused:

- *the curse of North Sea oil;*

- *the balance of payments constraints; and*

- *the Bacon and Eltis thesis.*

At first it might seem strange to refer to the 'curse' of North Sea oil. When it first came on stream it was seen as a windfall gain which would create prosperity for the British people (ignoring the fact that Scots saw it as Scottish oil). Unfortunately, Britain's oil experience was similar to the Dutch experience of North Sea gas a decade before. Britain suffered 'Dutch disease' as the benefits of oil were squandered. What happened was that the oil surplus of the early 1980s led to an artificially high pound, which undermined the competitiveness of British industry, and an increased ability to import manufactured goods.

The oil surplus was mirrored by a deficit on Britain's trade in manufactured goods: for the first time in 200 years Britain became a net importer. Unfortunately, Britain's ability to live off oil was strictly limited and pessimists wondered what industrial base would be left when the oil ran out.

In the early 1980s the New Cambridge School argued that strong economies enjoy dynamic economies of scale whereas weaker ones suffer a vicious circle of declining market share, declining profits, low investment and low competitiveness. A relentless cumulative process works in favour of the strong and against the weak. Britain's problem was that it could not enjoy growth without suffering import penetration. Consequently, the balance of payments acted as a constraint upon growth. The solution, as put forward in Labour's Alternative Economic Strategy of 1983, was a combination of Keynesian reflation and protectionism (to prevent leakage abroad). The New Cambridge School argued that as previous reflation tended to boost foreign economies (via exports to Britain) it was essential to keep the 'spending in'. When challenged about the harm protection would do to exports, they presented the 'paradox of import controls'. Import controls plus reflation will boost the economy to such an extent that the country would continue to import – but more materials for industry and fewer consumer goods to undermine British manufacturing. These ideas were not put into practice, but readers should appreciate that at this time (1983) there was a question mark over Britain's continued membership of the EC.

Bacon and Eltis attributed the problem to the growth of the non-market (mainly public) sector. The result of the unrestrained growth of these non-market activities is 'resource and financial crowding out'. When resources are scarce, the market sector may be unable to expand for lack of sufficient real resources. Similarly, the growth of government sector activities places a tax burden on the private sector – which has less money to spend. Alternatively, government borrowing from the non-bank sector pushes up interest rates, producing a crowding out of private sector investment.

The construction industry

The construction industry is one of the largest in the UK economy. It employs 1.5 million people, mainly in small firms (98 per cent of firms in this sector have fewer than 25 employees). In 1991 it had a turnover of £33 billion, or 7 per cent of national output.

The construction of commercial premises represents a form of investment which inevitably fluctuates with the state of the economy and perceptions of future trends. Not surprisingly, this sector has experienced a downturn during the recession of the 1990s. The housing sector is normally very buoyant given the high demand for houses in an era of rising real incomes. However, the housing market experienced a severe slump from 1989 onwards, attributed to high interest rates (during the period when sterling was in the ERM), rising unemployment coupled with the fear of unemployment, and the effect of a high level of personal debt. All these factors made people reluctant to buy new houses and therefore adversely affected the construction industry.

Public sector housebuilding declined to a trickle in the 1980s as a result of the government's right to buy scheme, restrictions on the use of council house receipts to build new properties, and general reductions in the level of local authority spending. The downturn in private housebuilding and the dwindling of public sector housebuilding are illustrated in Table 9.10.

Table 9.10 *Housing starts (000) 1986–92*

	Private	Housing association	Local authority
1986	180	13	20
1987	197	13	20
1988	221	14	16
1989	170	16	15
1990	135	18	8
1991	135	21	4
1992	121	33	3

The service sector

The term 'service sector' covers a multitude of activities, including finance, distribution, retailing, tourism and business services. The unifying feature is that these industries provide services rather than goods. A few basic statistics illustrate the significance of the sector: it contributes 65 per cent of GDP and employs 71 per cent of the workforce. Employment in the sector rose from 13 million in 1982 to over 15.2 million in 1991, although mainly in the form of part-time work. The publicly owned service sector has experienced some contraction as a result of public expenditure cuts and the policy of privatisation, but the privately owned has prospered.

As we saw in chapter 8, the service sector produces a surplus element within the UK balance of payments. In 1991 the surplus on invisibles amounted to £4 billion, resulting almost entirely from trade in financial services, which enjoyed a £10 billion surplus. There was a small surplus on interest, profit and dividends, which at £75.9 billion of earnings and £75.5 billion of payments is the largest item in the balance of payments. Whereas the UK share of world markets in goods has fallen, its share of world trade in services remains high. Britain's earnings from invisible trade are second only to those of the USA, and constitute 10 per cent of world trade in invisibles.

The continuing success of this sector can be attributed to:

- *the historical legacy of the fact that London became the world's financial centre in the 19th century;*

- *innovation in financial services, which has enabled the City of London to maintain its competitiveness;*

- *government supply-side policies, which have led to deregulation in many forms: abolition of exchange controls in 1979; the end of quantitative controls on bank lending; the abolition of hire purchase restrictions in 1982; the Building Societies Act 1986, which removed restrictions on building society activity;*

- *the reputation of the City, aided by a system of self-regulation which, admittedly, some would argue is ineffective but nevertheless maintains the freedom of financial institutions to compete in world markets;*

- *continued growth in the demand for services.*

The completion of the EC single market will benefit the financial service sector in opening up previously restricted markets. For instance, insurance companies are able to operate throughout the EC on the basis of authorisation in their home state.

Despite the continuing success of financial services, the sector was unable to escape the recession of the early 1990s. A combination of slow growth in the volume of business and increased use of capital equipment led to substantial job losses, especially in banking. This was one of the distinctive features of the recession of the 1990s compared with that of a decade before. The 1980s recession involved a massive shake-out from manufacturing and therefore was felt particularly in the main areas of industry. The 1990s recession has had a significant impact on the service sector in the South East.

PART THREE

EUROPEAN ECONOMY

CHAPTER 10

EC Institutions

Before looking in detail at EC policy we should understand the decision-making process within the Community and the nature of the EC. In this chapter we look at the major institutions and identify the so-called democratic deficit in the Community.

OBJECTIVES
1 To outline the role and functions of the main EC institutions.
2 To develop an understanding of the decision-making process within the EC.
3 To develop an understanding of the nature of EC law.
4 To identify the democratic deficit and to understand why it persists.

The EC institutions described in this chapter are the following.

1 The European Commission, which initiates policy, proposes legislation and is the executive arm of the Community.

2 The Council of Ministers, which is the main decision-making body of the Community.

3 The 518-strong Parliament, which has a role (albeit limited) in the legislative process of the Community, in the budgetary process and in control and supervision of the executive arm.

4 The European Court of Justice, which deals with disputes concerning Community law.

5 The Economic and Social Committee, which gives advice.

6 The Court of Auditors, which examines the regularity and soundness of Community financial management.

7 The European Investment Bank.

The European Commission

The Commission has a staff of 15,000, of whom 10,000 are based in Brussels. At the head of the Commission is a 17-strong College of Commissioners drawn from member states (two from each of the 'big five' and one from each of the other seven). Like a national cabinet the College of Commissioners has a head (known as the President of the Commission) and each commissioner has specialist responsibilities. However, decisions are taken on a collegiate or collective basis comparable with collective responsibility in a UK cabinet.

Although most commissioners are recruited from the ranks of senior politicians in member states, as commissioners they are required to act on behalf of the Community and not that of their country of origin. Once appointed they cannot be dismissed by their national government although the latter can refuse to reappoint 'its' commissioner when his or her four-(soon to be five-) year term is up for renewal. Prime Minister Thatcher did not reappoint Lord Cockfield in 1989, allegedly on the grounds that he had 'gone native' in Brussels and was adopting 'too European' a stance. The UK's usual practice is to appoint one commissioner from the ranks of the government party and one from the main opposition party. Hence Thatcher replaced Cockfield with former Conservative minister Leon Brittan and at the same time appointed former Labour cabinet minister Bruce Millan as the other commissioner from the UK. It is important to stress that neither Brittan nor Millan is the 'UK's commissioner' – they are EC commissioners nominated by the UK government. In the distribution of portfolios in 1989, Sir Leon Brittan (as he became) was made a Vice-President of the Commission and given responsibility for competition policy, a matter of great significance in a free market. Millan was made commissioner responsible for regional policy, an issue that Labour politicians, especially from regions away from the centre of Europe, regard as vital.

The Commission (whose treaty responsibilities are shown in Fig. 10.1) has a variety of functions, the most important of which are:

- *the 'guardian of the treaties';*
- *the initiator of policy and legislation;*
- *the executive arm of the Community.*

As guardian of the treaties the Commission acts to ensure that provisions of the treaties are applied. This might involve initiating legal action against member states that fail to comply with EC rules.

Fig. 10.1 *The EC Commission*

Membership:
Seventeen appointed by common accord of the governments of the member states for a term of four years: one from each of Belgium, Denmark, Greece, Ireland, Luxembourg, the Netherlands and Portugal; two from each of France, Germany, Italy, Spain and the UK.

Responsibilities:
(a) Proposing measures for the further development of Community policy.
(b) Monitoring observance and proper application of Community law.
(c) Administering and implementing Community legislation.
(d) Representing the Community in international organisations.

As initiator of policy and legislation the Commission is in a pivotal position in the EC. The legislative process starts with a Commission proposal to the Council of Ministers. Not only can the Council (or the Parliament for that matter) not initiate and draft legislation but amendments to Commission proposals are accepted only if either the Commission agrees or the Council votes unanimously to put forward an amendment. In other words, unless the Council overrules the Commission by a unanimous vote an amendment is not passed.

The role as the initiator of policy and legislation contradicts the frequent (and quite erroneous) claim that the Commission is merely the 'civil service' of the EC. In fact, it (or at least the College of Commissioners) has a highly political role. From the time of its establishment the Commission was expected to represent the interests of the Community (rather than national self-interests) and to become what has been called the 'motor for integration', deepening the role of the EC within member states. This political role has, not surprisingly, led to clashes with national governments. (Commission President Jacques Delors, for example, became something of a *bête noire* with Britain's Euro-sceptics, including Thatcher, and with the UK tabloid press during the late 1980s. Conservative Euro-sceptics spoke out against 'socialism through the back Delors'.)

As the executive arm of the EC the Commission is charged with the tasks of:

- *issuing decisions and regulations implementing treaty provisions or Council acts, and supervising the day-to-day running of Community policies;*

- *applying treaty rules to specific cases;*

- *administering the 'safeguard clauses' in the treaties (these allow treaty requirements to be waived in exceptional circumstances; the Commission has the power to grant such a waiver, known as a derogation);*

- *the administration of Community Funds such as the European Agricultural Guidance and Guarantee Funds, the European Social Fund and the European Regional Development Funds (jointly known as the EC Structural Funds).*

We have seen that at the head of the Commission is the 17-strong College of Commissioners. Each commissioner is assisted by his or her cabinet or personal office. The cabinet, uniquely in the Commission's organisational structure, is drawn mainly from the commissioner's country of origin, and many members are in fact seconded from domestic civil services. Cabinets provide support for commissioners, identifying the main issues for consideration. Cabinet staff from different commissioners meet in inter-cabinet committees known as Chefs de Cabinet.

The remaining Commission staff are organised into Special Units and Directorates-General (DGs). The DGs implement policy and report to the relevant commissioner. The number of staff employed in each DG varies considerably, to reflect policy importance, workload and specialisation within the DGs. In addition to these functional areas, there are units providing various support services, the most important of which is translation and interpretation. With 12 member states speaking nine different languages there is a considerable volume of translation and interpretation work. As and when the EC expands this work will inevitably grow as the number of language permutations increases (e g. not just English into French but Danish into Greek and – perhaps in the future – Spanish into Swedish).

Who's who in the Commission

Like the national cabinet, there is a periodic reshuffling of the EC Commission. The last occurred at the end of 1992, when some countries took the opportunity to nominate new commissioners and the Commission President Jacques Delors took the opportunity to reshuffle the 17 portfolios. Fig. 10.2 shows the commissioners at 1 January 1993. Jacques Delors became Commission President in 1985. (Fig. 10.3 lists the Presidents since inception.) Prior to that date he had been a civil servant and later Finance Minister in the French Socialist government that was elected in 1981. As Finance Minister he was forced to introduce austerity measures in 1983.

Fig. 10.2 *The EC Commission from 1 January 1993*

Commission:	Country of Origin:	Portfolio:
Jacques Delors	France	President
Henning Christophersen	Denmark	Economic, financial and monetary affairs
Manuel Marin	Spain	Development issues, humanitarian aid
Martin Bangemann	Germany	Industrial policy
Sir Leon Brittan	UK	External economic affairs (e.g. GATT, policy towards Eastern Europe)
Abel Matutes	Spain	Energy and transport
Peter Schmidhuber	Germany	Budget
Christiane Scrivener	France	Taxation and consumer affairs
Bruce Millan	UK	Regional policy
Karel Van Miert	Belgium	Competition policy
Hans van den Broek	Netherlands	External political affairs (i.e. enlargement of the Community)
Joao de Deus Pinheiro	Portugal	Culture, relations with the European Parliament and with EC governments
Padraig Flynn	Ireland	Social policy, internal and judicial affairs
Antonio Ruberti	Italy	Training and research
René Steichen	Luxembourg	Agriculture
Glannis Paleokrassas	Greece	Environmental and fisheries
Raniero Vanni d'Archirafi	Italy	Single market, small businesses, financial institutions

Fig. 10.3 *Presidents of the Commission*

1958–67	Walter Hallstein	Germany
1967–70	Jean Rey	Belgium
1970–72	Franco Maria Malfatti	Italy
1972–73	Sicco Mansholt	Netherlands
1973–77	François-Xavier Ortoli	France
1977–81	Roy Jenkins	UK
1981–85	Gaston Thorn	Luxembourg
1985–	Jacques Delors	France

The Economist says that:

> [Delors] has successfully heightened the profile of his office – much diminished by his two immediate predecessors – by moving into the centre of policy making, directly involving himself in many of its activities, and using his considerable personal authority to keep his fellow commissioners in line (more or less). He has pursued the creation of the Single Market and the realisation of economic and political union with characteristic energy and eloquence [*The Economist Dictionary of Political Biography*, p. 78].

In his forcefulness he has made many enemies – not just Conservative Euro-sceptics like Thatcher but also fellow commissioners such as Ray MacSharry, the former Commissioner for Agriculture.

In the December 1992 reshuffle Britain's commissioners remained in Brussels although one was given a new portfolio. Sir Leon Brittan (Britain's senior commissioner) had been a barrister, a Conservative MP and cabinet minister under Thatcher (Home Secretary and later Trade and Industry Secretary). He resigned from the Thatcher government after a leak of a confidential letter during the Westland affair. In 1989 he was appointed one of Britain's commissioners, responsible for competition policy and the single market in financial services. It is generally agreed that he was very successful in this task, formulating new EC merger rules and waging war against state aid to industry. Although this made him unpopular with the French, Spanish and Italians, he did demonstrate his Community credentials (without being accused of 'going native'). In the 1993 Commission Brittan was placed in charge of trade policy with the rest of the world and aid to Eastern Europe. The former responsibility involves GATT negotiations (which proved troublesome during 1992).

The other British commissioner, Bruce Millan, was also reappointed (to the surprise of many people who expected the former Labour leader, Neil Kinnock, to be given the post). Millan is a former Labour Secretary of State for Scotland and on appointment in 1989 was given the task of conducting the EC Regional Policy. The *Financial Times*, commenting on his reappointment, stated that 'he stays in a job he has done with the quiet efficiency of a Scottish accountant'.

Hans van den Broek was appointed Commissioner for External Affairs with effect from 1 January 1993. A former Dutch Foreign Minister, van den Broek played a key role during the 1991 Dutch Presidency that culminated in the Maastricht Treaty. A 'committed European and Atlanticist' (*The Economist Dictionary*, p. 288) he was given the tasks of developing the Common Foreign and Security Policy (CFSP) and leading the negotiations on enlargement. The allocation of work between Brittan and van den Broek represented a separation of the two strands (political and trade) previously under the authority of the same commissioner, the overworked retiring Dutch Commissioner Frans Andriessen.

The commissioner responsible for agriculture is the former Luxembourg Farm Minister René Steichen. Given the controversy over the CAP it is customary to give this portfolio to a commissioner from one of the smaller EC members rather than the more partisan French, Italian or British. The previous holder of this post was Ireland's Ray MacSharry, who worked to reform the CAP especially to satisfy Americans during the 1992 GATT negotiations. This strained relations with Delors and led to unpopularity in France.

The commissioner from Ireland appointed in 1993 is Padraig Flynn, a former Irish Justice Minister. Flynn, who achieved 'notoriety at home for his views against abortion, divorce and on the role of women' (*Financial Times*), was given the Social Affairs portfolio with additional responsibility for immigration and justice. In the Social Affairs post Flynn took over from Ms Vasso Papandreou of Greece, who had become a *bête noire* of the UK government since she was responsible for the Social Charter, to which British Conservatives took such exception.

Papandreou's retirement from the Commission meant that the only woman in the 1993 Commission is Christiane Scrivener from France. She is responsible for tax and customs policy and for consumer affairs.

The Competition Policy Commissioner appointed in 1993 was Karel Van Miert from Belgium. Previously Transport Commissioner, he worked to deregulate the airline industry. However, this Belgian socialist is more interventionist than Sir Leon Brittan, who previously held the post. Writing in the *Guardian*, John Palmer stated that this was 'a move which could signal a swing away from the ultra free market philosophy prevailing in Brussels in recent years'. Remember that Brittan had made himself unpopular with the French and others because of his opposition to state aid to industry.

The commissioner appointed for industrial policy in 1989 (and reappointed from 1993) is the German Liberal, Martin Bangemann. Despite his liberal background Bangemann is more interventionist than Brittan or British Conservatives. 'Bangemann, a German liberal who yet raged against Sir Leon's "ayatollahs" in the competition directorate, adds telecommunication and information technology to his industrial portfolio. This falls far short of his ambition to create an EC version of Japan's Miti but it gives a small fillip to efforts to develop an EC wide industrial strategy' (*Financial Times*).

The Commissioner for Economic Policy is a Dane, Henning Christophersen. This is a key role in the post-Maastricht EC since it involves responsibilities for the EC budget which now includes the administration of the Cohesion Fund.

The remaining commissioners are:

1 Manuel Marin from Spain, who has responsibilities for EC Development Aid both to the Lomé Convention countries and other parts of the developing world.

2 Joao de Deus Pinheiro, a former Portuguese Foreign Minister, has responsibilities for relations with the European Parliament and member states.

3 Antonio Ruberti from Italy has responsibilities for training and research.

4 Glannis Paleokrassas, a former Greek Finance Minister, was appointed as commissioner responsible for environmental policy.

5 The second Spanish commissioner, Abel Matutes, has responsibilities for energy and transport policy.

6 Vanni d'Archirafi is the commissioner responsible for policing the single market.

7 Finally, Peter Schmidhuber, the second German commissioner, is responsible for the EC budget, including the new Cohesion Fund.

The new intake of commissioners in 1993 strengthened the Commission. The *Financial Times* commented that Delors is now 'flanked by four or five political heavyweights, as against two or three in the outgoing Commission'. In any list of heavyweights Brittan, van den Broek and Bangemann (all non-socialists) would be included. John Palmer in the *Guardian* saw the 1993 intake as shifting the Commission to the right in its political composition. However, as was noted with reference to Bangemann the right does not necessarily mean non-interventionist in the Thatcher–Brittan sense.

The Council of the EC

The Council of the EC is made up of government ministers from each of the member states. Hence, alone of the key institutions the Council is an inter-governmental body. However, its membership alters with the subject being discussed. Consequently, if the Council is scheduled to discuss the common agricultural policy it takes the form of a meeting of ministers responsible for agriculture. Similarly, the transport ministers of member states will attend Councils scheduled to discuss transport issues. The complete list of functional councils is:

- *Foreign affairs*
- *Industry*
- *Economic and financial policy (ECOFIN)*
- *Transport*

- *Agriculture and fisheries*
- *Environmental policy*
- *Research*
- *Culture*
- *Education*
- *Health*
- *Employment and social affairs*
- *Internal market*
- *Consumer affairs*
- *Development*
- *Budget*
- *Telecommunications.*

The function of the Council is to take decisions which become Community law. Even though we normally associate legislative powers with a Parliament the legislative body of the EC is the Council. Its legislative capacity is in theory limited to deciding on proposals originating in the Commission. However, over the years ways have been developed to enable the Council to play a more active role in initiating proposals even though formally they must be presented through the Commission. The Council is supported in its task by working groups of officials from member states and the Committee of Permanent Representatives of Member States in Brussels, known as COREPER.

In addition to the specialist Councils there is also the twice-yearly meeting of heads of government, known as the European Council (this has nothing to do with the similarly named Council of Europe). The popular press tends to call these meetings Euro-summits and in many respects this is a good description. The European Council developed as a series of informal summit meetings but has now become an established institution. The heads of government deal with broad issues and the summit is 'an important focus for political activity and integration dynamics' (Archer and Butler, *The European Community: Structure and Process*, p. 31). In this role of taking the EC further down the path of integration we should note that the Single European Act, the Social Charter and the Treaty on European Union emerged respectively from summits held in Milan (1985), Madrid (1989) and Maastricht (1991).

In addition to dealing with matters within the treaty competency of the EC, the European Council will discuss other issues of general significance to the member states, e.g. German reunification, the Gulf crisis of 1991 and the disintegration of Yugoslavia. The London Conference (in relation to the 1992 crisis in the former Yugoslavia) was co-chaired by John Major (the then President of the European Council) and Dr Boutrous Ghali (Secretary-General of the United Nations). The EC involvement in seeking a solution to the crisis was an example of the Council going beyond its treaty competence to deal with an issue that had significant implications for the peace and security of Europe.

As the Council is composed of representatives of sovereign nation states, a unanimous vote in support of a proposal was in the past necessary at all Council meetings. This procedure enabled individual members to block any proposal that threatened national interest. It had the effect of slowing down the process of European integration to the 'pace of the slowest ship in the convoy'. On the basis of strict unanimity a block could be imposed by non-appearance at the Council (the so-called empty chair policy). To facilitate decision-making in the Council, three systems of voting are now used.

1 For all new developments in policy unanimity is required (it is also required when the Council wishes to amend a proposal against the Commission's wishes). Unanimity does *not* require all 12 to vote in favour of a proposal, merely that no one votes against it. Consequently, an abstention is in effect a vote in favour.

2 For procedural matters a simple majority of the 12 states is required for a proposal to be accepted.

3 For decisions required to implement or clarify proposals within existing guidelines a system of qualified majority voting (QMV) was introduced as part of the Single European Act. Under QMV each of the 12 member states has a fixed number of votes in Council meetings, related to the size of its population:

United Kingdom	10
Germany	10
France	10
Italy	10
Spain	8
Belgium	5
Greece	5
Netherlands	5
Portugal	5
Denmark	3
Ireland	3
Luxembourg	2
	76

Under QMV a proposal must receive 54 out of the 76 votes and thus 23 votes constitutes a 'blocking minority'. The arithmetic of QMV is such that if two of the large member states and one other (apart from Luxembourg) vote against, the proposal can be blocked but if only one of the big five (e.g. the UK) votes against the measure it is likely to be carried.

The European Parliament

In its original form the European Parliament (EP) was the Assembly of the European Coal and Steel Community. Following the 1957 Rome Treaties it

Fig. 10.4 *The European Parliament building*

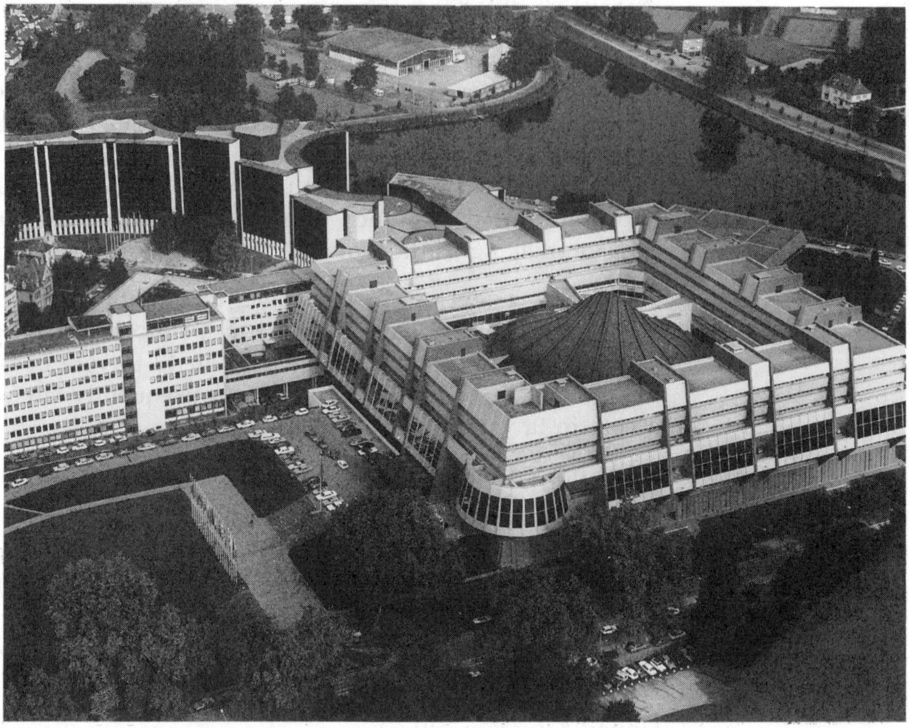

Source: *European Parliament UK office*

became the assembly of the three communities, and in 1962 adopted the title 'European Parliament'.

The relative ineffectiveness of the EP is the result of the reluctance of national parliaments and governments to surrender power to a supra-national parliament. For 20 years after the Treaties of Rome the EP was composed of representatives from the national parliaments. Consequently, the delegation from each country reflected the distribution of seats within the national parliament. Members of the European Parliament (MEPs) were also members of their own national parliament. Consequently, MEPs were merely part-time parliamentarians in Europe and were reluctant to pursue policies which detracted from the power of their own national parliaments.

In 1976 it was agreed by the Council of Ministers that future elections to the EP would be by direct universal suffrage. A directly elected EP would be more independent of national parliaments and national governments and would be more likely to acquire the powers associated with a parliament. It was also possible that the political composition of national MEPs would not reflect the composition of national parliaments. (In the 1989 election, for example, the Labour Party won 46 out of the 78 seats in Great Britain despite, or perhaps because of, the Conservative dominance of the Westminster Parliament.) The divergence in voting patterns for the two parliaments can be explained in terms of the following points.

1 There is a lower turnout in EP elections compared with those for Westminster. In general elections the anticipated turnout is 75 to 80 per cent, whereas that for the EP is significantly lower. The UK has the shameful record of the lowest turnout in each of the three direct EP elections to date. In 1989 only 36 per cent of the UK electorate bothered to vote (compared with an EC average of 58 per cent). A low turnout, especially when combined with a differential rate of abstention, is likely to produce unpredictable results. The low turnout might reflect a belief that the EP is unimportant and ineffective. Unfortunately for the EP (and its supporters), a low turnout also reduces the validity of its claim to represent the people of the whole Community.

2 The differences in the election cycle: EP elections are held every five years from 1979; a UK general election must be held no more than five years after the previous one. However, even governments with healthy majorities tend to seek a new mandate from the electorate after four years (those with small majorities often after a shorter period). Thus, EP elections were held in 1979, 1984 and 1989 with future dates set for 1994, 1999, etc. Westminster elections were held in 1979, 1983, 1987 and 1992, with the next one scheduled for 1997 or before if the Prime Minister of the day so decides. As governments tend to be unpopular in mid-term it is not surprising that the Conservatives 'lost' the British EP election of 1989.

3 There are differences in constituency size, compared with Westminster constituencies. Great Britain (that is, excluding Northern Ireland) is unique in using the single-ballot, majority voting by constituency system (the so-called 'first past the post' system). The other EC members and Northern Ireland use one or other of the so-called proportional representation systems. As is well known, the British voting system produces strange and, many would argue, unfair results. The fact that each of the 78 British Euro-constituencies combines an average of eight Westminster constituencies means that even if voting occurred on the same day it is possible that the result in terms of seats would be different. The unfairness of the electoral system is demonstrated by the fact that the UK Liberals (now Liberal Democrats) have never obtained a seat in the directly elected European Parliament. Table 10.1 gives the votes cast and seats won in the three EP elections.

Table 10.1 *Voting in European elections (Great Britain only)*

	1979	%	seats	1984	%	seats	1989	%	seats
Conservative	6,508,493	50.6	60	5,426,821	40.8	45	5,331,077	34.7	32
Labour	4,253,207	33.0	17	4,865,261	36.5	32	6,153,640	40.1	45
Liberal	1,690,599	13.1	0	986,292	6.2	0			
SDP				75,886	0.5	0			
Lib/SDP							2,591,635	19.5	0
Green							2,292,705	14.9	0
SNP	247,836	1.9	1	230,594	1.7	1	406,686	2.7	1
Plaid Cymru	83,399	0.6	0	103,031	0.8	0	115,062	0.8	0
Others	90,318	0.7	0	95,531	0.7	0	41,295	0.3	0
ELECTORATE	40,529,970	31.8		41,917,313	31.8		42,590,060	35.9	

British MEPs are less well known than their Westminster counterparts. This is due partly to the weakness of the EP and the fact that the route to political power in the UK still resides in membership of the Westminster Parliament. Consequently, with a few exceptions (e.g. Barbara Castle, who had been a senior cabinet minister in Britain), MEPs tend to be those:

- *embarking on the first stages of a political career which will take them to Westminster at the earliest opportunity;*

- *who failed to win seats at Westminster;*

- *with a mastery of the technical detail of their subject of expertise but who are not drawn to the 'rough and tumble' of Westminster politics.*

As mentioned above, before 1979 all MEPs were national MPs. Since direct election has been used it has become less common for people to combine membership of both national and European parliaments, partly because of problems of time and distance. In addition, the rules of the British Labour Party prevent members being at the same time MPs and MEPs (there is no such prohibition in the Conservative Party). However, as 'political high-flyers' gravitate towards Westminster and as Westminster MPs jealously guard their position as the electorate's representatives, the progress of the EP has been retarded.

MEPs sit not in national groups but in political groups reflecting alliances between political parties across national frontiers. Unlike Britain, where the two-party system dominates politics, European countries have developed an array of political parties representing different shades of opinion (*see* Fig. 10.5). Given this fragmentation, it is not surprising that the political groups in the EP are not as cohesive as parties at Westminster. Nevertheless, the following principal groups can be identified.

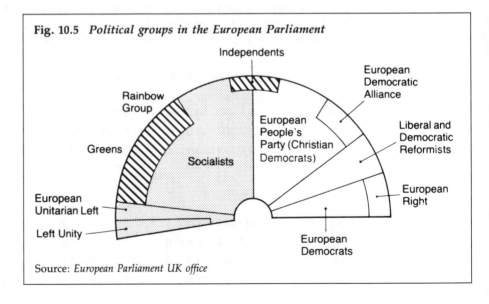

Fig. 10.5 *Political groups in the European Parliament*

Source: *European Parliament UK office*

1 The Socialist Group is the largest group in the European Parliament. It has 180 members (out of 518) including the 46 British Labour MEPs. The term 'socialist' covers a wide range of opinion (including opinion on the vital issue of the future direction of Europe) and as a result the Socialist Group has often been disunited.

2 The European People's Party Group is a centre right group consisting of 128 members. The Italian and German Christian Democrats provide the largest contribution to this group of MEPs. To the Group has now been added the former European Democratic Group of 34 members. This is primarily the 32 British Conservative MEPs with some Danish allies. Like the Conservative Party in the UK, the Group contains both Euro-sceptics as well as those more favourably disposed to further integration.

3 The Liberal Democratic and Reformist Group combines a variety of parties across most EC countries and has 45 MEPs (but none from the UK).

The other groups are:

- *European Unitarian Left, with 29 MEPs;*

- *the Greens, with 27 MEPs;*

- *European Democratic Alliance – a centre right group of French and Irish MEPs who number 21;*

- *Rainbow Group, of 15 MEPs. As the name suggests, this a miscellaneous group of politicians most of whom are concerned with regional and minority interests;*

Table 10.2 *Composition of the European Parliament*

	Total	B	DK	D	GR	E	F	IRL	I	L	NL	P	UK
Socialist Group	180	8	4	31	9	27	22	1	14	2	8	8	46
Group of the European People's Party	162	7	4	32	10	18	11	4	27	3	10	3	33
Liberal, Democratic and Reformist Group	45	4	3	5	–	5	9	2	3	1	4	9	–
Group for the European Unitarian Left	29	–	1	–	1	4	–	1	22	–	–	–	–
Green Group	27	3	–	6	–	1	8	–	7	–	2	–	–
Group of the European Democratic Alliance	21	–	–	–	1	2	12	6	–	–	–	–	–
Rainbow Group	15	1	4	1	–	2	1	1	3	–	–	1	1
Technical Group of the European Right	14	1	–	3	–	–	10	–	–	–	–	–	–
Left Unity	13	–	–	–	3	–	7	–	–	–	–	3	–
Non-attached	12	–	–	3	–	1	1	–	5	–	1	–	1
TOTAL	518	24	16	81	24	60	81	15	81	6	25	24	81

Source: DGI, May 1992

- *the European Right Group – a far right nationalist group of 14 MEPs;*

- *the Left Unity Group (Communist), of 13 MEPs.*

In Table 10.2 MEPs are shown by political group and member state.

The next EP election in 1994 is likely to produce a different distribution of seats and, given the fragmentation of European political parties, it is quite possible that parties will be allied in different ways.

This brief survey of EP political groups provides an insight into why British governments (and the British political parties) have been reluctant to extend the powers of the EP. Any increase in the power of Community institutions, including the EP, is seen as a diminution of national sovereignty. As the EP grows in strength, that of Westminster will decline. Moreover, the position in the EP is such that its party political make-up is likely to differ from that of the UK, as indeed it does today.

The influence of the EP is exercised in three ways: through the legislative process, through supervision of the Commission and through the budgetary process.

Legislation
The EP's powers in relation to legislation fall far short of the legislative powers of national parliaments. The traditional procedure involved the EP offering an 'opinion' on a Commission proposal and the Council of Ministers taking the final decision. The new co-operation procedure (*see* Fig. 10.6) was introduced in parallel with qualified majority voting under the Single European Act.

Under the co-operation procedure, the Council, on a proposal from the Commission and after obtaining the opinion of the EP, adopts a 'common position' on legislation. This is then referred back to the EP, which has three months in which it must endorse, reject or amend the proposal. The Commission has one month in which to decide whether or not to accept any amendments proposed by the EP. At the second reading stage unanimity in the Council is required if the EP has rejected the Council's common position. If Parliament has proposed amendments to the legislation, the Council votes by QMV where the Commission accepts the amendments but by unanimity where the Commission rejects them. The Council has to reach a decision within three months, otherwise the proposal fails.

The significance of the procedure is that it gives the EP some real legislative powers – but it should be noted that, despite this increase in power, legislation is enacted only if proposed by the Commission and accepted by the Council. The EP has no independent law-making powers; what is more, the EP is not consulted on all legislation and the Council can overturn EP amendments.

Supervision
Parliaments have the functions of controlling and supervising the executive (the government) and the EP is no exception. However, in addition to the common problems of controlling the executive that face all parliaments (e.g. inequality of access to information), the EP has a unique problem: national governments are responsible to national parliaments and not to it. The Commission's role is to propose and implement measures whilst the Council

Fig. 10.6 *Community legislative process: new co-operation procedure*

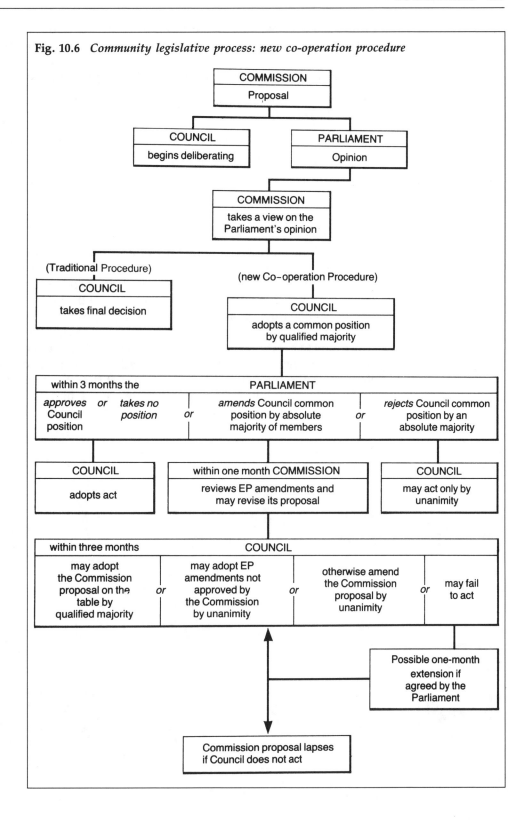

of Ministers decides; and the EP has little control over the Council – which is, after all, a meeting of the representatives of the governments of member states.

The EP does have some powers to control the Commission:

- *by a censure motion passed by two-thirds of votes cast, including a majority of all MEPs, it can dismiss the College of Commissioners;*

- *commissioners (like ministers at Westminster) can be questioned;*

- *the standing committees of the EP (see Fig. 10.7) attempt to supervise the Commission's work in specific areas.*

The budget   The EP has some powers in relation to the Community budget. The EP has the final word on all 'non-compulsory expenditure'. This is expenditure which is not the inevitable consequence of Community legislation (e.g. Social Fund, Regional Fund). The EP has the power to reallocate and to increase expenditure within certain limits. 'Compulsory expenditure' which flows from Community legislation takes up 64 per cent of the budget (mainly on the common agricultural policy). The EP can propose modifications to this expenditure although even these can be overturned by QMV.

The ultimate sanction is the EP's power to reject the budget as a whole and ask for a new one. It has this power provided that a majority of the 518 MEPs vote against the budget *and* two-thirds of votes cast are to reject it. Both criteria must be fulfilled. The power to reject the budget is potentially a powerful lever for the EP since rejection would place EC spending plans in

---

Fig. 10.7 *European Parliamentary committees*

Political

Agriculture, Fisheries, Rural Development

Budgets

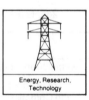
Economic, Monetary, Industrial

Energy, Research, Technology

External Economic Relations

Legal Citizens Rights

Social, Employment Working Environment

Regional Policy and Planning

Transport and Tourism

Environment, Health and Consumer

Youth, Culture, Education, Media, Sport

Development and Cooperation

Institutional Affairs

Budgetary Control

Procedure, Immunities, Credentials

Woman's Rights

Petitions

Source: *European Parliament UK office*

jeopardy. However, the fragmentation of the EP political groups coupled with the need to meet the two criteria means that this weapon remains merely a potential threat.

Over the years, especially since the direct election of MEPs, the EP has acquired an enhanced position within the European Community. Slowly it has acquired more powers to influence the course of Community action. However, 'the EP is still commonly regarded as being a rather special sort of advisory body rather than a proper parliament. The main reason for this is that its constitutional powers remain considerably weaker than those of national parliaments. It does not have full legislative powers, its budgetary powers are circumscribed and it cannot overthrow a government' (Nugent, *The Government and Politics of the European Community*, p. 165).

The European Court of Justice

The European Court of Justice (ECJ) is based in Luxembourg, and should not be confused with the European Court of Human Rights based in Strasbourg. The latter is a non-EC body dealing with issues of human rights, whereas the ECJ is concerned with the interpretation and application of Community law.

The 13 judges of the ECJ will hear cases brought by the Commission, national governments and by individuals. As 'guardian of the treaties' the Commission will bring cases of inaction or illegality by national governments to the Court. Member states can also take action against other states that fail to implement Community law. These types of cases are similar to the work of national appeal courts in that ECJ judgements not only settle particular cases but provide clarification of and guidance on Community law. In addition to these appeal cases the ECJ has power to review the legality of acts of the Council, Commission and the EP. This aspect of the ECJ's work is comparable with the American Supreme Court, which has powers to decide upon the legality and constitutionality of US legislation.

As well as the ECJ we should also note the Court of First Instance (established in 1988). This court has jurisdiction in:

- *disputes between Community institutions and their staff;*

- *matters relating to the ECSC Treaty;*

- *enforcement of the rules of competition.*

As the name Court of First Instance suggests, it deals not with appeals from national courts but with the first hearing of cases.

The Economic and Social Committee

Although called a 'committee', the Economic and Social Committee (ESC) has 189 members, drawn from the 12 member states roughly in proportion to size of population. The big four each have 24 members; the other states have fewer representatives, down to Luxembourg with only six. As a committee of 189 members it has some similarity with the Parliament (in fact it is sometimes called the 'other assembly'). However, members are not elected and they are not politicians in the party political sense. Rather, they are appointed to reflect sectional interests. Hence, within each national delegation a third are seen as employers' representatives, a third are trade unionists and the remaining third will be drawn from other interest groups (consumer groups, environmental organisations, the professions or agriculture).

The work of the ESC is undertaken in nine sections: Agriculture; Industry and Commerce; Economic, Financial and Monetary Questions; Social and Cultural; Transport and Communications; External Relations; Energy; Regional Development; and Environment, Public Health and Consumer Affairs. By organising into sections the ESC is able to give 'opinions' on Community-related issues. The treaties require the Council and Commission to consult with the ESC on particular issues, and they may choose to consult on others.

It might be asked why there is this 'other assembly' when the EP exists to represent the electorates of the member states. The ESC was established to ensure that there would be an effective forum for the views of the sectional interests that are directly affected by EC activities. However, it is in a relatively weak position: the range of issues on which consultation is mandatory is limited and its 'opinions' can be ignored by the Council and Commission. Moreover, the EP has slowly acquired a position of greater influence (especially since direct elections in 1979) whilst that of the ESC has declined correspondingly.

The Court of Auditors

The Court of Auditors was established in 1975 (replacing separate audit bodies for the various communities) to audit the Community's general budget and the ECSC's operating budget. Auditing means, first, ensuring that revenue has been raised and expenditure incurred in a lawful manner and, second, investigating the soundness of the financial management of Community institutions.

The auditing role is especially important when it is remembered that Community funds (like those of national governments) have been taken from the taxpayers of member states. The taxpayers, and their representatives in Parliament, are entitled to know if their money is being spent lawfully and efficiently. The widespread, if unjustified, image of the 'Euro-gravy train', with funds misappropriated for unlawful purposes, renders it essential for a body such as the Court of Auditors to be established to investigate and to report its findings.

The Court can investigate operations carried out by member states on behalf of the Community (e.g. expenditure on agriculture) and in non-member countries that receive Community aid (e.g. under the Lomé Convention).

European Investment Bank

Based in Luxembourg, the European Investment Bank (EIB) was established under the EEC Treaty of 1957. Although it can be regarded as an EC institution we should remember that it is a bank and not a grant-dispensing body. Consequently, it offers loans (admittedly at competitive and fixed interest rates) to facilitate the financing of projects (Article 30 of the Treaty):

- *for developing less-developed regions;*

- *for modernising or converting undertakings or for developing fresh activities called for by the progressive establishment of the common market, where these projects are of a size or nature that they cannot be entirely financed by various means available in the individual member states;*

- *of common interest to several member states which are of such a size or nature that they cannot be entirely financed by the various means available to individual member states.*

EIB loans must satisfy one or other of these criteria but, in addition, the project for which a loan is sought must be economically viable and the loan must be guaranteed by adequate security. Moreover, the EIB usually lends only 50 per cent (or less) of the cost of an investment project and so borrowers will need to seek other sources of finance. The Bank offers only large-scale loans (10 million ECUs or more) but smaller projects can receive EIB assistance via intermediary institutions, such as a regional development agency.

Community law

Like any other community the EC requires a framework of law to regulate its activities (*see* Fig. 10.8). Consequently, on accession to the Community, the member states 'voluntarily surrender their right across a broad range of important sectors, to be independent in the determination and application of public policy' (Nugent, *The Government and Politics of the European Community*, p. 166). Hence the European Communities Act of 1972 (in which the UK Parliament approved UK membership of the EC) states:

> All such rights, powers, liabilities, obligations and restrictions from time to time created or arising by or under the Treaties, as in accordance with the Treaties are without further enactment to be given legal effect or used in the United Kingdom and shall be recognised and available in law, and be enforced, allowed and followed accordingly . . .

The following can be regarded as the primary legislation of the Community, making up its written constitution:

- *Paris Treaty, establishing the ECSC (April 1951);*

- *Rome Treaty, establishing the EEC (March/April 1957);*

Fig. 10.8 *Sources of Community law*

Treaty law

Primary legislation
(Treaties establishing the Communities, Annexes and Protocols, amendments to the Treaties, Treaties of Accession)

General principles of law, customary law
International agreements

Secondary legislation

Regulations and implementing regulations
Directives/ECSC Recommendations
General and individual Decisions

Conventions between the Member States

Decisions of the representatives of the Member States meeting within the Council
Conventions creating uniform Community law

■ *Rome Treaty establishing Euratom (March 1957);*

■ *Single European Act (February 1986).*

The Treaty on European Union signed in Maastricht on 7 February 1992 will (or would have) become EC primary law but has yet to be ratified by member states. The treaties established the institutional structure for decision-making and, at the same time, enunciated general principles (e.g. the promotion of competition and the free movement of factors of production) and identified policy sectors to be developed (e.g. regional policy).

The laws that emerge from the Community institutions can be seen as secondary legislation. Basically, these measures translate the general principles laid down in the treaties into specific rules, and are of four kinds.

1 *Regulations* have general application and are directly binding in all member states. This means that they take immediate effect and do not have to be confirmed by national parliaments.

2 *Directives* are binding as to the result to be achieved but national authorities in member states have choice over the form and method of implementation. In other words, they are general requirements which the national authorities are required to translate into national legislation. In itself, a directive does not have legal force but particular provisions may take direct effect if it is not duly implemented.

3 *Decisions* are binding upon those to whom they are addressed. A decision might be addressed to a member state, a company or an individual.

4 *Recommendations and opinions* have no binding force (and in that sense do not formally constitute part of Community law), but state the views of the EC institution that issues them.

As we have seen, the legislative procedures of the EC involve the Commission (proposing), the Parliament and ESC giving an opinion and the Council taking the final decision. The role of the European Court of Justice is to interpret the law in specific cases. As the Community is more than an inter-governmental body, but is a supra-national body, it is necessary for Community law to enjoy primacy, or supremacy, over national law. Although the supremacy of Community law is not spelt out in the treaties, national courts have accepted its precedence, as required by the ECJ: 'Every national court must, in a case within its jurisdiction, apply Community law in its entirety . . . and must set aside any provision of national law which may conflict with it, whether prior or subsequent to the Community rule.'

Maastricht and Community institutions

This survey of Community institutions reveals that the Council, Commission and ECJ have power but that the (elected) European Parliament is relatively weak. The Commission is not fully accountable to the EP, which in turn has limited powers over the budget. The Council, rather than the EP, is the legislative body of the EC. This weakness of the elected assembly of the EC gives rise to what is known as the 'democratic deficit'. This provides Euro-sceptics with a justification for resisting further integration. After all, transferring the power of decision-making from national governments to EC institutions means a loss of democratic control.

It is not just Euro-sceptics who are critical of the democratic deficit. Euro-federalists also call for greater democracy within the EC. David Martin is Labour MEP for the Lothians and is the author of the EP's Report on Political Union. In his book *Europe: an Ever Closer Union* he states (at pp. 15–16) that it:

> remains something of an embarrassment and a cause for shame that the European Community itself is not yet a democracy properly understood; as it is not controlled by the EC's electorate, it is not a Parliamentary democracy. Indeed, if the EC was a state and was to apply to join itself, it would be turned down on the grounds that it was not a democracy.

Later (at p. 59) he argues that it 'must be of concern to all democrats' that 'although a great many decisions affecting the citizens of Member States are no longer made in their national Parliaments, they do not evolve from what we would understand as a democratic process at the European level'.

To rectify the 'democratic deficit' the EP sought to influence the wording of the Maastricht Treaty. In particular the Parliament called for:

■ *a common citizenship and a common framework for fundamental rights and freedoms;*

- *the establishment of a Regional Assembly to contribute towards and monitor policy affecting the regions of the EC;*

- *the right for the democratically elected representatives of the EC to initiate legislation;*

- *the right of the EP to appoint the President of the Commission;*

- *the establishment of joint decision-making between the EP and Council, thus ensuring that no EC law could be passed without the joint agreement of the Council, representing member states, and the Parliament, representing the Community electorate as a whole.*

Although EC governments were not prepared to go as far as the EP wanted, the Maastricht Treaty does introduce institutional changes to strengthen the democratic accountability of Community institutions.

1 National parliaments will play a larger role in EC affairs both in terms of scrutiny of EC legislation and by periodic conferences of parliaments (or assizes).

2 The ECJ was given new powers to fine countries that did not comply with its judgements.

3 The Court of Auditors was strengthened.

4 A new Committee of the Regions will advise the Commission and Council on issues concerning the regions.

5 A new European Ombudsman will investigate maladministration in European institutions.

6 European citizenship was created.

7 The principle of subsidiarity will limit the power of EC institutions, returning some matters to national governments and parliaments.

8 The European Parliament will be given new powers:

(a) to approve the appointment of the European Commission;
(b) to carry out enquiries into cases of maladministration of Community law;
(c) to have a greater say over some EC legislation;
(d) to act as a watchdog over the way the Commission implements the Community's budget.

CHAPTER 11

Britains European Partners

An understanding of the EC does require some understanding of the different national economies of Europe. This chapter focuses on profiles of Britain's 11 partners, and a statistical appendix compares the economies in various ways.

OBJECTIVES
1 To provide a profile of the economies of Europe.
2 To compare Britain with its partners.
3 To develop an understanding of the core and periphery within Europe (see Fig. 11.1).
4 To analyse the impact of Germany and German unification on the Community in general and Britain in particular.

Belgium

Basic statistics

Population (1991):	9.9 million
Population growth (1991):	0.2 per cent
Currency:	Belgian franc
GDP (1991):	$225 billion
GDP per head (1991):	$22,600
Exports to EC:	75 per cent of 1991 total
Exports to EFTA:	0.6 per cent of 1991 total

%	1991	1992	1993 (est)
Growth of GDP	1.4	2.0	2.7
Inflation rate	3.4	3.3	3.2
Unemployment	9.4	9.7	9.6
Current account of balance of payments as % of GDP	2.2	3.0	3.4

Commentary Belgium's position at the crossroads of Europe meant that it in the past was fought over, and suffered, but has greatly benefited from European integration. It has been at the forefront of moves to deepen the EC, especially as it accommodates the EC executive within its capital city.

Fig. 11.1 *Europe: core and periphery*

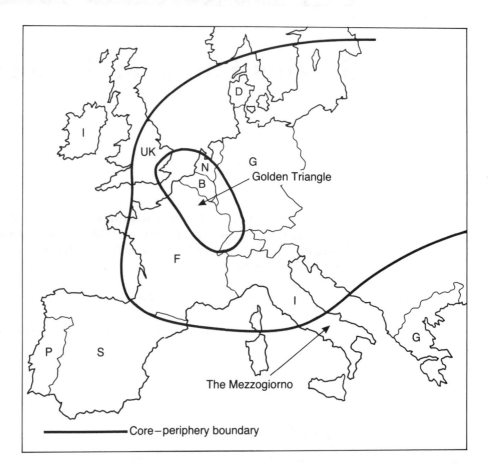

Belgium was one of the first continental countries to follow Britain's Industrial Revolution. Consequently, like Britain, it has a small agricultural sector (2.7 per cent of the workforce, 2.1 per cent of GDP) and a mature industrial sector based upon engineering, metal products, processed food, chemicals, metals, textiles, glass and petroleum. Industry accounts for 31 per cent of GDP and 28 per cent of the workforce. Hence, over two-thirds of both GDP and employment is in the service sector of the economy.

Belgian exports and imports are dominated by engineering products, chemicals, metals and foods. Its relatively small size, in the heart of the EC, renders inevitable the EC's domination of Belgium's overseas trade. But only 8.3 per cent of its imports come from the UK (which is the destination for 8.7 per cent of Belgian exports). This is substantially less than Belgium trades with its immediate neighbours: Germany, the Netherlands and France.

A major problem faced by Belgium is the large public sector debt. This currently amounts to 130 per cent of GDP and is aggravated by continuing budget deficits (5.2 per cent of GDP in 1992/3). This deficit poses problems for Belgium both in meeting the EMU criteria of the Maastricht Treaty and in reducing regional problems within the country. Belgium is formed by an (at times uneasy) alliance between the French-speaking Walloons and Dutch-speaking Flemings. Any reduction in public spending could cause further strains in this uneasy alliance.

Denmark

Basic statistics

Population (1991):	5.14 million
Population growth (1990):	0.1 per cent
Currency:	Kroner
GDP (1991):	$145 billion
GDP per head (1991):	$28,200
Exports to EC:	54 per cent of 1991 total
Exports to EFTA:	24.5 per cent of 1991 total

%	1991	1992	1993 (est)
Growth of GDP	2.0	2.5	3.1
Inflation rate	2.0	2.4	2.4
Unemployment	10.3	10.2	9.6
Current account of balance of payments as % of GDP	1.6	1.8	2.2

Commentary

Danes are often depicted as 'reluctant Europeans' in that they seem less enthusiastic about the deepening of EC relationships than are the citizens of the other smaller EC member states. Denmark joined the EC at the same time as the UK because it felt that it was important to retain the link with its neighbour across the North Sea. However, the Danes, like the British, insisted upon an opt-out from EMU if they considered it necessary in the future. In a 1992 referendum the Danish people rejected the Maastricht Treaty but this was reversed in a second referendum held in 1993. There was concern about the co-operation on defence and security and they were particularly hostile towards discussion of a European army, preferring instead to strengthen the NATO alliance.

The statistics given above show that Denmark enjoys very high living standards even by EC standards. Despite Britain's association of Denmark with bacon, agriculture contributes only 4.3 per cent to GDP and employs 5.5 per cent of the Danish workforce. Industry is responsible for 28 per cent of GDP and 20 per cent of employment. Major industries include food processing, machine making, textiles, furniture, wood products, chemicals and electronics.

These industries figure prominently in both Danish exports and imports. Trade with the EC is proportionally less than is the case with other EC countries. This is partly because of the continuing importance of Sweden and Norway (EFTA countries). The UK takes 10.7 per cent of Danish exports and provides 7.6 per cent of its imports.

France

Basic statistics

Population (1991):	57 million
Population growth (1991):	0.4 per cent
Currency:	Franc
GDP (1991):	$1,190 billion
GDP per head (1991):	$21,107
Exports to EC:	63 per cent of 1991 total
Exports to EFTA:	6 per cent of 1991 total

%	1991	1992	1993 (est)
Growth of GDP	1.2	2.1	2.7
Inflation rate	2.8	3.0	2.7
Unemployment	9.4	10.1	10.2
Current account of balance of payments as % of GDP	−0.7	−0.6	−0.5

Commentary

France has the second largest economy in the EC and a GDP 20 per cent greater than that of the UK. It has played a pivotal role in European affairs for centuries – not least in the EC, where it has always been a major player. During much of the 1960s and early 1970s, when the UK experienced slow growth, France achieved per capita growth of around 5 per cent a year and, although this slowed to 2 per cent by the 1980s, over the 1960–89 period as a whole annual per capita growth in France was 3.7 per cent, which exceeded that of West Germany.

Although agriculture is of greater importance in France than in the UK (providing employment for 6.4 per cent of the workforce and contributing 3.7 per cent of GDP) there has been a shift of population off the land: 6 million have left the land since the Second World War and the character of French farmers has changed from small peasant to larger-scale agri-buinessman. Nevertheless, a combination of CAP reform and low prices for farm products produces problems for French farmers, who tend to take militant action. In 1992, for instance, a promise to reduce farm subsidies was the price of a GATT agreement with non-EC countries (most importantly, the USA). French farmers led the protest against the agreement, thus reinforcing the view that French farmers are a small but vocal minority.

French industry consists of metallurgical industries (39 per cent of total industrial output), chemicals (17 per cent), electronics (17 per cent), textiles and leather (14 per cent) and paper and printing (10 per cent). Together with agriculture, these industries provide the bulk of France's exports, which go to Germany (17 per cent of the total), Italy (11 per cent), Belgium/Luxembourg and the UK (9 per cent each) and Spain (6 per cent). Imports, which take the form of similar goods, come from Germany (19 per cent), Italy (12 per cent), Belgium/Luxembourg (9 per cent), the USA (8 per cent) and the UK (7.3 per cent). Within the industrial sectors mentioned above there has been a shift to the high-tech sector which has had regional implications for France. The declining sectors have been concentrated in the north-east whereas the new high-tech industries are located in the south, in cities such as Grenoble and Toulouse.

France has a long tradition of state intervention in the economy. This *'tradition dirigiste'* developed under governments of all political persuasions and took the form of indicative planning, nationalisation, government ownership of shares in companies such as Renault and Crédit Lyonnais, and state aid for French industry. Although there has been some reversal of *dirigisme*, the French government favours intervention to an extent that British Conservative governments regard as unacceptable.

The French have developed a more integrationist approach to Europe. We saw in chapter 2 that General de Gaulle (president in the 1960s) saw the EC as an association of strong sovereign, but French-dominated, states which would be a bulwark against what he regarded as the unwelcome intervention of the USA in European affairs. Over the decades that concept of the EC has changed. President Mitterrand, head of state since 1981, still pursues an independent path on many foreign policy issues (e.g. preference for the Western European Union over NATO, and nuclear arms) but is a strong advocate of EMU. As we will see in chapter 15, France is one of the two EC states that have already complied with the Maastricht currency convergence criteria. This is as a result of austerity measures pursued since 1984, involving financial discipline, high interest rates, low inflation and maintaining the franc within the ERM (even during the turbulence of 1992–3). Mitterand's commitment to EMU is not shared by large numbers of French people, who in a referendum held in 1992 voted only narrowly in favour of the Maastricht Treaty. The price paid for this financial discipline in advance of the Maastricht timetable has been high unemployment.

Germany

Basic statistics

Population (1991):	80.9 million
Population growth (1991):	0.3 per cent
Currency:	Deutschmark
GDP (1991):	$1,488 billion
GDP per head (1991):	$18,878
Exports to EC:	54 per cent of 1991 total
Exports to EFTA:	15 per cent of 1991 total

%	1991	1992	1993 (est)
Growth of GDP	3.1	1.8	2.5
Inflation rate	4.5	4.5	3.9
Unemployment	4.3	5.0	5.1
Current account of balance of payments as % of GDP	−1.5	0.8	−0.7

Commentary At the end of the Second World War the German economy was in ruins, the country was divided and some lands had been lost to Poland. With the assistance of America and other Western countries, however, the Federal

Republic of (West) Germany was able to enjoy a *Wirtschaftswunder* (or economic miracle) during the 1950s when the economy grew by a most impressive 8.8 per cent a year. Although we are inclined to see this as merely rebuilding after the devastation, it is even more impressive when one remembers that this economic growth was sustained over a decade and was substantially in excess of the UK's annual 2.8 per cent, France's 5 per cent, America's 3.3 per cent and (the other devastated former enemy country) Japan's 4.2 per cent. Admittedly, West German growth slowed in the subsequent decades but it was consistently above the UK growth rate until the 1980s. As Fig. 11.2 illustrates, differential growth rates produce a widening GDP gap between countries. As a result of differential growth rates Germany became the dominant economy within the EC, with a national income substantially greater than those of its partners.

Not surprisingly, there has always been great interest in the reasons for German success. Over the years the following explanations have been offered.

1 The Second World War rid Germany of obsolete technology and attitudes. More than any other European nation Germany was able to start anew in 1945.

2 As a defeated power limitations were placed on Germany's military activities. These included a constitutional prohibition on action outside

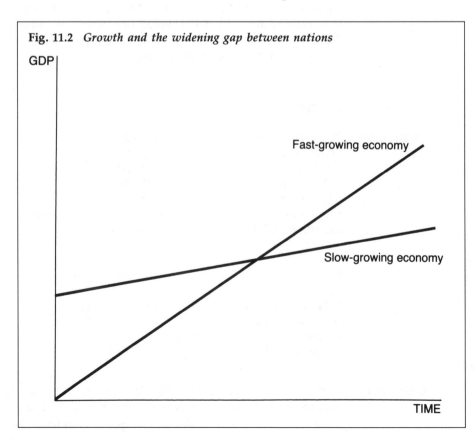

Fig. 11.2 *Growth and the widening gap between nations*

Germany and a prohibition on German possession of nuclear weapons. Barred from great power status in a military sense, it concentrated its energies on economic success.

3 A skilled and intelligent workforce has enabled Germany to be competitive both in price terms and in terms of quality.

4 Heavy investment in plant and equipment in the 1950s and 1960s provided Germany with a strong industrial base.

5 Superior labour relations (achieved in part by the extension of industrial democracy or worker participation) have maintained German competitiveness and quality.

6 A ready supply of guest-worker labour was available when required, especially in earlier decades.

7 The cautious monetary policy of the Deutsche Bundesbank has given Germany low inflation. Unlike the Bank of England, the Bundesbank is constitutionally independent of the government and is charged with the duty of providing low inflation and exchange rate stability. Independence has meant that interest rate policy is conducted without reference to the output/employment consequences of any action. Moreover, it gives the right signals in wage negotiations: the Bundesbank will not expand the economy to protect jobs when wage increases are excessive. The low inflation enjoyed by Germany has provided the basis for growth.

Like the UK, Germany has a small agricultural sector (1.6 per cent of GDP and 3.4 per cent of the workforce). However, unlike the UK, German industry accounts for 39 per cent of GDP and 41 per cent of the workforce. Hence, although Germany has experienced the same 'march through the sectors' as the UK, its falling share of manufacturing and employment has not been as dramatic. The strength of German industry is reflected in consistent visible balance surpluses: DM 106 billion in 1990, 22 billion in 1991 and 45 billion in 1992.

Germany's main exports are road vehicles (18 per cent of total), mechanical engineering products (16 per cent) and chemicals (13 per cent), and its main markets are France (13 per cent), Italy (9 per cent), the UK (8.5 per cent), the Netherlands (8.4 per cent) and Belgium (7.4 per cent). Major German imports include food (12 per cent of total), and electrical engineering products, chemicals and road vehicles (each 10 per cent). Again, Germany's main customer (France) is its main supplier (12 per cent) with the Netherlands (10 per cent), Italy (9 per cent), Luxembourg (7 per cent) and Britain (6.7 per cent) following behind.

In 1990 the *Länder* (provinces) of the former German Democratic Republic (DDR) joined the Federal Republic of Germany (FDR). This momentous event in history was brought about by the virtual collapse of the East German economy, a flood of migration to the West via the more liberal regimes of Czechoslovakia and Hungary, the changes in the former Soviet Union and (the great symbolic event) the dismantling of the Berlin Wall. The post-1945 division of Germany was an unequal one in terms of size, population and resources. This inequality grew as the FDR enjoyed growth in a market-based economy and the DDR suffered the inefficiencies of bureaucratic command planning. The eastern *Länder* contributed 7 per cent of German GDP but had 19 per cent of its workforce. This means that East German productivity was only one-third that of West Germany. East German goods were of a low quality, labour was low paid and, as in the case of other former 'hardline' Communist states, consumer goods were in short supply. Reunification opened up the state-owned enterprises to competition, the like of which they had never previously experienced.

The problem was compounded by the conversion rate between the old Ostmark and the Deutschmark: the one-to-one rate agreed for political and social reasons meant that East German industry found it difficult to compete in Western markets. Although state subsidies were given during the transitional period, they are contrary to EC rules on state aid to industry. In the long run they have to be phased out as the Treuhandanstalt (the privatisation agency) succeeds in its difficult task of selling off East German enterprise.

The currency conversion resulting from German EMU increased the money supply of the FDR by 10 per cent. As EMU was expected to raise FDR output by 14 per cent it was not expected to be inflationary. However, a combination of factors conspired to produce an inflationary impact.

1 East Germans (long deprived of consumer goods) took the opportunity to spend their money, thus increasing the velocity of circulation.

2 The slump in East German output meant that the real output of the new FDR did not rise by the expected 14 per cent.

3 The rise in the government's deficit added to the money supply and thus to inflationary pressures.

The Bundesbank is required to take action against inflation. This absolute commitment to combating inflation is the result of the folk memory of the 1923 hyper-inflation. Bundesbank action takes the form of raising interest rates to discourage borrowing and thereby reduce bank lending. High interest rates are deflationary on the German economy and therefore tend to limit German imports. More important, these actions were happening at the time when most EC currencies were in the ERM (Britain having recently joined). High interest rates attract 'hot' money from abroad. Consequently, to retain funds in London and keep sterling within the ERM band, Britain was forced to continue a policy of high interest rates as the country entered the longest recession since the Second World War. There is some justification for saying that part of the cost of German reunification was borne by its partners in the ERM.

EMU will not have the devastating impact on the EC that German monetary union has had on the German economy. This is because the timetable laid down in Maastricht (*see* chapter 15) calls for growing convergence before the final step. In addition, the productivity gap between Germany and the other EC states is not as great as that between the former West and the former East Germany. However, German experience does show the risks involved in EMU.

Greece

Basic statistics

Population (1991):	10.4 million
Population growth (1991):	0.6 per cent
Currency:	Drachma
GDP (1991):	$67 billion
GDP per head (1991):	$6,566
Exports to EC:	63 per cent of 1991 total
Exports to EFTA:	5.5 per cent of 1991 total

%	1991	1992	1993 (est)
Growth of GDP	1.2	1.3	1.6
Inflation rate	18.7	14.7	11.0
Unemployment	8.5	9.6	10.5
Current account of balance of payments as % of GDP	−2.4	−2.7	−2.8

Commentary

Greek admission to the EC (in 1981) was in part a reward for the restoration of parliamentary democracy in 1975, after years of military rule. However, Greece remains somewhat isolated from the rest of the EC. It is the only member not to share a land border with another member. (The UK shares a land border with the Irish Republic and from 1994 will be connected to France by a tunnel.) The conflict in the former Yugoslavia increases Greece's isolation, especially as the Macedonian issue provides a source of tension. Many EC states (especially Germany) favoured recognition of Yugoslavia's successor states but Greece was concerned that an independent Macedonia would pose problems for its own province of Macedonia. Greece is also in a state of intermittent tension with its eastern neighbour, Turkey.

There is a substantial gap in living standards between Greece and the other EC countries. Not only is income per head substantially lower but also Greece is less developed. This is reflected in the fact that agriculture contributes 17 per cent of GDP and employs 25 per cent of the workforce. These figures are high by European standards and point to the low productivity of Greek agriculture. Industry contributes 27 per cent of GDP and employs 21 per cent of the workforce in food and tobacco processing, textiles, chemicals, metal products, mining and petroleum.

The UK (with 7.2 per cent) is Greece's fifth largest export market but UK exports to Greece are lower than those of the Netherlands and Japan. On the positive side, at least the UK has a balance of trade surplus with Greece.

Tourism is a major part of the Greek economy: over 8 million tourists each year, although this trade is highly sensitive to economic and political factors. Another important service activity is shipping, which brings much-needed foreign currency. The inflation figures given above are very high by EC standards and suggest that Greece will not reach the EMU convergence targets without severe austerity measures, which will add to the problem of unemployment. Like the other weaker economies, European integration poses acute problems for Greece although it is aided by Structural Funds, the CAP and, in future, by the Cohesion Fund.

Republic of Ireland

Basic statistics Population (1991):   3.5 million
Population growth (1991):   −0.2 per cent
Currency: Irish punt
GDP (1991): $50 billion
GDP per head (1991): $14,700
Exports to EC: 74 per cent of 1991 total
Exports to EFTA: 5.5 per cent of 1991 total

%	1991	1992	1993 (est)
Growth of GDP	1.3	2.5	3.3
Inflation rate	3.1	3.0	3.0
Unemployment	15.8	16.5	16.0
Current account of balance of payments as % of GDP	3.0	1.8	2.0

Commentary Ireland is unique among the 12 member states in being neutral and not a signatory of the North Atlantic Treaty. Obtaining its political independence from the UK in 1922, Ireland has long sought economic independence from its larger and more affluent neighbour across the Irish Sea. Hence, although it joined the EC at the same time as Britain (like Denmark, to preserve links with its main trading partner) Ireland has attempted to demonstrate its European credentials by wholeheartedly embracing the EC. Ireland joined the ERM before the UK and managed to stay in (albeit with a devaluation) during the troubled period of 1992–3.

The Irish vote in favour of Maastricht was symbolically important in putting the treaty back on course for ratification. The major problem areas for Ireland are uniquely social and moral. EC social policy and free movement of people threaten Ireland's strict laws on contraception, abortion and divorce.

The statistics given above show that Irish living standards are low compared with those of its European partners. Agriculture contributes 11 per cent of GDP and employs 15 per cent of the workforce, both high figures by European standards. One result is that CAP reform will have an adverse effect on the Irish economy. Industry contributes 37 per cent of the GDP and employs 22 per cent of the workforce. The major industries are food processing, brewing, textiles, chemicals, pharmaceuticals, machinery, glass and crystal. These products also figure highly in Ireland's overseas trade, in which it enjoys a healthy surplus on visible items. One third of all Irish exports go to the UK, which provides 44 per cent of Irish imports.

The macro-economic statistic which gives greatest concern is the high unemployment rate. As one of the countries on the outer limits of the EC, there is a continual danger that European integration will result in a centrifugal movement, leaving the extremities in continuing poverty. Unemployment is a factor in the continued population decline in a country that has suffered outward migration on and off since the Great Famine of the 1840s.

Italy

Basic statistics

Population (1991):   58 million
Population growth (1991):   0.2 per cent
Currency: Lira
GDP (1991): $1,072 billion
GDP per head (1991): $18,575
Exports to EC: 59 per cent of 1991 total
Exports to EFTA: 9 per cent of 1991 total

%	1991	1992	1993 (est)
Growth of GDP	1.4	2.0	2.5
Inflation rate	7.1	5.8	5.2
Unemployment	11.0	10.8	10.7
Current account of balance of payments as % of GDP	−1.4	−1.5	−1.8

Commentary

Italy, like Germany, experienced an economic miracle in the decades following the Second World War. Although not quite reaching German levels, it was still most impressive. Labour productivity rose by a consistent 6 per cent a year during the 1960s, although it slowed down in the 1970s and 1980s. Output doubled between 1950 and 1970 and by the late 1980s Italy had overtaken the UK as the third largest economy in Western Europe. However, one problem with Italian statistics is the exceptionally large black (hidden) economy. Assumed to be around one-fifth the size of the official economy, statisticians add 28 per cent to GDP figures to account for the black economy. The strength of the Italian economy is undermined by its:

- *public sector debt;*
- *chronic budget deficits;*
- *need to import energy and raw materials;*
- *inflationary tendencies;*
- *cumbersome bureaucracy (which incidentally contributes to Italy's poor record in implementing EC directives);*
- *political instability and scandals;*
- *current account deficit;*
- *exchange rate weakness (which keeps Italy, alone of the original six, in the slow track of European integration).*

One problem in assessing the Italian economy is the tremendous contrast between north and south. The north, with cities such as Milan, Venice, Florence and Genoa, enjoys living standards comparable with much of Western Europe but the south (the Mezzogiorno) suffers acute economic and social problems. If the overall GDP per head in Italy were given an index value of 100, we would find that regional differences ranged from 133 in

Lombardy to 55 in Calabria. In other words, living standards in the northern region were twice as high as in the south. The figure for the north and centre (down to Rome) is 118.8, whereas that for the south as a whole is 67.3. (The statements above are all based on 1987 figures quoted by Paci, in Dyker (ed), *The National Economies of Europe*.)

Although regional differences occur in all countries, the extent of Italy's is unusual. It is as though Italian unification, which occurred in 1870, was merely political: as though economically and socially Italy remains two countries – the north an affluent Western European country and the south similar to Portugal and Greece as the poor and weak economies of the EC.

Agriculture accounts for 5 per cent of GDP but 9.3 per cent of the workforce, indicating low productivity, especially in the Mezzogiorno. Industry accounts for 37 per cent of GDP with machinery (32 per cent of the total), textiles (13 per cent) and food processing (8 per cent) the largest industries. Of Italy's exports, 19 per cent go to Germany, 16 per cent to France, 7.6 per cent to the USA and 7.1 per cent to the UK. Germany provides 21 per cent of Italian imports with France 14 per cent, the Netherlands and the USA 5 per cent each and Japan 2 per cent.

Luxembourg

Basic statistics

Population (1991):	0.38 million
Population growth (1991):	0.3 per cent
Currency:	Luxembourg franc
GDP (1991):	$10 billion
GDP per head (1991):	$27,320

Luxembourg's overseas trade is treated as part of Belgian trade for statistical purposes.

%	1991	1992	1993 (est)
Growth of GDP	2.5	2.9	3.3
Inflation rate	3.1	3.3	3.0
Unemployment	1.4	1.4	1.3
Current account of balance of payments as % of GDP	1.9	2.9	n/a

Commentary Luxembourg is the smallest of the existing member states and, consequent upon its size and position, is very 'European'. It is heavily dependent on trade with Belgium, with which it is already in an economic union (BLEU).

Agriculture contributes a minute 1.9 per cent to GDP although it employs 3.4 per cent of the workforce. Industry contributes 32 per cent to GDP and employs 31 per cent of the workforce. The sector is dominated by iron and steel (32 per cent of gross industrial value added) although the problems of the steel industry worldwide have affected Luxembourg badly. Other industries include food processing, engineering, glass and aluminium production. The macro-economic statistics given above show Luxembourg enjoys low unemployment, consistently mild inflation and, by recent EC standards, high economic growth. Luxembourg will have little difficulty in meeting any EMU convergence criteria and if a 'two-speed Europe' develops, there is no doubt that Luxembourg will join Germany, the Netherlands, Belgium and France in the fast track.

The Netherlands

Basic statistics

Population (1991):	15 million
Population growth (1991):	0.4 per cent
Currency:	Guilder
GDP (1991):	$330 billion
GDP per head (1991):	$21,400
Exports to EC:	76 per cent of 1991 total
Exports to EFTA:	6.5 per cent of 1991 total

%	1991	1992	1993 (est)
Growth of GDP	2.2	1.8	2.3
Inflation rate	3.1	3.2	3.3
Unemployment	6.1	6.4	6.3
Current account of balance of payments as % of GDP	3.7	4.3	4.6

Commentary

The Netherlands occupies a pivotal position in the Community as a result of development of Europoort – the main entry point for much of extra-EC trade into continental Europe. Being close to the heart of the EC, the Netherlands has greatly benefited from trade links with its immediate neighbours, especially Germany, which is responsible for over 25 per cent of the country's cross-border trade. The link is so close that we can regard the Netherlands as part of the greater German economy. The two countries enjoy a monetary quasi-union in that the guilder is closely linked to the Deutschmark through the ERM. The Netherlands does, with some justification, regard itself as leader in the process of European integration, and it was therefore fitting that the Treaty on European Union was signed in the Dutch town of Maastricht during the period of Dutch presidency of the EC Council of Ministers.

Agriculture occupies a tiny 1.5 per cent of the Dutch labour force but such is its productivity that it contributes 4.7 per cent of GDP. It is especially strong in dairy production and horticulture: its bulbs and flowers are world famous. Manufacturing industry occupies 21 per cent of the workforce and contributes 33 per cent of GDP, with machinery and food processing the leading industries. Gas production in the North Sea is also an important economic activity but, as we saw in chapter 9, the Dutch North Sea gas experience was similar to the British experience with North Sea oil. In both cases much of the benefit was lost through import penetration and resulting unemployment and high government expenditure.

The Netherlands is one of Europe's most trade-orientated economies, with foreign trade exceeding 60 per cent of GDP. Its exports of machinery, food, chemicals and fuel go to Germany (28 per cent of the total), BLEU (15 per cent), France (11 per cent) and the UK (10 per cent). Similar goods are imported from Germany (26 per cent of the total), BLEU (14 per cent), and the UK and the USA (8 per cent each).

Although seen as a successful and prosperous economy, the Netherlands has suffered a number of imbalances from the 1970s. Unemployment has been high by Western European standards and is tackled by tight controls over the growth of real wages. The public sector debt is high in relation to GDP, and during the 1980s the profitability of Dutch industry deteriorated. Nevertheless, there is little doubt that if Europe does proceed with EMU the Netherlands will be involved.

Portugal

Basic statistics

Population (1991):	10.5 million
Population growth (1991):	0.3 per cent
Currency:	Escudo
GDP (1991)	$80 billion
GDP per head (1991):	$7,600
Exports to EC:	75 per cent of 1991 total
Exports to EFTA:	9.7 per cent of 1991 total

%	1991	1992	1993 (est)
Growth of GDP	2.7	2.6	2.7
Inflation rate	14.3	13.5	12.5
Unemployment	3.9	4.5	5.3
Current account of balance of payments as % of GDP	−0.9	−1.9	−2.6

Commentary

For much of the 20th century Portugal's development was retarded by dictatorial rule and the burden of attempting to maintain its African colonies. A peaceful military coup in 1974 was followed by democratic government and, after 1983, economic liberalisation. The process of economic transformation was enhanced by Portugal's accession to the EC in 1986.

Despite the progress of the 1980s – between 1985 and 1990 it achieved a very respectable annual growth rate of 4.6 per cent – Portugal remains one of the poorest EC countries. Its low state of development is symbolised by the fact that, despite employing 19 per cent of Portugal's workforce, agriculture is responsible for only 6.2 per cent of GDP. Yields in Portuguese agriculture are low, contributing to the country's problems. Industry occupies 35 per cent of the workforce and contributes 38 per cent of GDP. However, much of Portuguese industry is low wage and low value added, e.g. food processing, textiles and clothing. These goods also feature in Portugal's exports, which go to Germany (17 per cent), France (15 per cent), Spain (13 per cent), the UK (12 per cent) and the Netherlands (6 per cent).

Imports include machinery, chemicals and fuel, supplied from Spain and Germany (14 per cent each), France (12 per cent), Italy (10 per cent) and the UK (7.6 per cent). The tourist industry is a crucial part of the Portuguese economy and helps to finance the visible trade deficit. Earnings from tourism are unreliable, however, and point to the need to diversify into other sectors.

Inflation has been a problem in Portugal. Throughout the later 1980s it averaged 14 per cent a year and although it fell in the early 1990s, it still remained high by EC standards. On the other hand, Portugal enjoys low unemployment, in part because of under-employment in the agricultural sector. The problem for Portugal is to reduce inflation and improve the balance of payments without suffering a rise in unemployment to the levels experienced by its Spanish neighbour.

Another worrying statistic about the Portuguese economy is the extent of its foreign debt: in 1991, $18 billion. As students of economics are aware, a national (or public) debt is not a burden when it is primarily internal, but an external debt represents a burden on the balance of payments. In effect a country with a large external debt is required to relinquish a large part of its national output each year as interest. The debt holders' claim on Portuguese output will neutralise assistance given from the EC Structural and Cohesion Funds.

Spain

Basic statistics

Population (1991):	40 million
Population growth (1991):	0.1 per cent
Currency:	Peseta
GDP (1991):	$540 billion
GDP per head (1991):	$13,600
Exports to EC:	70 per cent of 1991 total
Exports to EFTA:	4 per cent of 1991 total

%	1991	1992	1993 (est)
Growth of GDP	2.4	2.9	3.2
Inflation rate	6.9	5.8	5.0
Unemployment	16.3	15.2	14.6
Current account of balance of payments as % of GDP	−3.2	2.9	−2.9

Commentary

Spain is the largest of the EC southern states, and it sees itself as the leader of this group, especially on issues such as the allocation of EC funds. In terms of GDP per head, Spain ranks tenth in the EC. Only Greece and Portugal have lower living standards. Nevertheless, Spain has achieved considerable growth and could challenge the UK and Italy for the position of Europe's fourth largest economy.

The transformation of Spain from a weak, poor economy to a modern, successful one started in the late 1950s under the dictator General Franco. In the 1960s industrial output grew by 9 per cent a year although this high growth rate could not be sustained indefinitely. Franco liberated the economy and opened it up to overseas influence. In this, Spain was assisted by the development of the package holiday industry. Tourism accounts for 10 per cent of GDP and 11 per cent of the workforce, making it Spain's most important industry. The transformation was accelerated under Franco's successors (King Juan Carlos and Prime Ministers such as socialist Felipe Gonzalez). In the late 1980s Spain's GDP grew in real terms by 4.9 per cent a year – more than all the other EC economies apart from Luxembourg.

The agricultural sector accounts for 5.2 per cent of output but 11.8 per cent of the workforce, whereas industry accounts for 38 per cent of output and 24 per cent of the workforce. The major industries are machinery (24 per cent of manufacturing output), food processing (19 per cent) and textiles (8 per cent). Spain's industrialisation, which did slow down in the early 1990s, has not eliminated unemployment, which officially is at a rate of 16 per cent of the workforce although a large black (or hidden) economy means that it might be only 10–11 per cent. Industrialisation has not improved Spain's balance of payments since its growing incomes are spent on imports. Even the large surplus on services (tourism) is insufficient to prevent a current account deficit which, in the early 1990s, was around $18 billion per year. Spanish trade is heavily EC-orientated with France (21 per cent), Germany (13 per cent), Italy (10 per cent) and the UK (9 per cent) the major destinations for Spanish exports. In turn, Spain's major suppliers are Germany (16 per cent), France (15 per cent), Italy (10 per cent), the USA (8 per cent) and the UK (7 per cent).

Spain is very keen on European integration. This is because the modernisation and growth of the last three decades have convinced Spain that its future lies in closer links with Europe rather than any retreat to the past, when isolation and backwardness led to Spain being perceived by the World Bank as a developing country.

Further reading

D. Dyker (ed) (1992), *The National Economies of Europe*, LONGMAN.
D. Dyker (ed) (1992), *The European Economy*, LONGMAN.
The Economist (1992), *Pocket Europe*, ECONOMIST/CENTURY BOOKS.
E. Somers (ed) (1991), *European Economies: A Comparative Study*, PITMAN.

Statistical appendix

Table 11.1 *The ten largest free market economies*

		1990 GDP ($ billion)
1.	USA	5,420
2.	Japan	2,930
3.	Germany	1,493
4.	France	1,190
5.	Italy	1,070
6.	UK	970
7.	Canada	579
8.	Spain	490
9.	Brazil	350
10.	Australia	290

(GDP = gross domestic product or total value of output)

Table 11.2 *EC–EFTA economies by rank order*

		1991 GDP (billion ECUs)
1.	Germany	1,269
2.	France	967
3.	Italy	926
4.	UK	819
5.	Spain	425
6.	The Netherlands	231
7.	*Sweden*	*190*
8.	*Switzerland*	*184*
9.	Belgium	160
10.	*Austria*	*132*
11.	Denmark	105
12.	*Finland*	*101*
13.	*Norway*	*86*
14.	Greece	57
15.	Portugal	55
16.	Ireland	35
17.	Luxembourg	7.2
18.	*Iceland*	*5.2*
19.	*Liechtenstein*	*1.2*

EFTA countries in italics

Table 11.3 *Human development index*

Ranking in Europe	Country	Score
1	Iceland	98
	Sweden	98
	Switzerland	98
	Norway	98
	Netherlands	98
6	France	97
	UK	97
	Denmark	97
9	Finland	96
	Germany	96
	Belgium	96
	Austria	96
	Italy	96
14	Luxembourg	95
	Spain	95
	Ireland	95

(continued)

Table 11.3 *(continued)*

Ranking in Europe	Country	Score
17	Greece	93
18	Cyprus	92
	Czechoslovakia	92
	Malta	92
21	Hungary	91
22	Bulgaria	90
23	Yugoslavia	89
24	Portugal	88
25	Poland	86
26	Albania	82
27	Romania	76
28	Turkey	69

Note: The human development index combines into a single weighted score both quantitative and qualitative aspects of living standards. The latter include quality of life factors such as literacy and life expectancy. On world standards any score in the 90s is high.

Table 11.4 *Intra-Community trade (exports and imports) as percentage of external trade*

	1980	1991
EC 12	50.2	60.1
Portugal	44.9	73.1
BLEU	65.6	72.8
Ireland	74.5	71.9
The Netherlands	62.2	67.5
France	49.4	63.9
Spain	41.7	62.5
Greece	49.4	62.2
Italy	45.4	58.3
Denmark	49.5	54.2
Germany	47.5	54.2
UK	45.2	53.0

Note: The data points to greater economic integration as the Community deepens although whether this is at the expense of trade with the rest of the world is not revealed in the figures. The exception to the rule of increased proportion of intra-EC trade is Ireland: the exceptionally high figure is the result of strong trade links with the UK which pre-date Ireland's entry into the EC.

Source: Eurostat

Table 11.5 *External trade as a percentage of GDP 1991*

	Trade in goods	
	Total	Extra-Community
EC 12	22.9	9.1
BLEU	59.2	15.8
Ireland	53.5	14.3
The Netherlands	46.9	15.1
Portugal	30.2	8.0
Denmark	26.3	12.1
Germany	25.3	11.5
Greece	21.4	8.4
France	19.8	7.1
UK	19.3	8.9
Italy	15.4	6.3
Spain	14.5	5.4

Note: This is a measure of the importance of international trade throughout the Community. In the case of the Belgium–Luxembourg Economic Union (BLEU), international trade exceeds 50 per cent of GDP but is less than one-sixth of the GDP of Spain and Italy. The figure for extra-EC trade provides a measure of the significance of the rest of the world to the economies of the EC.

Source: Eurostat

CHAPTER 12

Customs Unions and GATT

Before looking in detail at the single market, we should understand the theory behind protection, free trade and customs union. A key feature of the analysis concerns the extent to which customs create or merely divert trade. For a country such as the UK, with links (albeit declining) with the wider world, it is important that increased trade with Europe is not at the expense of trade with the rest of the world.

OBJECTIVES
1 To outline trade theory and protectionism.
2 To introduce the theory of customs unions.
3 To analyse the relationship between GATT and the EC.
4 To analyse the issues of trade creation and trade diversion.

Trade theory and economic history

Seventeenth-century attitudes to trade were dominated by mercantilism. Mercantilists believed that gold and silver bullion was the source of wealth and power. Non-producers could acquire bullion only by exporting more goods and services than were imported. In the crude version of the theory, the nation should ensure that it ran a balance of trade surplus with each and every trading partner. Consequently, the English East India Company was disliked in the early 17th century because it imported more than it exported. In a more sophisticated version of mercantilism, a deficit with one country did not matter provided there was a trade surplus overall. To achieve a surplus in conditions of (it was assumed) a fixed quantity of trade, it was necessary to impose a series of controls on trade, for example:

- *under the Navigation Acts all trade involving England (and Wales) had to occur in English ships or ships of the country with which it was trading;*

- *trade in goods from English colonies had to involve English ports;*

- *the export of textile machinery was prohibited;*

- *there were heavy (sometimes prohibitive) duties on both exports and imports.*

Mercantilism was a system of protectionism designed to increase English (and

Welsh) power and wealth at the expense of rivals. It is not surprising that in the late 17th century there was a series of Anglo-Dutch wars, in which two great trading countries fought over trade advantages. Similarly, the 18th century was characterised by trade and colonial wars – although this time with France.

It was against the background of a structure of protectionist measures that Adam Smith wrote *An Enquiry into the Nature and Causes of the Wealth of Nations* (1776). Smith argued against equating wealth with the nation's stock of gold. The wealth of a nation is determined by the annual flow of goods and services available to its inhabitants. This wealth can be increased by countries specialising in those forms of production for which they are most suited and then engaging in trade with other nations.

Fig. 12.1 illustrates Smith's theory of economic growth, in which emphasis is placed on division of labour, increased output and productivity, increased wealth and capital accumulation. The process is enhanced if the enlargement of markets through trade increases the degree of specialisation of labour. Moreover, by concentrating on those forms of production in which the country has an advantage, world output would increase – to the advantage of all concerned.

Smith's trade theory was extended by David Ricardo, who developed the notion of comparative (as distinct from absolute) advantage. Trade between nations can be mutually advantageous even though one trade partner has an absolute advantage in producing all goods. A country has comparative advantage in the production of a particular commodity either when its superiority is most marked or when its inferiority is least marked. By inferiority or superiority we mean efficiency in use of resources. The rule is that provided the rate of exchange between commodities lies between the

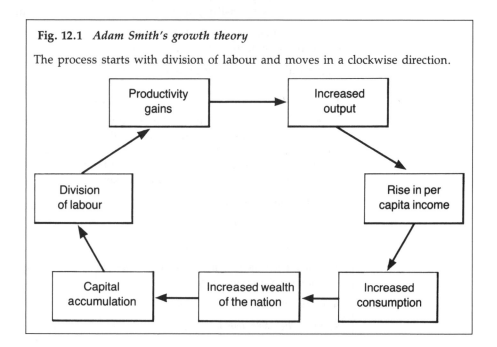

Fig. 12.1 *Adam Smith's growth theory*

The process starts with division of labour and moves in a clockwise direction.

opportunity cost ratios of the countries concerned, trade will benefit both countries (*see* Fig. 12.2). This is not to say that both countries benefit equally, but it does mean that both experience some positive benefit from specialising and trading. The rule also outlines the circumstances in which the benefits of trade are one-sided – that is, when one country benefits at the expense of another. If the rate of exchange lies outside the opportunity cost ratios, one country benefits whilst the other experiences negative results from trading. Belief that trade produces one-sided benefits for other countries has led some countries (especially in the developing world) to pursue a policy of autarky, or self-sufficiency, behind protective barriers. This is seen as an exception, however, and the main thrust of economic thinking in the UK has been to see trade as beneficial and, consequently, barriers to trade as harmful.

Fig. 12.2 *Trade theory and opportunity costs ratios*

In the graph opposite, Country A has an absolute advantage in both car and wheat production but a comparative advantage in car production. Country B is absolutely less efficient at both forms of production but nevertheless has a comparative advantage in wheat. This is because B's inferiority is less marked in the case of wheat whereas A's superiority is greater in cars. The theory of comparative advantage informs us that under specific circumstances trade will be mutually beneficial and, consequently, trade barriers mutually harmful.

Suppose the rate of exchange between the commodities was 1 car to 2 wheat. Consider the implications for the two countries:

Country A. By production, sacrifices 3 cars for 5 wheat
     By specialising and trading, can exchange 2 cars for 4 wheat

Country B. By production, sacrifices 4 wheat for 1 car
     By specialising and trading, can exchange 4 wheat for 2 cars

Trade is mutually beneficial because the exchange between commodities lies between the opportunity cost ratios, i.e.:

Opportunity cost ratio by production – A   3:5
                                                      – B   1:4
Trading ratio   1:2

If the trading ratio was outside the range we would have found that the benefits of trade were one-sided, thus justifying a measure of protection.

However, it is important to bear in mind that the theory of comparative advantage is based on a number of assumptions, the absence of which provides a reason for intervention in markets:

- *perfect mobility of factors;*

- *competition in all markets;*

- *no idle resources;*

- *constant returns to scale, i.e. no economies of scale, diseconomies of scale or diminishing marginal returns;*

- *no currency problems;*

- *relatively stable demand.*

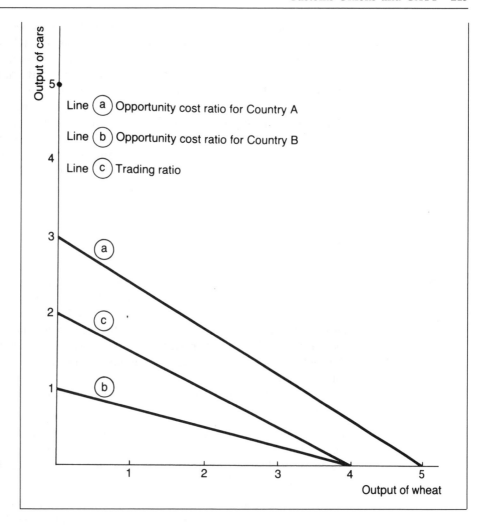

In the half-century after Smith and Ricardo, Britain moved in stages towards free trade. First Pitt, in the 1790s, and then Huskisson (1820s), Peel (1840s) and Gladstone (1850s), gradually removed the protectionist measures that impeded trade. The great symbolic victory of the free trade movement was the repeal of the Corn Laws in 1846. This removed the last measure of agricultural protection and represented a victory for the pro-free trade manufacturing community over the protectionist landed classes. With agricultural protection removed, the final completion of free trade was a relatively easy task and was achieved by 1860.

From 1860 there were no customs duties of a protective nature on imports into the UK. All export duties, prohibitions and quotas were also removed. As this was a time of expansion and growing prosperity, Victorians tended to equate free trade with prosperity. Consequently, even during the depressions of the late 19th century, there was no question of a return to protection. When the issue was put before the electorate in 1906, voters preferred the free trade Liberal Party to the Conservatives, who favoured tariffs and Imperial Preference.

Britain clung to its free trade policy during the 1920s despite the depression and despite the imposition of import controls elsewhere in the world. However, the world slump of the 1930s led to the abandonment of the policy. Tariffs, quotas and Imperial Preference characterised Britain's trade policy in the 1930s. Although this change in policy might have been necessary in the circumstances of the time, it did have unfortunate consequences. The competitive raising of tariffs reduced the volume of world trade: as a major trading and shipping nation, Britain consequently suffered. The considered view of most economists, historians and statesmen was that the 1930s protectionism slowed down world trade. Thus, there was a determination in the 1940s to learn the 'lessons of the 1930s'.

Protectionism

Ever since Adam Smith's *Wealth of Nations* there has been widespread acceptance of the desirability of free trade. By removing barriers each nation will specialise in those forms of production in which it has the greatest comparative advantage, and the result is likely to be mutually beneficial. Despite the benefits of free trade, protectionism is still widely practised – including by the EC countries, who erect barriers against non-EC goods. Before looking at the cases for and against protectionism, let us consider the forms it takes.

We can distinguish between traditional and new protectionism. The former includes:

1 *Tariffs* These import taxes do not prohibit imports but discourage them by raising their price. The effect of an import duty will depend upon the price elasticity of demand for the imported goods. The loss to the Community is illustrated in Fig. 12.3.

2 *Subsidies* These are given to home producers to enable them to compete in both home and overseas markets. Subsidies that artificially reduce the price of exports below cost price lead to 'dumping'.

3 *Quotas* These are quantitative controls on imports.

4 *Exchange controls* By denying residents access to foreign currencies, governments can control the quantity of imports and discriminate against certain forms of imports.

New protectionism (or non-tariff barriers) is a feature of the last third of the 20th century and has been used as a way of imposing import controls whilst remaining true to the letter, if not the spirit, of international obligations such as GATT. New protectionism, which tends to discriminate against particular countries and particular commodities, takes the form of:

1 *Administrative restrictions* Product safety laws have been used as a covert method of protection. Other bureaucratic procedures can be called into service, including the well-known example of France processing all imports of Japanese video recorders at the small and undermanned customs post at Poitiers.

Fig. 12.3 *The effects of tariffs*

1. In the absence of trade, equilibrium occurs at the intersection of the supply and demand curves.
2. When the domestic market is opened up, price falls to the world level of 0W. The line WW represents the supply curve for imports. At this world price quantity 0D is demanded but domestic producers are prepared to sell only 0A – hence imports are shown by the distance AD.
3. A tariff of WX is now imposed and the price rises to 0X. As a result there is:

   (a) a production effect in that domestic producers expand output to 0B (triangle P represents the loss in efficiency as a result of the increase in high-cost production);
   (b) a consumption effect in that, faced with a price rise, consumers reduce consumption to 0C (triangle C represents the cost in terms of reduced consumption);
   (c) a revenue effect in that the government gains revenue equal to box R.

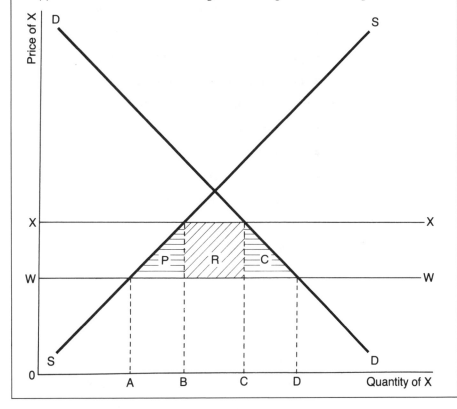

2 *Voluntary export restraints* EC countries have imposed voluntary export restraints on Japanese car producers. Although the inclusion of the word 'voluntary' suggests that both parties agreed, in practice the 'agreement' was the result of coercion. Failure to agree would have been followed by more damaging non-tariff barriers.

3 *Agricultural protection* The farm lobby in developed countries has demanded and gained protection, in the forms of state intervention in markets and import controls.

4 *Government contracts* In most economies the government is responsible for a high proportion of national expenditure, and in general there is a tendency to discriminate in favour of home producers and against foreign producers.

In relation to the EC it could be argued that the original conception of the common market involved the elimination of all traditional protectionism in intra-EC trade. The single market of 1993 eliminates all new protectionism from intra-EC trade.

The case against protection is based on the benefits of free trade and the costs of protection. It is argued that free trade results in:

- *specialisation by comparative advantage;*
- *production in the hands of efficient, low-cost producers;*
- *access to the cheapest source of supply;*
- *greater choice;*
- *global markets and economies of scale;*
- *dynamic gains from increased competition.*

On the other hand, import controls:

- *also act as export controls;*
- *protect inefficient, high-cost producers;*
- *reduce specialisation;*
- *raise prices to consumers;*
- *protect monopolists;*
- *result in complacency;*
- *reduce living standards;*
- *encourage resistance to structural change;*
- *push up exchange rates, thus adding to the problems of exporters;*
- *raise domestic costs, thus increasing the problems of selling in other markets;*
- *harm developing countries; and, most important of all,*
- *prevent specialisation by comparative advantage producing mutually beneficial gains from trade.*

The economic case for protectionism is based on the argument that market imperfections and externalities exist in the real world and the competitive model of trade theory is not valid. For instance, if trade is not mutually beneficial the nation that suffers as a result of trading will be inclined to impose tariffs. The principle of comparative advantage teaches us that trade is mutually beneficial provided the rate of exchange between commodities lies between the two opportunity cost ratios. Logically, if the rate of exchange lies outside the limits, trade produces one-sided benefits. This point is stressed to remind the reader that even classical theory does *not* conclude that trade is always beneficial.

We can list the arguments for protection:

- *to halt the drain of foreign currency reserves and thus improve the balance of payments;*
- *to prevent dumping;*
- *to promote the development of infant industries;*
- *to cushion the decline of major industries;*
- *to use as a bargaining weapon in trade negotiations;*
- *to prevent the benefits of a Keynesian reflationary package leaking abroad;*
- *to retaliate against import controls imposed against the country;*
- *to improve the terms of trade by imposing customs duties borne in part by the overseas supplier;*
- *to combat so-called 'unfair competition'.*

This last point is rather dubious in economic theory since, if foreign rivals possess the advantage of low-wage labour, it suggests that such countries do enjoy a comparative advantage in the form of production concerned. This being so it is hardly 'unfair'.

The economic validity of some of the other arguments is also in doubt but what we can say is that, although there might be a short-term case for protection, in the long run there is no justification. In the long run there is no sense in propping up monopolistic or inefficient producers of goods for which the country does not possess comparative advantage.

The theory of customs unions

The general thrust of economic theory is that free trade is preferable to restriction except in defined circumstances. Consequently, before 1950 economists assumed that, in the absence of universal free trade, partial free trade in the form of a customs union was preferable to restricted trade. This was based on the view that, being a step in the right direction, it must be preferable to restricted trade. However, such a view conflicts with the theory of 'second best'.

The general theory of second best states that 'unless all the conditions necessary for optimality can be achieved, it may not be desirable to achieve just some of them' (Winters, *International Economics*, p. 177). In other words, if universal free trade is the optimum situation it is a fallacy to believe that partial free trade is better than restricted trade. To illustrate this principle consider a cup of coffee: in the absence of sugar or milk, black and unsweetened coffee might be preferable to no coffee; in the absence of a spoonful of coffee, however, the combination of water, milk and sugar is not preferable to no drink at all.

The general theory of second best was applied to customs unions by Jacob Viner in 1950. He developed the idea of 'trade creation' as against 'trade diversion' in the analysis of customs unions. Organisations such as the EC create trade in that they increase the amount of trade. However, they also divert trade from non-union to union sources of goods. Consider the following:

- *in country X product A costs £10 per unit;*
- *in country Y it costs £8 per unit;*
- *in country Z it costs £6 per unit;*
- *X imposes a 100 per cent tariff on imports from Y and Z.*

In the situation above, country X has protected its home market against imports of product A by a high tariff which raises the price of imported goods above the domestic price. In these circumstances a customs union between X and Y would create trade since X would now import product A from Y. Thus a customs union is preferable to the pre-union situation.

Suppose that the tariff imposed by X was only 50 per cent. The price of domestic supplies of A remains £10, compared to £8 + 50% from Y and £6 + 50% from Z. Even with the 50 per cent tariff, supplies from Z are less expensive and so X would now import from Z. After the formation of the customs union between X and Y the situation changes. The price of domestic supplies remains £10 but supplies from Y are now free of tariff and are therefore priced at £8. This is cheaper than the £9 (£6 plus 50 per cent tariff) for imports from Z. Consequently, the effect of the customs union is to divert trade from Z (outside the customs union) to Y (inside the union). This situation arises in spite of Y being a higher cost producer than Z. This involves a social cost in that the second best is not preferable to the existing situation.

The theory of second best applied to customs unions can be summed up as follows.

1 Universal free trade improves resource allocation.

2 But limited free trade in the form of a customs union can, in certain circumstances, have the effect of reducing efficiency.

3 Whether the effect of the customs union is to increase or to reduce the efficiency of resource allocations depends upon the balance of trade creation against trade diversion. The former is preferred to the latter. In general, we can conclude that customs union is more likely to be beneficial:

(a) the larger the union;
(b) the higher the pre-union tariff;
(c) the lower the post-union external tariff;
(d) the greater the overlap between the production ranges of partners in the union.

These last points can be illustrated by reference to the EC. The greater the membership of the EC the greater the chance of including the lowest-cost producer. Hence the UK (one of the more outward looking and open of the EC economies) has always favoured enlargement of a looser customs union rather than a deepening of the relations of a small group of existing members. Taken to its logical conclusion the optimum situation is a customs union encompassing the whole world.

If tariffs within Western Europe were high prior to the formation of the EC there would have been considerable distortion in the European economy. The creation of the EC would have led to considerable trade creation. A high common external tariff would result in a high level of discrimination against non-EC producers and therefore the effect of the establishment of the EC would be trade diverting. It should be remembered that a factor in Britain's initial reluctance to join the EC was the effect on Commonwealth trade. This concern was partly political (the desire to tie the Commonwealth together by trade links) and partly economic. If membership of the EC resulted in trade diversion away from cheaper Commonwealth sources of supply it could be seen as detrimental to Britain.

The final point concerns the degree of overlap between the bundles of goods produced by union members. It is often said of the early EC that it was dominated by an alliance of German industry and French agriculture, suggesting that the economies of these two dominant members to an extent complemented each other. This led to considerable trade diversion towards German manufactures in France and French food in Germany. The development and enlargement of the EC have led to competition rather than complementing as the predominant characteristic of the EC economies. This increases the prospect of trade creation (additions to the volume of trade) rather than trade diversion (EC goods at the expense of non-EC goods).

General Agreement on Tariffs and Trade (GATT)

GATT emerged from the desire to avoid the mistakes of the 1930s. Competitive raising of tariffs had reduced world trade in the inter-war period and had prolonged the depression of the 1930s. Hence, parallel with the discussions that led to the International Monetary Fund, there were discussions on an International Trade Organisation (ITO), which was to have extensive powers over trade and the real economies of members. The ITO negotiations were inconclusive and this led 23 countries to sign a tariff reduction agreement, which became the General Agreement on Tariffs and Trade (signed in Havana, 1947).

The Preamble to GATT states that members enter into 'reciprocal and mutually advantageous arrangements directed to the substantial reduction of tariffs and other barriers to trade and to the elimination of discriminatory treatment in international commerce'. From this general statement we can identify a number of GATT principles for the conduct of trading relations.

1 *Non-discrimination* Discriminatory trade measures are contrary to GATT since each member state is required to grant 'most favoured nation' treatment to all other members. The Treaty of Rome, establishing the EEC, is contrary to the principles of non-discrimination: EC members *do* practise discrimination

in favour of fellow members and against non-members. However, the GATT agreement allows for regional groupings such as the EC. The most favoured nation clause is also in conflict with another basic principle in trade liberalisation: that of reciprocity. Readers with an understanding of 19th-century history will know that the moves towards free trade involved a series of reciprocity treaties, in which tariffs were reduced on a bilateral basis. The British intention was to prise open export markets by agreeing to reductions in import duties. The most favoured nation clause means that tariff reductions cannot be made bilaterally but must be offered to all other GATT members.

2 *National treatment* Once imports have crossed national boundaries they must receive equal treatment with domestically produced goods.

3 *Import quotas or quantitative controls* These are in general prohibited under GATT, although exceptions are permitted to alleviate a balance of payments crisis, or if a sudden rise in import causes serious injury to a competing domestic industry.

4 *Export subsidiaries* In the 1930s export subsidiaries were used by some governments as a way of ridding the country of surplus goods. This led to the practice known as dumping – or selling goods below cost price. Dumping is generally regarded as a 'beggar my neighbour' policy since it results in the 'export of unemployment'. Consequently export subsidiaries are generally prohibited except in the case of agricultural goods.

The work of GATT As well as being a treaty, GATT is also an international organisation. It has a staff of 400 based in Geneva. The main tasks of the GATT organisation are to:

- *monitor trade agreements;*

- *watch out for national policies that conflict with GATT agreements;*

- *arbitrate in trade disputes between members;*

- *provide the secretariat for meetings of ministers and/or their representatives in which further measures of trade liberalisation are discussed.*

These meetings have taken the form of eight (to date) 'rounds' of negotiations of GATT members (by 1992 membership had risen to 105 states).

The first five rounds were concerned with tariffs and substantial progress was made, especially in relation to trade in industrial goods. However, the concentration on industrial goods and the neglect of trade concessions in primary products caused dissatisfaction among the primary producing nations, who saw GATT as a 'rich man's club'.

The Haberler Report to GATT in 1958 emphasised that agricultural protectionism in industrial countries had 'minimised the benefits that the traditional food exporting countries could have expected to receive from their membership of GATT' (Kenwood and Lougheed, *The Growth of the International Economy 1820–1990*, p. 276). This report was written before the EC's CAP was established and before the decolonisation of Africa. The problem it highlighted was to grow in subsequent years despite:

- *the establishment of the Generalised System of Preferences (1971), in which OECD countries reduced tariffs on developing countries' manufactured exports below most favoured nation rates;*

- *the United Nations Conference on Trade and Development (UNCTAD). Established in 1964, UNCTAD is an organisation of developing countries which aims to improve their negotiating position* vis-à-vis *the developed countries.*

The Kennedy Round of GATT negotiations (1964–7) reduced tariffs on industrial goods by an average of 39 per cent but little progress was made in the agricultural sphere (because of the strength of the USA and the newly created EC). The Kennedy Round was followed by the Tokyo Round (1973–9). This Round was characterised by a greater desire to tackle the issue of agricultural protection. Nevertheless, the dominance of the USA and the EC meant that although tariff cuts on industrial goods averaged 30 per cent, there were smaller reductions on raw materials and temperate zone agricultural commodities (which in addition faced further non-tariff barriers).

The Tokyo Round did, however, attempt to deal with non-tariff barriers outside the agricultural sphere. These included public buying policies that discriminated against foreign suppliers, the use of technical standards as a way of blocking imports and the use of subsidies to enable domestically produced goods to undercut imports. Although some progress was made, it was less than hoped for:

> Given the extent to which non-tariff barriers ... had been introduced particularly in Europe to counter competition from Japan and the NICs [newly industrialising countries] the relatively minor agreements reached, highlighted the manner in which many of the fundamental trade problems which were supposed to receive the bulk of attention of the round, were side stepped in negotiations [Kenwood and Lougheed, *The Growth of the International Economy 1820–1990*, p. 282].

The latest round of multilateral trade negotiations is known as the Uruguay Round and dates from 1986. The developing countries, together with richer agricultural exporters such as Australia and Argentina (known as the Cairns Group), were determined that the Uruguay Round should result in substantial benefit for primary producers. As well as a simple north–south divide, the Uruguay Round was also characterised by a dispute between the USA and the EC (which negotiates on behalf of its member states). Before looking at the dispute in detail, we should appreciate some features of the EC which are contrary to the philosophy of GATT.

1 The EC customs union (allowed under the GATT) is discriminatory in that EC goods are given preference over non-EC goods.

2 The CAP involves protection for EC farmers against those from outside the Community (including the developing countries).

3 The EC has association agreements with EFTA and certain Mediterranean states. In addition, under the Lomé and Yaounde Conventions, the EC grants trade preference to specified countries in Africa, the Caribbean and the Pacific (the ACP countries). Such agreements favour certain countries at the expense of others and are therefore contrary to the 'most favoured nation' rule.

4 The Single European Act creates an internal market within the EC (by abolishing all non-tariff barriers). This means that there are non-tariff barriers against the non-EC members of GATT.

The task of negotiating on the EC's behalf rests with the External Affairs Commissioner (previously Frans Andriessen but now Sir Leon Brittan) and, given the importance of agriculture in GATT disputes, the Commissioner for Agriculture (formerly Ray MacSharry, now René Steichen).

The dangers of a failure of GATT negotiations

The Uruguay Round was bitter and protracted and on a number of occasions appeared to be on the brink of failure. One of the most contentious issues was the EC farm support policy, which was seen by both the Americans and the Cairns Group of food-producing nations as excessively protectionist especially as it involved subsidies for exports. The latter are always seen in a GATT context as 'dumping'. Success at GATT required an EC commitment to reduce support for farmers. As Director-General of GATT, Arthur Dunkel called for a 36 per cent reduction in export subsidies and a reduction in internal farm support.

As we will see in chapter 16, reform of the CAP is supported by the British government because of the burdens it places on the EC budget and because of the way it distorts the market. Consequently, many of the demands of the USA and the Cairns Group were acceptable to the British – but not to the French and other EC nations where agriculture is economically or politically important. The French and the EC negotiator feared that the GATT proposals would lead to a 40 per cent reduction in agricultural employment throughout the EC. Given the militancy of French farmers there was a reluctance to accept the GATT demands.

A compromise was reached on farm subsidies when the outgoing Commissioner for Agriculture, Ray MacSharry, agreed to reduce the volume of subsidised farm exports by 21 per cent by 1998 and to a freezing of the oilseed rape acreage. UK Prime Minister Major stated that the November 1992 compromise was 'the most important trade deal ever' but a final GATT settlement was still a long way off due to other disputes. And the French farmers are still unhappy about the November 1992 compromise. The final outcome of the Uruguay Round is still unclear, and we should be most aware of the costs to the British economy of a failure to agree.

Britain, like the other EC members, is not separately represented at GATT talks. The EC 12 are treated as a single bloc notwithstanding the differences in national interests. What concerns the UK is that the developed world will divide into three trading blocs: the EC, the North American Free Trade Area and the Pacific Rim countries. Although a rising proportion of its trade is with the other EC states, the UK is always anxious to keep open trade links with the rest of the world. Britain has always sought increased trade with the EC but, ideally, as an addition to, rather than instead of, trade with other countries. A division of the world into protectionist trading blocs will at the very least slow down the growth of world trade. Britain has always prospered in periods of growing world trade – and has always been especially harmed by any reduction in it. It is not just that UK exports to the *non*-EC world will suffer – any reduction in, say, German exports to the rest of the world could have a knock-on effect in terms of lost UK exports to Germany.

Britain is also concerned about GATT failure in terms of lost opportunities. The Uruguay Round promised a liberalisation of trade in services (which at present accounts for 19 per cent of world trade). If there is an agreement on the Uruguay Round, banks and insurance companies will operate freely across national boundaries; national telecommunications monopolies will be dismantled; shipping and civil aviation will be liberalised. As these are all areas in which the UK is particularly strong, a GATT agreement which includes such provisions would be especially beneficial to Britain.

Finally, a successful Uruguay Round will help lift the world out of the recession of the early 1990s, adding $4,000 billion to world output. Failure will prolong the recession in the same way that competitive tariff-raising prolonged the 1930s depression. However, one impediment to agreement during a recession is the protectionist instincts of some but not all national leaders. It seems that in the good times free trade supporters hold sway – in a downturn there is a swing to protectionism even though such measures are ultimately self-defeating.

Fig. 12.4 summarises what has been said about GATT.

Fig. 12.4 *General Agreement on Tariffs and Trade (GATT)*

Objectives
1. To reduce trade barriers
2. To prevent the establishment of new barriers
3. To prevent discriminatory trade practices
4. To prohibit subsidies and export quotas
5. To extend most favoured nation treatment
6. To promote consultation rather than unilateral action
7. To promote multinational trade links

Exceptions to GATT principles
1. Free trade area
2. Special circumstances such as a balance of payments deficit
3. Developing countries

The main concerns in the Uruguay Round
1. To bring trade in agriculture and textiles fully within the GATT system
2. To achieve further reductions in tariff and non-tariff barriers
3. To extend GATT to new areas such as intellectual property, investment and services
4. To strengthen the GATT system so that it can deal more effectively with trade distortions and disputes

CHAPTER 13

The Single Market

By the single market we mean a situation in which trade across national frontiers is conducted on the same basis as trade within a member state. European leaders set themselves the target of a single market, free of all barriers, by 1 January 1993. The benefits to firms, employees and – most of all – to consumers were claimed to be substantial: new market opportunities, increased efficiency through greater competition, and freedom from frontier checks.

OBJECTIVES 1 To outline the process leading to the Single European Act.
2 To explain the nature of non-tariff barriers.
3 To explain the benefits of the single market.
4 To explain and analyse EC law on competition and state aid to industry.
5 To analyse the impact on British business.

Background

Under the 1957 Treaty of Rome, member states (six at the time) agreed a timetable for the removal of tariff barriers and fixing a common external tariff. Forming a customs union was the first stage in the process of creating a common market. Progress toward the original ideal was rapid. In 1960 the Council of Ministers agreed to accelerate the removal of internal barriers and the erection of a common external tariff.

There was a marked slowing down in the process of the Community in the mid-1960s. The 1965 crisis in which France (led by President de Gaulle) withdrew from participation in the business of the EC led to a suspension of progress towards further European integration. By the time de Gaulle had been replaced by the more accommodating President Pompidou the economic environment had changed significantly. The early 1970s were characterised by stagflation and the 1973 crisis over oil prices. National governments were not able to raise tariffs or quotas against other members of the EC and consequently they devised non-tariff ways of reserving domestic markets for domestic producers. These non-tariff barriers (clearly contrary to the spirit and letter of the Treaty of Rome) took the form of:

- *state aid to industry;*
- *national specifications on product safety;*
- *customs formalities;*
- *public procurement policies.*

The Community institutions worked to enforce what had already been agreed. There was little scope for any progress on additional measures.

It should also be remembered that this was the period of the first enlargement of the EC, when the UK, Ireland and Denmark joined. Inevitably, effort was directed to the process of enlargement rather than to deepening the EC. After accession there was a period of adjustment to bring the newcomers to the same stage of integration as the original six. The dispute over the British contribution to the budget (settled at Fontainebleau in 1984) also delayed progress.

In 1985 a new Commission, headed by Jacques Delors, took office. One of the two commissioners from Britain was Lord Cockfield, who had been Secretary of State for Trade and Industry in the Thatcher government. Cockfield, given the key Commission portfolio of Trade and Industry, produced a paper on freeing the internal market from non-tariff barriers to trade in goods, services, people and capital. He specified 300 separate measures, which covered:

- *the harmonisation of technical standards;*
- *opening up public procurement to intra-EC competition;*
- *the removal of barriers to free trade in services;*
- *removal of exchange control to allow free movement of capital;*
- *the harmonisation of indirect taxation;*
- *the removal of physical frontier controls between member states.*

The Cockfield proposals fitted the non-interventionist philosophy of Thatcher and her government. This was one aspect of the process of EC deepening of which she would approve and Britain had the opportunity to demonstrate its credentials as a 'committed' rather than 'reluctant' European. Other member governments came round to the idea of the internal market after pressure from the European business community. Europe's industrialists and business leaders saw the advantage in removing non-tariff barriers.

The proposals were agreed at the Milan European Council of June 1985. However, against Thatcher's wishes the internal market proposals became linked with the question of institutional reform of the EC. Up to this point decision-making in the Council of Ministers and European Council (the Euro-summit) had been on the basis of unanimity. This meant that all members could veto any measure deemed contrary to national interests. In consequence, the progress of the EC was dictated by the pace of the 'slowest ship in the convoy'. Institutional reform would involve replacing unanimity with majority voting in which Britain (or indeed any other member) could be committed to a proposal against its wishes. The Milan Council led to an inter-governmental conference (IGC). Thatcher continued to oppose majority voting, but Foreign Secretary Geoffrey Howe persuaded her that other members would accept the Cockfield proposals only if there was an agreement on majority voting.

The IGC led to the Single European Act (SEA), which was signed in 1986 and ratified by national parliaments in 1987.

The Single European Act 1986

The SEA represented an important amendment to the Treaty of Rome. Its stated aims (*see* Illustration 13.1, which reproduces the Preamble) are to provide greater impetus to the achievement of the objectives of the founding treaties of the EC.

1 To transform relations between member states into a real European union.

2 To achieve a common foreign policy.

3 To promote democracy.

4 For the member states to speak with one voice.

5 To protect EC freedoms and human rights.

6 To extend the common policies.

7 To facilitate the exercise by the Commission of its powers.

8 To work towards economic integration with economic and monetary union.

9 To work towards the protection of the general and working environment.

Although wide-ranging, the key elements in the SEA relate to qualified majority voting (QMV) in the Council of Ministers and the completion of the single or internal market. QMV is important in that it is designed to speed decision-making by eliminating the national veto, except on issues of great importance to particular member states. The issue of QMV was dealt with in chapter 10 and the rest of this chapter will concentrate on the trade issues.

Article 13 of the SEA states:

> The Community shall adopt measures with the aim of progressively establishing the internal market over a period expiring on 31 December 1992 ...
>
> The internal market shall comprise an area without internal frontiers in which the free movement of goods, persons, services and capital is ensured in accordance with the provisions of this treaty.

Articles 14 and 15 lay down that the Council shall act by QMV to ensure balanced progress in all sectors concerned. Although derogations (exemptions) are permitted in order to take account of special national circumstances,

Illustration 13.1 *Preamble to the Single European Act 1986*

[The sovereign rulers of the twelve countries]

MOVED by the will to continue the work undertaken on the basis of the Treaties establishing the European Communities and to transform relations as a whole among their States into a European Union, in accordance with the Solemn Declaration of Stuttgart of 19 June 1983,

RESOLVED to implement this European Union on the basis, firstly, of the Communities operating in accordance with their own rules and, secondly, of European Cooperation among the Signatory States in the sphere of foreign policy and to invest this union with the necessary means of action,

DETERMINED to work together to promote democracy on the basis of the fundamental rights recognized in the constitutions and laws of the Member States, in the Convention for the Protection of Human Rights and Fundamental Freedoms and the European Social Charter, notably freedom, equality and social justice,

CONVINCED that the European idea, the results achieved in the fields of economic integration and political cooperation, and the need for new developments correspond to the wishes of the democratic peoples of Europe, for whom the European Parliament, elected by universal suffrage, is an indispensable means of expression,

AWARE of the responsibility incumbent upon Europe to aim at speaking ever increasingly with one voice and to act with consistency and solidarity in order more effectively to protect its common interests and independence, in particular to display the principles of democracy and compliance with the law and with human rights to which they are attached, so that together they may make their own contribution to the preservation of international peace and security in accordance with the undertaking entered into by them within the framework of the United Nations Charter,

DETERMINED to improve the economic and social situation by extending common policies and pursuing new objectives, and to ensure a smoother functioning of the Communities by enabling the institutions to exercise their powers under conditions most in keeping with Community interests,

WHEREAS at their Conference in Paris from 19 to 21 October 1972 the Heads of State or of Government approved the objective of the progressive realization of Economic and Monetary Union,

HAVING REGARD to the Annex to the conclusions of the Presidency of the European Council in Bremen on 6 and 7 July 1978 and the Resolution of the European Council in Brussels on 5 December 1978 on the introduction of the European Monetary System (EMS) and related questions, and noting that in accordance with that Resolution, the Community and the Central Banks of the Member States have taken a number of measures intended to implement monetary cooperation,

HAVE DECIDED to adopt this Act

these derogations 'must be of a temporary nature and must cause the least possible disturbance to the functioning of the common market'.

Non-tariff barriers

The single market initiative is designed to eliminate the non-tariff barriers which impede trade between member states. These barriers are of three kinds.

1 *Physical barriers* This refers to lengthy delays at border crossings and the documentation associated with movement between member states. For as long as frontier, customs and immigration controls continue to exist, trade between members will be different from trade within a member state.

2 *Technical barriers* This term covers a range of regulations relating to product specifications. For instance, differences between member states' regulations on product safety or pollution controls impede trade between member states. In fact, such rules on product specification can be and have been manipulated as a form of import control. Also included in technical barriers are policies relating to public sector procurement (i.e. government contracts with private sector firms for construction work or the supply of materials). Traditionally, governments have discriminated in favour of domestic suppliers with the result that a high proportion of a member state's national expenditure was blocked to non-nationals including fellow members of the EC. Under the SEA such discrimination is prohibited and public sector announcements for the tendering of goods and services have to be placed in the Official Bulletin of the EC.

3 *Fiscal barriers* Different rates of expenditure taxes, most notably VAT, can result in discrimination against products of other member states. For instance, a high tax on wine but low tax on beer is discriminatory: it will result in a stimulation of beer sales to the detriment of wine sales. In effect it protects domestic UK producers of alcoholic products by reducing imports of wine from fellow member states such as France, Italy and Germany.

The benefits of the single market

Although most government pronouncements on the single market (e.g. the DTI's Enterprise Initiative) have concentrated on the effect on business, the benefits of the single market may be expressed in terms of increasing consumer welfare by:

- *eliminating inefficient producers;*
- *eliminating monopoly power and monopoly profit;*
- *reducing prices;*
- *increasing per capita national income.*

The most important study of the likely benefits of the single market was undertaken by a group led by Paolo Cecchini. The Cecchini Report was published (by Wildwood House) as *The European Challenge 1992: The benefits of a Single Market*. In his report Cecchini analysed and quantified the 'costs of non-Europe': the costs resulting from the failure to complete the internal market. From this he was able to quantify the benefits of completing the single market.

Cecchini's conclusions are summarised in Tables 13.1 and 13.2, but it is necessary to explain how he reached the overall conclusion. Cecchini estimated that frontier delays add 1.8 per cent to the price of traded goods; technical barriers a further 2 per cent. Once these obstacles are removed not only will costs and therefore prices fall but there will be an increase in trade between member states. This will lead to increased competition and further cost and price reductions as the efficient producers drive out the inefficient. As the efficient increase in size they will benefit from further economies of scale. In total, Cecchini estimated that the single market will add around 6 per cent to Europe's GDP, thus benefiting the peoples of the EC. In addition, the creation of a single market will result in the development of EC producers

Table 13.1 *Single market: estimated gains*

Source of gain	Billion ECU	% GDP
Barriers to trade	8–9	0.2–0.3
Barriers to production	57–71	2.0–2.4
Economies of scale	61	2.1
Increased competition	46	1.6
Total EC-7 (1985 prices)	127–187	4.3–6.4
Estimate EC-12 (1988 prices)	174–258	4.3–6.4
Mid-point	216	5.3

Source: Cecchini Report

Table 13.2 *Estimated macro-economic consequences of completion of single market*

Source of gain	GDP % change	Consumer prices % change	Employment change (mn)	Budget balance change (% points of GDP)	External balance change (% points of GDP)
Customs barriers	0.4	−1.0	200	0.2	0.2
Public procurement	0.5	−1.4	350	0.3	0.1
Financial services	1.5	−1.4	400	1.1	0.3
Supply effects	2.1	−2.3	850	0.6	0.4
AGGREGATE	4.5	−6.1	1,800	2.2	1.0

Source: Cecchini Report

large enough to compete with the industrial giants of the USA and Japan, adding to the economic advantages of completing the internal market. In terms of these dynamic effects Cecchini might indeed have underestimated the impact of the single market.

However, it is necessary to add a note of caution. First, it is likely that residual non-tariff barriers will persist, especially in those member states concerned that the removal of frontiers will enable terrorists and drugs to move more freely between member states. Critics of Cecchini's research argue that the lower figure in each band in Table 13.1 is the more probable effect of the single market. Second, a two-speed Europe exists whether or not it is officially recognised. Europe consists of an inner core of fully integrated states and an outer group where non-tariff barriers persist. This will reduce the overall benefit of the 1992 initiative for the simple reason that the process will not be fully completed.

Third, economic and monetary union will not be completed under the SEA. It is doubtful whether the potential benefits of a single market can be realised when member states operate independent monetary and exchange rates policies. 'These may continue to distort the allocation of resources in the Community and depress the overall level of economic activity in the interests of maintaining some specific policy objectives in one member state which are incompatible with those in other countries' (Vickerman, *The Single European Market*, p. 14).

Fourth, the impact of the single market measures will vary from sector to sector. A major determinant of the impact of the SEA on particular sectors is the extent to which trade is currently constrained by non-tariff barriers. Cecchini grouped 12 industrial sectors according to the height of technical barriers:

1 *High*
   Electrical engineering
   Mechanical engineering
   Pharmaceuticals
   Food, alcohol and tobacco

2 *Medium*
   Automobiles
   Office equipment
   Rubber products
   Metallic products

3 *Low*
   Oil refining
   Footwear and clothing
   Plastics
   Paper and printing

The industries in the high barrier group will experience the greatest effect of the completion of the single market. Fortunately for the UK, it possesses comparative strength in three of the four sectors (the exception being mechanical engineering). The completion of the single market will thus present opportunities (rather than threats) to British firms in these sectors. It does, however, assume that UK firms continue to be efficient and are geared up to take advantage of the 1992 opportunities.

Dismantling technical barriers to trade

Differences in national laws on product safety constitute technical barriers to trade. Harmonisation is thus essential to the achievement of a single market. Current directives on this issue are based on the 'New Approach to Technical Harmonisation and Standards' agreed by the EC Council of Ministers in 1985. 'New approach' directives set up essential requirements, expressed in general terms, which must be met before products may be sold anywhere in the Community. European standards fill in the detail and are the main way for businesses to meet the essential requirements. Products meeting the requirements carry the 'CE' mark, which means that they may be sold throughout the Community.

Consider toy safety as an example of technical harmonisation: under the UK Toys (Safety) Regulations 1989, children's toys supplied in the UK must:

- *be made wholly to BS 5665 (or the equivalent standard in other EC countries); or*

- *be made to a prototype approved by an independent body;*

- *carry the CE mark and other information (generally about the manufacturer); and*

- *in some cases, carry warning notices.*

There are penalties (£2,000 or up to six months' imprisonment) for supplying toys which do not satisfy these requirements. UK toy manufacturers may well incur costs in complying with the standards laid down. However, having complied, harmonisation will ensure that exports will not be impeded by technical barriers elsewhere in the 12 member states.

As well as eliminating existing barriers to trade and establishing a single market, the EC is concerned to prevent any new technical barriers arising. Therefore EC directives of 1983 and 1988 set out procedures for the provision of information on new technical standards and regulations. Under the procedure member states must send a draft of any new technical regulation to the Commission. Except in an emergency, there is a three-month stand-still before the draft regulation can be enforced. During that time other member states or the Commission can make comments, which must be taken into account before the final regulation is issued. If the comments constitute a 'detailed opinion', including reasons for believing the proposed regulation would constitute a barrier to the free movement of goods, the stand-still can be extended for a further three months. If the proposed regulation relates to a subject covered by a proposal for an EC directive or regulation, a 12-month stand-still applies. Obviously, in the final analysis a dispute on technical standards can be referred to the European Court of Justice for a final decision.

Fiscal harmonisation

To complete the single market it is necessary to introduce some degree of harmonisation in the taxation systems of EC member states. The Commission has proposed a number of measures of fiscal harmonisation but all have been the subject of controversy. Before looking at specific issues we need to understand why harmonisation is necessary.

Alcohol is subject to a specific excise duty in the UK. This applies both to drinks produced in the UK and to imported drinks. The fact that it is imposed on domestic and imported supplies suggests that it is not discriminatory and is therefore consistent with the principle of the customs union. Suppose, however, that the rate of duty on wine was high and that on beer and whisky low. Admittedly, the high rate on wine applies equally to English and to French wine but the UK is not a major wine producer, whereas it is a major producer of beer and Scotland is the home of whisky production. The different rates of duty result in beer and whisky being cheaper than would otherwise be the case, and wine substantially more expensive. This distorts the market against the imported product (wine) and in favour of the home-produced drinks (beer and whisky). Distortion of the market by such policies is clearly contrary to the single market.

Value added tax (VAT) was adopted as a Community-wide system of indirect taxation and is charged on the supply of a wide range of goods and services. The tax is charged on the additional value of each transaction in the chain of production. A business pays VAT on its purchases of inputs, and charges VAT on sales of its outputs – and in the UK accounts to Customs and Excise for the difference. In the end the tax is borne by the final consumer. Within the EC it is charged on the destination principle (at the rate which applies in the country where it is sold) rather than the origin principle (the rate in the country of production). Although the basic system is Community-wide there are major differences between member states in both the VAT base and the rates of VAT (*see* Table 13.3).

The Commission has directed most of its efforts to harmonising the VAT base rather than tackling the difficult task of harmonising VAT rates. EC directives have listed goods and services that should be exempted from VAT, e.g. health and education services. This is in keeping with practice in member states and is not a source of great controversy. What has been acrimonious, however, is the issue of zero-rating. As Table 13.3 shows, zero-rating is widely used in Ireland and the UK but not elsewhere in the Community. Zero-rating is not the same as being exempt: zero-rated goods are subject to VAT but at a rate of 0 per cent. Thus suppliers can claim back VAT paid on inputs (which is not the case with suppliers of goods exempt from VAT). Zero-rating applies to

- *food (but not chocolate, crisps or snacks);*

- *books, magazines, newspapers;*

- *fuel and power to final consumers (but domestic fuel will be subject to VAT from 1994);*

- *transport;*

Table 13.3 *VAT across the Community*

	Standard rate (%)	*Increased rate (%)*	*Reduced rate (%)*	*Extent of zero-rating*
Belgium	19.5	None	1, 6, 12	Minimal
Denmark	25.0	None	None	Minimal
France	18.6	None	2.1, 5.5	None
Germany	15.0	None	7	None
Greece	18.0	None	4, 8	Minimal
Ireland	21.0	None	2.7, 10, 12.5, 16	Wide
Italy	19.0	38	4, 9, 12	Minimal
Luxembourg	15.0	None	3, 6	None
The Netherlands	18.5	None	6	None
Portugal	16.0	30	5	None
Spain	15.0	28	6	Minimal
UK	17.5	None	None	Wide

Source: *Single Market News*, Winter 1992

- *medicines;*

- *children's clothing and footwear;*

- *exports.*

The system of zero-rating distorts the market in favour of zero-rated goods and this is why the Commission and other members are anxious to end the anomaly. The UK argued against Commission proposals on the basis that:

- *the rates and coverage of taxation are matters for national governments and parliaments – not for a supra-national organisation;*

- *zero-rating applies to basic necessities and primarily benefits low-income groups. In fact the Thatcher government argued that the removal of zero-rating from necessities (which absorbed a high percentage of the expenditure of low-income groups) would penalise the less well off in society. The spectre of the EC forcing the UK to tax children's shoes outraged the Euro-sceptics, especially in the tabloid press. VAT on books and newspapers was also 'denounced as a tax on knowledge'.*

Compromise was eventually reached at an ECOFIN meeting in 1991. Britain and Ireland were permitted to retain their zero-rating, but:

- *the range of zero-rated goods was reduced (e.g. water, fuel and power supplied to other than final consumers became chargeable);*

- *no extension of zero-rating to other goods and services would be permitted;*

- *once a good or service ceases to be zero-rated, it cannot resume its privileged status without approval by the Council of Ministers.*

Fig. 13.1 *Completion of the single market*

1985: European Community launches plans for single market; 282 necessary measures outlined.

1987: Political backing provided as the Single European Act comes into force.

1989: A market worth 15 per cent of the EC's GNP begins to open with first competitive tenders to public contracts.

1990: Money moves freely as exchange controls are lifted in most of the EC.

1991: Graduates' qualifications increasingly recognised across the Community.

January 1993: No border checks for goods as the frontier-controlled VAT and excise system is abolished, together with 60 million tax forms.
Government curbs on air fares lifted.
Banks free to set up branches anywhere in the Community.
Exchange controls to end, but Greece given extension.
Pending: Passport checks for internal EC flights should end in December 1993, but UK, Denmark and Ireland may resist.

1994: Higher education diplomas recognised throughout the EC.
Open competition for all public authority contracts, including utilities.
Insurance companies free to set up and sell policies across frontiers.

1996: Stockbrokers get 'single passport' to operate anywhere in the EC.
Banks able to deal on all EC stock exchanges except in Greece, Portugal and Spain.

1997: Single VAT system applied to traders and consumers, if member states agree to a permanent change.
Airlines can fly any route within the EC.

1999: Duty-free sales end on internal flights and ferry crossings.

2000: Free internal market in cars – deadline for removing all controls on Japanese imports.

Continuing problems:
Original plan: Five per cent of 1985 measures still to be adopted at Community level.

National measures: EC directives cannot be fully implemented unless they are transformed into national legislation. Between 20 and 30 per cent of EC measures have still to be enacted in most countries.

Energy: No agreement in sight for consumers to buy gas and electricity from any Community supplier.

Telecommunications: Competition in equipment and services, but no legislation yet to open up monopolies in ordinary telephone calls.

Postal services: Gradual liberalisation promised, but no legislation drafted so far.

Company law: Directive harmonising take-over procedure under review; voluntary European Company Statute for multinationals stalled.

Monetary union: By 1999, according to Maastricht, depending on strict economic conditions.

Source: Adapted from the *Financial Times*, 4 January 1993

The extent of the agreement on rates is that the standard rate of VAT should be in the 14–20 per cent band (to which the UK complies). A reduced rate of not lower than 5 per cent is available on a specified list of goods and services:

- *foodstuffs;*
- *water supplies;*
- *pharmaceutical products;*
- *medical equipment;*
- *passenger transport;*
- *books, newspapers;*
- *social housing;*
- *admission to performing arts, libraries, exhibitions, etc.;*
- *farm inputs;*
- *hotel accommodation;*
- *charities;*
- *street cleaning;*
- *funeral undertakings.*

Three points should be made about the reduced rate list. First, member states are permitted, but not required, to impose VAT at the reduced rate on these items. Second, Britain's zero-rate is an exception to the minimum rate (which should not be lower than 5 per cent). Finally, by specifying the goods and services to which it could apply an attempt is being made to prevent or at least reduce distortions in the market.

Fig. 13.1 summarises the steps taken – and those yet to be taken – towards completing the single market.

EC competition law

According to the EC publication *EEC Competition Policy in the Single Market*, EC competition law:

> provides for the establishment of a system to ensure that competition in the common market is not distorted. The objective of market integration is as important as the traditional role which competition plays in free market economies ensuring efficient allocations of resources, stimulating enterprises to make the best use of their know-how and skills and encouraging them to develop new research techniques and products.

Article 85 of the Treaty of Rome prohibits, as incompatible with the common market, agreements which have as their object or effect the prevention, restriction or distortion of competition within the common market and which may affect trade between member states. The article then goes on to list as examples of prohibited agreements, those which:

- *fix prices;*

- *limit output;*

- *limit technical development;*

- *limit investment;*

- *share out markets;*

- *apply dissimilar conditions to equivalent transactions with other trading parties, thereby placing them at competitive disadvantage;*

- *make the conclusion of contracts subject to acceptance by other parties of supplementary obligations.*

The article makes void agreements which do any of these things. However, like the UK 'gateways' (*see* chapter 4), exemptions are allowed if they:

contribute to improving the production or distribution of goods or to promoting technical or economic progress, while allowing consumers a fair share of the resulting benefit, and which do not:

a. impose on the undertakings concerned restrictions which are not indispensable to the attainment of these objectives
b. afford such undertakings the possibility of eliminating competition in respect of a substantial part of the products in question.

Article 86 relates to dominant firm situations. Again, it states that abuse of a dominant position within the common market (or in a substantial part of it) is incompatible with the common market in so far as it may affect trade between member states. Two points emerge from this: EC law is concerned with the abuse of a dominant position in the market, but only when such practice affects trade between member states.

EC regulation of mergers is a more recent innovation. With effect from 1990, all cross-border mergers of undertakings with a combined worldwide turnover of 5 billion ECUs or more, or an EC-wide turnover of 250 million ECUs, must be notified to the Commission to gain approval. The regulation defines merger as 'taking control' and therefore it includes a variety of ways of joining firms together other than outright merger. The only exception allowed under the Merger Regulation is where the firms concerned undertake two-thirds of their business in one and the same member state.

In EC competition law the Commission plays a pivotal role. It can:

- *issue regulations which have direct effect in member states;*

- *issue directives requiring national legislation;*

- *issue notices (to the government of a member state requiring it to put an end to the infringement of a regulation);*

- *enforce competition law;*

- *impose fines;*

- *declare void anti-competitive practices;*

- *demand information;*

- *organise 'dawn raids' to search premises.*

Obviously, any Commission action in these matters can be the subject of an appeal to the European Court of Justice, which is charged with the duty of interpreting the provisions of the treaty (in this case articles 85 and 86) and the actions of EC institutions.

State aid to industry

All state aid to firms or to industry is discriminatory, in that it benefits specific undertakings at the expense of others. As a result, state aid distorts the market and, where it affects trade across national borders with the EC, can be judged incompatible with the common market. Like other aspects, if the state aid has a purely local impact with no ramifications for inter-member trade, the EC is not involved. However, where inter-member trade is affected, the Commission is able to require the state concerned to abolish or alter the offending forms of state assistance.

The relevant part of the Treaty of Rome 1957 is article 92-4, which states that 'aid . . . in any form whatsoever which distorts or threatens to distort competition by favouring certain undertakings or the production of certain goods shall, in so far as it affects trade between Member States, be incompatible with the Common Market'. The treaty goes on to list aid which *is* compatible with the common market:

- *aid having a social character, granted to individual consumers, provided such aid is granted without discrimination related to the origin of the products concerned;*

- *aid to make good the damage caused by natural disasters;*

- *aid granted to the economy of certain parts of the Federal Republic of Germany affected by the division of Germany (obsolete since reunification).*

In addition, other forms of aid may be considered to be compatible with the common market:

- *aid to promote the economic development of areas where the standard of living is abnormally low or where there is serious unemployment;*

- *aid to promote the execution of an important project of common European interest or to remedy a serious disturbance in the economy of a member state;*

- *aid to facilitate the development of certain economic activities or certain economic areas, where such aid does not adversely affect trading conditions to an extent contrary to the common interest;*

■ *such other categories of aid as may be specified by decision of the Council acting by a qualified majority on a proposal from the Commission.*

Examples of such aid include aid to:

■ *correct regional imbalance;*

■ *help accelerate industrial growth and/or change;*

■ *neutralise distortions of competition due to outside factors;*

■ *allow certain industries to be run down without too much social distress. Aid for declining industries must, however, preserve the status quo, be part of a reorganisation plan, and any investment assistance must not expand capacity.*

The treaty clearly gives the Commission considerable discretion on decisions relating to the validity of state aid. Although there are exemptions to the prohibition on state aid, there has recently been a tendency for the

---

Illustration 13.2 *British Aerospace and Rover v. EC Commission*

In 1974 the ailing motor manufacturer British Leyland was taken into public ownership because of the importance of the company both to the balance of payments and to employment. After restructuring, considerable plant closure and job losses the car company, now called Rover, was prepared for privatisation. Because of its past history and the continuing problems of the British motor industry a share issue was not considered an appropriate way of privatising Rover and in 1988 it was sold to the already privatised British Aerospace (BAe). What was not revealed at the time was a £44-million financial concession made by the UK government to BAe. This concession (labelled 'a sweetener' by the press) was heavily criticised by opposition politicians (who tended to see it as an example of giving away rather than selling the family silver) and by the EC Commission, which argued that it constituted illegal aid under article 92(1) of the Treaty of Rome. The article states:

Save as otherwise provided in this Treaty, any aid granted by a Member State or through State resources in any form whatsoever which distorts or threatens to distort competition by favouring certain undertakings or the production of certain goods shall, in so far as it affects trade between Member States, be incompatible with the Common Market.

The Commission ordered BAe to pay the £44 million back to the UK government because it was illegal aid and because it was in breach of a previous decision (17 July 1990) which had stipulated various conditions surrounding the sale of Rover to BAe.

BAe and Rover applied to the European Court of Justice for an annulment of the Commission decision relating to repayment of the £44 million. The Court accepted the applicants' contention that there had been a procedural violation in the Commission's decision of July 1990 – in other words, because of a technicality BAe would not be forced to repay the money.

Commission to look more critically at it – especially when Sir Leon Brittan was commissioner responsible for competition policy (1989–92). The powers of the Commission extend beyond requiring member states to desist: it can order a member state to recover the illegal payments (e.g. the *British Aerospace/Rover* case; *see* Illustration 13.2). From the perspective of an individual member state, EC regulations on state aid act as a constraint on economic policy-making, but help to ensure that its business enterprises compete on a 'level playing field' throughout the EC.

Free movement of workers

The free movement of workers provided for under the Treaty of Rome has both social and economic implications. Enabling workers to move freely within the Community allows employers to draw on a larger pool of labour whilst at the same time permitting EC residents to move in search of work and improved pay. Logically, it should lead to a movement from areas of high unemployment (such as some of the impoverished parts of the southern member states) to areas of high employment.

Article 48 of the treaty states that freedom of movement shall be secured by the end of the transitional period (allowed to each new member before all the rules apply – now expired for all 12 members) and that such freedom of movement shall entail the abolition of any discrimination based on nationality as regards employment, pay and conditions (although there is a derogation relating to employment in the public sector). The article grants EC nationals the right to:

- *accept work in other EC states;*
- *move freely within member states;*
- *stay in a member state for the purpose of employment under the same provisions governing the employment of nationals of that state;*
- *remain in the country after employment in that state.*

The treaty entitles citizens of EC countries to move freely within the Community, but we know that there are constraints on the movement of workers (e.g. the tax and benefit system, children's education, etc.). Consequently, if the right of free movement is to be meaningful, it is essential that measures are taken to enhance the mobility of labour to ensure that advantage can be taken of the right. This required secondary legislation relating to:

- *conditions of employment;*
- *rights of residence;*
- *the families of migrant workers;*
- *equality in conditions of employment;*
- *taxation;*

- *entitlement to social benefit;*

- *children's education.*

Of particular interest in relation to the last point, children of migrant workers are to be admitted to the host state's general educational, apprenticeship and vocational training courses under the same conditions as the nationals of the host state.

The EC and the environment

The EC involvement in environmental issues is based on two considerations.

1 Pollution does not respect national frontiers.

2 To achieve a single market it is essential to create a 'level playing field' rather than one which discriminates in favour of the low-cost polluter.

The Community's environment objectives, as set out in the Single European Act, are to:

- *preserve, protect and improve the quality of the environment;*

- *contribute towards protecting human health; and*

- *ensure a prudent and rational utilisation of natural resources.*

EC environmental measures include directives and regulations covering:

- *air quality standards;*

- *power station emissions;*

- *waste incinerator emissions;*

- *ground level ozone;*

- *carbon dioxide (the main 'greenhouse' gas) emissions;*

- *the quality of drinking water;*

- *the availability of unleaded petrol;*

- *vehicle exhaust emissions;*

- *human and environmental risks from chemical accidents (the so-called Seveso Directive);*

- *hazardous waste.*

In addition, the EC and its member states have signed international agreements on marine pollution and the phasing out of chlorofluorocarbon gases (CFCs) and other ozone-depleting substances. Finally, in October 1991 the Commission set out a proposed strategy for meeting the Community objectives, based on a combination of national strategies, Community programmes on, for example, energy efficiency and renewable energy, and a Community-wide energy tax.

In May 1992 the Commission issued further proposals for an energy tax, the adoption of which would require unanimity among member states. The Commission proposes that adoption should be conditional on the EC's major competitors taking similar action to limit emissions, a view supported by the British government.

The single market and British business

We saw earlier that the Cecchini Report predicted increased trade, output and living standards as a result of the creation of the single market. However, the predictions were on a Europe-wide basis rather than a national basis. The extent to which the UK economy and UK business will benefit is debatable. The fruits of growth are often distributed unevenly through an economy. Hence even if all derive some positive benefit there is no guarantee that all will benefit equally. It is likely that some European economies will enjoy a disproportionate share of the benefits. It is even possible that the single market will pose a threat which is greater than the opportunities it presents. It must be remembered that the single market has opened the door to imports as well as to exports. The pessimistic view is that the UK's long-term structural weaknesses and its somewhat peripheral position away from the heart of the Community could lead to a vicious circle of cumulative decline involving further import penetration, low investment, low productivity and slow growth. The optimistic view is that all members will be swept along by the EC-wide growth that flows from the single market. Admittedly, some businesses will suffer as they face a greater blast of competition than they have known before. After an initial period of adjustment, however, they will emerge more efficient than before, able to compete more effectively in European and world markets.

For students of business rather than economics the approach to the single market is somewhat different. Rather than any macro-economic analysis of the benefits of demolishing trade barriers the student of business is concerned with strategies to enable the individual business to cope with the increased export opportunities and the threat of increased import penetration.

Business managers analyse the situation by identifying:

- *strengths;*

- *weaknesses;*

- *opportunities; and*

- *threats.*

This is known as SWOT analysis: the strengths and weaknesses refer to factors internal to the firms; threats and opportunities are external. The single market poses the threat of increased competition in home markets but also the opportunity of increased access to export markets. How individual firms are affected and react varies.

1 For the purely local firm selling goods to a local market the single market might appear irrelevant. This is even more so in the case of a local firm

supplying services. Although there is a measure of truth in this view, it should be remembered that the Single European Act has meant greater Europe-wide standardisation of laws and other regulations concerning product specification. Hence, even these firms are not immune from the impact of the single market.

2 For a larger firm supplying a UK regional market or the national market, there is the threat of import penetration. The shock has been greatest for those firms previously protected by non-tariff barriers, such as those supplying goods and services to the public sector. Continued success for these larger regional and national firms depends upon their efficiency and ability to respond to the needs of the market. From SWOT analysis it should be possible to identify weaknesses and, hopefully, to rectify them.

3 For the larger firm currently engaged in or contemplating entering the export market the response must be to defend the home market from further encroachment whilst taking the opportunity to export to the rest of the single market. This again means ensuring that price, quality and delivery are all sufficiently competitive to capture and retain the market.

CHAPTER 14

Maastricht and the European Union

The Treaty on European Union has been called the unknown treaty in the sense that its precise terms are unknown to the majority of British people. Despite or perhaps because of this ignorance, the treaty has become the most controversial that a UK government has signed since 1972. Although most of the terms are political rather than economic it does represent a further stage in a deepening relationship with Britain's European partners. Hence it is an important treaty to understand. This chapter concentrates on the general aspects of Maastricht, but leaves the monetary clauses to chapter 15.

OBJECTIVES
1 To survey the concept of a European Union.
2 To analyse the three pillars of the European Union.
3 To analyse the concepts of federalism and subsidiarity.
4 To analyse the economics of the Social Charter.

Britain and Europe since 1979

June 1984	Fontainebleau agreement on budget rebate.
June 1985	White Paper *Completing the Internal Market* published by the Commission.
December 1985	Luxembourg meeting of European Council. Agreement on completing the internal market by 1992.
July 1987	Single European Act comes into force.
September 1988	Bruges Speech. Mrs Thatcher criticised the centralising tendency of the EC.
April 1989	Delors Report: three-stage programme for economic and monetary union (EMU).
June 1989	Madrid meeting of European Council: agreement to start Delors stage 1 in July 1990.

1989/90	A series of UK cabinet resignations over European issues:

- *Chancellor Lawson over Alan Walters (the Prime Minister's adviser) and the Exchange Rate Mechanism (ERM);*
- *Trade Secretary Ridley over his comments about German domination of the EC;*
- *Deputy Prime Minister Howe over Thatcher's approach to Europe.*

June 1990	Agreement to hold inter-governmental conference (IGC) on political union.
October 1990	Britain becomes a member of the ERM.
October 1990	Agreement to start stage 2 of EMU in 1994.
November 1990	Thatcher replaced as Conservative leader and Prime Minister by John Major.
December 1990	Two IGCs held, on EMU and political union.
December 1991	Maastricht IGC ended in agreement.
1992	National ratifications of Maastricht Treaty.
June 1992	Danish rejection in a referendum.
September 1992	British membership of ERM suspended.
Autumn 1992	Growing opposition to Maastricht.
December 1992	Swiss reject the European Economic Area (EEA) in referendum.
1993	Danes accept Maastricht in a second referendum.

The Treaty on European Union

The Treaty on European Union, usually known as the Maastricht Treaty, was agreed at an EC Council meeting held in the Dutch town in December 1991. It was the culmination of a long series of negotiations that took place in inter-government conferences (known as IGCs) on (a) economic and monetary union and (b) political union.

The negotiations took place against the background of the imminent completion of the single market (under the SEA of 1986). Supporters of greater European union favoured progress towards monetary union and a single currency (or, as preferred by the UK government, a common currency). However, EMU would significantly increase the powers of Community institutions that were already criticised over what was known as the democratic deficit (their – notably the Commission's – inadequate account-ability to democratic control). All the Maastricht participants had their own, often conflicting preoccupations, and these are summarised in Fig. 14.1.

Other factors were at work. The failure of Europe to act in a decisive and united way over the Gulf crisis of 1991, coupled with the growing problem in the former Yugoslavia, convinced many people that greater co-operation was needed in the foreign and security policy field. To this was added a desire to allow EC citizens to share common and political rights.

From these desires to extend the EC into new areas and to redefine the powers and functions of Community institutions came the Treaty on

Fig. 14.1 *Preoccupations of the participants at Maastricht*

State	Preoccupations
Belgium	1. Federalist
	2. Concerned about workers' rights and EC role in immigration policy
Denmark	1. Concerned about changes which might weaken NATO
	2. Common defence policy posed a problem
France	1. Favoured the three-pillar concept because it cuts the Commission and EP out of two of the pillars
	2. Strong supporter of social policy
Germany	1. EMU based on German design
	2. Less keen on political union
Greece	Balkan instability
Ireland	1. Five per cent of national income is EC aid. Hence Ireland supports union
	2. Concern over EC and abortion issue
Italy	1. Federalist
	2. Strong on social policy
	3. EMU seen as providing much-needed monetary discipline
Luxembourg	1. Federalist
	2. Keen on EMU. Hoped to gain new central bank
	3. Worried about voting rights for EC citizens in local elections in view of large non-national population
The Netherlands	1. Federalist
	2. Keen on EMU
	3. As Council President, the Netherlands sought a triumph at Maastricht
Portugal	1. Supported Spain over Cohesion Fund
	2. Reservations over political union
	3. Concerned that QMV means that small countries can be ignored
Spain	1. Leader of southern states in demanding assistance under proposed Cohesion Fund
	2. Strong on European citizenship
UK	1. Opposed a. extension of EP powers
	b. Social Charter
	c. greater use of majority voting
	2. Opted out of EMU
	3. Objected to the word 'federal'
	4. Sought to emphasise subsidiarity

European Union together with 17 associated protocols and 33 declarations. The protocols are separate, additional agreements between some (but not all) members. For instance, the UK government refused to accept the Social Charter; consequently, it was not included in the main treaty signed by all 12 but became a separate protocol. A declaration does not have legal force but it does outline the ways in which treaty provisions should be interpreted or implemented.

Although the treaty was signed in February 1992 it does not have the force of law until it is ratified by all 12 member states. The Danish people rejected the treaty in the first Maastricht referendum held in 1992. The French narrowly accepted the treaty in a referendum later in that year. The narrowness of the French vote demonstrates the controversy aroused by the treaty in what has been one of the most pro-European member states. At the time of writing (late 1992) the British government has delayed the process of ratification (mainly because of internal problems within the Conservative Party). Although it appears that all 12, including the Danes, will eventually ratify the treaty it is possible that some of the Maastricht measures will not be fully implemented.

Assuming that Maastricht is ratified (and implemented) it will amend the Treaty of Rome and affect the workings of the Community. It is to the substance of the Maastricht Treaty, summarised in Fig. 14.2, that we now turn.

The Maastricht Treaty is more correctly entitled the Treaty on European Union. Notice that the 'Community' has been replaced by 'union'. There is a reason for this change in wording (and it is not the Trojan horse of federalism that Euro-sceptics would argue). The European Union comprises three pillars of co-operation under the European Council (the Euro-summit of heads of government), shown diagrammatically in Fig. 14.3. The three pillars are:

1 The European Community – established by the Treaty of Rome and amended by the Merger Treaty (1965), the SEA (1986) and the Maastricht Treaty itself. The European Community comprises the institutional structures outlined in chapter 10 and the rules and procedures that emanate from them.

Fig. 14.2 *Summary of the Maastricht Treaty*

1. Three pillars: a. European Community
   b. Common Foreign and Security Policy
   c. Co-operation on interior and judicial issues

2. Citizenship of the European Union

3. Subsidiarity: action should be taken at Community level only if objectives cannot be achieved by individual state action; constraints on EC competence in certain defined areas

4. Institutional reforms

5. Economic and monetary union by 1999

6. Social Charter excluded from the main treaty but attached as an 11-member protocol

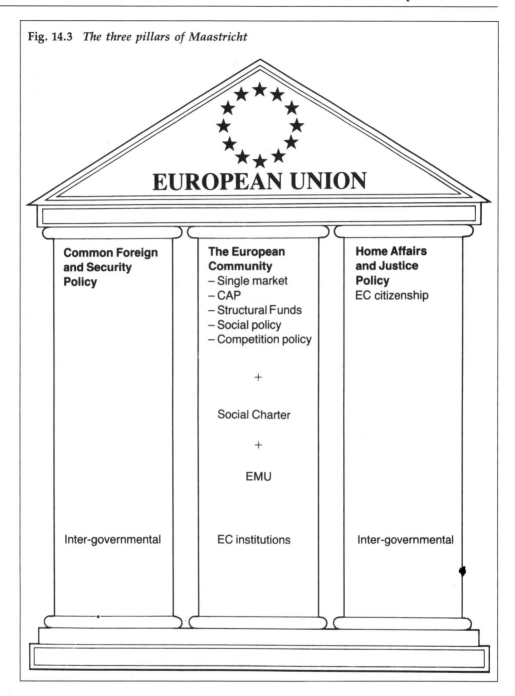

Fig. 14.3 *The three pillars of Maastricht*

EUROPEAN UNION

Common Foreign and Security Policy	The European Community	Home Affairs and Justice Policy
	– Single market	EC citizenship
	– CAP	
	– Structural Funds	
	– Social policy	
	– Competition policy	
	+	
	Social Charter	
	+	
	EMU	
Inter-governmental	EC institutions	Inter-governmental

2 Common Foreign and Security Policy, which is to be dealt with on an inter-governmental basis with only limited involvement of EC institutions such as the Parliament, Commission and the ECJ.

3 Home affairs and justice policy, which again is to be decided on an inter-governmental basis.

> **Illustration 14.1** *Preamble to the Treaty on European Union 1991*
>
> [The sovereign rulers of the twelve countries]
> RESOLVED to mark a new stage in the process of European integration undertaken with the establishment of the European Communities,
> RECALLING the historic importance of the ending of the division of the European continent and the need to create firm bases for the construction of the future Europe,
> CONFIRMING their attachment to the principles of liberty, democracy and respect for human rights and fundamental freedoms and of the rule of law,
> DESIRING to deepen the solidarity between their peoples while respecting their history, their culture and their traditions,
> DESIRING to enhance further the democratic and efficient functioning of the institutions so as to enable them better to carry out, within a single institutional framework, the tasks entrusted to them,
> RESOLVED to achieve the strengthening and the convergence of their economies and to establish an economic and monetary union including, in accordance with the provisions of this Treaty, a single and stable currency,
> DETERMINED to promote economic and social progress for their peoples, within the context of the accomplishment of the internal market and of reinforced cohesion and environmental protection, and to implement policies ensuring that advances in economic integration are accompanied by parallel progress in other fields,
> RESOLVED to establish a citizenship common to nationals of their countries,
> RESOLVED to implement a common foreign and security policy including the eventual framing of a common defence policy, which might in time lead to a common defence, thereby reinforcing the European identity and its independence in order to promote peace, security and progress in Europe and in the world,
> REAFFIRMING their objective to facilitate the free movement of persons, while ensuring the safety and security of their peoples, by including provisions on justice and home affairs in this Treaty,
> RESOLVED to continue the process of creating an ever closer union among the peoples of Europe, in which decisions are taken as closely as possible to the citizen in accordance with the principle of subsidiarity,
> IN VIEW of further steps to be taken in order to advance European integration,
> HAVE DECIDED to establish a European Union

The second and third pillars are new and they were established outside the structure of EC institutions. The effect of the two new pillars is to strengthen the role of member states without slowing down the momentum towards economic integration. Despite such sentiments the Euro-sceptics remain convinced that the new pillars will eventually be incorporated into Community institutions.

The preamble to the Maastricht Treaty

The preamble to a treaty states the overall aim of the participants in drawing up the treaty. The Maastricht Preamble, reproduced in Illustration 14.1, states that the heads of state of Community countries have resolved to proceed to a new stage in the process of creating an ever closer union of the peoples of Europe. Like the earlier treaties, emphasis is laid upon political aims such as liberty, democracy, respect for human rights and peace. Economic prosperity will help to ensure the attainment of these important political goals.

Economic prosperity is to be achieved by economic integration – including monetary union. The convergence of economies would be aided by a single currency (although it is also true to say that a single currency without convergence will cause hardship). Also to be added were a common foreign and security policy (CFSP) and common policies on internal affairs. These two, and the EC, represent the pillars of the new European Union.

In the early drafts there was reference to a federal Europe but this was unacceptable to a number of governments (especially that of the UK) and, instead, emphasis was switched to 'subsidiarity', which basically means taking decisions as close as is practical to the citizens. It was the stress on subsidiarity, and the fact that the CFSP and common internal affairs policy were to be decided on an inter-governmental rather than Community basis, that made the treaty acceptable to the British government.

The first pillar: the European Community

Maastricht completes the process by which the European Economic Community has become the European Community dealing with an increasing number of political, environmental and social issues. Article 2 of Maastricht amends the Treaty of Rome by stating that:

> The Community shall have as its task by establishing a common market and an economic and monetary union and by implementing common policies ... , to promote throughout the Community a harmonious and balanced development of economic activities, sustainable and non-inflationary growth respecting the environment, a high degree of convergence of economic performance, a high level of employment and of social protection, the raising of the standard of living and quality of life and economic and social cohesion among Member States.

The equivalent article in the Treaty of Rome refers to 'the harmonious development of economic activities, continuous and balanced expansion, stability and the raising of living standards'. Maastricht clearly goes further than was envisaged in 1957 and reflects changing preoccupations (e.g. with the environment). It also lists the activities of the EC that aim to achieve the purposes set out in article 2:

- *elimination of all trade barriers;*

- *a common commercial policy;*

- *free movement of people, capital, services and goods;*

- *common policies for agriculture, fisheries and transport;*

- *a system to ensure that competition in the internal market is not distorted;*

- *the approximation of laws of member states to the extent required for the function of the common market;*

- *a social policy, including the European Social Fund;*

- *the strengthening of economic and social cohesion;*

- *a policy on the environment;*

- *the strengthening of the competitiveness of Community industry;*

- *the promotion of research;*

- *the encouragement of trans-European networks;*

- *health protection;*

- *a contribution to education, training and the 'flowering of the cultures of Member States';*

- *assistance to development of associate countries;*

- *'measures' in the spheres of energy, civil protection and tourism;*

- *a strengthening of consumer protection.*

Most of the activities listed above are, of course, features of the existing, pre-Maastricht EC. What was a significant development was the commitment to EMU. Article 3a of Maastricht commits signatories to:

- *co-ordination of member states' economic policies;*

- *the irrevocable fixing of exchange rates;*

- *the introduction of a single currency (the ECU);*

- *a single monetary policy, whose objective was to maintain price stability.*

To achieve the goal of monetary union the member states are required to comply with the principles of stable prices, sound public finances and sustainable balance of payments.

As is well known, the UK government negotiated an opt-out (or more correctly an opt-in) to the third stage of EMU. This is not in the main treaty but is in a protocol attached to it. The protocol clearly states that the UK shall not be obliged or committed to the third stage of EMU without a separate decision to do so by government and Parliament. Unless the UK government notifies the EC Council that it intends to move to the third stage it is under no obligation to do so. If the UK chooses not to opt in it will retain its powers in the field of monetary policy but will be barred from decision-making relating to the progress of EMU.

The UK is not alone in having an EMU opt-out. Denmark, like Britain often portrayed as a reluctant European, also has a protocol on EMU. This is a consequence of the Danish Constitution, 'which may require' Denmark to hold a referendum prior to the third stage of EMU. Therefore, even though the Danes have ratified the Maastricht Treaty as signed in 1992 they can still opt out of EMU.

Chapter 15 gives more detail on EMU.

The second pillar: common foreign and security policy (CFSP)

In all federal states foreign and defence policy is determined at the centre rather than in the individual states or provinces. Hence, American foreign policy is a matter for the federal government and Congress in Washington rather than for individual states such as Texas or California. Any move toward an EC foreign policy would be seen as a clear move towards a federal 'United States of Europe'.

At the time of the drafting of the Maastricht Treaty there were a number of foreign policy issues which concerned many, if not all, EC states.

1 The end of Communist rule in Eastern Europe was a potential source of instability. Although the Cold War (1945–89) was prolonged and tense, it did impose a form of stability. Relaxation of the controls could open up old tensions and disputes.

2 The EC states had an interest in the peace process in the Middle East and in the Iraqi crisis of 1990.

3 The dissolution of Yugoslavia led to war on the European continent for the first time since 1945.

America was anxious to reduce its global commitment and looked to its European allies to take the lead in this crisis (Yugoslavia) on the borders of the EC. The need for an agreed Community policy was illustrated by differences of opinion over recognition of the breakaway states. Germany was anxious to recognise the independence of Slovenia, Croatia and Bosnia whereas Britain was more reluctant, fearing that it would encourage the dissolution. The former Yugoslav republic of Macedonia posed a particular problem for the EC since Greece objected to the name because Macedonia was also the name of a Greek province. Greece feared that the independent Macedonia would receive support from its own Macedonian people. After the commencement of the Croatian and Bosnian wars Europe (especially the countries of the EC) faced the biggest refugee problem since the end of the Second World War. German policy was to allow refugees to enter the country (this created social tensions and contributed to neo-Nazi violence) whereas British policy was to provide help in the homelands of the refugees. One can argue the merits for and against these different approaches; however, the desirability of a common approach is not in dispute.

A Community foreign and defence policy as part of the institutional structure of the EC was favoured by the Commission and smaller states such as the Netherlands. However, there were major problems.

1 Some but not all EC countries are in NATO.

2 Ireland is a neutral state.

3 France has signed the NATO treaty but is not part of the integrated military structure of NATO.

4 A clause in the Constitution of the Federal Republic of Germany prohibits its forces from acting outside Germany.

5 Denmark was unhappy at moves towards a common defence structure.

6 Britain was also unhappy at the removal of foreign and defence policy to Brussels.

In the Maastricht Treaty CFSP has been constructed as a pillar of the European Union outside the EC institutions. In other words, it was placed on an inter-governmental footing rather than a supra-national one. This means that unanimity rather than majority support (simple or qualified) will be the basis of the policy. It was agreed that where supreme national interest is at stake, a country can be set free of a Union-wide decision although it is accepted that this right of veto will not be used over detailed implementation of policy initiatives.

A related issue is co-operation over defence – leading perhaps to a European army. As we saw in chapter 2, there was an abortive proposal for a European Defence Community before the signing of the Treaty of Rome. French and German support for a common defence policy was countered by:

- *Dutch and British fears that NATO would be undermined;*
- *Danish fears of conscription into a European army; and*
- *Irish desires not to compromise its neutrality.*

Because of these concerns, the Maastricht Treaty does not assign a defence role to the Community institutions. Instead the Western European Union was assigned the task of elaborating and implementing decisions and actions of the Union which have defence implications. Hence, although the treaty assigns a limited role for the Parliament and the Commission, it is clear that the EC will not (for the immediate future at least) be a defence community with a common army.

The third pillar: justice and home affairs

The Maastricht Treaty makes interior policy (justice and home affairs) a part of the European Union. What prompted the move into this area of policy was the realisation that relaxation of frontier controls in the single market made it imperative to work together against international crime. At the same time, the prospect of increased immigration from Southern and Eastern Europe was likely to impose new pressures on member states. Germany has operated a very open policy on refugees and economic migrants but the large influx of the early 1990s added to its own problems in the aftermath of reunification.

In the original drafts of the treaty, immigration policy was to be removed from national governments and entrusted to the EC. However, the UK government refused to accept any proposal that removed from national governments control over the immigration of third-country nationals. In this it was supported by others, especially Denmark. As a result the provisions relating to home affairs and justice merely commit signatories to inform and consult with one another and when there is agreement to collaborate by means of joint action. Inter-governmental co-operation in the Council of Ministers is provided for but the role of the Commission in these matters is strictly limited.

The matters to be dealt with under the third pillar are:

- *asylum policy;*
- *the external frontiers of the Union;*
- *immigration policy;*
- *the fight against drugs;*
- *international fraud;*
- *judicial co-operation;*
- *customs co-operation;*
- *co-operation between police forces.*

All this seems innocuous – the government and Europhiles argue that the fact that these issues are treated as a separate pillar of the Union rather than as part of the EC itself means that national governments retain ultimate control over these sensitive issues. However, this separate pillars idea does not impress a Euro-sceptic like William Cash. In his book *Europe: the Crunch* he writes (at p. 40):

> the institutions of the Community are always involved in the formulation of policy, even in the pillars. The Commission is fully associated with the preparation of foreign policy and justice and home affairs. Thus the central institutions of the Community will sit sometimes as the Union ... and sometimes as the European Community. Given that the Community itself has a myriad of different modes of operation ... the difference between a pillar and the European Community proper will be largely invisible. Indeed, it will not be long before they are all harmonised into one structure, since by then people will argue, with some justification, that the difference between the Union and the EC itself is little more than a technicality.

What Cash is arguing is that, irrespective of the claims that interior, security and foreign policy are dealt with outside the EC framework, there will be a tendency for the Commission (the *bête noire* of Euro-sceptics) to take the lead and for creeping federalism to occur.

European citizenship

Article 8 of the Maastricht Treaty states that 'every person holding the nationality of a Member State shall be a citizen of the Union', and spells out what this means in practice. Three new rights are provided for.

1 The right to vote and stand in elections (but not a general election) in the country of residence irrespective of one's nationality.

2 Union citizens are able to raise complaints of maladministration by EC institutions with a new EC Ombudsman. The Ombudsman can investigate the complaint and publish a report on his findings.

3 Union citizens will enjoy the diplomatic protection of EC countries where their own country is not represented but another EC state is.

Clearly, these practical features of Union citizenship are attractive for the people of Europe. It is claimed that citizenship will bring a sense of European identity as well as providing the EC with a more human, less distant, face. Maastricht supporters argue that European citizenship is additional to, not instead of, national citizenship. On the other hand, opposition is based on sentiment and emotion: we are British or Irish or Danish rather than 'European'.

The government's case for acceptance of Maastricht

Euro-sceptics have opposed Maastricht on the basis that it represents a move towards a federal Europe. The change in name from European Communities to European Community to European Union suggests a movement towards federalism. However, the UK government has argued that the aim is to create a more efficient community without centralisation or a weakening of national political institutions. In particular the government points to the following features of the treaty.

1 The close co-operation on foreign, defence and internal policies will be on an inter-governmental basis without the Commission or the ECJ performing the roles they enjoy under the Treaty of Rome.

2 The new European citizenship establishes new rights for EC citizens but does not detract from national citizenship rights.

3 Community involvement in social affairs is carefully defined and therefore delineated.

4 The Commission will be more accountable and the European Parliament will have a more significant role.

5 The treaty strengthens the ECJ's ability to act against those who do not implement agreed EC rules. The suggestion here is that other states fail to implement the rules.

6 The treaty will facilitate action on the environment and development aid.

7 The treaty enshrines the principle of subsidiarity.

Subsidiarity

This is the key word in John Major's 'selling' of the treaty to the British

Parliament and people. He argues that the Maastricht Treaty is not federalist inspired because (unlike the other key treaties) it enshrines the principle of 'subsidiarity'. A problem is the lack of a clear definition of the word. It is usually taken to mean that decisions should be made at the lowest practical level. In areas where objectives cannot be achieved by individual action the Community will act; if it is practical to leave a matter to individual members, it should be. In addition, the principle of subsidiarity dictates that Community action in any field must not go beyond that which is necessary to achieve treaty objectives.

The principle of subsidiarity:

- *prevents the Community straying into areas where it is not needed;*

- *excludes Community action which exceeds that required to achieve objectives;*

- *reserves certain matters for 'inter-governmental co-operation' rather than EC action.*

To appreciate the last point, remember that qualified majority voting applies in the Council whereas inter-governmental co-operation requires unanimity.

The government's interpretation of subsidiarity was not accepted by others – both Euro-federalists and Euro-sceptics. The latter believed that, irrespective of high-sounding principles, Maastricht was part of the move toward a federal Europe. Their suspicions were reinforced when Commission Vice President Bangemann stated that a federal Europe was an essential precondition for the application of the principle of subsidiarity.

The search for an agreed definition was on the agenda at a special European Council summit in Birmingham in October 1992. Although there was no clear statement on subsidiarity it was agreed that the EC should:

- *be more open, to ensure a better informed public debate on its activities;*

- *respect the history, culture and traditions of individual nations, with a clearer understanding of what member states should do and what needs to be done by the Community;*

- *take action at the Community level only when necessary;*

and that:

- *Community legislation should be more limited, clearer and better explained;*

- *the Commission should consult more regularly and widely;*

- *national parliaments should be more closely involved in EC business and, for example, should be able to scrutinise the Commission's work programme each year.*

Federation

The UK is a unitary state in the sense that sovereignty is concentrated in a single place (the Crown-in-Parliament) and is not shared with other centres of power. Even though there are Secretaries of State for Scotland, Wales and

Northern Ireland (each with his or her own civil service departments) there is only one Parliament for the whole of the UK. In a federal system sovereignty is shared between the central (or federal) parliament and government and those of the constituent states.

The USA, Canada, Australia, Germany and India are all federal states. Foreign, defence and economic policy are normally determined at the centre whilst education, law and order and health care are dealt with at a state level. A major problem in all federal countries is the division of powers between the centre and the states. If the constitution specifies the powers of the centre with the residue in state hands, the result is a rather loose confederation. More probably, the constitution will lay down the matters to be dealt with at a state level, with the residue at the federal level. The likely result of this is a tendency for the centre to acquire more and more power. This was the case in the USA, which started in 1776 as a loose confederation but gradually became more centralised.

Fervent Europeans (the Europhiles or Eurofanatics, depending on the reader's own view) envisage the creation of a confederation – a United States of Europe perhaps. Although not on the immediate political agenda, this might be seen as the logical outcome of the Treaty of Rome, the Single European Act, the Maastricht Treaty and EMU.

The Major government is reputedly more pro-Europe than was the Thatcher government. However, even the most 'European' ministers in the Major cabinet (e.g. Douglas Hurd, Kenneth Clarke) do not advocate a federal Europe. Consequently, in the Maastricht debates Major has laid great emphasis on 'subsidiarity': an ill-defined concept that basically means taking decisions as close to the people as is practical. Hence, if an issue can be dealt with at a national level it should be. Fig. 14.4 summarises the main areas of disagreement in the debates.

The Maastricht Treaty amends the Treaty of Rome by, *inter alia*, the insertion of article 3b, which states: 'The Community shall act within the limits of the powers conferred upon it by this Treaty and of the objectives assigned to it therein.' This article seems to place a limit on the powers of EC institutions, with the clear implication that anything not covered is the concern of national institutions. However, Euro-sceptics stress that this same article goes on to state:

> In areas which do not fall within its exclusive competence, the Community shall take action, in accordance with the principles of subsidiarity, only if and in so far as the objectives of the proposed action cannot be sufficiently achieved by the Member States and can therefore by reason of the scale or effects of the proposed action, be better achieved by the Community.

The vagueness and open-endedness of this statement alarm Euro-sceptics such as Michael Spicer, Conservative MP for South Worcestershire and a former junior minister. Spicer's opposition to the Maastricht Treaty is contained in a book whose title was clearly inspired by the classic account of allied airborne landings at Arnhem in 1944. Just as Arnhem was 'a

Fig. 14.4 *The debate over political union*

Euro-sceptics	*Pro-Europeans*
1. A federal Europe is contrary to the tide of history. Euro-sceptics point to the disintegration of federations in Eastern Europe.	European union is being undertaken voluntarily by democratic nations. It will avoid the over-centralisation that contributed to disintegration in the East.
2. Maastricht and EMU form a 'conveyor belt' to a federal Europe.	Federalism does not mean centralisation. 'Subsidiarity' is a key concept in Maastricht.
3. The old tensions in Europe have disappeared, making political union unnecessary.	Instability in Eastern Europe coupled with American withdrawal from Europe make political union necessary.
4. Deepening should not be at the expense of widening (i.e. enlargement).	Deepening is needed to enable the EC to meet the needs of a wider community.
5. There is a 'democratic deficit' in the EC.	The democratic deficit results from the unwillingness of member states to reform EC institutions.
6. UK MEPs are in a permanent minority.	This is true for all members. UK MEPs have joined with like-minded MEPs from other states to exert influence on the Commission.

bridge too far', so, according to Spicer, Maastricht is *A Treaty too Far*. He argues that:

> the word [subsidiarity] has the strength and weakness that no one quite knows what it means . . .
> The inclusion of 'subsidiarity' in the Maastricht Treaty on European Union has been presented as a great victory for those who wanted to see the centralising, Federalist, and irrevocable proposals of the Treaty given some sort of counterbalance for the rights of nation states. Subsidiarity does no such thing. Indeed, it merely reinforces the Federalist tendency.

Spicer goes on to argue that the vagueness of the wording and the absence of a general legal meaning to the term mean that almost anything could be included under Community-wide action.

Another Conservative MP who has written and spoken extensively on this issue is William Cash (MP for Stafford). Cash is closely associated with the Bruges Group – a group of academics and others founded to support

Thatcher's views, expressed at the College of Europe in Bruges (Belgium) in 1988. In his book *Against a Federal Europe* Cash argues (p. 85) that:

> federal states ... have been unable to resist the tendency to centralise .... There is little evidence to support the claim that federal states are decentralised. Some federal states [and here he cites Austria] are so centralised that it is doubtful that one should continue to refer to them as federal.

He is therefore saying that even if a post-Maastricht Europe does have a clear division between EC and national responsibilities, there will be a tendency over time to accumulate more power in the centre.

One point made by the anti-federalists is that the most successful states of the late 20th century are nation states such as Japan, South Korea and Hong Kong. The nation state is clearly not obsolete. In fact the federations are the states in difficulty. The Soviet Union broke up, to be replaced by a very loose confederation known as the Commonwealth of Independent States (whose own future is uncertain). Czechoslovakia was dissolved at the end of 1992 and the break-up of Yugoslavia has brought warfare to Europe, the like of which has not been seen since 1945. Elsewhere, the future of Canada, India and Nigeria is uncertain.

The USA is a successful and united federation. However, according to Dr Alan Sked ('A Proposal for European Union', reproduced in Minford (ed), *The Cost of Europe*), the claim that:

> there is an analogy between a United States of Europe and a United States of America, is quite misleading. It fails to recognise that the American colonists were a fairly homogeneous group who were starting Government from scratch. Europe today is definitely not starting from scratch, rather it contains nations whose histories go back almost a thousand years.

The Social Charter

It is important to remember that social policy within the EC refers primarily to employment matters. Reference to social objectives is present in the founding treaties: one of the objectives of the ECSC, for example, is 'to improve living and working conditions ... for the workers' in the coal and steel industries. The Euratom Treaty refers to the need to protect workers and the general population from the hazards associated with nuclear power.

The Treaty of Rome made more extensive reference to social and employment issues. It made provision for:

- *the gradual achievement of free movement of workers within the Community, accompanied by guaranteed eligibility for social security benefit;*

- *the exchange of young workers;*

- *collaboration between member states over issues such as employment law, working conditions, vocational training, social security, health and safety, trade union rights and collective bargaining;*

- *equal pay for men and women undertaking the same work;*

- *the establishment of a European Social Fund (ESF) to promote employment opportunities and improve labour mobility.*

In the first decade of the EC the major social provisions of the founding treaties (freedom of movement, rights of migrant workers, action on working conditions, etc.) were implemented, and the ESF was established. Despite progress there was a growing feeling that a more active social dimension was necessary if the Community was to progress beyond a simple common market. There was concern about the unevenness of economic growth, with peripheral areas of south-western France and the Mezzogiorno of Italy lagging behind (and this was before the accession of Greece, Spain, Portugal and Ireland). There was also concern about the social costs of economic growth (e.g. pollution, and the quality of life).

To meet these concerns, in 1974 the Council of Ministers adopted a Social Action Programme. This involved:

- *reform and enhanced status of the European Social Fund;*

- *moves towards a common vocational training policy;*

- *co-ordination of national employment policies;*

- *equal treatment of men and women, including equal pay for men and women doing work 'of equal value';*

- *improvements to health and safety legislation;*

- *greater protection of workers' interests (including Directive 77/187, which specifies that workers' rights arising from a collective agreement or labour contract must be maintained in the event of a company transfer);*

- *an anti-poverty programme;*

- *an attempt, in the so-called Vredeling Directive, to require large companies to include workers on the board of directors.*

The Social Action Programme had only limited success mainly because:

> not all member governments share the social protectionist aims of the Commission and its rather dirigiste approach towards implementation of the Social Action Programme. In particular, there was a major rift after 1979 between the British Conservative Government, whose macro-economic policy was based upon deregulation of the labour market, and the Commission, which refused to endorse the abolition of workers' legal rights in the name of greater labour flexibility (Lintner and Mazey, *The European Community: Economic and Political Aspects*, p. 121).

'Dirigiste' comes from the French word *dirigisme*, meaning control by the state in economic and social spheres. It is the antithesis of the *laissez-faire* approach favoured by the Thatcher and Major governments. This attitude can be illustrated by extracts from *Britain in the European Community* (HMSO, pp. 69–70, 72):

The British Government believes that the Community has a role to play in supporting action to promote employment, labour flexibility and helping the unemployed back to work. It therefore supports Community efforts to improve training, raise health and safety standards at work and increase labour mobility. It also believes that the Community could have a more prominent role in identifying and disseminating information on effective practice in helping people back to work.

However, the Government is opposed to measures which would, in its view, impose arbitrary restrictions and unnecessary costs upon employers, thereby damaging Community competitiveness in world markets.

The British Government is opposed to binding Community legislation in the field of employee involvement. It believes that in Britain such arrangements should be agreed voluntarily between employers and employees. The benefit of the voluntary approach is the flexibility it allows for employers to develop schemes which are best suited to their own business needs and circumstances and the needs of their employees.

A number of factors contributed to a major transformation of the EC in the 1980s. In 1983 the EC heads of government (including Thatcher) committed member states to the creation of a 'European Union'. Although its exact meaning is unclear, it surely is more than the deregulated market the Thatcher government favoured. The Single European Act of 1986 provided not just for the completion of a single market by the end of 1992 but also for qualified majority voting in which national desires can be overridden. It was also felt necessary to make the single market a 'citizens' and workers' Europe' rather than merely an entrepreneurs' Europe.

The entry of Greece, Spain and Portugal also posed problems. To ensure harmonious development it was essential to provide social and regional assistance for these southern states. Moreover, there was concern in the richer north that investment, and therefore jobs, might be transferred to the low-wage producers of the south.

To meet these varied concerns, the Commission adopted a statement on the 'social dimensions' of the internal market. It proposed a series of measures to accompany the single market programme:

- *mutual recognition of qualifications;*

- *European training certificate;*

- *reform of the Structural Funds;*

- *a new anti-poverty programme;*

- *education and training programmes;*

- *rights of part-time workers;*

- *greater worker participation; and*

- *a Community Charter of the Fundamental Social Rights of Workers (Social Charter – see Illustration 14.2).*

In 1989 the Commission presented the Council with a draft Charter on Social Rights. This was a declaration of intent to improve social and working conditions in the EC by statutory provisions on issues such as equal opportunities, minimum wages, working hours, trade union rights and the rights of migrant workers. Although many of the matters dealt with in the Social Charter are relatively uncontroversial, with member states already enacting similar measures themselves, it was rejected by both the Thatcher and Major Conservative governments. They argued that the Charter represented EC interference in what should be purely domestic policy and was contrary to the 'supply-side' measures taken by UK governments in the 1980s.

As a result of UK opposition, the Social Charter was not incorporated into the main Maastricht Treaty but as a protocol. In effect, the Charter was a separate agreement between 11 member states.

The aim of the Social Charter is stated in article 1 of the protocol:

> The Community and the Member States shall have as their objectives the promotion of employment, improved living and working conditions, proper social protection, dialogue between management and labour, the development of human resources with a view to lasting high employment and the combating of exclusion. To this end the Community and the Member States shall implement measures which take account of the diverse forms of national practices, in particular in the field of contractual relations, and the need to maintain the competitiveness of the Community economy.

Article 2 allows the Council to adopt directives relating to minimum requirements on:

- *health and safety;*

- *working conditions;*

- *consultation between management and employees;*

- *equality between men and women in terms of labour market opportunities and treatment at work.*

These measures can be enacted by qualified majority voting and therefore can be imposed on reluctant member states. QMV in this instance means 44 votes or more in a Council of 11 members (the UK naturally being excluded). However, the protocol does state that implementation should have regard to conditions in member states and that the directives shall avoid 'imposing administrative, financial and legal constraints in a way which would hold back the creation and development of small and medium sized undertakings'.

Illustration 14.2 *The Social Charter*

Community Charter of the Fundamental Social Rights of Workers (Based on the Community Charter of 9 December 1989)

Freedom of movement Every worker of the European Community shall have the right to freedom of movement throughout the territory of the Community, subject to restrictions justified on grounds of public order, public safety or public health.

The right to freedom of movement shall enable any worker to engage in any occupation or profession in the Community in accordance with the principles of equal treatment as regards access to employment, working conditions and social protection in the host country.

Employment and remuneration Every individual shall be free to choose and engage in an occupation according to the regulations governing each occupation.

All employment shall be fairly remunerated.

Every individual must be able to have access to public placement services free of charge.

Improvement of living and working conditions The completion of the internal market must lead to an improvement in the living and working conditions of workers in the European Community. The improvement must cover, where necessary, the development of certain aspects of employment regulations such as procedures for collective redundancies and those regarding bankruptcies.

Every worker of the European Community shall have a right to a weekly rest period and to annual paid leave.

The conditions of employment of every worker of the European Community shall be stipulated in laws, a collective agreement or a contract of employment, according to the arrangements applying in each country.

Social protection Every worker of the European Community shall have a right to adequate social protection and shall, whatever his status and whatever the size of the undertaking in which he is employed, enjoy an adequate level of social security benefits, according to the arrangements applying in each country. Persons who have been unable either to enter or re-enter the labour market and have no means of subsistence must be able to receive sufficient resources and social assistance in keeping with their particular situation.

Freedom of association and collective bargaining Employers and workers of the European Community shall have the right of association in order to constitute professional organizations or trade unions of their choice for the defence of their economic and social interests.

Employers or employers' organizations, on the one hand, and workers' organizations, on the other, shall have the right to negotiate and conclude collective agreements under the conditions laid down by national legislation and practice.

The right to resort to collective action in the event of a conflict of interests shall include the right to strike, subject to the obligations arising under national regulations and collective agreements.

Vocational training Every worker of the European Community must be able to have access to vocational training and to benefit therefrom throughout his working life.

Equal treatment for men and women Equal treatment for men and women must be assured. Equal opportunities for men and women must be developed.

Information, consultation and participation of workers Information, consultation and participation of workers must be developed along appropriate lines, taking account of the practices in force in the various Member States.

This shall apply in companies or groups of companies having establishments or companies in two or more Member States of the European Community.

Health protection and safety at the workplace Every worker must enjoy satisfactory health and safety conditions in his working environment.

The provisions regarding implementation of the internal market shall help to ensure such protection.

Protection of children and adolescents The minimum employment age, subject to derogations limited to certain light work, must not be lower than the minimum school-leaving age and, in any case, not lower than 15 years.

Young people who are in gainful employment must receive equitable remuneration in accordance with national practice.

The duration of work must, in particular, be limited – without it being possible to circumvent this limitation through recourse to overtime – and night work prohibited in the case of workers of under 18 years of age, save in the case of certain jobs laid down in national legislation or regulations.

Following the end of compulsory education, young people must be entitled to receive initial vocational training of a sufficient duration to enable them to adapt to the requirements of their future working life; for young workers, such training should take place during working hours.

Elderly persons Every worker of the European Community must, at the time of retirement, be able to enjoy resources affording him or her a decent standard of living.

Any person who has reached retirement age but who is not entitled to a pension or who does not have other means of subsistence, must be entitled to sufficient resources and to medical and social assistance specifically suited to his needs.

Disabled persons All disabled persons, whatever the origin and nature of their disablement, must be entitled to additional concrete measures aimed at improving their social and professional integration.

In addition to these matters subject to QMV, the protocol also details matters which require unanimous acceptance:

- *social security and social protection of workers;*

- *protection of workers where their employment contract is terminated;*

- *representation and collective defence of the interests of workers and employers, including co-determination;*

- *conditions of employment for third-country nationals legally residing in Community territory;*

- *financial contributions for promotion of employment and job creation, without prejudice to the provisions relating to the Social Fund.*

In all cases, the directives will lay down minimum conditions. This does not prevent member states maintaining or introducing more stringent protective measures if they so choose. The other point that should be appreciated is that the protocol does *not* refer to the rights of association (i.e. trade union membership), to strike or to impose lock-outs.

The British government's objection to the Social Charter is described in *Britain in the European Community* (HMSO, p. 73):

> The British Government opposed the Charter on the grounds that it did not take into account differences in national practice and that it failed to address the overriding concerns of job creation and competitiveness. It also believed that many of the areas covered in the Charter should be decided at national rather than Community level.

The first point can be criticised on the basis that an aim of the Community is greater uniformity. The second point is valid if one accepts the free-market, supply-side economics of British government. The third point is based on the principle of subsidiarity.

The economics of the Social Charter

The UK government claims that acceptance of the Social Charter will result in job losses. Conversely, the Christian Democrat (Conservative) government of Germany supports the Charter as a way of preserving living standards and international competitiveness. How do we account for these differing interpretations of the likely impact of this highly controversial aspect of the Maastricht Treaty?

The British government's opinion is based upon micro-economic analysis of price and wage fixing coupled with the supply-side ideas that have become widely held in the closing decades of the 20th century. Fig. 14.5(a) shows the well-known analysis of the impact of minimum price or wage regulation. At the legally imposed minimum wage, supply exceeds demand, resulting in unemployment. The only way to reduce unemployment is to allow wages to fall and, by a combination of extension of demand and contraction of supply, equilibrium will be restored.

Fig. 14.5(b) is based on the analysis of imperfections in the labour market. To secure additional labour employers must offer higher wages not just to the additional workers but to all previous workers. As a result the marginal cost of employing extra labour exceeds the average cost (wage). Assuming profit-maximising behaviour by employers, the effect of the imperfections is to cause a contraction in the demand for labour and unemployment equal to ab. As we saw in chapters 3 to 5 the UK government adopts a non-interventionist, or supply-side, approach to unemployment and other macro-economic problems. Hence for the government the Social Charter is an anathema.

The German position is based on the dangers of 'social dumping', which is a translation of the unfair competition argument for import duties in the era of the single market. The single market opens up the high-wage economies of Germany and elsewhere to greater competition from the low-wage producers of the southern states of the EC. In particular, there will be

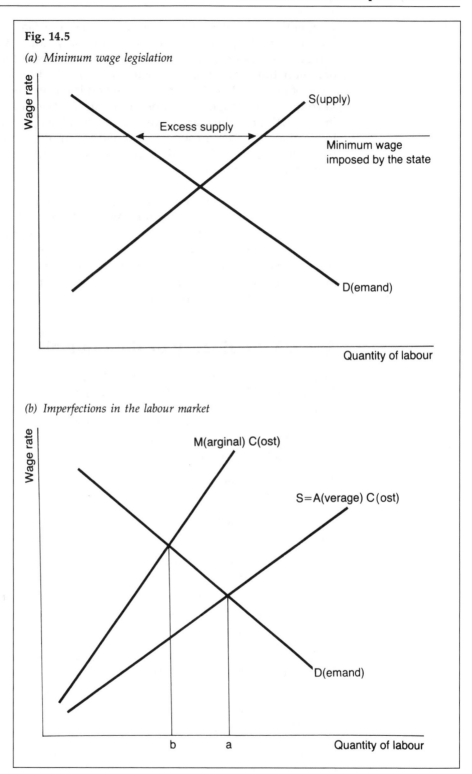

Fig. 14.5

(a) Minimum wage legislation

Wage rate

Excess supply

S(upply)

Minimum wage
imposed by the state

D(emand)

Quantity of labour

(b) Imperfections in the labour market

Wage rate

M(arginal) C(ost)

S=A(verage) C(ost)

D(emand)

b   a

Quantity of labour

competition from countries such as Portugal and Greece, where wages are low and working conditions poor. Not only could this undermine the competitiveness of firms in the more affluent parts of Europe but, in an age of multinational corporations, there is a danger that capital will migrate to the areas of low-cost labour. Conservative politicians in Germany and elsewhere in continental Europe tend to be more interventionist than their equivalents in the UK and they argue that a 'level playing field' necessitates the imposition of minimum standards of work and minimum wages throughout the Community. Enthusiastic supporters of the free market argue that the migration of capital in search of low-cost labour and inputs is what is supposed to happen in the market. The UK government hopes that by not acceding to the Social Charter the country will continue to attract a large share of inward investment into Europe. When challenged on the 'level playing field' argument the government's reply is that the Social Charter was a voluntary arrangement between the other 11. When challenged by opposition parties and trade unions on the argument that the UK will become the low-wage, low-conditions economy of the EC, the reply is that the alternative is continuing high unemployment.

The UK Presidency of the Council – 1992

In a 12-member Community, each member state occupies the six-month Presidency of the Council of Ministers once every six years. The UK occupied that position in the second half of 1992. During its presidency, the ministers of the state chair meetings of the Council, take the lead in discussions and in setting the agenda, and host the European Council. The UK's turn came at a particularly difficult moment.

1 The Danish referendum vote against the Maastricht Treaty threatened to de-rail the Maastricht process.

2 Currency turbulence forced Britain and Italy out of the European Exchange Rate Mechanism and cast doubt on EMU.

3 The war in the former Yugoslavia (with its accompanying refugees) posed a problem for the EC as both the USA and the United Nations looked to it to provide a lead in diplomatic moves to solve the dispute.

4 Negotiations over the GATT Uruguay Round led to confrontation between the USA and the EC over the issue of agricultural protection.

5 The recently reunited Germany sought an increase in its representation in EC institutions, thus threatening the principle of the equality of the 'big four'.

6 The southern states, led by Spain's Felipe Gonzalez, demanded assistance under the Cohesion Fund. This reopened the whole question of the budget and UK contributions.

7 Britain, seen by the others as lukewarm on Maastricht, sought a clear declaration on the meaning of 'subsidiarity' in the Maastricht Treaty.

These problems for the UK Presidency were in addition to domestic, economic and political problems. Rather than setting the agenda, the UK was forced to respond to the series of problems that were thrown up. In the early autumn Major was co-host at a London Conference on the former Yugoslavia. A special European Council held in Birmingham attempted to deal with what Major called the 'fault lines' that had opened up in the ERM. Little was achieved and it became clear that sterling's suspension from the ERM was not purely temporary. By the end of the autumn it appeared that, rather than progressing towards EMU, 1992 represented a significant retreat.

The regular European Council meeting was scheduled for December, in Edinburgh. These meetings have a history of acrimonious discussion, talk of crisis but compromise at the last moment. Edinburgh was no exception – although not all issues were resolved, there was considerable agreement.

1 *The Danish question* With the backing of the British, the Danes were allowed to opt out of the defence and monetary clauses of Maastricht, thus enabling the Danish government to put the treaty to the Danish electorate in a second referendum.

2 *The European Parliament* Germany was given 18 extra seats to reflect the rise in the population after reunification. To pacify the other three of the big four, they each received six extra seats. This means that from 1994 the UK will have 87 seats to Germany's 99.

3 *Subsidiarity* Although issuing no clear statement of its meaning, the Commission agreed to drop or to repeal around 20 initiatives which were considered matters to be dealt with at a national rather than Community level.

4 *Migration from outside the EC* There was an agreement on tighter restrictions on economic migrants. It was also agreed that the displaced peoples of the former Yugoslavia were to be helped in their home areas. This had been Britain's policy throughout the crisis although many had criticised it.

5 *Budget* There was agreement to increase the Community budget (from £47 to £64 billion) and, in particular, to transfer resources from the rich North to the poorer South.

6 *Enlargement* The 12 agreed to formal talks with Austria, Norway, Sweden and Finland over accession. However, the talks will not start until after Maastricht had been ratified. The UK is a firm supporter of enlargement but seemed, to the others, to be dragging its feet over ratification.

7 *Recovery* The heads of government agreed on co-ordination of strategy for economic recovery, thus paving the way for £14 billion of investment in capital projects.

8 *The single market* The summit declared the single market to be an irreversible achievement, completed in all essential respects. However, there was no agreement on the siting of the European Central Bank. London's claim was obviously jeopardised by the ERM crisis and by the UK's opt-out of the EMU clauses of Maastricht. Germany's case appears overwhelming but, for political reasons, it should not be in Frankfurt, home of the all-powerful Bundesbank.

Most commentators stated that Major managed to salvage the European credentials of the UK government by achieving some agreement after what appeared to be an unpromising start. Although European unity had taken a battering in 1992, reports of the EC's demise were clearly exaggerated.

Economic and Monetary Union

At the very least, monetary union involves irrevocably fixed exchange rates. This measure, seen by some as the only way to achieve the full benefits of a single market, is highly controversial because of its effect on the autonomy of national monetary policy. At present the EC has a halfway stage to EMU (through the Exchange Rate Mechanism) but currency crises in 1992/3 would suggest that the aim of EMU by 1999 is further off than when Europe's leaders signed the Maastricht Treaty, which commits most but not all members to this far-reaching goal.

OBJECTIVES
1 To analyse the costs and benefits of EMU.
2 To analyse the European Monetary System.
3 To explain why the ERM went wrong.
4 To explain the convergence criteria for EMU.

Monetary union: an overview

There are two requirements for complete monetary union.

1 Capital market integration, by which we mean that all obstacles to the free movement of financial capital between union members have been removed.

2 Exchange rate union, by which we mean that participants agree to the permanent fixing of exchange rates. This can be contrasted with the Exchange Rate Mechanism of the European Monetary System. Under the ERM currencies float within a limited band (6 per cent either side of the central rate, in the case of sterling between 1990 and 1992). Moreover, the ERM arrangement was clearly not permanent since Britain and others were allowed to suspend their membership when maintaining the currency within the band proved impossible or where the domestic costs were unacceptably high. If exchange rates are permanently fixed with no margin of fluctuation, in effect we have a single currency: the logical conclusion of the process of monetary union.

To sustain monetary union, harmonisation of monetary policy becomes essential. In the case of union by means of permanent fixed exchange rates between separate national currencies, all members must control the rate of monetary growth in line with one another (after allowing for differences in productivity between members). Differences in monetary growth will lead to differing rates of inflation, which would undermine the permanence of the exchange rate.

A single currency necessitates a union-wide central bank to control the supply of the single currency and to manage the exchange rate of the single currency against third-country currencies. Whatever form monetary union takes, it means the end of an independent monetary policy.

Benefits of European monetary union

Stimulus to trade   The rationale behind the EC is that by removing trade barriers there will be an increase in intra-EC trade, with the result that there will be an increase in the prosperity of member states. The SEA was designed to create a Europe without frontiers and yet the EC cannot be a truly single market when there are national currencies which fluctuate against one another. A single market requires a single currency as a common medium of exchange.

Savings in business costs   The present system of national currencies involves a cost for business. Resources are used up in monitoring exchange rate movements, hedging against adverse movements and in currency conversion. The elimination of exchange rates within the EC will produce significant savings for business. The Commission estimates that the adoption of a single currency would produce annual savings in transaction costs of 10 billion ECUs (or 0.5 per cent of GDP).

Efficient allocation of resources   The removal of exchange rate fluctuations and all controls over capital movements will lead to a better, more efficient allocation of capital. Capital (as well as labour) will move to areas of high marginal productivity, which will raise output thus adding to economic prosperity. What prevents this happening at present is the existence of fluctuations in exchange rates and residual controls over capital movement (although not by the UK government – which abolished all exchange controls in 1979).

Economising on foreign currency reserves   The elimination of national currencies will obviate the need for national governments and national central banks to hold reserves of foreign currencies. The task will be undertaken by the union-wide central bank. It is likely that the union reserves will be lower than the combined former reserves of the member states.

To understand the significance of this it is necessary to introduce the concept of seigniorage. In the days of dollar supremacy the rest of the world had to run balance of payments surpluses (whilst America ran a deficit), to acquire dollars. The French in particular argued that because the rate of interest on dollars accumulated by the rest of the world was low, the Americans were able to borrow at a low rate of interest. The benefit that accrued to the country issuing the reserve currency (in this instance, America) is known as seigniorage.

If a single currency means that holdings of dollars can be reduced, a lower seigniorage benefit is transferred from the EC to the USA. Moreover, a single European currency would be a major world currency, thus producing a seigniorage benefit to the European Union.

Low inflation

German participation in any EC monetary union is clearly imperative. The Germans would not participate unless the union-wide central bank enjoyed the same independence from political interference for which the Bundesbank is famous, and was constitutionally committed to price stability. It is therefore argued that monetary union would provide the member states with the kind of price stability enjoyed by Germany but denied to Italy, Spain, Portugal, Greece and the UK.

Lower interest rates

A combination of low (if not zero) inflation expectations coupled with exchange rate certainty would lead to low interest rates.

Precondition for future integration

The adoption of a single currency is a precondition for future moves towards economic and political union. Whether one regards this as an advantage, however, depends upon one's view of the desirability of future steps towards union.

Costs of monetary union

Loss of autonomy over economic policy

Acceptance of a single currency means that countries are no longer free to determine their own monetary policy.

If one accepts the Phillips curve trade-off (in the short run at least), it is possible for national governments to reduce unemployment by accepting a rise in the inflation rate. Under monetary union, member states will have the same inflation rate. Consequently, for those countries willing to accept more inflation to reduce unemployment (albeit temporary), the effect of union is to force them to accept more unemployment than they would prefer.

This problem of loss of autonomy over macro-economy policy does not present a problem to those people who reject even a short-run Phillips curve trade-off. For them (who include some but not all monetarists) the real test is whether the monetary union can deliver price stability more successfully than the national central bank.

The loss of exchange rate as a policy instrument

Devaluation of the currency is a method of correcting a balance of payments deficit (by an extension of demand for exports and a contraction of demand for imports) and stimulating growth and employment. Monetary union removes the possibility of using the exchange rate in this way. Once again, it represents a loss of national autonomy in economic policy.

The loss of inflation tax Irrespective of pronouncements from governments, inflation produces some benefits for them. First, it raises the average rate of taxation (assuming that other factors remain unchanged). Second, it reduces the real value of outstanding public sector debt. These benefits accruing to governments can be called an 'inflation tax'. Monetary union with a commitment to price stability will reduce the inflation tax of member states. Moreover, it removes the ability (and temptation) to inflate, to reduce the real value of debt.

Regional differences As factors of production move to high productivity areas there could be some undesirable social consequences of monetary union. Peripheral areas could lose out in the process unless monetary union is accompanied by regional policy measures to assist development in the less favoured regions (*see* the final section in this chapter, on the Cohesion Fund).

History of EMU within the EC

The Treaty of Rome does not mention economic and monetary union, although reference is made to:

- *unrestricted currency convertibility;*

- *the abolition of restrictions on capital movements;*

- *co-ordination of economic policy.*

Perhaps one reason there was no mention of EMU is that this was the period of managed exchange rates. Under the Bretton Woods system (1945–71) all major currencies were managed within narrow bands. However, as we saw in chapter 8, the system was breaking down. Not only was sterling devalued (in 1967 when Britain was not an EC member) but so was the franc (1969) and the Deutschmark was revalued. Changes in exchange rates had implications for EC budget transfers as well as providing governments with the means to affect trade flows.

Early efforts at EMU centred on the Werner Committee, set up to decide between two competing strategies to achieve it. The first strategy was known as the 'monetarist position' (it was not in any way related to Friedman or the monetarist counter-revolution). The monetarists favoured a commitment to the pooling of exchange reserves and to fixed exchange rates. The alternative strategy (known as the economist strategy) was to concentrate on economic co-ordination (convergence) before the final stage of EMU was reached. This reflected German concerns that, under a system of fixed exchange rates, inflation could be imported from abroad. Policy to reduce disparities, especially inflation rates, has been a persistent preoccupation of German governments.

The Werner Committee produced a compromise between monetarists and economists. It was known as parallelism: co-ordination of economic policies would be accompanied by narrowing exchange rate margins and integration of capital markets leading to a common currency and central bank. The outcome of these proposals was the 'snake in the tunnel'. Under the Smithsonian Agreement of 1971, the Bretton Woods system was altered to allow wider margins for currency fluctuation (a 4.5 per cent band). The EC countries limited the range of their own currencies to a band of 2.25 per cent. This was the snake within the tunnel. However, the system was unstable: sterling (which was included in advance of Britain's accession) withdrew in 1972, with the lira following one year later.

Currency turbulence led to the abandonment of the Smithsonian Agreement, which in retrospect appears a doomed attempt to patch up Bretton Woods. From 1973 the residue of the 'snake' ceased to be in the 'tunnel' and even then there were further realignments.

The next major initiative on EMU dates back to 1977, when Roy Jenkins was President of the Commission. Jenkins argued that his proposed European Monetary System (EMS) would help to alleviate the macro-economic problems of simultaneous high inflation and high unemployment. As the Phillips curve trade-off was no longer valid or accepted, Jenkins argued that the EMS could deliver lower inflation throughout the Community. From this base lower unemployment would eventually follow. Jenkins gained the support of German Chancellor Helmut Schmidt (who had been concerned about the adverse effects of over-valuation on German exports) and French President Giscard d'Estaing (who was anxious to prevent further decline in the value of the franc and was keen for France to remain in the first division of world economies). For all major initiatives in the EC, German and French support is essential and, with this gained, most of the other members fell in line although for a variety of reasons.

Italy saw the EMS system as likely to produce more effective discipline on the economy than seemed available internally. Over the years the Dutch have developed a close identity of interest with Germany and could be relied upon to join. The Irish took the opportunity to detach the punt from sterling, thus achieving greater economic independence than ever before. The UK was the great exception – but before looking at why it did not become a full member of the EMS in 1979, it would be useful to describe the system.

The European Monetary System (EMS)

> It was the intention of the founders of the EMS to create an area of stability in Europe with the lowest rate of inflation and the most stable exchange rates possible. The EMS is designed to improve economic co-operation between Member States and to cushion the impact of external economic shocks, such as the repeated excess fluctuations in the dollar rate, for individual member countries (*What is the EMS*, Commission leaflet).

To achieve these objectives the EMS has two main features: the European currency unit (ECU) and the Exchange Rate Mechanism (ERM).

The ECU The ECU is the basic monetary unit used in Community transactions. Although there was a coin in medieval France called an *ecu*, the link is purely coincidental. The modern ECU is the successor to the common unit of account and it dates from the establishment of the EMS in 1979. The ECU is a basket-type currency made up of specific amounts of member states' currencies. The weighting of each currency takes into account the proportion each state represents of Community GNP and of intra-Community trade. This is revised every five years or on the request of a member state if its exchange rate varies by more than 25 per cent.

The 1989 weightings were as follows:

Deutschmark	30.1
French franc	19.0
Sterling	13.0
Italian lira	10.15
Dutch guilder	9.4
Belgian franc	7.9
Spanish peseta	5.3
Danish kroner	2.45
Irish punt	1.1
Greek drachma	0.8
Portuguese escudo	0.8

Based on this weighting, the ECU in September 1989 was equal to the sum of the following:

Deutschmark	0.6242
French franc	1.332
Sterling	0.0878
Italian lira	151.8
Dutch guilder	0.2198
Belgian franc	3.301
Spanish peseta	6.885
Danish kroner	0.1976
Irish punt	0.0085
Greek drachma	1.440
Portuguese escudo	1.393
Luxembourg franc	1.130

The ECU is issued by the central banks of the EMS in return for the deposit of 20 per cent of their gold and dollar reserves with the Europe Monetary Co-operation Fund.

The role of the ECU

The ECU is not a fully fledged currency because:

- *it is not legal tender;*

- *there is no European central bank responsible for it;*

- *no ECU banknotes have been issued and ECU coins (minted in Belgium, France and Spain) are more a collector's item and a symbolic gesture to EMU than a medium of exchange.*

Despite these limitations the ECU plays a crucial role.

1 It is the basis for EC accounting for:

(a) the common customs tariff;
(b) intra-Community payments;
(c) agricultural prices;
(d) loans and subsidies from Community funds;
(e) Community credits;
(f) fines imposed by the Commission;
(g) repaying debts between central banks.

2 It is the accounting currency of the European Investment Bank (*see* chapter 17).

3 It plays a pivotal role in the EMS, which was set up in 1979 to establish a zone of monetary stability. The key feature of the EMS is the Exchange Rate Mechanism (ERM), in which member states' currencies fluctuate within limited bands. The ECU is the benchmark for fixing the central rates on which calculation of the permissible fluctuations is based. It is the point of reference for an early warning system for action to be taken to keep currencies within the permitted bands. It is the denominator for payments between central banks resulting from purchases and sales in support of exchange rates. Finally, it is the denominator for Community balance of payments assistance to member states in economic difficulties.

4 The ECU is increasingly used for private purchases. It has taken on this role because it is increasingly accepted by banks, companies and individuals in the EC countries and elsewhere (remember there is only one essential characteristic of money: it must be acceptable). Hence, the ECU is used as a currency for loans, for inter-bank lending, and for settlement between multi-national corporations and in foreign trade. ECU traveller's cheques and bank cards are available although private use is confined mainly to large banks and corporations. Nevertheless, the importance of the ECU is demonstrated by the fact that, in 1990, 8.5 per cent by value of all international loans were ECU loans. Only the American dollar, the yen and the Swiss franc were more important for international loans. Sterling was of equal importance to the ECU, and each was more important than the Deutschmark.

The ERM In many respects, the ERM is similar to the 'snake' and to the worldwide Bretton Woods system of an earlier era. In all cases currencies are managed: they are allowed to fluctuate within a defined band but government action is required if there is any danger of moving outside the band. The government action will take the form of central bank intervention in foreign exchange markets and adjustment to monetary policy (e.g. interest rate changes)

These similarities should not be allowed to hide a number of essential differences. First, although the ERM is a 'snake', there is no 'tunnel'. The ERM currencies jointly float against all other currencies. The second difference is the role of ECU in the system. Third, each currency in the ERM has a value against the ECU and a series of cross-rates against all other ERM currencies. The permitted band is 2.25 per cent either side of the central rate (or 6 per cent in exceptional circumstances). However, in practice the permitted margin of fluctuation is less when referring to fluctuation against the ECU. This is because as the value of the currency falls against the ECU the value of other ERM currencies rises – thus altering the value of the ECU. The greater the weighting of a currency in the EMS, the smaller are its effective margins of fluctuation against the ECU before it reaches the limits allowed against other currencies.

The mechanism for keeping currencies within the bands takes the following form.

1 Commitment to central bank intervention in foreign exchange markets: when a currency reaches the upper or lower limits of its permitted range of values against another ERM currency both central banks are required to act. The intervention will take the form of buying weak currencies and selling strong ones.

2 Credits and pooling reserves: there are agreements for credits to be made available to central banks seeking foreign exchange to buy weak currency. As well as direct swaps between central banks, there is also the European Monetary Co-operation Fund (EMCF). EMS members deposit 20 per cent of their gold and foreign exchange reserves, receiving ECUs in return. Through the EMCF short-term credit is available.

3 Divergence indicators: set at 75 per cent of the permitted fluctuations, these provide an early warning system. It is expected that action will be taken when the divergence indicator is reached.

4 Convergence of economic policy is expected of members.

5 Some limited redistribution via the European Investment Bank is also available.

Fig. 15.1 *ERM membership*

Advantages
1. Exchange rate stability reduces uncertainty.
2. Monetary discipline; under the ERM the course of monetary policy is determined by the most conservative of central banks.
3. A high exchange rate reduces the importation of inflation.
4. Controls wage costs in that excessive pay rises will lead to job losses.
5. Exchange stability is an essential part of a single market.

Disadvantages
1. The loss of the exchange rate as a policy weapon.
2. Acts as a constraint on economic policy.
3. Interest rate policy becomes subservient to exchange rate goal.
4. A tight monetary policy involving high interest rates is essential when the currency is weak.
5. Unemployment will result from the failure to control costs.
6. The currency becomes a hostage to speculative currency movements.
7. A strong Deutschmark pulls up the value of other currencies against non-ERM currencies, thus leading to overvaluation.

Fig. 15.1 summarises the advantages and disadvantages of joining the ERM.

Britain's aloofness from the ERM

From 1979 the UK was a member of the EMS in the sense that sterling was part of the basket of currencies making up the ECU. However, it was not part of the Exchange Rate Mechanism. Neither the outgoing Callaghan (Labour) government nor the incoming Thatcher (Conservative) government favoured ERM membership at the time. Arguments against membership included the following.

1 As sterling was a petro-currency (its value depending upon the price of oil) it would be inappropriate to tie it to the non-petro-currencies of the ERM.

2 Sterling was an international currency with substantial flows of mobile funds into and out of the City of London. These funds are sensitive to interest and exchange rate changes and this could destabilise the ERM.

3 Conflict with domestic policy: the outgoing Labour government feared that with the UK's propensity for inflation and its high marginal propensity to import, ERM would force deflationary policies on the country. With import controls and exchange rate adjustment no longer available (except in a crisis), British governments would be forced to inflict further unemployment on the country as an 'import control'. The incoming Thatcher government was committed to an application of strict monetarism. The ERM might have forced it to adopt a more expansionary monetary policy than it was prepared to introduce. Both these points reflect the concern that ERM membership would represent a loss of autonomy in monetary policy.

During the 1980s the UK remained outside the ERM. Prime Minister Thatcher was particularly opposed to membership, arguing that 'you can't buck the market'. However, a growing amount of opinion (academic economists, the CBI, the City, opposition parties, the TUC) favoured entry as the decade wore on. Some people feared that Britain would be 'left behind' in a two-speed Europe. Others argued that ERM would impose the discipline to eliminate inflation (and inflationary expectations) once and for all. Nigel Lawson (Chancellor of the Exchequer from 1983 to 1989) favoured membership but the only concession Thatcher would make was to define the conditions under which 'the time would be right' for entering: the UK's inflation must be reduced to that of its EC partners, and Italy and France must dismantle all exchange controls.

Thatcher's economic adviser (Professor Alan Walters) was opposed to membership and this difference of opinion led eventually to Lawson's resignation – an event which marked an important point in Thatcher's own downfall. Lawson's replacement was John Major, who had served as Chief Secretary to the Treasury (a cabinet post with responsibilities for public spending – in effect, deputy chancellor). Major was seen as a possible successor to Thatcher and he was less abrasive in his attitude to Europe. It was Major who took Britain in to the ERM in October 1990 (the Thatcherite

Lord Tebbit has remarked, perhaps rather unkindly, that in this terminal stage of the Thatcher era, the Prime Minister was not in full control of her cabinet).

ERM entry, albeit at the wide band, was widely supported by politicians, industrialists, the City and many economists. Major (soon to be Prime Minister) argued that it was not a soft option but would provide for greater currency stability and would deliver lower inflation by the imposition of discipline on markets. For instance, a determination to keep within the permitted bands forces governments to pursue appropriate monetary policy. Both sides of industry would soon realise the consequences of excessive pay rises.

For nearly two years the government kept sterling within the permitted bands. At one stage Major, rather foolishly in retrospect, told journalists of his vision of sterling replacing the Deutschmark as the anchor currency of the ERM. Within a few weeks of this unguarded comment, sterling was forced out of the ERM.

ERM crisis in September 1992

In September 1992 massive currency movements placed downward pressure on those currencies of the ERM perceived to be weak. These included the lira, the peseta and the escudo as well as sterling. The government stated its commitment to maintain sterling within the 6 per cent band either side of the central rate of DM 2.95. This was a key feature of the policy of achieving zero inflation. On 13 September, when there was a realignment of weaker currencies, the Chancellor of the Exchequer, Norman Lamont, rejected devaluation of sterling. He hoped that a resolute stand by the government, involving a willingness to take whatever action was necessary, would prevent sterling falling below its ERM floor. The German government was willing to allow interest rates to fall, thus increasing the attractiveness of sterling. However, the Bundesbank, famed for its independence from the government, was prepared to reduce rates by only 0.25 per cent. Consequently, the pressure on sterling continued. (*See* Illustration 15.1.)

On 16 September heavy selling of sterling forced the UK government to raise interest rates from 10 to 12 per cent and again to 15 per cent. Even this historically unprecedented increase (two rises in one day, by a total of 50 per cent) was insufficient to stem the selling. In the early evening of 16 September Lamont abandoned the attempt to stay within the ERM at DM 2.95 plus or minus 6 per cent. It soon became clear that the UK's ERM membership was to be suspended for a period of months and years rather than days. Eurosceptics saw the events of 'Black Wednesday' (as it became known) as proof of their argument against not only the ERM but the monetary clauses of the Maastricht Treaty.

We can divide the causes of the crisis into two groups: a combination of unique historical factors operating in the autumn of 1992; and underlying weaknesses in a system of relatively fixed exchange rates. Looking more closely at the first of these, the particular factors were:

1 The UK's late admission to the system. This meant that the British economy had not had time to adjust to the ERM before it faced its first massive test. The

Illustration 15.1 *Countdown to Black Wednesday 16 September 1992*

June	Danish referendum rejects Maastricht Treaty. French government decides to hold referendum. Rise in Italian interest rates.
July	Lamont makes a speech in which he rules out all options other than keeping sterling in the ERM. Rise in German and Italian interest rates.
August	Discussions on realignment of ERM currencies. Opinion polls in France suggest a majority against Maastricht in forthcoming referendum.
28 August	Devaluation ruled out.
4 September	UK government takes out a 10 billion ECU loan to add to reserves.
10 September	Italian government takes on emergency powers to cut the budget deficit.
13 September	Italian lira devalued. Bundesbank says that it will reduce interest rates.
14 September	0.25 per cent cut in German interest rates.
15 September	Heavy selling of sterling, which falls close to its ERM floor. Treasury and Bank of England consider pre-emptive rise in interest rates before markets open. German Finance Minister states that the realignment of 13 September did not go far enough.
16 September	Intense pressure on sterling when markets open. Heavy intervention by Bank of England. UK reserves of foreign currency used to buy sterling.
11 a.m.	Minimum Lending Rate set at 12 per cent. Heavy selling continues despite: ■ *central bank intervention in markets;* ■ *rise in interest rates.*
2.15 p.m.	Crisis meeting of cabinet ministers agrees on rise in MLR to 15 per cent.
7.30 p.m.	Lamont announced suspension of ERM membership and rescinds the 15 per cent MLR.
Night of 16/17 September	EC monetary committee meets. Lira leaves ERM, peseta devalued.
17 September	MLR reduced to 10 per cent. Sterling falls sharply and ends the week at DM 2.61, or 15 per cent below the old ERM floor.

lateness of British entry can be attributed to Thatcher's opposition to the ERM over a long period. In this opposition she was supported by Euro-sceptics within the Conservative Party and her advisers, such as Walters.

2 The choice of DM 2.95 as the central rate at which sterling entered and the government's inflexibility in maintaining this rate. Devaluation was scorned as the 'easy option' taken by Labour governments in 1949 and 1967. As Chancellor at the time of entry and Prime Minister for most of the period, Major clearly has responsibility for the choice of sterling central rate. The fact that exit from the ERM was followed by a fall in value demonstrates that sterling was overvalued.

3 The fundamental weakness of the UK economy was coupled with a lack of government action in summer 1992. The 'green shoots' of recovery heralded by Lamont in 1991 had withered away in 1992.

4 The Danish rejection of Maastricht in a referendum held in June 1992 was followed by considerable uncertainty over the outcome of the constitutionally unnecessary French referendum. This uncertainty over the future development of the EC contributed to the movement of currency across the foreign exchanges.

5 Events in Germany also played a major role in the crisis. Reunion with East Germany produced monetary and economy problems. The union of the Deutschmark (West Germany's currency) and the Ostmark (East Germany's) was at an exchange rate which overvalued the latter. Consequently, Germany's money supply rose at a faster rate than the target of 3.5 to 5.5 per cent. This led to high interest rates to reduce inflationary pressure. High German interest rates forced up rates in the rest of Europe, thus preventing the UK government kick-starting the economy by interest rate cuts.

At the same time the Governors of the Bundesbank seemed reluctant to prop up sterling and the lira to the same extent as the French franc was supported. The German defence of their action (or inaction) was that the heavy buying needed to support sterling would have further endangered Germany's money supply targets. The more xenophobic elements in Britain saw this as German unhelpfulness and perhaps a German preference for a two-speed Europe.

To the peculiar circumstances of September 1992 we should add the following underlying causes.

1 In an open economy with free movement of capital, the potential currency movements are beyond the capacity of national governments to tackle. Even if all ERM members acted to support a weak currency it would still be insufficient where the market perceives a fundamental weakness in the currency. Moreover, any inkling of devaluation (euphemistically known as realignment) will increase pressure on the weak currency.

2 The absence of a sufficient degree of convergence between ERM members. If exchange rates are to remain stable, members of the system should pursue similar policies and be at similar stages in the business cycle. Any divergence – whether differential rates of inflation, interest rates or monetary growth – will cause exchange rate movements and pressure on the system.

Illustration 15.2 *The impact of devaluation*

1. Exports become cheaper; there is therefore an extension of demand.

2. Imports become dearer; there is therefore a contraction of demand.

3. The balance of payments will improve if:

   (a) demand for exports and imports changes sufficiently to counteract the deterioration in the terms of trade. The Marshall–Lerner Condition for successful devaluation is that the sum of the price elasticities of demand for imports and exports should exceed one;

   (b) the supply of exports is sufficiently elastic to satisfy the additional demand. In conditions of full employment this will require deflationary measures to create spare capacity.

4. Additional demand will provide a boost to output and employment.

   But

5. Higher import prices will add to inflationary pressures.
   Unfortunately the experience of previous devaluations is not promising:

Period	Depreciation (%)	Export growth (%)	Import growth (%)
1967–9	14	35	7
1972–4	25	22	16.5
1981–3	20	4.5	18
1987–9	14	13	21

   Source: Central Statistical Office, quoted in the *Sunday Times*, 8 November 1992

Exit from the ERM provided the UK government with the opportunity to pursue economic policy less constrained by commitments to other countries. Sterling no longer had to be kept within a specific band and was allowed to fall. Within days it had been effectively devalued by 15 per cent. (The possible impact of this is outlined in Illustration 15.2.) Interest rates could now be reduced to stimulate investment and spending. Coinciding with the publication of a major biography of Keynes came renewed interest in Keynesian economics. There was even a subtle change in the government's inflation objective: commitment to zero inflation was replaced by a commitment to low inflation, suggesting that mild inflation was tolerable if it led to other benefits. In the 1992 Autumn Statement Lamont announced a PSBR in excess of £40 billion – the sort of figure that would frighten strict monetarists.

EMU and Maastricht

The 1970 Werner Report defined monetary union as:

- *total and irreversible convertibility of currencies;*

- *complete liberalisation of capital transactions and full integration of banking and financial markets;*

- *elimination of margins of fluctuation and irrevocable locking of exchange rate parities.*

This definition was used in the Delors Report, which then defined economic union in terms of:

- *the single market within which persons, goods, services and capital can move freely;*

- *competition policy and other measures aimed at strengthening market mechanisms;*

- *common policies aimed at structural change and regional development;*

- *macro-economic policy co-ordination, including binding rules for budgetary policies.*

The Delors Report formed the basis of the EMU provisions of the Maastricht Treaty. Article 3 obliges the member states to adopt 'an economic policy based on the close co-ordination of . . . [their] economic policies' in accordance with the principles of an open market economy and free competition in order to achieve the economic convergence necessary for monetary union. It also commits the member states to an irrevocable fixing of exchange rates, which will lead to the introduction of a single currency (the ECU), and the definition and conduct of a single monetary policy and exchange rate policy. The primary objectives of these exchange rate/monetary policies will be to maintain price stability and to support the general economic objectives of the Community.

Finally, article 3 sets out guidelines as to the kind of principles which must underlie these economic policies, including stable prices, sound public finances and monetary conditions and a sustainable balance of payments.

The movement towards EMU is in three stages (*see* Illustration 15.3). Stage 1 started in 1990 and involved action to co-ordinate economic policy, to strengthen both the EMS and ECU, and to extend the role of the Committee of Central Bank Governors. Stage 2 is set to commence in 1994 with the establishment of the European Monetary Institute, which will co-ordinate economic policies of member states. Convergence criteria have been established and will be used to assess whether to move to Stage 3. The criteria are:

- *price stability: a rate of inflation no more than 1.5 per cent above the average of the three best performing member states;*

- *interest rates should not be more than two percentage points above the average of these three best performing states over the previous 12 months;*

- *there should be no excessive government deficit, i.e. not above 3 per cent of GDP; public debt should not exceed 60 per cent of GDP;*

- *exchange rate fluctuations in the EMS should not exceed their normal margins (i.e. must have remained in the ERM narrow band) for at least two years.*

At the time of the signing of the Maastricht Treaty in 1991, only France and Luxembourg satisfied all criteria, whilst Denmark and the UK (the two

Illustration 15.3 *The Delors three stages to EMU*

Stage 1: single market

Stage 1 would be based on *consolidating the single market*. It would involve:

- *the complete removal of physical, technical and fiscal barriers;*
- *the strengthening of competition policy and the reduction of state aids such as subsidies to industries;*
- *the reform of Structural Funds, which offer regional aid, and the doubling of their resources;*
- *closer co-ordination of economic and monetary policies;*
- *the deregulation of financial markets and the establishment of a single financial area, through the implementation of directives on banking, securities and insurance services;*
- *all Community currencies joining the Exchange Rate Mechanism of the EMS in the narrow band;*
- *the removal of all impediments to the private use of the ECU;*
- *consultation with Committee of Central Bank Governors.*

Stage 2: transitional stage

Stage 2 would be a transitional stage and would involve the revision of existing institutions and setting up new ones, including the European System of Central Banks (ESCB), although, throughout Stage 2, ultimate responsibility for policy decisions would remain with national authorities:

- *movement towards common monetary policy;*
- *less reliance on currency realignments;*
- *reduction in ERM bands;*
- *European System of Central Banks established.*

Stage 3: monetary union

Stage 3 would involve:

- *possible further strengthening of Community structural and regional policies;*
- *a move to irrevocably locked exchange rates;*
- *creation of a single EC currency in the long run;*
- *binding constraints on national budgets;*
- *the EC would act as single entity in international policy measures;*
- *responsibility for monetary policy to pass to ESCB;*
- *common regional policy.*

allegedly reluctant Europeans) satisfied most of the conditions. Germany, indispensable for the whole operation, did not satisfy the deficit criterion, although this can be explained by the unique circumstances of reunification. The southern states will have to make substantial progress on debt, combating inflation and achieving greater currency stability before they will be ready. Even countries like the Netherlands (seen as participating in a quasi-EMU with Germany), Ireland (always anxious to be a good European) and Belgium will have to reduce their public sector debt if they are to qualify. Fig. 15.2 shows which countries satisfied which criteria in 1991.

Since Maastricht was signed European currencies have experienced great turbulence – sterling left the ERM, the lira and punt were devalued. This means a number of the signatories to Maastricht are now further off satisfying the convergence criteria. Moreover, the experience of 1992 has strengthened the argument of the opponents of EMU. High interest rates were the price of staying in the ERM – the price of EMU would be devastating unless British industry improved both its price and non-price competitiveness.

Stage 3 will begin at the end of 1996 if the European Council decides that enough member states have met the criteria. By 1998 (or before) the European Central Bank (ECB) and the European System of Central Banks (ESCB) would be established. At this point all participating members will agree the conversion rates at which their currencies will be exchanged for the ECU, which will take on the role of a currency in its own right.

The basic tasks of the ESCB will be to:

- *define and implement monetary policy;*

Fig. 15.2 *Who satisfied the criteria in 1991*

	Public debt	Budget deficit	Inflation rate	Long-term interest rates	ERM	Score
Belgium	×	×	√	√	√	3
Denmark	×	√	√	√	√	4
Germany	√	×	×	√	√	3
Greece	×	×	×	×	×	0
France	√	√	√	√	√	5
Ireland	×	×	√	√	√	3
Italy	×	×	×	×	×	0
Luxembourg	√	√	√	√	√	5
Netherlands	×	×	×	√	√	2
Portugal	×	×	×	×	×	0
Spain	√	×	×	×	×	1
UK	√	√	√	√	×	4

√ = criteria satisfied
Source: European Commission

Fig. 15.3 *EMU timetable under Maastricht*

On ratification	No further change in currency composition of the ECU basket.
1 January 1993	Single market established.
By 31 December 1993	Abolition of all exchange controls within EC. Cohesion Fund established.
1 January 1994	*Stage 2*: European Monetary Institute established. All EC currencies in narrow band.
After January 1994	Work toward central bank independence. Members to avoid excess budget deficit.
By 31 December 1996	Decide whether to move to Stage 3 and who qualifies.
1 January 1997	*Start of Stage 3*: European Central Bank, Economic and Financial Committee, single currency.
1998	Decision on irrevocable conversion rates.
1 January 1999	Last date for start of Stage 3.

- *conduct foreign exchange operations;*

- *hold and manage official foreign reserves of participating member states.*

The ECB will have the exclusive right to authorise the issue of ECU banknotes in the participating member states, respecting as far as possible existing practices for both issue and design. Each member state will be able to issue ECU coins subject to the ECB's control on volume, and to the harmonisation necessary for smooth circulation.

The ECB and national central banks must be independent both of Community institutions and national governments.

Fig. 15.3 sets out the EMU timetable.

Britain's concern over EMU

During the Maastricht negotiations the UK government sought to ensure that:

- *there would be no commitment by Britain to move to a single monetary policy or to a single currency;*

- *monetary policy would remain unambiguously a national responsibility until the Community moved to a single currency and monetary policy;*

- *member states would retain primary responsibility for their own economic policy; and*

- *the arrangements for EMU would be practical and workable and, in particular, there should be clear and quantifiable convergence conditions which would have to be met by each member state before it could move to a single currency and monetary policy.*

These reservations about EMU resulted in a protocol to the treaty which recognised that Britain would not be obliged or committed to Stage 3 without a decision to do so by the government and Parliament.

If Britain exercises its option not to join, sterling will remain the national currency and Britain would retain its own monetary policy. However, it was assumed that sterling outside EMU would continue to be linked to the ECU by the ERM. If Britain opted out the door to EMU would remain open and the Bank of England would still be represented on the ESCB.

The Commission's statement of the benefits of EMU

Moving to a situation in which the exchange rates of member states' currencies were permanently fixed or in which there were a single currency would yield the following benefits, according to the Commission's publication *Economic and Monetary Union*.

1 Reducing the uncertainties and risks due to currency fluctuations will stimulate industrial and commercial investment, economic growth, company profitability, and employment.

2 Economic and monetary union will increase price stability.

3 Interest rate cuts in several countries, which should reduce the cost of servicing the public debt.

4 Employment, which is already responding to improved growth prospects, will receive a boost from regional and structural policies and, ultimately, from

---

Illustration 15.4 *Benefits of a single currency over irrevocably fixed exchange rates*

1. **Transaction costs**: a single currency would eliminate all the costs arising to firms and individuals from conversions from one Community currency into another.
2. **Transparency of prices**: as goods and services would be priced in the same currency, this would further strengthen the pro-competitive effect of the single market.
3. **Economies of scale**: a single currency would lead markets for the same categories of financial instruments to merge, yielding benefits in terms of market depth and efficiency.
4. **Credibility**: from the outset, a single currency gives maximum credibility to monetary union.
5. **Visibility**: a single currency would, for all Community agents, be a visible sign of the creation of EMU and would make those agents more conscious of the associated wage and price discipline.
6. **External benefits**: only with a single currency can the EMU lead to a recasting of international currencies and to a more balanced international monetary regime.

the adjustments that will have taken place. Furthermore, within an economic and monetary union, a number of countries will benefit from the removal of the constraint imposed at national level by the external current-account balance.

5 Those member states which already have only modest inflation will also gain from the reduction in the other member states. As a result, their trade will probably become more buoyant but, more importantly, the phenomenon which economists refer to as 'imported inflation' will recede as the rise in import prices slows down. Member states will also gain from the establishment of a Community-wide market and the introduction of a single currency.

6 The Community as a whole will benefit from the adoption of a single currency, the ECU, which could become as important internationally as the dollar or yen.

Illustration 15.4 identifies the benefits of a single currency over irrevocably fixed exchange rates.

The Cohesion Fund

The optimistic interpretation of EMU is that, once established, the benefits will spread out to all regions of the Community. In a 'trickle-down' way the greater integration of the European economy will mean that capital – and therefore output and income – will be dispersed over a wide area. The opposing interpretation is that EMU will result not in a virtuous circle to engulf all in greater prosperity but, instead, the peripheral and disadvantaged areas will experience a vicious circle of decline. Britton and Mayes (*Achieving Monetary Union in Europe*, p. 66) sum up the distinction between the virtuous and the vicious circle as follows:

> if the initial adjustment process is positive, it sets in motion a virtuous circle of increased profitability for firms, enabling increased investment and R&D, which in turn brings new products and more efficiency, which enables a further gain in profitability and a rise in real wages and so on indefinitely.
> . . . those regions requiring a downward adjustment to achieve convergence . . . can get themselves locked into a downward spiral . . . With free movement of labour and capital, both are attracted by the regions of higher returns, and because of the imperfections in the system and the dynamic nature of the gains, these flows are not sufficient to equalise the position and bring divergence to a halt . . . Transport costs and economies of scale would tend to favour a shift in economic activity away from less developed regions, especially if they were at the periphery of the Community, to the highly developed regions.

Examples of EMU in history point to the damage to disadvantaged and peripheral areas. EMU in the reunited Germany has caused major problems because of the divergence in the two economies prior to union. In the British

Isles there have been two examples of EMU: the Act of Union with Scotland (1707) and the Act of Union with Ireland (1801). In both cases it could be argued the peripheral area in the union suffered – and without the prospect of devaluation to restore its competitive position: 'it has been widely argued that EMU with Great Britain led to a progressive decline in Ireland's relative position in a cycle of cumulative causation, as British competitive advantage was continuously reinforced' (Britton and Mayes, p. 66).

Because of this concern over the future of disadvantaged and peripheral regions it was decided to establish a new fund alongside the existing Structural Funds (chapter 16). This new fund, established under article 130 of the Maastricht Treaty, is to be called the Cohesion Fund. Assistance is to be given to disadvantaged regions in member states whose GDP is less than 90 per cent of the Community average. As the Cohesion Fund is linked to EMU it is available only to those states which commit themselves to the Delors Stage 3. Ireland and the three southern newcomers will qualify for assistance under the Cohesion Fund, with money earmarked for expenditure on projects in 'the fields of environment and trans-European networks in the area of the transport infrastructure'.

As the next poorest EC member the UK might qualify for assistance but only if it commits itself to EMU. This is a further source of aggravation among Euro-sceptics, who argue that Britain will be forced to contribute to the EC budget to enable the southern states to achieve sufficient convergence with the affluent states to proceed to the Delors Stage 3. The Cohesion Fund and the demands of Spain, Portugal and Greece have reopened the contentious issue of the budget and British contributions.

CHAPTER 16

EC Budgetary Issues

The EC budget and Britain's contributions to it have long been a source of controversy. The method of assessing the contributions coupled with the dominance of the common agricultural policy (CAP) with the EC has led to Britain being a net contributor. As one of the poorer countries in Europe this is inequitable. As well as looking at the system of own-resource financing this chapter looks at the expenditure through the CAP and the Structural Funds.

OBJECTIVES
1 To explain and analyse the system of own-resource financing.
2 To explain and analyse the CAP.
3 To investigate the CAP.
4 To explain the common fishing policy.
5 To survey the EC Structural Funds and the role of the European Investment Bank.

EC funds

When studying EC budgetary matters, a key concept to understand is that of 'EC own resources'. By this we mean the right of the EC to levy a tax remitted to the Commission by national governments not as a gift, but as an entitlement of the EC. This concept is crucial for understanding the Commission's position in relation to the controversy over the British contribution.

The Coal and Steel Community was set up before the other Communities and was financed in a different way. From the outset the ECSC had its own resources: this was the first 'EC tax' and took the form of levies on the production of coal and steel. The High Authority of the ECSC (now the Commission), has the right to impose a levy of up to 1 per cent of the value of output from the industries. A higher rate requires majority approval in the Council but no such approval is needed for levies below 1 per cent.

In the early days of the ECSC the two industries made roughly equal contributions, but over the years the share borne by the steel industry has risen, whilst that from coal has fallen (to 24 per cent of total in 1989). As the coal industry has received a larger percentage share of ECSC funds, there has effectively been a transfer of resources from the steel industry to the coal industry and this produces 'constant recriminations from the steelmakers' (Strasser, *The Finances of Europe*, p. 76).

On a national basis contributions vary according to the relative sizes of the two industries concerned. Germany and the UK provide 85 per cent of the coal levy. The steel levy results in greater (but not complete) equality in contribution. Over the two industries as a whole contributions are:

- *Germany 32 per cent;*
- *UK 20 per cent;*
- *Italy 14 per cent;*
- *France 12 per cent;*
- *Spain 9 per cent;*
- *Belgium 6 per cent;*
- *Other EC countries 7 per cent.*

In addition to the levy the ECSC has been financed by

- *income from investment of ECSC funds;*
- *contributions from member states (unlike the levy, these contributions require agreement in the Council);*
- *contributions from the EC budget;*
- *fines and late-payment surcharges, e.g. those imposed on producers who fail to observe production quotas;*
- *ECSC borrowing guaranteed by the ECSC's own resource (namely the levy).*

The other two Communities were at first financed in a way different from the ECSC. The Commission proposed and the Council approved the overall budget and contributions were collected according to agreed proportions. In the period of the 'six', Germany, France and Italy each contributed 28 per cent, the remainder coming from the small Benelux countries. Despite a rise in the budget from 11 million units of account in 1958 to 3,385 million in 1970, the system worked.

'Own-resource' financing was allowed for under article 201 of the Treaty of Rome, which specified a system based on the Common Customs Tariff. When the Commission attempted to introduce own-resource financing in the 1960s there was a crisis within the EC. This was the period of the French 'empty chair' (1965–6) when any member could block progress by refusing to attend Council meetings. Despite the controversy the Commission persisted in its attempt to obtain its own resources. Agreement finally came in April 1970, when, under the Luxembourg Agreement, the customs duty, agricultural levies and 1 per cent of VAT (calculated on a uniform basis) were assigned to the EC. There were delays in implementing these measures and, coupled with growing expenditure on agriculture, they led to budgetary imbalance. Consequently, from time to time financial 'top-up' contributions from member states were necessary, and these were based on GNP, at market prices. This conflicted with the principle of financial autonomy based on EC own resources since these top-up payments required unanimous agreement in the Council.

The Commission sought a rise in the 'own-resources' finance in the form of increasing the VAT percentage from 1 to 1.4. However, this change became embroiled with a number of other issues that persist in EC financial arrangements:

- *budgetary discipline – in particular control over agricultural spending;*

- *the necessity of developing new policies – especially in relation to the Structural Funds and now the Cohesion Fund;*

- *the costs involved in enlargement – especially as the EC was enlarged to take in poorer nations in the Mediterranean parts of Europe;*

- *the question of 'budgetary imbalances' – this is a code for 'the UK problem'. The UK is one of the poorest members of the EC yet the second biggest net contributor. This reflects the facts that as UK agriculture is efficient but a small part of the economy the UK gains little from CAP spending, and as an open economy with links beyond Europe, the UK makes a disproportionately high contribution to the tax on non-EC goods.*

During the early Thatcher years European Council meetings were characterised by angry disputes over the budget. The Commission and other members argued that the proceeds of the EC 'taxes' were not Britain's money but were EC own resources. Thatcher argued that Britain's budgetary contribution was inequitable. At the Fontainebleau Council in 1984 there was agreement on EC own resources and on the 'British problem'. The VAT rate was raised to 1.4 per cent on a national harmonised base. The harmonisation is designed to take account of national differences not least in the rates of VAT. However, a ceiling was set on 'own-resource' VAT – this was set at 0.55 per cent of a member state's GNP.

Despite this increase in own resources and an expressed determination to control expenditure on agriculture (especially with the accession of the poorer countries of the South) budgetary imbalance continued. Inter-governmental agreements in the mid-1980s led to top-up contributions to finance the deficit. The Commission argued for a fourth own resource, not linked to the existing tax base. The problem with agricultural levies was that as the EC became increasingly self-sufficient in food the yield from levies on non-EC food fell. VAT yield failed to rise sufficiently as consumption went down as a proportion of GDP. The Commission proposed a fourth own resource based on a limit of 1.4 per cent of Community GNP (in fact the Council limited it to 1.2 per cent). From the Brussels Council of 1988 the four 'own resources' are:

- *levies collected on trade in agricultural products between the Community and the rest of the world;*

- *customs duties collected under the common external tariff on imports into the Community;*

Table 16.1 *General Community budget 1991*

	Billion ECUs	%
Customs duties	12.8	20.5
Agricultural levies	1.3	2.2
Sugar levies	1.2	2.0
VAT	34.2	54.4
GNP-based own resource	14.3	22.7
Other revenue	0.3	0.5
Less collection costs	(1.5)	(2.4)
TOTAL	62.8	100.0

- *a levy on VAT revenue, at a rate of up to 1.4 per cent on a notional harmonised base, which is capped at 0.55 per cent of a member state's GNP; and*

- *a share of the Community's GNP up to an amount required to balance the budget within an own-resources ceiling of 1.2 per cent of GNP.*

Table 16.1 shows the breakdown of budget revenues for 1991.

Britain's contribution to the budget

Illustration 16.1 describes the EC budget procedure.

At the time when the Heath government negotiated British membership it was recognised that the 'own resources' of finance developed by the six would produce an unbalanced situation in which Britain would be the loser.

Illustration 16.1 *EC budget procedure*

- The Commission draws up a preliminary draft budget which it sends to the Council.

- On this basis the Council prepares a draft, which it sends to Parliament for a first reading.

- Parliament delivers an opinion on the draft budget: it may approve it, or send the Council a modified text. In the field of compulsory expenditure, Parliament can only submit proposals for modification to the Council. Where non-compulsory expenditure is concerned, however, Parliament has a genuine right of amendment.

- The Council examines this new draft, which it may amend in its turn. Modifications of compulsory expenditure are final but other amendments are sent on to Parliament for a second reading.

- In the final stage Parliament can reamend the changes made by the Council to its initial amendments. At the end of the procedure, the final adoption of the budget – or its rejection – falls to Parliament.

The Accession Treaty included lengthy transitional measures and it was accepted that if any member state found itself in an unacceptable position, the Community would take remedial action.

In 1979 the UK government asked for special measures to replace the transitional arrangements that were coming to an end. The UK was likely to be a major net contributor because of the import duties on non-EC goods and because EC expenditure was dominated by the CAP, from which Britain would gain little. The early 1980s were plagued by battles in the European Council over the British contribution. Both the Commission and Britain's partners argued that 'own resources' cannot be viewed as state contributions. Nevertheless there was an acceptance of the unfairness of the budget. Hence, after hard bargaining, the principle of financial compensation was agreed at the Fontainebleau Council in June 1984.

Under the Fontainebleau arrangement, Britain was to receive an abatement (a 'refund') of 66 per cent of the difference between what Britain would have paid to the budget had it been financed entirely by uncapped VAT and its share of receipts. The cost of compensation is borne by the other member states in proportion to their GNP, with reductions granted to Germany (the other major net contributor) and Spain and Portugal during their own transition phases.

By the end of 1992 the cumulative value of the abatement was £12 billion. Nevertheless Britain remains a major net contributor despite being one of the five EC states whose per capita GDP is below the EC average. In 1992 net payments and receipts per person were as shown in Table 16.2.

In his study *The EC Budget* (Royal Institute of International Affairs) Michael Franklin calculated net receipts/net payments if EC own resources were based on GDP per head in member states. The result (shown in Table 16.3) is that there will be more net contributors, including relatively affluent states such as Luxembourg and Denmark.

Table 16.2 *EC budget recipients and contributors 1992*

Net recipients	ECU per head
Luxembourg	1,897
Ireland	678
Greece	375
Belgium	165
Portugal	104
Denmark	97
Spain	73
Italy	10
Net contributors	
The Netherlands	7
France	26
Britain	52
Germany	140

Table 16.3 *EC budget recipients and contributors if based on per capita GDP*

Net recipients	ECU per head
Greece	327
Portugal	302
Ireland	254
Spain	187

Net contributors	
Britain	7
Italy	17
Belgium	21
The Netherlands	26
France	73
Denmark	77
Germany	134
Luxembourg	271

Agriculture in the Treaty of Rome

Articles 38 to 47 of the Treaty of Rome provide the framework for the common agricultural policy (CAP). In the treaty it is stated that the 'common market shall extend to agriculture and trade in agricultural products'. Agricultural products were defined as the products of the soil, of stock farming and of fisheries and products of first stage processing directly related to the products. It goes on to state that the common market for agricultural products must be accompanied by the establishment of a common agricultural policy among the member states.

The objectives of the CAP are:

- *to increase agricultural productivity by promoting technical progress and by ensuring the rational development of agricultural production and the optimum utilisation of the factors of production, in particular labour;*

- *to ensure a fair standard of living for the agricultural community, in particular by increasing the individual earnings of persons engaged in agriculture;*

- *to stabilise markets;*

- *to ensure the availability of supplies;*

- *to ensure that supplies reach consumers at reasonable prices.*

Why is agriculture afforded special treatment? The CAP has absorbed a very high proportion of the EC budget: at one stage as much as 75 per cent although now it is around 66 per cent (*see* Table 16.4). This is despite the relative unimportance of agriculture in the European economy. We need to consider why agriculture is afforded special treatment.

Table 16.4 *The EC budget 1973 and 1992 (% of total)*

	1973	1992
Agriculture and fisheries	80.6	53.0
Structural funds	5.5	27.0
Research and development	1.6	5.0
Development co-operation	1.4	5.1
Miscellaneous and administration	11.0	10.0
TOTAL (billion ECUs)	4.5	62.4

Politically and strategically, agriculture has an importance greater than its share in Europe's GDP. Of the founding members France and Italy have relatively large agricultural sectors which employed (and still employ) large numbers of people. In addition, an even greater number of people in those countries remain 'close to the land'. This is because they either work in industries related to agriculture or are only one generation removed from the land. They often have close relations on the land and return to their home villages for long periods during the summer. This explains why the agricultural sector has substantial influence in these countries. In the UK (which joined the EC when the CAP was already in place) agriculture assumes a smaller role in the economy but nevertheless the landed classes have social and political influence which exceeds their economic importance (even though the modern Conservative party is more a party of urban business and professional people than one of rural landowners and farmers).

Agriculture provides us with the basic essentials of life. It should be remembered that the founding fathers of the EC experienced the privations of war and post-war collapse. Consequently, they were determined to establish a system of agricultural support which would enable Europe to be self-sufficient in food and therefore not dependent upon outside sources of supply. The French, in particular, were determined to pursue policies which enabled them to be independent of the USA.

To some extent the CAP was a *quid pro quo* for the establishment of a free trade area in industrial goods. Germany, anxious to secure access to the markets of Europe, agreed to the CAP, which inevitably was to benefit French agriculture. Hence German manufacturers could sell goods to France, which in turn obtained support for its socially, politically and economically important agricultural sector.

In addition to these political arguments in favour of agricultural protection there are other points rooted in economic theory. First, agriculture suffers from unplanned fluctuations in supply, because farmers are unable to control their physical environment (the weather) to the same extent as manufacturers can theirs. The fluctuations in supply result in fluctuations in prices and therefore incomes; these are made worse by the inelastic demand for agricultural products. As shown in Fig. 16.1 price fluctuations are exaggerated when demand is price inelastic.

Agricultural support There are various ways in which support can be given to the agricultural sector.

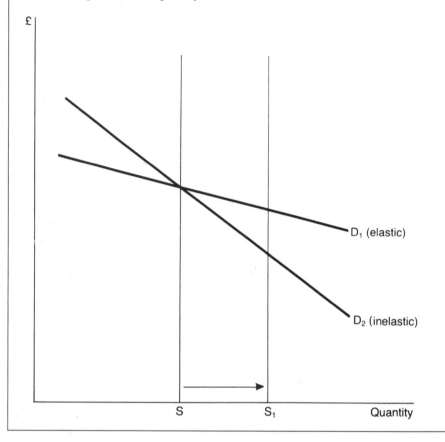

Fig. 16.1 *The effect of unplanned fluctuations in supply on a market where demand is inelastic*

An unexpected increase in supply from S to S_1 results in a fall in market price. However, as the demand for agricultural goods tends to be price inelastic the price fall is especially dramatic.

1 Import duties protect domestic producers against foreign competition by raising the price of imported goods. This protects the farmer at the expense of the consumer.

2 Buffer stock schemes involve the purchase of surplus products at a predetermined price. The aim is to stabilise both price and output at the same time, but the idea suffers from a major flaw: a guaranteed price for the purchase of any surplus will encourage overproduction.

3 Subsidies can be given to high-cost domestic producers. This was the system used in the UK before accession to the EC. As illustrated in Fig. 16.2, it has the advantage of protecting domestic producers without inflicting higher prices on consumers. The cost of agriculture protection (and there is always a cost to be paid) was imposed not on the consumer but on the taxpayer. At a time when taxes were progressive this represented income

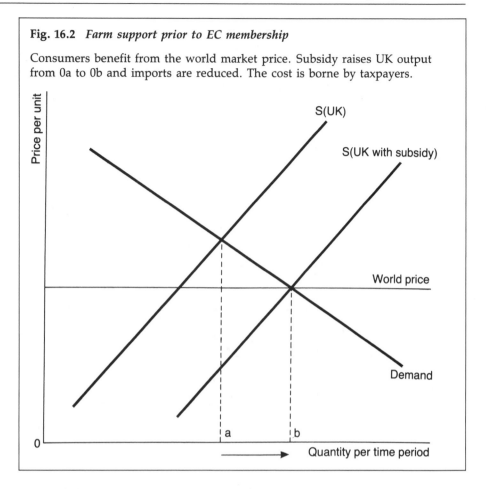

Fig. 16.2 *Farm support prior to EC membership*

Consumers benefit from the world market price. Subsidy raises UK output from 0a to 0b and imports are reduced. The cost is borne by taxpayers.

redistribution towards not only farmers but also the less well-off sectors of the community. There was considerable support for the traditional subsidy policy in the UK and consequently the CAP (established in the absence of the UK) was a source of controversy both at the time of entry and since.

The CAP: a graphical analysis

Before dealing with the finer points of the CAP let us look at the essence of the scheme and how economists analyse it. The graph in Fig. 16.3 refers to the market in butter (by changing values, weight, etc., it is possible to employ the same graph to analyse the market in other farm products). We start at the present world price of butter – 2 ECUs per kg. Non-EC producers will supply any amount of butter to the EC at this price. At the intersection of the supply curve ('World supply') and the demand curve (D) price settles at 2 ECUs and a quantity of 200 million kg will be sold per time period.

EC producers are willing to produce only 100 million kg at this price but to assist them a tariff will be imposed on non-EC butter. With a tariff of 1 ECU the price now rises to 3 ECUs.

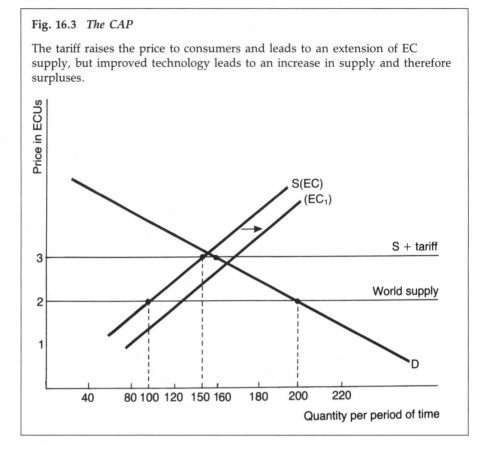

Fig. 16.3 *The CAP*

The tariff raises the price to consumers and leads to an extension of EC supply, but improved technology leads to an increase in supply and therefore surpluses.

At the new, higher price, there is some contraction of demand (to 160 million kg) but an extension of supply by EC farmers (to 150 million kg). The effect of the tariff is to raise the price to the consumer but enable domestic producers to sell more than they would have done in the absence of the CAP and, what is more, to sell it at a higher price.

Remember that one of the aims of the CAP is to raise agricultural productivity. If this occurs the supply curve of EC butter will shift to EC_1 which intersects the demand curve at a price below 3 ECUs. As price stability is another aim of the CAP it is necessary for EC agencies to buy up the surplus over the 160 million kg demanded, at the 3-ECU price. The purchase of surpluses has created the EC food mountains. There is a reluctance to allow a fall in price because it would cause a fall in farm incomes as Europe's farmers produced less and sold it at a less favourable price.

How the CAP works

From the graphical analysis we can identify the main components of the CAP system.

1 Target or basic prices are set each year by the Council of (Agricultural) Ministers after taking advice from the Commission. The target price is the basic price for each commodity which should be attainable under normal market circumstances. Below the target price is what is called the threshold price: the minimum import price at which supplies from non-EC countries can be delivered at Community ports. The threshold price differs from the target price in that transport costs are added from the port to inland destinations. If import prices are below the threshold price the difference is made up by agricultural levies.

2 Levies are varying duties imposed in imports of farm produce from non-EC countries. They serve to raise the price of these goods to the threshold price fixed under the CAP.

3 Intervention prices are set for many agricultural products. This is the price at which national intervention agencies are obliged to purchase agricultural commodities offered to them. Intervention prices are 10 to 20 per cent below target price. In the UK intervention is undertaken by an executive agency known as the Intervention Board. Incidentally, the fact that the buying up of surpluses is undertaken on a national basis demonstrates the fallacy of the single EC butter mountain or wine lake. The surpluses are held throughout the Community.

4 Exporters of certain farm products can receive a subsidy if world prices are below target prices. These subsidies are known as export restitution payments.

5 The finances of the CAP are administered by the European Agricultural Guidance and Guarantee Fund (EAGGF, or FEOGA in French). The Guarantee Section deals with intervention and price support. The Guidance Section is concerned with structural changes in agriculture and with the development of rural areas.

6 The support prices and export restitution payments are set in ECUs but farmers receive money from EAGGF in their own currencies. The conversion from ECU to national currency is not at the current market rate of exchange but at fixed rates of exchange (known as green rates). The green rates can be out of line with market rates and this leads to different real support price levels in the different EC states. To overcome this problem, a system of monetary compensatory amounts (MCAs) was applied on intra-EC trade in agricultural goods. MCAs were based on the difference between the green and market rates of exchange. When the market rate was less than the green rate they acted as import subsidies and export levies; in the reverse situation as import levies and export supplies.

If the green currency and MCA appear complicated, it shows that to overcome the problems arising from interference in the market it is necessary to introduce other and yet more complex measures. Obviously the green currency system will not be needed if and when EMU is achieved. Movements towards EMU coupled with the high cost and abuse of the system led to the elimination of MCAs in 1992, although the currency crises of that year mean that the problems currency movements inflict on the operation of the CAP remain.

Reform of the CAP

The CAP has been subject to much criticism, especially from the British government. The main criticisms are:

1 The CAP penalises consumers, who are diverted from cheaper non-EC goods sold in the world market to higher-cost supplies from within the EC. The inflationary aspect of the CAP was an issue at the time of British accession and the cost to the UK taxpayer and consumer remains a source of grievance.

2 As the EC is protectionist, especially in relation to agriculture, the CAP is an impediment to greater liberalisation of trade on a worldwide basis (*see* chapter 12 on GATT).

3 The CAP destabilises world markets through the system of export restitution payments (export subsidies).

4 Intervention in the form of purchase of surpluses encourages farmers to maximise their output. The production of surplus goods for which there is no (effective) demand represents a misallocation of resources. Economic welfare would be increased by switching resources to the production of goods sought by the consumer.

5 The CAP is a major factor in the budgetary problems of the EC. High, and at times uncontrolled, expenditure on agricultural support has increased the cost of EC membership to countries such as the UK. Moreover, the high demands that agriculture places on the EC budget have limited the development of spending on other activities, especially the Structural Funds from which the UK benefits.

6 The CAP represents a transfer of finance (and therefore resources) from the net contributors (e.g. the UK) to the net beneficiaries (e.g. France).

7 Price support related to volume of produce benefits mainly the larger farmer. Conversely, those farmers with little to sell will benefit proportionately less. Therefore, the smaller or disadvantaged farmers (such as hill farmers) derive less benefit from the system of price support.

In the numerous demands and proposals for reform the UK government has consistently been in the forefront:

Britain has consistently pressed for reform in order to:

- bring demand and supply into better balance;
- increase the role of market forces in agriculture; and
- make environmental considerations an integral part of agricultural policy (*Britain in the European Community*, HMSO, p. 65).

In Commission reform proposals 'three main targets of reform have been proposed: a) cutting rewards to farmers; b) limiting the EC's liability; and c) restricting the amount farmers sell' (Marsh, in Lodge, *The European Community and the Challenge of the Future*, p. 157).

Price reductions   Proposals for price reductions (or, more likely, reductions in real prices) are designed to produce a contraction of supply, thus reducing the surpluses of agricultural products. Proposals to reduce prices have always led to controversy, with opposition from France with its vocal (and sometimes militant) farm lobby. This has limited the size of reductions.

An alternative way of achieving the same end is the system of co-responsibility levies. They were introduced first for milk and later for cereals. The levy takes the form of a tax on the sales made by farmers to the EC intervention schemes. This reduces the price farmers receive and forces them to contribute to the cost of disposing of surplus products (e.g. through a Community subsidy for school milk). Generally these schemes have proved inadequate to prevent surpluses being generated.

Reduction in EC liability   This takes a number of forms:

- *imposing more rigorous quality standards;*

- *delaying or shortening the period during which intervention occurs;*

- *suspending export restitution or subjecting it to competitive tender.*

Output restrictions   The best-known output limitation scheme is the milk quota. This was introduced in 1984 after the co-responsibility levy proved inadequate to prevent a surplus and when dairy support accounted for 30 per cent of all guarantee expenditure. Although quotas conflict with free market principles they were still introduced. Under the quota the output of each farmer is pegged to only 1 per cent above 1981 levels.

Since 1988 there has been a limit on CAP market support for most agricultural products. If the output of specific products exceeds the maximum guarantee quantity (MGQ) the amount of CAP support is automatically reduced. This stabiliser mechanism has the great advantage of being triggered automatically without the need for lengthy and acrimonious discussion in the Council of Ministers.

Other schemes   As well as these general schemes there have been others designed to achieve other objectives. Aid for farmers operating in difficult terrain is designed to reduce the imbalance. Peripheral parts of the UK with large numbers of hill farmers have derived benefit from the scheme. As mentioned above, the Guidance Section of EAGGF aids investment projects related to agriculture, food processing and the rural infrastructure.

More radical schemes are based on the recognition that the root problem is not just excess output but too many resources being devoted to farming. In 1968 Commissioner Mansholt argued for a shift of 5 million people out of the agricultural sector of the original six members. Measures have included the following.

1 The farm retirement scheme, in which the EC contributes to the pension of farmers who retire early (over 55). The scheme was designed to overcome the difficulties that older farmers faced in adapting to changed conditions.

2 Set-aside, in which farmers are paid a premium to compensate for loss of income if they take at least a fifth of their arable land out of production for five years. In effect, farmers are paid for not producing arable crops but, instead, using the land for fallow, forestry or non-agricultural purposes.

The common fisheries policy

Like the CAP, the common fisheries policy (CFP) is a source of tension between member states and non-EC countries. Indeed, Norway's rejection of membership in 1972 was based on concern over the emerging CFP. Twenty years on the CFP still poses a problem for Norwegian entry. Under the CFP the first six miles of territorial waters (out from the coast) are reserved for the fishing fleets of the member state concerned. The second six miles are opened up to the fleets of other member states that have 'traditionally fished there'. The remaining part of the Community waters (up to 200 miles into the Atlantic) is open to the fleets of all member states.

Concern over fish stocks has placed the conservation and management of resources at the centre of the CFP. Overfishing led to a 'sector in crisis' which could be remedied only by restricting fishing activities. This is done by fixing total allowable catches (TAC). Allocation of quotas between member states takes account of traditional fishing activities, the specific needs of regions dependent upon fishing, and any loss of fishing grounds in the waters of third countries. In addition to controlling quantity there are regulations on:

- *the size of fish caught;*

- *the minimum mesh size for the nets;*

- *the permitted areas for fishing;*

- *the maximum amount of time vessels can spend at sea.*

Under the CFP, the EC also attempts to 'adjust and redirect capacity'. Adjustment takes the form of subsidies for the breaking up and laying up of vessels. This can be seen as the fisheries equivalent of set-aside under the CAP. Redirecting capacity takes the form of grants and subsidies to encourage the fishing of unexploited species and/or new areas.

Fish caught by non-EC vessels is subject to a common external tariff although preference is given to specific countries (e.g. EFTA and ACP (African, Caribbean and Pacific) countries). The EC (recognised as 'competent' as regards international relations in connection with fishing) has concluded fisheries agreements with other states involving mutual access to waters subject to quotas. Agreements have been made with Norway, Sweden, the Faroe Islands and Greenland.

The final aspect of the CFP which should be mentioned is the common marketing organisation, with aims as follows:

- *to encourage the rational marketing of fish products;*

- *to implement common marketing standards (e.g. over quality and packaging);*

- *to ensure market stability by adjusting supply to market requirements;*

- *to guarantee a fair income to producers.*

The last objective has led to the establishment of guide and intervention prices. The former is fixed by a formula linked to average prices over the last three years and the intervention price is set at 70–90 per cent of guide price. The extreme perishability of fish means that surpluses are even less desirable than they are for agricultural products. Consequently, it is important to set prices to stabilise markets without creating surpluses.

EC Structural Funds

The Structural Funds are intended to support development and adjustment in both less-developed regions and the regions of industrial decline. The term 'Structural Fund' covers three distinct schemes.

1 The European Social Fund (ESF) supports training and employment measures for young people and the long-term unemployed.

2 The Regional Development Fund (ERDF) supports infrastructure projects and gives aid to industry.

3 The Guidance Section of the EAGGF supports agricultural restructuring and rural development.

Held back by the budgetary problems for many years, help for the regions was given greater emphasis following the commitment to achieving the single market by the end of 1992. This is because greater economic and social cohesion is a necessary corollary of the single market (and even more so of the economic and monetary union). In 1988 there was a major reform in the administration of the funds, accompanied by a doubling of available funds, from 7 billion ECUs (£5.7 billion) in 1987 to 14 billion ECUs in 1993.

Assistance is concentrated on the most disadvantaged regions, with five priority objectives being specified.

1 Promotion of economic development in the poorest regions. These are defined as areas (such as Greece, Ireland and Corsica) where per capita GDP is less than 75 per cent of the Community average. Hence the emphasis is placed on 'catching up' by improvements in the infrastructure and investment in human capital.

2 Converting regions suffering from industrial decline – this is helped by EC financial support for training, improvements to the environment and employment creation.

3 Combating long-term unemployment.

4 Facilitating the integration of young people into the labour market.

5 Promoting development in rural areas by way of the modernisation of agriculture structures and diversification of economic activity away from the purely agricultural.

In many cases the problems are greater than can be solved by individual, local, regional or even national measures. Hence Community involvement in problem solving. However, the EC facilitates action by means of support – it does not undertake the work itself.

Three concepts are important in the administration of regional aid:

- *'partnership' with national, regional and local authorities;*

- *'subsidiarity', or responsibility as close as possible to the level of concrete reality;*

- *'additionality', which means that EC assistance is designed to supplement local and national efforts but not to replace them.*

The Commission's publication *Working for the Regions* states:

> The Community's assistance is based on three phases in which the Community collaborates with the Member States and the regions:
>
> 1 Development plans identifying the main priorities of the region are prepared by competent authorities ... These are then submitted to the Commission by the Member States
>
> 2 Next, the Commission draws up the Community Support Frameworks (CSFs) on the basis of the development plans, in agreement with the national or regional authority concerned, within the framework of a real partnership. The CSFs are agreements [which] define priorities, the forms of assistance and the multi-annual financial support provided by the Community
>
> 3 Lastly, the Member State submits operational programmes for each priority.

Once adopted by the Commission, implementation is in the hands of national or regional authorities, subject to monitoring by all parties concerned. Table 16.5 gives details of the amounts paid to the member states from the Structural Funds in 1990. Projects in the UK that have been supported by the Funds range from over £37 million towards the construction of the Kielder water reservoir to £40,000 towards the Bournemouth Enterprise Centre. Others include:

- *electricity supply in the Highlands and Islands £24.8 million;*

- *road improvements in West Glamorgan £12.6 million;*

- *a new bridge across the River Loughor £5.2 million;*

- *restoration of Lichfield Cathedral £1 million;*

- *construction of a terminal at Humberside Airport £323,000;*

- *restoration of the 13th-century Cressing Barn in Essex £70,000.*

Fig. 16.4 lists the vocational training programmes initiated by the EC.

Table 16.5 *The Structural Funds in 1990 (ECU million)*

Country	ERDF	ESF	EAGGF	Total
Belgium	67	65	23	155
Denmark	18	40	19	77
Germany	114	211	186	511
Greece	562	339	271	1,172
France	443	400	387	1,230
Ireland	292	307	131	730
Italy	837	509	279	1,625
Luxembourg	3	2	5	10
The Netherlands	46	86	11	143
Portugal	534	284	249	1,067
Spain	1,802	722	312	2,836
UK	469	538	100	1,107

ERDF – European Regional Development Fund
ESF – European Social Fund
EAGGF – European Agricultural Guidance and Guarantee Fund

1973

Fig. 16.4 *Vocational training programmes*

Programme	Objective
1. Comett (Community Action Programme in Education and Training for Technology)	To improve technological training
	To encourage co-operation between industry and universities
	To encourage cross-border co-operation
2. Erasmus (European Action Scheme for the Mobility of University Students)	To increase the number of students studying in another member state
	To foster co-operation between universities throughout the EC
3. Force (*Formation Continuée en Europe*)	To foster greater investment in and a better return from continuing vocational education
4. Eurotecnet	To promote innovation in basic and continuing vocational training
5. Lingua	To promote knowledge of and competence in foreign languages in the Community
6. Tempus	To provide assistance for the development of higher education in Central and Eastern Europe in order to facilitate their adaptation to the requirements of the market economy
7. Youth for Europe	To promote exchange (outside schools) among young people living in the EC

The European Investment Bank

Article 130 of the Treaty of Rome states that the task of the European Investment Bank (EIB):

> Shall be to contribute, by having recourse to the capital market and utilising its own resources, to the balanced and steady development of the common market in the interests of the Community. For this purpose the Bank shall, operating on a non-profit basis, grant loans and give guarantees which facilitate the financing of the following projects in all sectors of the economy:
>
> a. projects for developing less developed regions
> b. projects for modernising or converting undertakings or for developing fresh activities called for by the progressive establishment of the common market, where these projects are of such a size or nature that they cannot be financed by the various means available in the individual Member States
> c. projects of common interest to several Member States which are of such a size or nature that they cannot be entirely financed by the various means available in the individual Member States.

The EIB was therefore established to provide medium- and long-term loans for investment projects designed to further the economic development of disadvantaged regions and to improve communications between member states, but it has also participated in EC co-operation policies with non-member countries. Between 1987 and 1991, the following formed the EIB's lending priorities.

1 Regional development remains the main objective of EIB activities. Between 1987 and 1991 the EIB granted loans amounting to 31.8 billion ECUs for the purpose of aiding the disadvantaged regions. The funds were used for projects relating to industry, agriculture, services, transport, telecommunications and energy. EIB loans supplement grants from the EC Structural Funds.

2 Transport and communications projects are vital for the completion of a truly single market. Consequently, these projects have attracted an increasing amount of EIB loans (12 billion ECUs between 1987 and 1991).

3 Projects to enhance industrial competitiveness have also attracted EIB loans. Of the 14 billion ECUs granted for this purpose between 1987 and 1991, 38 per cent went to large firms and 62 per cent to small and medium-sized enterprises (SMEs), especially to those in the assisted regions. For large projects and larger firms, the EIB lends directly but, for SMEs, EIB loans are made available through banks and other financial institutions.

4 Between 1987 and 1991 8.3 billion ECUs of EIB loans was used for environmental projects, especially those related to conservation and management of water supplies. In addition, a condition for any EIB loan is compliance with current environment legislation.

5 Finally, the EIB finances capital investment to develop indigenous energy resources, reduce dependence upon oil imports and foster greater efficiency in the use of energy. Some 9.7 billion ECUs of lending was available to secure more reliable energy supplies.

As mentioned above, the EIB also grants loans to non-members:

■ *the 69 ACP countries can seek EIB loans from its own resources and risk capital drawn from the European Development Fund;*

■ *Mediterranean countries outside the EC can obtain EIB loans, especially for environmental projects;*

■ *loans are also available to Central and Eastern European countries in their transition to a market economy.*

To finance its lending activities, the EIB borrows on the capital markets through the issue of public bonds. Because it is 'owned' by the 12 EC member states, and thanks to the quality of the projects it funds, the EIB is able to borrow throughout the world on very favourable terms. It borrows in some 15 different currencies (including non-EC currencies such as the yen, dollar and Swiss franc) and disburses these currencies in its loans. However, the ECU is the single largest currency borrowed, and by its activities the EIB promotes the use of the ECU.

Research and development

In a dynamic world economy, research and development (R & D) is essential if domestic producers are to compete with rivals abroad. R & D provides the new products and new processes that are needed for continued prosperity in the long run. Unfortunately, its high cost – compounded by uncertainty over results – makes it difficult not only for private sector firms, but increasingly for relatively small individual states, to finance large R & D projects. As no individual European state is able to meet the challenge of Japan and the USA, with their large domestic markets, so EC collaborative research projects are essential.

Community involvement in research is set out in the EC Framework Programmes. These set objectives, define priorities and fix funding levels for each area. The 1990–4 Framework Programme (the third of its kind) identifies the areas of action (and the amounts, in million ECUs, to be budgeted):

■ *information technology   1,325;*

■ *communications technology   489;*

■ *telematic systems (development of a trans-European electronic information exchange infrastructure)   380;*

■ *industrial and material technologies   748;*

■ *measurement and testing   140;*

■ *environment   104;*

■ *marine science   104;*

- *biotechnology 164;*

- *agricultural and agro-industrial research 333;*

- *life sciences and technologies for developing countries 111;*

- *non-nuclear energies 157;*

- *nuclear fission safety 199;*

- *controlled nuclear fusion 458;*

- *human capital and mobility 518.*

The actual research is undertaken either on a contract basis (with the EC funding projects up to 50 per cent of total costs) or in one of the four EC joint research centres. The JRCs are financed entirely out of Community funds and draw staff from different countries. Research in the nuclear field takes up 50 per cent of all JRC expenditure.

EC projects tend to have colourful names, many based on acronyms, including:

- **Delta**: *Developing European Learning through Technological Advance;*

- **Diane**: *Direct Information Access Network for Europe;*

- **Echo**: *European Commission Host Organisation (this supports the use of on-line information in Europe);*

- **Esprit**: *European Strategic Programme for Research and Development in Information Technology (its aim is to help provide the European IT industry with the key components of the technology it needs to be competitive in world markets);*

- **Eureka**: *this takes in the EFTA states as well as EC members, and aims to improve European performance in the production of high-tech goods;*

- **JET**: *Joint European Torus (based at Culham, JET is a Euratom project which seeks to establish the feasibility of nuclear fusion technology).*

CHAPTER 17

The EC and the Outside World

As a customs union the EC is inevitably discriminatory. However, each of the members is anxious to preserve trade links with non-EC countries, none more so than the UK, which has always looked beyond Europe to a wider world. Consequently, the EC preserves special relations with four groups of non-EC countries, one of which (EFTA) has joined the single market via the EEA. The reasons for these special relationships varies but all are designed to offer the parties privileged access to one another's markets. It is to these groups of countries that this chapter is directed, and it concludes with another issue close to Britain's heart: the enlargement of the Community.

OBJECTIVES
1 To analyse the European Economic Area and to profile the countries involved.
2 To survey assistance given to the EC's neighbours in Europe.
3 To survey and analyse the EC's relations with former colonies in the APC group.
4 To analyse the prospects for enlargement.

The European Economic Area

The European Free Trade Association (EFTA) now consists of seven Alpine and Nordic states: Austria, Finland, Iceland, Liechtenstein, Norway, Sweden and Switzerland. As we discovered earlier, EFTA dates from the same era as the EC but has the more limited aim of securing free trade in industrial goods. The EFTA countries have expressed interest in full membership of the EC, but problems in the past, or continuing anxieties, have prevented this. In view of the importance of the EC in European trade (*see* Table 17.1), the EFTA countries sought closer association with the 12. The result is the European Economic Area (EEA), which is at one and the same time a halfway house to EC membership and a mutually beneficial arrangement in its own right. The EEA consists of 19 countries (12 EC plus seven EFTA countries) covering the whole of Western Europe. It has a population of 375 million people, or 30 per cent of world population. In 1991 its combined GDP was around $7,000 billion and it is responsible for 40 per cent of world trade.

Table 17.1 *The importance of the EC in the exports of EFTA countries*

	% of Exports sent to EC 1991	% of Exports sent to other EFTA countries 1991
Austria	66	9
Finland	50	20
Iceland	67	9
Liechtenstein	43	21
Norway	66	15
Sweden	55	18
Switzerland	59	6

The aim of the EEA is to extend the EC single market to the EFTA countries. This means that most EC single market legislation will apply to all 19 countries. Hence free movement of goods, services, capital and persons will apply throughout the EEA. This will create increased opportunities for UK business enterprise, although it should be remembered that:

- *the EFTA countries are relatively small, and so the large majority of the 375-million population live in the EC member states;*

- *existing EC–EFTA agreements provide for tariff-free trade in industrial goods and some processed agricultural products.*

The EEA agreement further reduced tariffs on processed agricultural products and it liberalised trade in fish. The EEA has also meant a reduction in non-tariff barriers. This means extending EC technical and safety regulation to EFTA, prohibiting discriminating taxation on goods, and opening up public procurement.

Under the EEA agreement new EC measures will be applied to the whole area by joint decision of the EC and EFTA. Consultation with EFTA is provided for, but the EFTA countries have no voting or veto rights. EC competition rules (relating to restrictive practices, monopoly abuse, mergers, take-overs and state aid) now apply throughout the EEA, to ensure equal terms of trade. The free movement of capital has created investment opportunities in those EFTA countries that traditionally maintained a restrictive policy on inward investment. The free movement of people has given EEA citizens the right to work and to establish business enterprises throughout the area.

The closeness of the EC–EFTA relationship should not lead readers to assume that (from 1 January 1993) the EC consists of 19 countries. The EFTA countries have merely joined in the trade liberalisation measures of the single market. Other aspects of the EC (e.g. the CAP, the Maastrict Treaty) do not apply to them. The EFTA countries have not committed themselves to the Exchange Rate Mechanism although certain of the countries have chosen to 'shadow' the Deutschmark. EFTA states will be consulted on single market measures but will not participate in the institutions of the EC.

Although the EEA agreement does not enlarge the Community it will facilitate the entry of EFTA countries if and when they decide to become full members. For those Alpine states that accept the single market and informally 'shadow' the Deutschmark, full membership will require little adjustment, whilst at the same time admitting them to the decision-making institutions of the EC. As we will see later in this chapter, the EFTA states are the most obvious candidates for membership in a larger Community.

Profiles of the EFTA countries

In the profiles that follow, all figures are for 1991 unless otherwise specified.

Austria

Currency:	Schilling
Population:	7.5 million
GDP per capita:	$16,600
UK exports:	£0.77 billion
Main categories:	Office machinery, chemicals and related products, road vehicles
UK imports:	£0.9 billion
Main categories:	Paper products, textiles and clothing

%	1991	1992	1993 (Projected)
Rise in GDP	2.8	2.6	2.7
Inflation rate	3.2	3.4	3.2
Unemployment	3.4	3.8	4.0
Current account of balance of payments as % of GDP	−0.3	−0.4	−0.5

Austria applied to join the EC on 17 July 1989.

Although portrayed as a country of mountains, lakes and tourism, Austria has a highly developed and prosperous industrial economy. Of its 3.4 million working population, 40 per cent is employed in industry, mainly in small and medium-sized enterprises. The data above shows that Austria enjoys a surplus in trade with the UK, which used to be Austria's third largest supplier but now has only a 2.7 per cent share of the Austrian market and ranks only ninth in terms of imports to Austria.

Naturally its close proximity to, and language and cultural links with, Germany have drawn Austria into the 'greater German' economy. These links have contributed to Austria's low inflation and low unemployment rates and to its high standard of living. In fact, its current status as an EFTA rather than EC country is due entirely to the 1955 Peace Treaty, which committed the Austrian state to neutrality. The end of the Cold War made this obsolete and so Austria now has applied for EC membership.

Finland Currency: Finnmark

Population: 5 million

GDP per capita: $23,250

UK exports: £0.85 billion

Main categories: Office machinery, fertilisers, electrical machinery, vehicles, textiles and chemicals

UK imports: £1.5 billion

Main categories: Paper products, iron and steel, office equipment, general industrial machinery

%	1991	1992	1993 (Projected)
Rise in GDP	−5.2	−0.4	3.8
Inflation rate	4.1	−0.3	1.4
Unemployment	7.7	9.8	9.3
Current account of balance of payments as % of GDP	−4.7	−3.3	−2.0

Finland applied to join the EC on 18 March 1992.

Finland is a highly industrialised country, producing a range of capital and consumer goods. The standard of living is one of the highest in Europe, although the data above demonstrates that in the early 1990s Finland has experienced negative growth and rising unemployment.

As in the case of Austria, Finland had to pursue a policy of neutrality during the Cold War but the changes in Eastern Europe have provided the opportunity for closer relations with Western Europe, which is responsible for the bulk of Finland's overseas trade. In 1991 the UK had a 7.6 per cent share of the Finnish market.

Iceland Currency: Icelandic Króna

Population: 0.25 million

GDP per capita: $20,500

UK exports: £0.1 billion

Main categories: Machinery and transport equipment, miscellaneous manufactured items, chemicals and related products

UK imports: £0.24 billion

Main categories: Fish and fish preparations, non-ferrous preparations, animal feed, iron and steel

%	1991	1992	1993 (Projected)
Rise in GDP	1.4	−1.6	0.5
Inflation	7.6	7.0	8.0
Unemployment	1.6	2.0	2.0
Current account of balance of payments as % of GDP	−4.4	−4.3	−4.8

Iceland, which joined EFTA in 1970, has a high standard of living but has only a limited industrial base. Its economy is highly dependent upon fish, with the result that any decline in fishing would have a significant impact. The creation of the EEA will allow Iceland's fish products greater access to EC markets but it will still jealously guard its 200-mile fishing limit.

EC countries will have greater export opportunities as a result of the EEA but it must be remembered that:

- *the Icelandic market remains small because of its small population size;*

- *European countries have always provided Iceland with manufactured products;*

- *the prosperity of the Icelandic economy fluctuates with the state of its fishing industry.*

Norway

Currency:	Norwegian Krone
Population:	4.2 million
GDP per capita:	$21,340
UK exports:	£1.36 billion
Main categories:	Machinery and transport equipment, supplies to the offshore industry, minerals, fuels, lubricants and manufactured goods
UK imports:	£4.23 billion
Main categories:	Petroleum and petroleum products, gas, non-ferrous metals, iron and steel, specialised machinery, transport equipment

%	1991	1992	1993 (Projected)
Rise in GDP	4.1	2.0	2.9
Inflation	1.5	3.3	3.3
Unemployment	5.3	5.1	4.8
Current account of balance of payments as % of GDP	5.0	5.5	5.8

'Norway is relatively rich, and has a potentially strong economy based on the natural resources of oil and gas, hydro-electric power, fish, forests and mineral oil. Its GDP per capita is the third highest in the OECD, almost twice as high as the UK's' (*Single Market News*, Autumn 1992). The statistics above show that both inflation and unemployment are not high by UK standards. However, both have risen in the late 1980s/early 1990s.

Norway's industrial base is relatively narrow (e.g. food, fish and forestry products, oil and gas) and, as a result, it provides a good market for its European neighbours. With an 8.9 per cent share of the market, the UK is the third most important supplier of goods to Norway – after Sweden and Germany.

Sweden Currency: Swedish Krona

Population: 8.5 million

GDP per capita: $22,360

UK exports: £2.5 billion

Main categories: Petroleum, electrical machinery, office machinery and ADP equipment, general manufactured goods and industrial machinery

UK imports: £3.1 billion

Main categories: Paper products, road vehicles, cork and wood, iron and steel, general industrial machinery

%	1991	1992	1993 (Projected)
Rise in GDP	−1.4	0.2	1.5
Inflation	7.5	3.1	4.0
Unemployment	2.7	4.1	4.1
Current account of balance of payments as % of GDP	−1.9	−1.7	1.3

Sweden applied to join the EC on 1 July 1991.

In terms of living standards Sweden ranks in the top ten economies of the world: 'The economy is a high cost and high quality one [but] after several prosperous years in the 1980s, the economy went into recession in 1991' (*Single Market News*, Autumn 1992). Curbs on public expenditure were designed to reduce inflation from its high 1991 level and, as can be seen, unemployment started to rise. The Conservative government (after decades of Social Democratic governments) has pursued a policy of encouraging private enterprise to enable Sweden to improve its competitive advantage.

Anglo-Swedish trade links are close: Britain is Sweden's second most important trading partner. Sweden is the UK's largest market outside the USA and EC. It takes more UK exports than Japan, Canada and Australia and, in per capita terms, only Ireland, Switzerland and the Benelux countries buy more UK goods.

Switzerland Currency: Swiss franc

Population: 6.5 million

GDP per capita: $26,350

UK exports: £2.1 billion

Main categories: Office machinery and ADP equipment, electrical machinery, road vehicles, iron and steel and non-ferrous metals, telecommunications, organic chemicals

UK imports: £3.75 billion

Main categories: Electrical machinery, textile yarns, organic chemicals, pharmaceuticals

%	1991	1992	1993 (Projected)
Rise in GDP	−0.5	1.2	1.8
Inflation	5.2	4.5	3.5
Unemployment	1.0	1.6	1.4
Current account of balance of payments as % of GDP	3.9	4.9	5.2

Switzerland applied to join the EC on 26 May 1992.

Despite its small size, lack of natural resources and limited amount of agriculturally productive land, Switzerland enjoys a very high living standard. It has a significant industrial sector (chemicals, pharmaceuticals, foodstuffs, telecommunications) and is the world's 14th largest exporter of goods. Nevertheless, it runs a deficit on visible trade which is made good through earnings from the invisible sector.

The statistics above reveal that Switzerland experienced negative growth in 1991 and that, unusually for the Swiss, inflation started to move up. Despite these difficulties, Switzerland remains strong and prosperous.

Anglo-Swiss trade is substantial, with UK exports to Switzerland amounting to £2.1 billion. Switzerland is the UK's 12th largest export market whilst the UK is Switzerland's fifth largest supplier (a 5.5 per cent share of the Swiss market). However, there is still a trade surplus in Switzerland's favour.

Switzerland has applied to join the EC (now that concern over its neutrality is no longer considered a problem) but in December 1992 the Swiss voted against joining the EEA single market. Analysis of the voting suggested that the urban Swiss (especially in the financial centre of Zurich) favoured the EEA but the more insular rural Swiss voted against. The Swiss vote has placed a question mark on the EEA as well as on Swiss accession to the EC.

Liechtenstein The seventh EFTA country is the Principality of Liechtenstein. This very small state of 28,000 people entered into a customs union with Switzerland in 1923. For statistical purposes it is treated as part of Switzerland.

Despite its small size Liechtenstein has built up an industrial base (machinery, precision instruments, textiles, chemicals, pharmaceuticals). More important than manufacturing is Liechtenstein's financial sector (banking, investment trusts, offshore sales companies), which employs 40 per cent of the workforce and accounts for 60 per cent of national revenue. One interesting feature of the economy is that 60 per cent of the workforce are foreigners and 31 per cent commute daily from Switzerland and Austria.

Links with the Mediterranean countries

The EC has co-operation agreements with most of the countries that surround the Mediterranean. The only exceptions are Albania (the most closed of Communist countries until the revolutions of 1989/90), Libya and, since its dissolution and war, Yugoslavia. The links with the remaining countries are a consequence of:

- *close historical and cultural ties;*

- *the desire to extend already close trading links;*

- *the desire to contribute to political stability in the area;*

- *the importance of co-operation for environmental reasons.*

There are association agreements with Turkey, Cyprus and Malta, which have led to the establishment of a customs union between the states and the EC. The association agreement with Turkey is seen as the prelude to eventual full membership although there are still a number of problems (both in the EC and in Turkey) before that occurs.

There are co-operation agreements with Israel, the Maghreb countries (Algeria, Morocco and Tunisia) and the Mashreq countries (e.g. Jordan, Syria and Lebanon). Each of these agreements gives duty-free access to the EC for the industrial products from these countries – readers should, however, bear in mind that these countries are not major industrial powers. Concessions are available for specified agricultural goods from these countries, and there are reciprocal concessions to allow goods into them.

The EC provides financial aid to the Mediterranean countries through direct grants and EIB loans. Under the EC Action Programme for the Mediterranean (1991) there is renewed effort to reduce the economic imbalance between the northern and southern Mediterranean by means of:

- *measures to back up the process of economic adjustment;*

- *incentives for private investment;*

- *increased EC financing;*

- *improved access to the EC;*

- *economic and political co-operation.*

The EC and the former Communist states

In 1989–90 the Communist regimes of Central and Eastern Europe collapsed as the peoples of these regions sought greater freedom (especially of movement), a democratic system of government and a market system which would provide them with the consumer goods denied to them for decades. In the transition to a market system, the EC was anxious to assist for a number of reasons:

- *fear that they would return to old Communist ways;*

- *the pain and difficulty of the transition;*

- *fear that instability would threaten the peace of Europe;*

- *the potential refugee/economic-migrant problem that would be created;*

- *economic reform in Eastern Europe would open up new markets, new investment possibilities and new sources of supply.*

In 1991 the EC signed the first 'European agreements', with Poland, Hungary and Czechoslovakia (now the Czech Republic and Slovakia). These agreements involve political as well as economic co-operation:

- *free trade with the EC;*

- *industrial, technical and scientific co-operation;*

- *a long-term programme of financial support;*

- *a mechanism for political dialogue.*

The European agreements are not a transitional phase for full membership of the EC, although the possibility of it in the future is not excluded.

The first European agreements were concluded with these more industrial states which had travelled furthest on the road to reform. Other trade and co-operation agreements have been signed with other, less industrialised countries: Bulgaria and Romania as well as the Soviet Union (now CIS). Agreements with Yugoslavia were suspended by the civil war that engulfed much of the territory of the former federation. However, relations with some at least of the successor states (Slovenia and Croatia) will be close.

The EC provides assistance for higher education and training in the former Communist states (e.g. Tempus Scheme) and is involved in the OECD Phare Scheme. Although Phare stands for 'Poland and Hungary Assistance for Economic Restructuring', the scheme now extends to other states, including the previously isolationist Albania. The Phare programme finances projects to aid the reform process in these countries.

European Bank for Reconstruction and Development (EBRD) The EBRD was founded in 1991 with 41 shareholders including the European Commission, the EIB, and all the EC and EFTA states as well as other states in Europe and elsewhere. With capital of 10 billion ECUs, the EBRD's object is 'to contribute to the progress and reconstruction of the countries of central and eastern Europe which undertake to respect and put into practice the principle of multiparty democracy and a market economy, to encourage the transition of their economies to a market economy and to promote private initiative and the spirit of enterprise' (article 1 of the EBRD statute).

Clearly, the the EBRD (which has a similar role to that of the World Bank) has both a financial and political mission since it seeks to promote the market economy and political democracy. To this end it offers unsecured loans at favourable rates of interest. Sixty per cent of these loans must involve the private sector. The EBRD is also involved in the privatisation of enterprises in Central and Eastern Europe.

The Lomé Conventions

Ten of the 12 member states of the EC (the exceptions being Ireland and Luxembourg) were colonial powers. To some extent the EC can be seen as an association of once mighty colonial powers, now grouped together in the post-colonial era. When France and Belgium signed the Treaty of Rome in 1957, they each had a large empire in Africa, although the early years of the EC coincided with an acceleration in the pace of decolonisation.

France in particular was anxious to secure an arrangement between the EC (as opposed to individual member states) and the overseas countries and territories (OCTs) of member states. Under an annex to the Treaty of Rome, the OCTs were granted 581 million ECUs from the European Development Fund. Most of the money went towards infrastructure development in franco-phone Africa. By 1963 the francophone parts of Africa (as well as most of English-speaking Africa) had achieved independence and were therefore no longer entitled to development aid under the treaty annex. However, both the former colonial powers and the ex-colonies wished to continue their association. Hence, by the Yaounde Convention, 18 countries of the Associated African States and Madagascar negotiated a convention with the EC.

The first Yaounde Convention (1963) established a new European Develop-ment Fund (EDF) of 800 million ECUs to provide loans and grants. In addition, there were preferential trade agreements and the establishment of joint institutions at ministerial and parliamentary level. A second Yaounde Convention was concluded in 1969. Again, this provided for a EDF, which was allocated 900 million ECUs together with EIB loans of 100 million ECUs and trade preferences. Some of the benefits under the convention were extended to other newly independent countries. Consequently, the countries of former British East Africa (Kenya, Uganda and Tanzania) became associated with the Yaounde arrangements (three years before Britain's accession to the EC).

The Yaounde Conventions expired in 1975, by which time the UK had acceded to the Treaty of Rome. Britain was by now an ex-colonial power but had continuing links with former colonies through the British Common-wealth. Given the large number of Commonwealth countries that would seek association in a manner similar to that enjoyed by former French colonies, it was necessary to conclude a new arrangement. This became known as the Lomé Convention, signed in 1975 by 46 developing countries and the EC.

The recipients of aid are known as the ACP countries since they are in Africa, the Caribbean or the Pacific. It is significant that the Lomé agreements were not made available to certain developing countries (e.g. the larger and more industrially advanced countries of southern Asia such as India and Pakistan). However, membership of the ACP group has increased over the years to 69, and includes Namibia, which was never a British colony but was in effect a South African colony until it achieved independence. Under the Lomé Convention the EC and ACP states concluded 'a co-operative conven-tion in order to promote and extend the economic, cultural and social development of the ACP states and consolidate and diversify their relations in a spirit of solidarity and mutual interest'.

To date, four Lomé Conventions have been signed. Their time coverage and amount of aid are:

- *Lomé 1 – 1975 to 1980, 3,450 million ECUs;*

- *Lomé 2 – 1980 to 1985, 5,700 million ECUs;*

- *Lomé 3 – 1985 to 1990, 8,500 million ECUs;*
- *Lomé 4 – 1990 to 2000, 12 billion ECUs.*

The aid takes the form of loans from the EIB and grants and risk capital from the EDF. The EDF has five specific funds:

- *structural adjustment – for countries undergoing economic reform, which in effect means changing from planned to market economies;*
- *refugee aid – for serious refugee problems;*
- *emergency aid – for disaster relief;*
- *Stabex – this involves cash transfers to offset serious losses on agricultural exports: when the export earnings of an ACP state for a given product represent at least 5 per cent of its total export earnings, that state has the right to request a cash transfer if its earnings from exporting one of these products to the EC are at least 5 per cent below the reference level, which is the average of the previous four years;*
- *Sysmin – this is similar to Stabex but applies to mining industries in difficulties.*

The aid arrangements under Lomé are accompanied by preferential trade arrangements.

1 The EC provides funds to promote the trade of ACP countries.

2 There is a guarantee to purchase up to 1.3 million tonnes of ACP sugar. This is designed to help small cane sugar producers of the Caribbean find a market in the beet-dominated European market.

3 Duty- and quota-free access to the EC for almost all products of ACP countries. This last concession is less substantial than it might appear since ACP economies complement rather than compete with those of the EC.

Enlargement of the EC

Enlargement means extending membership of the EC. As we have seen, the EC has already been enlarged on four separate occasions – but the next decade could see substantial further enlargement. This is the result of the EC's perceived success, which encourages others to seek membership. At the same time the end of the Cold War has allowed neutral states to contemplate membership. Moreover, the end of Communism in Eastern Europe has led to the emergence of democratic states with market economies. These countries have also expressed interest in membership.

The EC is an association or club. Like all clubs it has entry qualifications. Those possessing the qualifications have a right to apply for membership. Whether or not the application is accepted is a matter for existing members. Article 237 of the Treaty of Rome states: 'Any European State may apply to become a member of the community.' The Maastricht Treaty contains a clause that is identical save for substituting the word 'Union' for 'community' (article O). In treaty terms, the only qualification necessary to apply for membership is that the country is European. However, as the Community (Union) is composed of democracies which respect human rights it is accepted that only European democracies with a demonstrable respect for fundamental human rights are eligible to apply for membership. The EFTA countries are therefore eligible. However, although the former Communist states of Eastern Europe have made substantial progress in terms of democracy, human rights and the development of market economies, they have yet to demonstrate sufficient long-term commitment to these values to satisfy existing members. As an unwritten rule, the EC will not accept as a member a country which generates tension with existing members or one that is in dispute with its own neighbours. The first point makes Turkey ineligible, the second would block any negotiations with Croatia, Romania or Ukraine.

States eligible to apply have to consider the advantages of EC membership against the obligations that it implies. Membership of the EC means more than acceptance of trade liberalisation. Newcomers are committed to EC institutions, the single market and the budget arrangements. If Maastricht is implemented, membership will also entail acceptance of the CFSP, the EC policy on citizenship, justice and immigration, the Social Charter and EMU. In other words, new applicants must accept the framework developed by existing members over the years since 1957. A newcomer today is required to accept a much closer Community than the one that Britain joined in 1973.

Accession to the single market will create export opportunities for newcomers and this explains the attraction of joining. However, the two-way traffic through the open door will pose a serious threat to weak and less efficient sectors of the economy. Membership of the EC has posed major problems for the Greek economy. Another example is industry in the former East Germany. Following reunification in 1991 the East German economy experienced a painful and rapid transformation from strict planning under Communist rule to a market economy inside the EC. Industry in East Germany was unable to compete against more efficient rivals in both the rest of Germany and the wider Europe. German unification demonstrates the problems that will follow if there is too hasty accession by ex-Communist countries.

Eligibility coupled with desire to join does not guarantee accession since entry has to be acceptable to existing members. Both the Treaty of Rome and the Maastricht Treaty state that applications should be addressed to 'the Council, which shall act unanimously after consulting the Commission and after receiving the assent of the European Parliament which shall act by an absolute majority of component members'. In other words, enlargement requires not only a majority vote in the EP but also unanimous support of existing members. Consequently, a single member state can veto the application of a new member (as France did to the UK twice during the 1960s). When assessing an application for membership, MEPs and member governments are likely to consider the benefits of accepting the applicant into the Community. Any enlargement will increase market opportunities. Consequently, for the UK government, concerned more about the free trade aspect of the EC than wider issues, new members are likely to be welcomed.

However, it is necessary to consider the consequences of any new member on EC finances and political union.

Newcomers will obviously contribute to the EC budget through VAT and customs duty. They will also be eligible to receive grants from the Structural Funds. As the CAP takes the lion's share of Community funds, existing members might be reluctant to accept those states with a large agricultural sector which will need substantial support. This factor might count against Poland when it makes a formal application for membership. Conversely, the new Czech Republic with its relatively strong industrial base could prove more acceptable.

Enlargement will affect the functioning of EC institutions. It is likely that the EP will be enlarged to include new members (and the united Germany might take the opportunity to claim more seats as a state substantially larger than Britain, France or Italy). It will be more difficult to develop a common foreign and security policy in an enlarged Community. Moreover, EMU is likely to prove more difficult if more of the economically weak states of Europe join. Enlargement might also be at the expense of a federal Europe (i.e. enlargement as an alternative to a deepening of the Community). For anti-federalists, such as the UK government, enlargement is seen as attractive for this very reason.

Candidates for membership

The candidates for membership can be divided into three groups: the EFTA countries, the former Communist countries, and some Mediterranean countries. Those states that have applied (and two likely applicants) are shown in Fig. 17.1, with a summary of the problems facing them.

The EFTA countries The EFTA countries are the most likely candidates for early entry. They are relatively small and therefore easily absorbed. They enjoy high living standards, political stability, good human rights records and deeply embedded democratic instincts. By their acceptance of the EEA arrangement they have already adjusted to the single market. Full membership will thus pose relatively few problems. It might, however, be necessary to devise transitional arrangements for the agricultural and (for Norway) fishing sectors of their economies. The fisheries issue was a major factor in the Norwegian people's rejection of membership in 1972. Alpine and Nordic farmers in the EFTA countries tend to be smaller scale and less efficient than other EC farmers. Hence entry to the EC could pose a problem unless transitional arrangements are made. Another possible problem is (or was) Swiss, Austrian and Swedish neutrality. In the past EC membership was seen as incompatible with neutral status. However, changes in Europe have reduced the importance of neutrality to the countries concerned and have opened the way to full membership.

The former Communist countries Revolution swept through Central and Eastern Europe in the years 1989–91. From the collapse of the Communist system there emerged new democracies and market systems. A number of the states have expressed interest in EC

Fig. 17.1 *Applications for EC membership*

Country	Date of application	Main problem(s)	Likely entry
Turkey	1987	Islam	After 2000?
		Relative poverty	
		Human rights	
		Relations with Greece	
Cyprus	1990	Division of island	After 2000?
Malta	1990	Mini-state	After 2000?
		Libya	
Austria	1989	Neutrality	1996
Sweden	1991	Neutrality	1996
Finland	1992	Neutrality	1996
		Agriculture	
Norway	1992	Fisheries	1996
		Whaling	
		Agriculture	
Iceland	–	Agriculture	?
Switzerland	–	Neutrality	1996

membership although it is unlikely that they will be ready for membership until the first decade of the 21st century. Hungary, Poland, the Czech Republic and Slovakia are the most likely first candidates for membership. Their economies are stronger than those of other ex-Communist countries and they have enjoyed greater stability in the post-Communist period.

The Balkan states of Romania and Bulgaria are less developed industrially and will face greater difficulties in satisfying EC conditions. Other Balkan states such as those emerging from the former Yugoslavia will not be considered until stability is restored to the region.

Some constituents of the former USSR are possible candidates. First, the three Baltic states of Estonia, Latvia and Lithuania are industrialised and have links with the Nordic states. Provided they successfully decouple themselves from Russia, economically as well as politically, they could become serious candidates. Second, Byelorussia, Moldova and Ukraine are all European states currently in the Commonwealth of Independent States (CIS). Although membership is out of the question in the foreseeable future, in the 21st century it is possible that they might look westwards and reduce their links with Russia. The Russian Federation itself is an unlikely member. First, it is only partly a European country. Second, it is so large that it could be a successful single market in its own right. Third, its size means that its membership would dominate EC institutions and finances.

The Mediterranean states

This is a mixed group of countries with little in common apart from location on or in the Mediterranean Sea. Turkey (with a toehold in Europe – hence fulfilling the first qualification for entry) has sought full membership since

1963. Although association agreements have been signed with it, full membership has been blocked. In 1989, for instance, the Commission declared that neither Turkey nor the EC was ready to open enlargement negotiations. The Commission felt that the size and rapid growth of the Turkish population, coupled with its economic problems, meant that it would not be able to adjust to membership. Moreover, the democratic institutions of Turkey were insufficiently developed and its record on human rights left something to be desired. Lastly, continuing tension with Greece (e.g. over Cyprus) was another reason for rejecting Turkey. Turkish membership is unlikely before the turn of the century, but its eligibility has been established.

Malta has had association agreements with the EC since 1970, and in 1990 applied for full membership. However, despite the success of its tourist-based economy there are grave problems with its membership. In part they spring from Malta's policy of non-alignment and its close links with near-neighbour, Libya. A more fundamental problem concerns its size, as a 'micro-state' of 350,000. Full membership would give tiny Malta equal rights in the Council (when dealing with matters requiring unanimous agreement) with Germany, with its 80 million people.

Cyprus – or to be more exact the Greek Cypriot Republic – applied to join the EC in 1990. However, the major problem is the division of the island between an internationally recognised Greek Cypriot Republic and a Turkish Cypriot Republic established in the aftermath of a Turkish invasion of northern Cyprus in 1974. These political problems prevent early accession of Cyprus, either whole or divided. Moreover, Cyprus remains a point of tension between Greece and Turkey and is therefore a major factor in the denial of EC membership to Turkey.

CHAPTER 18

Conclusion: An Evaluation of the Impact of EC Membership

This book has looked at various aspects of the UK economy and membership of the EC. It is now necessary to draw some conclusions about the impact of the EC on the UK and its economy.

OBJECTIVES
1 To highlight those aspects of the EC which have had a beneficial effect on the economy of the UK.
2 To highlight those aspects of the EC which have had an adverse effect on the economy of the UK.
3 To weigh up the costs and benefits.

On 1 January 1993 the UK completed 20 years as a member of the European Community. This landmark was treated with neither rejoicing nor protest but with massive indifference. The fact is that the EC has not captured the imagination of the British people. For the great majority the EC has not had the beneficial impact claimed by supporters, nor has it produced the catastrophe claimed by its detractors. Perhaps the obscure complexities of the EC inevitably lead to the tabloid-like concentration on the 'Brussels threat' to 'the great British breakfast' or to the daily pint of milk. Very often EC attempts to create a 'level playing field' are seen as foreign interference with 'our' beaches, 'our' livestock and 'our' traditional working practices. The real issues are often overlooked.

Among the more politically and economically aware sections of the population the EC evokes stronger emotions. There are some (like Tony Benn on the Labour left or Enoch Powell to the right of the Conservative Party) who were opposed to British membership in 1972 and have remained opposed to the EC. At the other extreme there are the Europhiles (or Eurofanatics) who favour the ever closer union promised in the Treaty of Rome. These people are found in the Liberal Democratic Party and parts of the Conservative and Labour Parties.

Between these two extremes there are those whose view of the EC can be best summed up as 'thus far, but no further'. These people accept the benefits of the initial concept of the common market, and even the single market, but do not want to proceed any further down the road of European integration. The Conservative government of John Major can be classed as part of this group: they favour the Treaty on European Union but without the Social

Charter and with no commitment to EMU. Conservative Euro-sceptics (or Europhobes, depending on your view) claim to support the free market, customs union aspects of the EC but do not wish to go further. For them, Maastricht is 'a treaty too far', to quote Michael Spicer. For others, the Single European Act was 'a treaty too far' and they would have preferred to halt the process before the SEA.

Problems of evaluating costs and benefits

Many people (especially in the 'thus far but no further' group), tend to see the EC as desirable but ... At this point they qualify their support of the EC with an adverse comment about the CAP, Brussels bureaucracy, the ERM or one or other of the harmonisation policies. Fortunately or unfortunately, we cannot pick and choose about the EC. We should see it as a complete package and evaluate the costs and benefits as a whole. Some aspects of EC membership produce an adverse effect on the economy or particular parts of it. Rather than arguing, for example, that the EC harms British farmers, however, we should weigh up the total gains and set them against the total costs. This will produce a conclusion to the effect that on balance EC membership has harmed/benefited the British economy or British people.

One problem to be mentioned is that it is not possible to conclude what would have happened in the absence of British membership of the EC. It would not be valid to conclude that the trends in the economy present since 1973 were solely the result of EC membership. It is quite likely that many of the trends would have been present if Britain had remained outside the Community. Moreover, some might have been substantially worse.

With these points in mind we should see the EC as a complete package and not attribute all trends to EC membership. Let us now look at various aspects of British involvement with the EC.

Aspects of UK membership

Budgetary issues In chapter 16 we saw that Britain was a net contributor to the EC. British contributions to EC own resources exceed the assistance gained from the EC Structural Funds. As a result Britain relinquishes part of its national income to others, who thus have a claim on British output. This clearly represents a cost of British membership, but the EC should not be seen in terms of balancing budgetary contributions with receipts. After all, if all 12 received the same out of EC funds as they paid in, there would be little point in maintaining EC budgetary arrangements. Member states could finance the same projects out of national taxation. The only justification for EC budget arrangements is that there should be some net contributors and some net recipients. Equity demands that net contributors should be the more affluent members and net recipients the poorer members. Unfortunately, this does not happen and our conclusion must be that, on budgetary issues, the EC harms rather than helps Britain. However, before concluding that the EC is harmful to Britain's interests, let us consider other aspects.

EC rules on competition and state aid

On legal issues, the EC does act as a constraint on national governments. Laws are essentially negative in that they prohibit certain types of activity. The UK government is unable to give various forms of state aid (e.g. to mining) because of EC rules. We should, however, remember the free-market stance of the Thatcher and Major Conservative governments. They are more opposed to state aid to industry than the most *laissez-faire* of Brussels commissioners. Consequently, we can hardly claim that Brussels acts as a constraint on government action which would not have taken place in any event had Britain been governed by Thatcher or Major outside the EC. Community rules on competition and state aid for industry are beneficial to a free-market government because they prevent others aiding their industries. Community rules are designed to create a 'level playing field' and to prevent various forms of dumping.

Community rules on product safety

These add to the costs of production and could thus be seen to be harmful to business enterprise. However, the rules are imposed for the safety of consumers and others and, unless they are unnecessarily restrictive, should be seen as beneficial. The same rule could of course have been introduced by a national government outside the EC. Nevertheless, the imposition of a common set of rules through the Community provides protection for consumers and also protection for producers from less scrupulous competitors elsewhere.

EC social policy

This is often condemned as unnecessary interference adding to production costs. However, as we saw in chapter 14, social and employment measures (including the Social Charter to which the Major government objects) provides the more affluent countries of the EC with protection against cheap labour output from the southern member states (i.e. social dumping).

The EC as a constraint on economic policy

In a number of policy areas the EC does act as a constraint on economic policy. UK regional policy is constrained by EC rules on state aid for industry. The moves towards fiscal harmonisation will act as a constraint on fiscal policy (e.g. Britain is not permitted to extend zero rating for VAT purposes even if it wanted to do so). The customs union means that import controls are no longer available on a national basis. In a variety of ways the UK government has lost autonomy in the conduct of economic policy.

The Common Agricultural Policy

Few people would defend the CAP in its present form. It is the major cause of EC budgetary problems, it has raised food prices at the expense of consumers and the production of surpluses is inefficient. The CAP has always been a negative feature in the balance sheet of costs and benefits. If Britain had been a member from the outset, it could perhaps have secured a superior form of farm support. As it was, in 1973 Britain joined an existing club and was obliged either to accept the existing arrangements or to decline to join.

The Exchange Rate Mechanism

After the events of September 1992, ERM membership appears to have been misguided. In an ultimately futile attempt to maintain sterling within its ERM band, Chancellor Lamont was forced to keep interest rates high and then to expend billions of pounds of foreign currency reserves. The ERM meant the loss of autonomy in monetary policy and placed the UK economy at the mercy of decisions made in the Bundesbank.

Despite the problems of Britain's ERM membership, we should remember that it had widespread support because of the greater certainty that it gave. In particular, the external financial discipline (emanating from the Bundesbank) provided a bulwark against inflation. It was unfortunate that a particular combination of events conspired to drive Britain from a system that had great merits even though there were flaws in its details.

European peace

In the founding treaties and subsequently, the EC has stood for peace, harmony and democracy. Given the turbulent history of Europe, especially in the first half of the 20th century, it has been a considerable achievement for old enemies such as Germany and France to work together for mutual benefit. For Britain, never a 'European power' but often drawn into European conflict, the peace and security of Europe have been a positive benefit of the EC.

The EC customs union

So far our balance sheet has suggested that EC membership either involves costs or has produced few tangible and quantifiable benefits. If it could be shown that there were substantial benefits in terms of trade, output and incomes, this could outweigh all the negative features such as the budget and the CAP as well as the irritants such as Brussels pronouncements on product specification.

We know that UK membership of the EC has been accompanied by growing trade with the EC countries. However, this started prior to UK membership and would have occurred whether or not Britain joined the EC. It is impossible to quantify the extent of increased trade as a result of British membership. At the same time it is difficult to quantify the extent of any loss of trade with non-EC countries following British accession to the EC customs union. As we saw in chapter 12, a crucial issue in the evaluation of a customs union is the extent of trade creation against trade diversion.

We know from the Cecchini Report that substantial advantages flow from the single market. There is every reason to believe that Britain will gain a share of these benefits, although much depends upon the ability of British industry to compete over price, performance, quality and delivery dates. In other words, the door is open both ways and it is up to industry to ensure that the EC is an opportunity rather than a threat.

A detailed quantification of cost and benefits is beyond the scope of this book and is left to more advanced works such as those quoted in the appendix. The present writer is convinced that Britain's future lies with an ever closer union with the other members of the EC and with new members as and when they accede to the treaties. For the peace and prosperity that the Community has brought to Europe, we owe a substantial debt to the founding fathers and to others such as Sir Edward Heath who took us into it.

Euro-glossary

Accession treaties The treaties by which states joined the EC and acceded to the founding treaties.

Adoption Formal agreement of a proposal by the Council of Ministers.

Africa, Caribbean and Pacific countries (ACP) States associated with EC through the Lomé and Yaounde Conventions.

Assembly Former name of the European Parliament.

Association agreements Agreements with non-EC countries.

Benelux Economic Union of Belgium, the Netherlands and Luxembourg.

Berlaymont Building Commission headquarters in Brussels.

Bulletin of the EC Official report on the activities of Community institutions.

Cecchini Report 1988 report on the benefits of the single market.

Cohesion Fund Structural Funds used to ensure that less well off regions shared in the benefits of growth.

Commission Often seen as the EC civil servants, in fact the Commission proposes and drafts EC legislation.

Commissioner One of the 17 members of the Commission. Appointed for four-year terms, they are required to act in the Community, rather than their own national, interests.

Common agricultural policy A complex system of farm support designed to maintain farm incomes and ensure adequate supplies of food.

Common commercial policy Common policy on trade with non-EC countries. One aspect of CCP is a common external tariff.

Common foreign and security policy One of the three pillars of the Maastricht Treaty. CFSP is the new name given to 'political co-operation'.

Communautaire Being Community-minded and a 'good European'.

Competence The right in law of the Commission to act in a particular area.

COREPER Committee of Permanent Representatives (or national ambassadors to the EC).

Council of Ministers Final decision-making body for adoption of directives or regulations.

Decisions Formal agreements and rulings addressed to specific governments or organisations.

Deepening Development of closer links with other member states.

Delors Plan Plan for three stages of EMU.

Democratic deficit Gap between current practice and democratic control of Community institutions.

Derogation Exemption from an EC directive.

Directive Instruction to member states to introduce legislation within a specified period.

Distortions Measures such as quotas and state assistance which prevent normal free trade.

ECOFIN Council of Ministers to deal with economic and financial matters.

Economic and monetary union (EMU) Common currency plus common monetary and fiscal policy.

Economic and Social Committee (ECOSOC) Committee of 189 specialists who advise the Commission and Council. Often referred to as the 'other Parliament'.

Enlargement Increase in size of EC by accession of new members.

European Agricultural Guidance and Guarantee Fund Mechanism for financing the CAP.

European Atomic Energy Community EURATOM was established to promote the peaceful use of nuclear technology.

European Bank for Reconstruction and Development Fund for the reconstruction of Eastern Europe.

European Coal and Steel Community ECSC, the original Community, is a single authority for the coal and steel industries.

European Communities Collective name for EEC, ECSC and EURATOM.

European Council Twice yearly 'Euro-summit'. Not to be confused with the Council of Europe.

European Court of Justice Court to interpret and ensure observance of EC law. Not to be confused with the (non-EC) European Court of Human Rights.

European currency unit (ECU) Monetary unit used in EC transactions.

European Development Fund Provides grants and loans to ACP countries.

European Economic Community Established in 1957 to create a common market.

European Free Trade Association EFTA is a free trade area (in industrial goods) involving Nordic and Alpine countries. From 1993 EFTA countries will participate in the single market via the European Economic Area.

European Investment Bank (EIB) Provides loans for capital investment in poorer regions of the EC.

European Monetary System (EMS) A system to stabilise currencies. It is composed of:

- *the ECU;*
- *the Exchange Rate Mechanism (ERM), in which currencies can fluctuate only within narrow bands;*
- *the European Monetary Co-operation Fund.*

European Parliament A parliament of 518 MEPs which gives opinions, adopts resolutions and scrutinises the Commission.

European Regional Development Fund One of the Structural Funds established to help less prosperous regions.

Harmonisation Movement towards common laws and standards for all member states.

Inter-government(al) conference Meeting of governments of member states.

'Level playing field' Equal and undistorted competition.

Lomé Convention Agreement between the EC and ACP countries.

'Non-Europe' Assessment of additional costs resulting from the continuation of trade barriers.

Non-tariff barriers Obstacles to trade other than through import duties.

Opinion Formal view of EC institutions.

President/Presidency

   1 The President of the Commission (e.g. Jacques Delors).

   2 The President of the EP.

   3 The rotating presidency of the Council of Ministers.

Proportionality An EC principle that a remedy must be sufficient to achieve its objective but must not be excessive.

Qualified majority voting (QMV) Under the Single European Act certain decisions of the Council can be made via QMV, in which members have a weighted vote linked to their size.

Recommendation Non-binding declaration of the Commission.

Referendum A popular vote on a specific proposition.

Schengen Treaty A proposed agreement (later aborted) for closer links between Benelux, France and the then West Germany. Often regarded as an example of a two-speed Europe.

Single European Act (SEA) Amendment to Treaty of Rome, involving QMV and increased powers of the EP.

Single market or internal market 1985 initiative to complete the process of eliminating non-tariff barriers by 1 January 1993.

Social Charter/Social Chapter Improvement of social and working conditions. It started as a charter and was included as part of the Maastricht Treaty (but from which the UK opted out).

Structural Funds Collective name for the Social, Regional Development and Agricultural Guarantee and Guidance Funds.

Subsidiarity The principle that decisions should be taken at the lowest possible level and that the EC should become involved only in matters that cannot be dealt with at the national level.

Technical barriers Trade obstacles caused by differences in legal and technical standards (e.g. on product safety).

Transparency Equivalent to perfect knowledge about prices, origin and nature of goods and services.

Two-speed Europe An EC in which some countries can press ahead with union whilst the others participate in the process at a more modest pace.

Reference books on Euro-terms

S. Crampton, *1992 Eurospeak Explained,* ROSTERS LTD.
F. Gondrand (1992), *Euro-speak: A User's Guide,* NICHOLAS BREALEY.

Select Bibliography and Further Reading

Economics textbooks

A. Anderton (1991), *Economics*, CAUSEWAY.

B. Atkinson (1989), *Economics: Themes and Perspectives*, CAUSEWAY.

J. Beardshaw with A. Ross (1992), *Economics: A Student's Guide*, PITMAN.

D. Begg, S. Fischer and R. Dornbusch (1991), *Economics*, McGRAW-HILL.

J. Creedy, L. Evans, B. Thomas, P. Johnson and R. Wilson (1984), *Economics: An Integrated Approach*, PRENTICE-HALL.

A. Dunnett (2e, 1992), *Understanding the Economy*, LONGMAN.

A. Dunnett (2e, 1992), *Understanding the Market*, LONGMAN.

J. Eatwell, M. Milgate and P. Newman (eds) (1992), *The New Palgrave: A Dictionary of Economics*, MACMILLAN.

D. Gowland (1990), *Understanding Macroeconomics*, EDWARD ELGAR.

B. Harrison, C. Smith and B. Davies (1992), *Introductory Economics*, MACMILLAN.

D. Heathfield and M. Russell (1992), *Modern Economics*, HARVESTER.

A. G. Kenwood and A. L. Lougheed (3e, 1992), *The Growth of the International Economy 1820–1990*, ROUTLEDGE.

R. Lipsey (1989), *An Introduction to Positive Economics*, WEIDENFELD AND NICOLSON.

R. Lipsey and C. Harbury (2e, 1992), *First Principles of Economics*, WEIDENFELD AND NICOLSON.

F. Livesey (1989), *A Textbook of Economics*, LONGMAN.

P. Maunder, D. Myers, N. Wall and R. L. Miller (1991), *Economics Explained*, COLLINS.

M. Parkin and D. King (2e, 1992), *Economics*, ADDISON-WESLEY.

A. Perry (1988), *Approaching Economics*, THORNES.

J. Sloman (1991), *Economics*, HARVESTER-WHEATSHEAF.

L. A. Winters (4e, 1991), *International Economics*, ROUTLEDGE.

The UK economy

B. W. E. Alford (1988), *British Economic Performance 1945–75*, MACMILLAN.

M. J. Artis (13e, 1992), *Prest and Coppock's The UK Economy: A Manual of Applied Economics*, WEIDENFELD AND NICOLSON.

G. B. J. Atkinson, *Developments in Economics: An Annual Review*, CAUSEWAY.

P. N. Balchin (1990), *Regional Policy in Britain*, PAUL CHAPMAN.

R. Blackhouse (1991), *Applied UK Macroeconomics*, BLACKWELL.

N. Crafts and N. Woodward (eds) (1991), *The British Economy since 1945*, OXFORD UNIVERSITY PRESS.

P. Curwen (2e, 1992), *Understanding the UK Economy*, MACMILLAN.

P. Donaldson and J. Farquhar (1988), *Understanding the UK Economy*, PENGUIN.

F. Green (1989), *The Restructuring of the UK Economy*, HARVESTER-WHEATSHEAF.

A. Griffiths and S. Wall (3e, 1993), *Applied Economics: An Introductory Course*, LONGMAN.

C. Harbury and R. Lipsey (3e, 1989), *An Introduction to the UK Economy*, PITMAN.

P. Hardy (1991), *A Right Approach to Economics: Margaret Thatcher's United Kingdom*, HODDER AND STOUGHTON.

N. Healey (ed) (1992), *Britain's Economic Miracle: Myth or Reality?*, ROUTLEDGE.

G. C. Hockley (1992), *Fiscal Policy: An Introduction*, ROUTLEDGE.

C. Huhne (1990), *Real World Economics*, PENGUIN.

C. Johnson (1991), *The Economy under Mrs Thatcher*, PENGUIN.

C. Johnson (1988), *Measuring the Economy: A Guide to Understanding Official Statistics*, PENGUIN.

R. Layard (1986), *How to Beat Unemployment*, OXFORD UNIVERSITY PRESS.

J. Michie (ed) (1992), *The Economic Legacy 1979–1992*, ACADEMIC PRESS.

D. Morris (ed) (1990), *The Economic System in the UK*, OXFORD UNIVERSITY PRESS.

M. Mullard (1992), *Understanding Economic Policy*, ROUTLEDGE.

J. G. Nellis and D. Parker (1990), *The Essence of the Economy*, PRENTICE-HALL.

G. C. Peden (1985), *British Economic and Social Policy: Lloyd George to Margaret Thatcher*, PHILIP ALLAN.

D. Smith (1992), *From Boom to Bust: Trial and Error in British Economic Policy*, PENGUIN.

D. Smith (1987), *The Rise and Fall of Monetarism*, PENGUIN.

R. Stutely/The Economist (1991), *The Economist Guide to Economic Indicators: Making Sense of Economics*, ECONOMIST/CENTURY BUSINESS.

G. P. Thomas (1992), *Government and the Economy Today*, MANCHESTER UNIVERSITY PRESS.

G. Thompson, V. Brown and R. Levacic (1989), *Managing the UK Economy: Current Controversies*, POLITY PRESS.

A. Walters (1990), *Sterling in Danger: The Economic Consequences of Pegged Exchange Rates*, FONTANA/IEA.

Studies in the Heinemann UK Economy series

(Series Editor B. Hurd)

H. Armstrong and J. Taylor (1990), *Regional Economics*.

P. Bennett and M. Cave (1991), *Competition Policy*.

S. Blazen and T. Thirlwall (1989), *Deindustrialisation*.

A. Clark and R. Layard (2e, 1993), *UK Unemployment*.

R. Crum and S. Davies (1991), *Multinationals*.

K. Glaister (1989), *The Entrepreneur*.

N. Healey and R. Levacic (2e, 1992), *Supply-side Economics*.

D. Heathfield (1992), *UK Inflation*.

B. Hill (1991), *The European Community*.

B. Hurl (1988), *Privatisation and the Public Sector*.

R. Levacic (1988), *Supply-side Economics*.

I. Morison and I. Shepherdson (1991), *Economics of the City*.

NIESR (2e, 1993), *The UK Economy*.

C. Smith (1992), *UK Trade and Sterling*.

D. Smith (2e, 1992), *Mrs Thatcher's Economics*.
D. Whynes (1992), *Welfare State Economics*.

The Macmillan Economics Today series

(Series Editor A. Leake)

J. L. Barsoux and P. Lawrence (1990), *The Challenge of British Management*.
A. Beharrell (1992), *Unemployment and Job Creation*.
F. Burchill (1992), *Labour Relations*.
K. Durham (1992), *The New City*.
A. Leake (1992), *The Economic Question*.
J. Wales (1990), *Investigating Social Issues*.
J. Wigley and C. Lipman (1992), *The Enterprise Economy*.
M. Wilkinson (1992), *Taxation*.

The EC: history and politics

C. Archer and F. Butler (1992), *The European Community: Structure and Process*, PINTER.
W. Cash (1991), *Against a Federal Europe*, DUCKWORTH.
W. Cash (1991), *Europe: the Crunch*, DUCKWORTH.
S. George (1991), *Britain and European Integration since 1945*, BLACKWELL.
S. George (1991), *Politics and Policy in the European Community*, OXFORD UNIVERSITY PRESS.
S. Greenwood (1992), *Britain and European Co-operation since 1945*, BLACKWELL.
R. O. Keohane and S. Hoffman (1990), *The New European Community: Decision Making and Institutional Change*, WESTVIEW.
V. Linter and S. Mazey (1991), *The European Community: Economic and Political Aspects*, McGRAW-HILL.
J. Lodge (ed) (1989), *The European Community and the Challenge of the Future*, PINTER.
D. Martin (1991), *Europe: an Ever Closer Union*, SPOKESMAN.
W. Nicoll and T. C. Salmon (1990), *Understanding the European Communities*, PHILIP ALLAN.
N. Nugent (1989), *The Government and Politics of the European Community*, MACMILLAN.
M. Spicer (1992), *A Treaty Too Far*, GUARDIAN/FOURTH ESTATE.
H. Wallace (ed) (1991), *The Wider Western Europe: Reshaping the EC/EFTA Relationship*, PINTER/RIIA.

The EC: economics

I. Barnes with J. Aeston (1988), *The European Community*, LONGMAN.
S. A. Budd and A. Jones (1989), *The European Community: A Guide to the Maze*, KOGAN PAGE.
S. Bulmer, S. George and A. Scott (eds) (1992), *The UK and EC Membership Evaluated*, PINTER.
A. Britton and D. Mayes (1992), *Achieving Monetary Union in Europe*, SAGE.
P. Cecchini (1992), *The European Challenge 1992: The Benefits of the Single Market*, WILDWOOD.
M. El-Agraa (1989), *The Economics of the European Community*, PHILIP ALLAN.
M. Emerson and C. Huhne (1991), *The ECU Report*, PAN.

S. F. Goodman (1990), *The European Community*, MACMILLAN.

A. Griffiths (ed) (1992), *European Community Survey*, LONGMAN.

D. Gross and N. Thygeson (1992), *European Monetary Integration: From EMS to EMU*, LONGMAN.

J. Harrop (1992), *The Political Economy of Integration in the European Community*, EDWARD ELGAR.

B. Hill (1991), *The European Community*, HEINEMANN.

T. Hitiris (1989), *European Community Economics*, HARVESTER-WHEATSHEAF.

V. Linter and S. Mazey (1991), *The European Community: Economic and Political Aspects*, McGRAW-HILL.

F. McDonald and S. Dearden (1992), *European Economic Integration*, LONGMAN.

S. G. Makridakis and Associates (1991), *Single Market Europe*, JOSSEY-BASS.

P. Minford (ed) (1992), *The Cost of Europe*, MANCHESTER UNIVERSITY PRESS.

R. Minikin (1993), *The ERM Explained*, KOGAN PAGE.

W. Molle (1990), *The Economics of European Integration: Theory, Practice and Policy*, DARTMOUTH.

B. Morris, K. Boehm and M. Geller (1992), *Business Europe: The Essential Guide to Who's Who and What's What in Europe*, MACMILLAN.

J. Neilson, H. Heinrich and J. Hansen (1989), *An Economic Analysis of the EC*, McGRAW-HILL.

R. Owen and M. Dynes (1992), *The Times Guide to the Single European Market*, TIMES BOOKS.

A. Roney (1991), *The European Community Fact Book*, KOGAN PAGE.

D. Strasser (1991), *The Finances of Europe*, EC COMMISSION.

D. Swann (7e, 1992), *The Economics of the Common Market*, PENGUIN.

L. Tsoukalis (1991), *The New European Community: The Politics and Economics of Integration*, OXFORD UNIVERSITY PRESS.

R. Vickerman (1992), *The Single European Market*, HARVESTER-WHEATSHEAF.

The EC: business studies aspects

S. J. Berwin and Co. (1992), *Competition and Business Regulation in the Single Market*, MERCURY/CBI.

R. Bennett (1991), *Selling to Europe: A Practical Guide to Doing Business in the Single Market*, KOGAN PAGE.

R. Brown (1991), *Doing Business in Europe*, HODDER AND STOUGHTON.

F. Bradley (1991), *International Marketing Strategy*, PRENTICE-HALL.

J. W. Dudley (1990), *1992: Strategies for the Single Market*, KOGAN PAGE.

P. Gibbs (1990), *Doing Business in the European Community*, KOGAN PAGE.

R. Lynch (1990), *European Business Strategies: An Analysis of Europe's Top Companies*, KOGAN PAGE.

R. Lynch (1992), *European Marketing: A Guide to New Opportunities*, KOGAN PAGE.

S. G. Makridakis and Associates (1991), *Single Market Europe*, JOSSEY-BASS.

B. Morris, K. Boehm and M. Geller (1992), *Business Europe: The Essential Guide to Who's Who and What's What in Europe*, MACMILLAN.

R. Owen and M. Dynes (1992), *The Times Guide to the Single European Market*, TIMES BOOKS.

Collin Randlesome *et al.* (1990), *Business Cultures in Europe*, HEINEMANN.

A. Roney (1991), *The European Community Fact Book*, KOGAN PAGE.

A. A. Scott (1992), *European Studies*, PITMAN.

R. Welford and K. Prescott (1992), *European Business: An issue-based Approach*, PITMAN.

Index